NAPOLEON III

The Second Empire

G. P. GOOCH
C.H., D.LITT., F.B.A.

LONGMANS

LONGMANS, GREEN AND CO LTD
6 & 7 CLIFFORD STREET, LONDON W1
THIBAULT HOUSE, THIBAULT SQUARE, CAPE TOWN
605–611 LONSDALE STREET, MELBOURNE C1
443 LOCKHART ROAD, HONG KONG
ACCRA, AUCKLAND, IBADAN
KINGSTON (JAMAICA), KUALA LUMPUR
LAHORE, NAIROBI, SALISBURY (RHODESIA)

LONGMANS, GREEN AND CO INC
119 WEST 40TH STREET, NEW YORK 18

LONGMANS, GREEN AND CO
20 CRANFIELD ROAD, TORONTO 16

ORIENT LONGMANS PRIVATE LTD
CALCUTTA, BOMBAY, MADRAS
DELHI, HYDERABAD, DACCA

© G. P. GOOCH, 1960

First published 1960
Second impression 1961

PRINTED IN GREAT BRITAIN BY
WESTERN PRINTING SERVICES LTD BRISTOL

PREFACE

THIS book is neither a history of the Second Empire nor a biography of Louis Napoleon. For the former, with its wars and its tortuous diplomacy, we turn to the massive surveys of Ollivier, La Gorce and Seignobos; for the latter to Simpson, Sencourt and Thompson. Its purpose is to transmute mere names into men and women of flesh and blood; to study the Emperor's complex character in sunshine and storm; to assess the influence of his wife and relatives, legitimate and illegitimate; to watch his Ministers at work and his critics in attack; to recapture something of the atmosphere of the two colourful decades which separate the drab Bourgeois Monarchy from the equally drab Third Republic.

Inevitably there is overlapping, for the highlights of the drama are described in different contexts. Yet every chapter adds a few touches to the portrait of 'Napoleon the Little'—'a blend of Don Quixote and Machiavelli', an echo of the mighty Emperor but an infinitely better man. Close acquaintance reveals the most humane of dictators, part idealist, part adventurer, sincerely desiring the welfare of his country and a fairer lot for the common man. Émile de Girardin, the most influential journalist of the time, described him as *Napoléon le bien intentionné*, a title subtly blending compliment with criticism. No one could have been more different from the popular conception of a ruthless autocrat than this kindly ruler who never lost his temper nor raised his voice. Neither a superman nor a rogue—as Francis Joseph described him—he is best described in Queen Victoria's verdict, after his visit to Windsor in 1855, as 'an extraordinary man'. Though there were other Bonapartes of the second generation, he alone possessed the drive and the quasi-mystical faith to secure a niche in the temple of fame.

There was nothing new either in the nature of the experiment, the success of the *début*, or the humiliating collapse. Dictator is a Latin term, but the type had flourished in Greece, where the feverish life of the City States threw up the Tyrannos as a recurring phenomenon—a real or counterfeit Leader who seized power in an emergency and was tolerated or even welcomed by a majority of his fellow-citizens. Emerging as the saviour of society, his function was to restore tone to the system in an hour of confusion, to steady the nerves of the community after a shock. Throughout the ages the pattern has never changed. When the times are out of joint, when the legitimate ruler appears unequal to his task, when public affairs are tangled in a knot, when masses of people are hungry or disillusioned or alarmed, there is a call for a strong hand at the helm. Too much, however, is promised by, and expected from, the autocrat who deteriorates as the years pass. 'All power tends to corrupt, and absolute power corrupts absolutely.' There is always a touch of uncertainty in the air, and the Man of Destiny usually disappears as suddenly as he came. He is a tree without roots. The glamour fades, for the system, even at its best, challenges the finest traditions of Western civilization: the rule of law is overthrown and liberty is denied. Since man does not live by bread alone, the citizen tires of the totalitarian state which he has acclaimed and looks round for an alternative.

No autocrat was more conscious of the fragility of his power than Napoleon III when his health—and with it his self-assurance —began to fail. France, declared the veteran statesman Odilon Barrot, when the performance was over, wanted liberty and peace; the Emperor gave her tyranny and war. George Sand classified him as a somnambulist, and such semi-pathological types are apt to make extremely dangerous guides. He has recently been labelled the most liked and the most hated ruler of modern France, and hatred is a far stronger emotion than liking. Dictators usually dig their own graves. The moral of these pages is that no human being is good enough and wise enough to be entrusted with the unfettered control of the destinies of a nation. Few Frenchmen today would challenge the declaration of Thiers, himself a monarchist, after the *débâcle*: *La République, c'est ce qui nous divise le moins*. That the tragi-comedy of the Second Empire continues not only to attract the student but to fascinate the general reader is indicated by the unceasing flow of histories and monographs, biographies and autobiographies. The serried array of volumes containing the correspondence of Mérimée, Flaubert and Sainte-Beuve, and the unabridged version of the de Goncourt journals, tell a similar tale.

Portions of this volume have appeared in the *Contemporary Review*, and my thanks are due for permission to reprint.

G.P.G.

CONTENTS

Part I: THE FAMILY

		PAGE
1.	THE EMPEROR	2
2.	THE EMPRESS	34
3.	'CHERCHEZ LA FEMME'	57
4.	THE MEXICAN FIASCO	73
5.	DUC DE MORNY, THE HALF-BROTHER	85
6.	PRINCE NAPOLEON, *l'enfant terrible*	99
7.	PRINCESS MATHILDE, *Notre dame des Arts*	119
8.	COUNT WALEWSKI, THE POLISH COUSIN	129

Part II: THE MINISTERS

9.	PERSIGNY, *Loyal Serviteur*	138
10.	THREE LAWYERS: ROUHER, BAROCHE, MAGNE	154
11.	OLLIVIER AND THE LIBERAL EMPIRE	173
12.	DURUY AND THE SCHOOLS	191
13.	HAUSSMANN AND THE BOULEVARDS	198

Part III: FRIENDS AND FOES

14. THE ARMY   210
    Fleury, Cavaignac, Changarnier, Lamoricière, Saint-Arnaud, Randon, Canrobert, Castellane

15. THE CHURCH   230
    Falloux, Montalembert, Veuillot, Dupanloup

16. THE PARTIES 252
    Thiers, Duc d'Aumale, Berryer, Favre, Rochefort,
    Gambetta, Mme Adam, Clemenceau, Proudhon,
    Blanqui

17. THE WORLD OF LETTERS 282
    Victor Hugo, Mérimée, Sainte-Beuve, George Sand,
    Flaubert, the Goncourt brothers, the World of
    Learning

    BIBLIOGRAPHICAL NOTES 310

    INDEX 315

ILLUSTRATIONS

frontispiece

NAPOLEON III

(*from a lithograph. Department of Prints and Drawings, British, Museum*)

facing page 48

THE EMPRESS EUGENIE

(*from an engraving by E. Weber after a painting by Winterhalter, Department of Prints and Drawings, British Museum*)

facing page 96

DUC DE MORNY

(*by courtesy of Librairie Hachette*)

PART ONE

THE FAMILY

I

THE EMPEROR

I

NAPOLEON THE LITTLE, as Victor Hugo called him, was a pocket edition of his mighty uncle but a far better man. Josephine called her grandson *Oui Oui* because he was so good-tempered; Bismarck thought his intellect overrated, his heart underrated. The greatest of soldiers was the super-egoist of all time—'as great as a man can be without virtue' in Tocqueville's incisive phrase. Taine's verdict—'a *condottiere* of the fifteenth century'—fits him like a glove. France was his instrument, not his fatherland. 'If you would rule mankind,' he declared, 'the heart must break or turn to stone.' For him the choice was easy. The heart of Louis Napoleon never turned to stone. 'I love and respect him,' declared Conneau, the faithful doctor who stood at his side from youth to old age and knew all his failings. 'He loved the people,' declares La Gorce, the fairest of his judges, 'not particularly his own, but all peoples, that is to say the poor, the weak, the disinherited.' Could that have been said of any previous ruler of France, even of Henri IV? There was a benevolence, occasionally an almost feminine gentleness, in him which we miss in the executioner of the Duc d'Enghien. His greatest qualities, testifies Véron, the influential Editor of *Le Constitutionnel*, were gratitude and generosity. The Fourth Estate was knocking at the door, and he earnestly strove to improve its lot. 'La guerre,' exclaimed the fallen Emperor to the youthful Lord John Russell on a visit to Elba, 'c'est un bon jeu, une belle occupation.' 'I hope some day to command a great army,' confided the prisoner at Ham to his former playmate Hortense Cornu. 'I know I should distinguish myself. I feel I possess every military quality.' Yet when at Solferino he saw what war was like his heart bled at the butchery. When all is said for the most humane and the most likeable of dictators it would have been better for France and the world had he never been born. Uncle and nephew alike were gamblers who plunged their country into avoidable conflicts and had to learn at the expense of France that, in Byron's words, 'tempted fate would leave the loftiest star'. That they died in exile unmourned by their former subjects tells its own sorry tale.

When Napoleon divorced Josephine he remained on excellent terms with her family, and liked to have Hortense and her boys about the Court. Her youngest son retained dim memories of the man whose words and deeds filled his mind and fashioned his career. On the eve of the Emperor's departure for his last battle the boy knelt before him and burst into tears. 'My governess says you are going to the wars,' he cried. '*Ne partez pas, ne partez pas.*' The Emperor, deeply moved, embraced him, saying to someone in attendance: 'He will have a good heart. Perhaps he is the hope of my race.' When the curtain fell at St. Helena in 1821 the boy of thirteen wrote to his mother: 'In Paris I was so young that it is only in my heart that I have any memory of him. When I do wrong, if I think of this great man I seem to feel his spirit within me bidding me be worthy of his name.' To his aged grandmother he wrote: 'You can imagine how welcome is the blessing of the mother of the Emperor, for I venerate him as a god.' They were all pygmies compared with him, he exclaimed, but even a pygmy might carry on a giant's work.

Born in 1808, Louis Napoleon scarcely knew his morose father who, after a brief span on the throne of Holland, retired to sulk in Florence, leaving his younger son with Hortense. On the fall of the Empire the Duchess of Saint-Leu, as she was called, made her home at Arenenberg at the northern end of Lake Constance, where she devoted herself to music, painting and society. Though she dearly loved her son, she and his first governor, Abbé Bertrand, did nothing to train his mind. A wiser choice was made when the lad was twelve, for Philippe le Bas, son of Robespierre's comrade in the National Convention, brought a rare combination of qualities to his task—tact, patience, enthusiasm, wide culture, a deep sense of responsibility and a loving heart. For the next eight years master and pupil were inseparable,

at home, on travel, and during his schooldays at Augsburg. His
difficulties and triumphs are recorded in the tutor's correspondence with his family published in 1903. From the first he was
amazed by the contrast between the warmth of his pupil's heart
and the almost unbelievable inertia of his brain. 'I am very
satisfied with my pupil,' he wrote after six weeks. 'Docility and
an excellent heart would make a personality of distinction if they
were accompanied by industry and quicker apprehension. At
twelve he is like a boy of seven, unfamiliar with even the simplest
things and finding it extremely difficult to express even what he
does understand. I don't think it is a lack of intelligence but
rather an inactive and inattentive mind. With patience it will
improve but it will not be easy. I already notice some progress
and so does the dear child. The difficulty will be to make him love
his lessons.' At the close of the year 1820 he reported a further
advance. 'The obstacle would have baffled anyone with less
courage than myself. An excellent heart, sweet-tempered, but a
horror of work and a desolating ignorance.' Now there were signs
of interest in history and literature, and he had begun to read
with enjoyment. Twelve months later he had become a model
pupil. The tutor's first impression was correct: there was plenty
of intelligence. What had been lacking was the complete incapacity of his former tutor to make lessons interesting. When master
and pupil parted in 1828 the latter was interested in many things
and ready to play his part in the world.

His faith in his star was sustained by a series of occurrences
which gave him his chance. His elder brother had died in childhood, the next was struck down by fever during the Carbonari
rising in 1831, and in the following year his cousin the Duc de
Reichstadt faded away at Schönbrunn. When *l'Aiglon* was gone,
he became the recognized standard-bearer of the Bonapartist
cause. Meeting him for the first time in his mother's house in
Rome in 1829, Lord Malmesbury described him as 'a wild,
harum-scarum youth, riding at full gallop down the streets to the
peril of the public, fencing and pistol-shooting, and apparently
without serious thoughts of any kind, though even then he was
possessed with the conviction that he would some day rule over
France. His face was grave and dark, but redeemed by a singularly bright smile.' Of the superman's brothers, Joseph had no

son, Lucien had ceased to count after Brumaire, and Louis was
a sour misanthrope without a friend. The road was open. Realizing
that France had had enough of war, he turned his thoughts to the
problems of peace. His ideal of government was an efficient and
paternal autocracy resting on nation-wide assent. The great
Emperor had promised constitutional reform in the *Acte Additionel* during the Hundred Days, though whether his pledge
would have materialized had the verdict of Waterloo gone the
other way we may doubt. His nephew coquetted with a similar
notion, and the promise of a Liberal Empire was implemented
in a rather half-hearted way at the close of his reign. While the
Petit Caporal had regarded the masses primarily as cannon-fodder,
his successor thought of them as subordinate partners in a
national task. Inheriting the conception of paternalism from the
Enlightened Despots of the eighteenth century, he aspired, not
wholly without success, to deserve the proud title assigned to
himself by Frederick the Great: *le premier domestique de l'état*.

'Our history from 1789 to 1830,' wrote Tocqueville in 1851,
'seen in broad perspective is the story of a desperate struggle
between the *ancien régime* and the new France led by the middle
class. The triumph of the latter was definitive and complete.' The
expulsion in 1830 of Charles X, the last of the elder branch of the
Bourbon line, and the accession of Louis Philippe cleared the
road for further changes. The son of the regicide Égalité steered
a middle course between outmoded dynastic autocracy and nascent
democracy in the long afternoon of the Restoration era. Sharing
the conviction of Guizot, the greatest of his Ministers, that the
interests of France were best served by the *juste milieu*, the leadership of the educated middle class, and that the country needed
peace to recover from the revolutionary storm, he believed that
his subjects cared far more about money than politics. It was a
profound miscalculation. The old King was colourless, the Court
was dull, foreign affairs were unexciting except for the conquest
of Algeria, and Lamartine pronounced the devastating verdict
La France s'ennuie. There was a general impression that the July
Monarchy, which had begun with a revolution, would end in the
same way. In that event who would take the helm? The Comte de
Chambord, grandson of Charles X, was living in retirement in
Austria, and was considered too fettered to the *ancien régime* to be

seriously considered; the Orleanist heir, the Comte de Paris, was a child of six. Only a few intellectuals, mostly socialists, wished for a Republic. 'I have no apprehensions,' declared the King; 'I am a necessity.'

With the rise of a new generation memories were dimming of the price paid for the luxury of a superman, and the Napoleonic legend began to take shape in the stirring verses of Béranger, the brisk narrative of Thiers, and above all in the writings of his nephew. His earliest manifesto, *Rêveries Politiques*, published in 1832, traced the *malaise* of Europe to the lack of confidence in its rulers who had broken their promises.

> Everywhere the peoples asked and the Kings refused, so force had to decide. Regarding their throne as their personal property, they thought every concession a robbery, every amelioration an incipient revolt. Frenchmen, be grateful to him who, springing from the people, did everything for its prosperity. If one day the people obtain freedom they will owe it to him. Do not blame his dictatorship, for it led us to liberty, as the iron plough prepares the way for the harvest. He carried civilization from the Tagus to the Vistula, and established in France the principles of the Revolution—equality before the law, the recognition of merit, the prosperity of commerce and industry, the liberation of all the peoples.

Unhappily he could not reap all he had sown.

> Though my principles are republican, I think monarchy best suited to France. My ideal constitution would be the division of power between the people, the Legislature and the Emperor—the people to elect, the Legislature to deliberate, the Emperor to rule. A country will be happy when there is harmony between these three. The Legislature should be elected by universal suffrage, and the sovereignty of the people would be guaranteed since each successive ruler would need its sanction.

That the Emperor had left tens of thousands of French corpses in the Russian snow, had been routed at Leipzig and Waterloo, and had spilled more French blood than Louis XIV, was discreetly ignored. Only the few who knew him well, like his mother and Persigny, took the young dreamer seriously. After a visit to Arenenberg Talleyrand's niece, the Duchesse de Dino, reported that he was 'no greater danger to the July Monarchy than a student at the École Polytechnique, a good mathematician, a good horseman, but timid and silent like a well brought up girl.'

Convinced that he alone was able to give France what she needed, the Pretender raised his standard in a *putsch* at Strasbourg in 1836. After the bloodless fiasco which lasted two hours he received the mild sentence of banishment to the United States. 'A deplorable acquittal,' commented Metternich obsessed by memories of the First Empire. 'What lies ahead? Disorder followed by the despotism of the masses or of individuals.' Returning to Europe in the following year to close his mother's eyes, he settled in London where he studied the working of Constitutional Monarchy and composed the longest and most important of his political tracts, *Les Idées Napoléoniennes*, published in 1839. Utilizing the narratives of the Napoleonic era which were pouring from the press, he piled incense on the hero's altar. The Emperor was gone, declared the Preface, but his spirit survived.

> He was the child of the Revolution, pledged to continue and complete its work, not only in France but throughout Europe. He cleansed it by sifting its truths from its passions, buttressed the Monarchy by rendering power respectable, and ennobled the peoples by giving them a consciousness of their strength and institutions which enhanced their stature. The masses had long done him justice, and his great conceptions were like beacon fires in the darkness. His aim was liberty, yes liberty. Every law prepared the way for it, but equality, order and respect for the law had to come first. The soil had to be planted and time allowed for the seed to sprout. Anchored in the assent of the people, he had proceeded to abolish all unjust laws, to heal all wounds, to reward all merit, to bring all Frenchmen to collaborate in the prosperity of France. Beginning with the recall of the *Émigrés*, the restoration of the Church and the drafting of the Codes, he proceeded to reform the administration of the judiciary, finance and the army while encouraging agriculture and commerce. He established new industries, modernized education, and carried out public works. His glory, like that of the sun, could only be contested by the blind. Though called a despot, power was necessary for his creative tasks and was the expression of the nation's confidence. No sovereign sought so much advice. Could he be a despot who by his codes had substituted law for caprice?

In the sphere of foreign affairs he merely wanted the independence of France: never an aggressor, he had to repel hostile coalitions. If at times he seemed to forestall attacks it was because initiative was the condition of success. 'He was one of those extraordinary beings created by Providence as the majestic instrument of its impenetrable designs. His aims expanded with his victories till they embraced the regeneration of Europe.' His greatest difficulty was to digest his conquests. In 1812 the struggle became more terrible. To achieve and consolidate universal peace England and Russia had to be persuaded by reason or force. His lofty plans were nearing success when he marched on Moscow. Alas! winter intervened and European association became impossible. All France's wars had come from England, who repulsed every offer of peace, who saw in him merely a despot, who failed to recognize that he was the chosen of the people and the representative of all the moral and material interests for which France had fought since 1789. He had laid the foundations of liberty when he was overthrown. He fell because he tried to accomplish in a decade the work of centuries. Despite his fall his ideas had germinated everywhere: even the victors had accepted them. The people were striving to regain what he had given them, and France ceaselessly demanded the implementation of his ideas under other forms. If some great measure is passed or some enterprise is carried out it is generally one of his projects. His memory waxes from day to day. The Napoleonic idea is not military but social, industrial, commercial, humanitarian. Now that the smoke of battle has cleared away, we see the civil glory greater and more lasting than that of arms.

The gospel was proclaimed anew in a shorter treatise, *L'Idée Napoléonienne*, on the eve of his raid on Boulogne in 1840. For twenty-five years France had exhausted herself in vain efforts to create a durable situation. The causes of the trouble remained, and society alternated between feverish agitation and apathy. The great movement of 1789 had two distinct characters, social and political. The social revolution had triumphed despite France's reverses; the political revolution had failed despite the victories of the people. Under Napoleon the floods receded, the ruins disappeared, order and prosperity emerged from the crater in which they had been momentarily engulfed.

Thus the great man solved for France and Europe the gravest of problems without disorder or excess, conducting the transformation from the old to the new, laying the broad foundations required to ensure the triumph of the social and political revolution. But no sooner had the Empire fallen than all the discordant elements and outmoded claims reappeared and with them the revolutionary excesses they caused. The *régime* established in 1800, guided by a superior genius, established progressive institutions on the principle of order and authority, but in 1814 and 1815 the *ancien régime* donned a liberal mask. This corpse clothed itself in new garments, and the shroud was mistaken for the swaddling clothes of a promising child. The disguise caused fatal confusion; foreign oppressors were hailed as liberators; the glorious remnants of the armies of the Republic and Empire were labelled brigands. Admirers of the oligarchic system of England were called liberals, while the title of partisans of absolutism was affixed to those who thought nostalgically of the power, at once authoritative and popular, of the plebeian hero who assured the independence of the peoples and was the true embodiment of our Revolution.

Some had hoped that the era of uncertainty and disillusion had passed with the revolution of 1830. Alas! it had sown new seeds of discord, presenting a scene of vague theories, petty interests and sordid passions.

Corruption, lies, hatred everywhere, such is our plight. In this chaos of mind and suffering there was no idea capable of rallying a majority, no man sufficiently popular to embody the general interest. This conflict of opinion, this lack of great designs, this apathy of the people, prove the insufficiency of the ideas of 1815. Instead of doctrinaires and rhetoricians we should become apostles of the man who was even greater as a legislator than as a warrior. Great men never wholly die. Their spirit survives, and the Napoleonic idea has sprouted from the tomb of St. Helena as the moral message of the Gospel rose triumphant from Calvary. The Napoleonic idea springs from the Revolution like Minerva from the head of Zeus. It stands for the reconciliation of order, liberty, the rights of the people and the principles of authority, obeying neither the uncertain lead of a party nor the passions of the crowd. Towering above political coteries and national prejudice, it sees in France brothers to reconcile, in the nations of Europe members of a single family. It gives to each his task according to his capacity. Its only concern is to render the country prosperous by work, not by words. It levels mountains and rivers, builds bridges, improves communications, reconciles peoples. Conscious of its strength it rejects corruption and lying, makes demands on the people but never flatters them. It appeals to reason, not to force. But if it becomes the sole refuge of the glory and honour of the country, then, picking up its helmet and lance, it would say to the people what Saint Rémi said to his sovereign: Burn what you have adored and adore what you have burned.

In these flamboyant expositions of the Napoleonic saga there was no mention of the author's readiness to serve his country, but the manifesto had little point unless some individual were available to implement it.

A fourth appeal, *Aux Manes de l'Empereur*, was a cry of distress from the fortress of Ham inspired by the transfer of the Emperor's remains to the Invalides.

> Sire, you return to your capital and the crowds salute you. From the depth of my dungeon I can merely catch a glimpse of the sun which shines on your *cortège*. Do not blame your family for its absence. Your exile and misfortunes ended with your life; ours remain. You died on a rock, far from your country and your family; no son's hand closed your eyes, no relative wears mourning. The people press round you as of old, acclaim you as if still alive. But the great ones, while paying you homage, whisper to themselves: Oh God, do not awake him. In vain do they say you were a meteor which leaves no track. In vain they deny your civil glory; they will not disinherit you. Sire, December 15 is a great day for France and for me. From your sumptuous *cortège*, disdaining some of the homage you receive, you cast a glance at my humble dwelling, and, mindful of your caresses in my childhood, you say to me: Friend, you suffer for me; I am pleased with you.

Louis Napoleon was no orator but he knew how to handle a pen. 'If the Emperor cares for my verdict,' declared Béranger, 'tell him that I regard him as the first writer of the century.' While dictators usually start from scratch, he sailed into fame under his uncle's flag. The Napoleonic saga was taking shape. *Parle-nous de lui, grand-mere, Parle nous de lui*, chanted Béranger. In the words of Victor Hugo, his candidature dated from Austerlitz. To bring back his bones was a good beginning, but why not bring back his throne? He had learned every detail of the twilight years at St. Helena direct from Gourgaud and Montholon; the demigod obsessed him. It was almost a case of dual personality. *Toujours Lui, Lui partout*. His picture was found in the peasant's cottage beside that of Christ and the Virgin Mother.

The five and a half years in the fortress of Ham, though alleviated by study, authorship and visitors, might well have broken an ordinary mortal, but the Prince's belief in his destiny was unimpaired. General Montholon, who had shared the Emperor's exile at St. Helena, Conneau, the family doctor, a valet, and a village girl who bore him two sons, were a consolation. Hortense Cornu, daughter of his mother's former lady-in-waiting, procured him books and looked up references, and he dabbled in chemical experiments. Literature, except for Schiller's stirring dramas, gave him little pleasure. When in later years people expressed surprise at the extent of his knowledge he answered with a smile: 'Do you forget my years of study at the university of Ham?' He was never a man to be idle and he knew how to wait. 'I have no wish to be elsewhere,' he wrote during the first winter. 'Here is my right place. With my name I must be either in the gloom of a dungeon or in the glare of power.' 'I have faith,' he wrote to a friend in 1842, 'the faith which makes men endure all things with resignation and makes them trample underfoot all joys, the faith which alone can move mountains.' 'If I have miraculously escaped every danger,' he added three years later, 'if my soul is steadfast in face of so many disappointments, it is because I have a mission.' To his cousin Prince Napoleon he wrote:

> I pass my time in studying, reflecting and hoping. I regret nothing I have done. I am sure the shade of the Emperor protects and blesses me. I am not unhappy, for I do not feel that my sufferings are in vain. I am convinced that I have done my duty—the only member of the family to do so—for I have sacrificed my youth, my fortune, my life to the triumph of the cause which we cannot desert without dishonour.

The tribute to himself was deserved, for no other member of the clan lifted a finger to revive its fortunes. When offered release in return for renunciation of his claims and a promise to abstain from further attempts to overthrow the *régime*, the pariah of Europe, as he described himself, declined. In addition to contributing to the provincial press he published booklets on the extinction of pauperism and unemployment by agricultural colonies, on the sugar beet industry, on artillery, and on the desirability of a Nicaraguan canal.

'I found him little changed,' reported Lord Malmesbury in April 1845. 'He confessed that though his confidence and courage were unabated he was weary of his prison, from which he saw no chance of escaping, as he knew that the French Government gave him opportunities of doing so that they might shoot him in the act.' 'My power is in an immortal name and in that only; but I have waited long enough, and I cannot endure imprisonment any longer.' His visitor returned to London deeply impressed with his calm resolution. 'Very few in a miserable prison like this, isolated and quasi-forgotten, would have kept their intellect braced by constant studies and original compositions.' A year later, when repairs were needed in his rooms, he disguised himself in the clothes of a workman brought in by his valet, shaved off his beard and moustache, rouged his pale face, carried a plank on his shoulder, walked quietly out, and entered Belgium with a British passport supplied by a friend. Turning up unexpectedly in London he was welcomed by old friends, among them Disraeli and other members of Lady Blessington's lively circle in Kensington, and served as a Special Constable when the Chartist demonstrations in 1848 alarmed the capital. 'Evidently a weak fellow,' commented Cobden, 'but mild and amiable.' Still waters run deep.

When the Monarchy collapsed in 1848 the King, who had lost his nerve and in the opinion of Lord Normanby, the British Ambassador, was distrusted by all the statesmen, fled to England and a Republic was proclaimed. 'Monarchy is gone for ever,' lamented Thiers, and he was right. It had received its death sentence in 1789 and now it was buried. The Pretender crossed to Paris and offered his services to the Provisional Government, but he was requested to leave. Back in London within the week he issued a protest which was also a manifesto: 'I thought that after thirty-three years of exile and prison I had a right to find a home in my native land. You think my presence might be an embarrassment, so I retire for the moment. You will see in this sacrifice the purity of my intentions and my patriotism.' With bitter memories of Strasbourg and Boulogne to warn him against premature action he was willing to bide his time, for the life of the Second

Republic seemed likely to be brief. Lamartine hailed the Republic which he had helped to establish as 'pure, holy, immortal, popular, peaceful', but the bright dawn was quickly over and the longer it lasted the more unpopular it became. The Constituent Assembly elected in April by manhood suffrage was divided into warring groups—Legitimists and Orleanists, Republicans and Socialists. He was urged by his supporters to stand, but he contented himself with selling the remainder of his father's estate and borrowing money from English friends.

Meanwhile the Provisional Government was unwittingly fostering his cause, as every aspiring Dictator needs the luck of the deal. The invasion of the Chamber on 15 May revealed the weakness of the Executive and the peril of mob rule. When supplementary elections were held in June to fill vacant seats the Prince, though not a candidate, was returned in four Departments. Cries of *Vive Napoléon*, *Vive l'Empereur*, were heard, Bonapartist journals were founded, portraits appeared with the simple caption *Lui*, and some people chanted *Nous l'avons, nous l'avons, Louis Napoléon*. The timid Government carried a resolution to arrest him if he returned to France; but Jules Favre, an eloquent Republican lawyer, persuaded the Chamber to annul its decision on the ground that every elected member had a right to sit and that the Prince would be a simple citizen like the rest of them. Seizing his opportunity, he wrote from London a letter to be read in the Chamber. 'If the people impose duties on me I should be ready to fulfil them.' The duties of which he spoke, it was clear to friend and foe, travelled far beyond the routine occupations of a Deputy. When this unabashed advertisement of political ambitions stung some of the members to anger he dispatched a second letter resigning his seat on the ground that he had no wish to cause disorder. 'You ask me about my intentions,' he wrote to Prince Napoleon. 'Considerations too long to be explained in this letter have decided me to refuse this honourable mandate. I am extremely flattered by the good opinion of me, but at this moment of exaltation I prefer to remain in the shadow.' Now that the rills had begun to flow he never doubted that they would swell into a torrent. The chess-player was matched against clumsy opponents, but he planned his moves with amazing skill.

A few days later the Government reaped the harvest of its

folly in starting National Workshops for the unemployed in the capital. Beginning with 6,000 in March, the numbers rapidly swelled to 100,000, far beyond the capacity of the authorities to supply with work, and hordes of loafers who streamed into the capital received a small daily wage for doing nothing. When the Government, appalled by the growing danger of civil war, ordered them into the army or back to the provinces, they refused to go. Barricades were erected and for four days in June the streets ran with blood. The revolt was suppressed by Cavaignac at the cost of thousands of casualties, and he was appointed President of the Council by the grateful Chamber; but his unbending republicanism alienated the royalist majority and his influence waned.

When thirteen vacant seats had to be filled in September the Prince, standing for the first time, was elected in five constituencies and returned to Paris, accompanied by his devoted mistress 'Miss Howard', who had helped him with his debts and his political campaigns. A Republican Constitution, with a single Chamber elected by manhood suffrage, became law in October, the most significant feature of which was the choice of a President for four years by a plebiscite, only one consecutive term being allowed. Though Cavaignac and Lamartine could boast of conspicuous services, Louis Napoleon headed the poll with $5\frac{1}{2}$ million votes against $1\frac{1}{2}$ for Cavaignac. He migrated from his hotel to the Elysèe and took the oath read aloud by the President of the Chamber. 'In the presence of God and in the face of the French people represented in the National Assembly, I swear to remain faithful to the democratic Republic and to fulfil all my constitutional duties.' 'I swear,' replied the Prince. 'I take God and man to witness this oath,' added the President of the Chamber. The new Chief of State proceeded to read his first discourse. 'The nation's votes and my oath will determine my course. My duty is clearly defined, and I will fulfil it as a man of honour. I shall regard as enemies of the country all who may try to change by violent means what the whole of France has established. Between you and myself there cannot be real disagreements. Our wishes are the same. Like you I wish to replace society on its foundations, to strengthen democratic institutions, and to seek every means calculated to assuage the sufferings of this generous and intelligent people who have given me such a striking demonstration of their confidence. We have a great mission, citizens—to found a Republic in the interest of all and a government, both just and firm, neither reactionary nor utopian but progressive.' The whole Assembly stood up and cried *Vive la République*. It was an excellent start, and Odilon Barrot, a moderate Liberal, was a wise choice to head the new Ministry.

At first he played for safety, but on his Presidential tours cries of *Vive l'Empereur* were heard and he was astonished at his popularity, partly due to his gracious ways and kindliness. The constitution gave him considerable powers, and he was determined to use them to the full. France, he rightly believed, had no desire for a *roi fainéant*. 'My name,' he declared, 'is a complete programme in itself. It stands for order, authority, religion, the welfare of the people, national dignity, particularly in the country districts.' A majority of Frenchmen believed him and were ready to follow his lead. The well-to-do bourgeoisie had been thoroughly rattled by the riots—not a mere political revolution like the fall of the monarchy, but a social convulsion inspired by Proudhon's war-cry *La propriété c'est le vol*; and the peasants flocked to his standard. 'My true friends,' he declared at St. Quentin in 1850, 'are in the cottages, not in the palaces,' and he was right. He made full use of Article 64 of the Constitution empowering him to appoint and dismiss Ministers, Generals, Prefects, Diplomatists and Colonial Governors, at his pleasure. Since his uncle had advanced from the position of First Consul to the Consulate for life and finally to the Imperial title he resolved to copy his time-table. The only obstacle—a very formidable one—was his solemn oath to the Constitution, but this he hoped to remove by a free vote of the Chamber. Though the masses were soon to show that they were ready for a change, Orleanists such as Thiers, republicans like Cavaignac, and intellectuals such as Victor Hugo detested Personal Government in every form, and their resistance could only be overcome by force. The Legislative Assembly elected in May 1849 contained as few Bonapartists as its predecessor the National Assembly and was no more inclined to smile on the President's plans. He too found it difficult to leap into the gulf. He had been described a thousand times as *honnête homme* who could be trusted to play the game, and he was nervous about the frowns of posterity. On the other hand he honestly believed that France not merely needed him but wanted him. Returning to Saint-Cloud from a ride in the summer of 1851 he was accosted by an artisan with the words: 'I hear that down there in the Chamber they don't want you. Well, we do. We know you love the people and the working-man. Count on us.' All hesitation vanished in July when a proposal to make the President re-eligible in the following year was rejected. The man described by Thiers at this moment as *absolument nul* knew not only how to wait but when to strike.

At this moment a new actor with a thicker skin strode towards the centre of the stage. Louis Bonaparte, King of Holland, and Queen Hortense parted company soon after the birth of their youngest son. Before long Hortense, starving for affection, fell in love with a dashing young officer, Comte de Flahault, an illegitimate son of Talleyrand, and gave birth to a boy who was registered in the name of Demorny. Not till many years later did Louis Napoleon meet his half-brother, who was never acknowledged by his mother. The *coup d'état* of 2 December 1851, the anniversary of Austerlitz, tore up the Constitution, muzzled the press, and inaugurated a dictatorship. Of the Ministers Saint-Arnaud alone was in the secret. Leading politicians—both royalists and republicans—and generals were arrested in their beds, troops filled the streets before dawn, and posters informed the capital that France had a master once more. *Tout vient à qui sait attendre.* He might have said with Chatham, 'I know that I can save my country and that no one else can.' He would give it all that was sound in the French Revolution, steer his course by the principles of 1789, and combat disorder in every form. Sporadic opposition, not on 2 December but two days later, was suppressed with bloodshed, but there was no premeditated massacre. 'The firing was not ordered by anyone,' declared Marshal Canrobert in reply to Victor Hugo's charges in *Histoire d'un Crime*; young and inexperienced troops panicked when stray shots fell in their midst. The casualties probably exceeded the official figures of 215 supplied by Maupas, Prefect of Police, but in any case were less than a tenth of the victims in June 1848. 26,000, mainly republicans, were arrested and tried by special commissions on the pretext that the numbers were too great for the courts, and about 200 were exiled to Africa or Cayenne. Neither Morny, the directing brain, nor Saint-Arnaud, the military arm, broke his heart about the slaughter, but the Dictator often brooded over the catastrophe. Though he had hoped to avoid the shedding of blood he bears the responsibility before history on the principle *qui veut la fin veut les moyens*, and his reputation never recovered. 'You wear December 2 like a Nessus shirt,' exclaimed Eugénie one day when her husband looked depressed. 'Yes,' he replied, 'it is always on my mind.' If a case could be made for the *coup*, the mass arrests and deportations were inexcusable. On 20 December, however, a plebiscite authorized a Presidential term of ten years by $7\frac{1}{2}$ million votes to 650,000, and there is no reason to believe that the result was due to government pressure. Mortally wounded, the Republic lingered on for another year, but everyone understood that the Second Empire was waiting in the wings, and the Dictator described himself as 'the result of 1848'. The wheel of fortune had come full turn.

A vivid portrait of the Prince is painted in the correspondence of Lord Cowley, who arrived in Paris as British Ambassador a few weeks after the *coup*. 'To fathom his thoughts or divine his intentions would try the powers of the most clear-sighted. No one's advice seems to affect him. He seems a strange mixture of good and evil. Few approach him who are not charmed by his manners. I am told that an angry word never escapes him. His determination of purpose needs no comment.' The portrait by Hübner, the Austrian Ambassador, is much the same. 'What a singular man! What a mixture of opposites! Calculating and naïve, pleasure-loving and fond of marvels, sometimes sincere, sometimes impenetrable, ever a conspirator.' The new Constitution announced in January 1852 inaugurated a *régime* as unashamedly monolithic as that of the First Empire. The President was to appoint the Ministers, who were responsible to him alone, and he alone could initiate legislation. The Senate, a nominated body, was to sit in secret. The proceedings of the Assembly, elected by manhood suffrage for six years, reached the public exclusively through authorized reports. When the new Chamber met in March 1852 they found that many decrees, some of them embodying plans of social reform long cherished by the Dictator, had already been issued. Most of them were widely approved, but a jarring note was quickly heard. That the Orleans family was ordered to sell their landed property, following the precedents of the treatment of the Bonapartes by Louis XVIII and of the Bourbons by Louis Philippe, was natural enough; but a second decree nullified a large donation to his sons by Louis Philippe on the eve of his accession while reserving a life interest for himself. Though the Dictator claimed to be correcting an illegality and allotted the proceeds to social betterment, his action was almost universally condemned as vindictive and of doubtful legality. Four Ministers resigned in protest, among them Morny, Minister of the Interior, who declined the offer of a seat in the Senate. The new Chamber was packed with government candidates, only eight opposition members finding their way in.

A year later the Empire was proclaimed, and Napoleon III, as he styled himself, migrated to the Tuileries where he had been born. To adopt the phraseology of Disraeli on his first appointment as Prime Minister, he had climbed to the top of the greasy pole; all the world wondered how long he would stay there and what he would do. 'When France has a cold,' remarked Metternich, bitterly after the revolution of 1830, 'all Europe sneezes.' 'When France is satisfied,' declared Louis Napoleon in 1852, 'the world is at ease.' But was France satisfied with the map of Europe as drawn in 1815? Her new master had never pretended to be. His sympathy with the ideals of nationalism was notorious, and he needed prestige for the Second Empire, wherever he thought it might be found. All Europe was watching him. 'Will the Emperor keep the peace or start a war?' wrote Ranke to Manteuffel on 12 July 1852. 'I don't believe that a static government will in the long run satisfy restless France, but Europe will not tolerate French aggression. This man, the child of the sovereignty of the people, will he be able to keep her within the limits which Europe has traced? If not, will he prevail?'

II

A Court required a hostess, the Emperor an heir. Princess Mathilde, who had attracted him as a young man, had married a

Russian millionaire. The Tsar Nicholas, who refused to address the *parvenu* ruler as *mon frère*, could not allow a Russian princess to share a shaky throne, for everyone remembered the fate of the Empress Marie Louise. Unable to break into the charmed circle of royalty, the ruler was compelled to lower the target. Meeting Eugénie de Montijo at a dinner-party in 1850 at the house of Princess Mathilde, he was fascinated by her beauty and invited her to the Elysée and St. Cloud. Her father Count Montijo, a grandee of Spain, had died when she was a child. Her ambitious mother, once a lady-in-waiting to Queen Isabella, had married her elder daughter to the Duke of Alba, the leading nobleman of Spain, and she cherished even loftier ambitions for the younger. The ladies revisited Paris in the autumn of 1852 and after the proclamation of the Empire were invited to Compiègne where the attentions of the host became embarrassing. '*Oui quand je serai Impératrice*,' replied Eugénie, who had remarked to the Belgian Ambassador, 'I am not a La Vallière.' The engagement was promptly announced. In safeguarding her reputation she had won his respect. 'I have preferred a woman whom I love and respect to one unknown to me,' he declared. 'Endowed with all the qualities of soul, she will be an ornament of the throne and in the hour of danger one of its courageous supports.' 'Miss Howard' reluctantly withdrew to a large estate near Paris with the title of Comtesse Beauregard.

The marriage took place at Notre Dame within a month. Infinitely more than a lovely doll, the Empress was an outstanding personality in her own right, with passionate religious and political convictions and a character beyond the reach of scandal. Though ambition counted for more than love, she dedicated herself to France and the glory of the Empire. Miscarriages were followed by the birth of the Prince Imperial in 1856, during the Congress at Paris which closed the Crimean War. It was the happiest moment of the Emperor's life—victory at Sebastopol, peace, the succession assured. With the passing years he realized ever more fully how much he owed to the fair consort who made Paris the social capital of Europe and the English *couturier* Worth the arbiter of fashion. Louis Philippe, declared Sainte-Beuve, was too like a bourgeois to win the respect of the bourgeoisie. 'The King of France in old times had been the first gentleman of the kingdom; Louis Philippe was merely the first bourgeois. There was nothing royal about him, nothing to strike the imagination.' It was the task of the Emperor and the Empress to strike the imagination, to revive the *panache* of the *ancien régime*, and one of the most reserved of men might have failed without her help. 'He can be charming if he likes,' reported Hübner; but for Eugénie to charm required no effort. *L'Espagnole*, needless to say, had her enemies, captained by Prince Napoleon, who disliked her clericalism and detested her as he would have detested any other woman for blocking his path to the succession. Princess Mathilde resented the loss of her position as the first lady of the land, and made little attempt to hide her jealousy. Morny was never her friend, and Persigny deplored her political influence. Complaints were heard of both extravagance and stinginess. She had a few loyal friends, among them Mérimée and Princess Metternich; but she was more envied than beloved, for she had a sharp tongue.

Though the Faubourg Saint-Germain boycotted the parvenu Court and gazed across the frontier to the Comte de Chambord or the Comte de Paris, the Emperor was supported by the army, the Church, and the great majority of the middle class and the peasants, but not by the urban manual worker. In the election of 1857, the first since the proclamation of the Empire, Paris stubbornly ignored official pressure and planted the germ of a Parliamentary Opposition known as *Les Cinq*, with two eloquent republican lawyers, Jules Favre and Emile Ollivier, at their head. The tide was beginning to turn. 'We must reflect seriously about the result of the elections,' wrote the Emperor. 'It is a question of how to reduce the number of malcontents in Paris and Lyons, but that will be difficult.' It was to prove impossible. He told Palmerston on a visit to Compiègne in 1859 that he would like to confine the franchise to married men.

The Emperor devoted as much energy to enriching the country as to increasing his prestige. His uncle confessed that he was afraid of nothing except a hungry Paris, and the nephew resolved that the capital, like Imperial Rome, should have *panem et circenses* in plenty. His primary task was the development of the national resources by public works—railways, canals, roads, ports, bridges, drainage of marshes—to be financed by the newly founded *Crédit Foncier*, *Crédit Mobilier* and *Crédit Lyonnais* as well as by the *Banque de France*. *Enrichissez-vous* was a slogan which everyone could understand. In consequence there was no serious unemployment throughout the reign, though wages rose less rapidly than prices. Deeply interested in applied science, he fostered the silk industry as his uncle had fostered sugar beet, and he welcomed the fruitful discoveries of Pasteur. Lacking the *laissez-faire* inhibitions of our Victorian statesmen, he improved the housing of the workers, promoted Friendly Societies, built almshouses, thus earning Sainte-Beuve's complimentary title of Saint-Simon on horseback. Impressed by the results of Free Trade in England, he made possible the Cobden Commercial Treaty of 1860, to the delight of French wine-growers and the dismay of many industrialists.

The most spectacular achievement was the reconstruction of Paris by Baron Haussmann. Prosperity encouraged speculation, and money was as lavishly spent as it had been quickly made. 'The country is a vast public and private Casino,' complained Flahault in 1863, whose son the Duc de Morny had a finger in many a financial pie. One of the ironies of the era was the prosecution of the author of *Madame Bovary* during the reign of a ruler whose immorality was notorious. Except for Mérimée, an old friend of the Montijo family, Octave Feuillet, and Sainte-Beuve, who coveted a well-paid seat in the Senate, most of the Intellectuals disapproved the Empire. That the Dictator was a lonely man was partly his own fault. 'The Emperor is not communicative,' noted Count Horace de Vieil-Castel in his journal in 1857. 'He remains for whole days without opening his mouth, absorbed in his inmost thoughts. Calm and impenetrable even to those most in his confidence, his soul seems as adamantine as his face. Esteeming no one, no one is allowed to share his thoughts. One cannot pretend to judge him by his acts alone, for their real meaning often baffles the wisest.'

'His mind is as full of schemes as a warren is full of rabbits,' exclaimed Palmerston, and the redrafting of the map of Europe on the principle of nationality had long obsessed him. Like Mazzini he dreamed of sovereign states based on racial and linguistic unity collaborating in the general purposes of prosperity and peace. For Poland in 1863 or Denmark in 1864 he could do nothing, but his share in the making of Italy was his outstanding achievement. Louis Philippe had collapsed, he remarked to Hübner, the Austrian Ambassador, because he had let France fall into disrepute, adding 'I must do something.' Having enhanced the prestige of French arms in Turkey and being saluted by Victor Cousin as the Emperor of Europe, he proceeded to plan with Cavour in their secret meeting at Plombières in July 1858 the eviction of Austria from Italy as soon as a plausible *casus belli* could be found or invented. When the Sardinian Minister had congratulated the newly elected President in 1848, he had received the reply: 'Now I can do what I like I will do something for Italy; tell your Government.' The time had now arrived to redeem his pledge. Countess Castiglione was dispatched to seduce the inflammable ruler, and the siren played her part with zest. A more sensational factor was Orsini's bombs, for the conspirator's appeal, 'Let him liberate my country,' stirred youthful memories: but for the unanimous protest of his Ministers he would have pardoned the assassins. A third method of cementing the alliance was the marriage of Prince Napoleon to Princess Clotilde, daughter of Victor Emmanuel. It was impossible to be the friend of the Italians and also of the Pope, declared Pio Nono, but the Emperor had made his choice.

In May 1858 the Emperor gave orders to prepare for a war with Austria, and a hint was dropped at the New Year's reception of the Corps Diplomatique in 1859. 'I regret that our relations with your Government are not so good as formerly,' he remarked to the Austrian Ambassador, 'but I beg you to tell the Emperor that my personal sentiments for him have not changed.' Did it mean war? Most observers thought so. Count Hübner recorded his hopes and fears in his journal and dispatches almost from day to day. Prince Napoleon desired it, unlike the Empress, Persigny, Morny and Walewski. The Emperor kept his own counsel till the moment to strike arrived. Baron Rothschild remarked prophetically to a Minister, who repeated the warning to the Emperor '*La paix, c'est l'Empire; pas de paix, pas d'Empire.*' Prefects reported that war would cause consternation, and a bishop exhorted him not to ally himself with an enemy of the Pope. Junior officers, on the other hand, scented the chance of promotion.

Five weeks after the fateful New Year's declaration the first indication of the programme was given in the Emperor's address at the opening of the session. 'For some time the fate of Italy and the abnormal situation in which order can only be maintained by foreign troops have caused just anxiety though not sufficient to anticipate war.' Much more light was afforded a fortnight later in a brochure by the journalist La Guéronnière entitled *L'Empereur Napoléon III et l'Italie*, inspired and revised by the ruler himself. Italy, it declared, must be liberated from Austrian domination and form a federation under the Pope as Honorary President who, in return for the increase of his prestige, might diminish both his territorial possessions and his political responsibilities by establishing a lay administrator, a civil legislature and an independent magistracy. The purely ecclesiastical government of the Papal States was an active cause of discontent and constituted a permanent threat of revolution.

When Austria answered Piedmontese provocation by a declaration of war the Emperor led 200,000 men into Italy. Mérimée declared that the soldiers marched off as if they were going to a ball. 'The Bourse is against me,' commented the Emperor, 'but the people are on my side.' They had not said so, for they were allowed no opportunity to express their wishes. It was a case of planned aggression, justified in the eyes of the plotters by the argument that Italy had a right to become a nation-state and that there was no other way of evicting Austria. As Cavour observed: 'If we did for ourselves what we do for our countries what rascals we should be!' The struggle was brief. Appalled by the slaughter at Solferino, which led Henri Dunant to found the Red Cross, the Emperor made peace with Francis Joseph on the basis of the cession of Lombardy. One of the proudest days of his life was that on which he rode with Victor Emmanuel through cheering crowds in Milan.

Cavour resigned in protest against leaving Venetia to Austria, but there was no real choice. The 'quadrilateral' of Austrian fortresses would have required greater sacrifices in blood and money than France was prepared to make, and the massing of Prussian troops in the Rhineland threatened invasion while the French army was busy beyond the Alps. The bill for facilitating the aggrandisement of Piedmont was the cession of Savoy and the district of Nice. 'Nobody can deny that the Emperor is a most extraordinary man,' commented Lord Cowley, 'and that he has raised France to a position in Europe which she had long ceased to occupy.' The issue of a comprehensive political amnesty testified to his confidence in the stability of the *régime*.

In addition to Lombardy, the richest province of Italy, the victory of the House of Savoy opened the way to further changes and was quickly followed by the absorption of Tuscany, Parma, Modena and two-thirds of the extensive Papal States. In these dramatic events the Emperor took no part though he had made them possible. After the campaign of 1859 he had hoped for an accord between Victor Emmanuel and Pio Nono and aspired to keep the goodwill of both, but neither of them was in a mood for compromise. While the former dreamed of a united Italy with its capital in Rome, the Pope regarded the maintenance of the Temporal Power with its inherited boundaries as the sole guarantee of his spiritual independence. Cavour's offer of 'a free church in a free state' was no consolation for loss of territory, since promises could be broken as easily as they were made. The Emperor was in partial disagreement with both parties. He disapproved the eviction of the Bourbons from Sicily and Naples by Garibaldi and his redshirts, and he rejected the argument that the Papal States were essential to the security and prestige of the Papacy. At the end of 1859 he sponsored a second brochure by La Guéronnière entitled *Le Pape et le Congrès*. Some form of Temporal Power, indeed, was necessary, but the less the better. 'The smaller the territory the greater the sovereign.' The secular tasks of government were not the *métier* of the priest, and the legitimate rights of the Papacy would be preserved by the Catholic Powers. Romagna was lost, could only be regained by force, and had long been an embarrassment. 'It is Rome that matters; the rest is secondary.' From this attitude the Emperor was never to depart, and his fidelity to the maintenance of the Temporal Power on a limited scale was to prove one of the causes of his downfall. The brochure was denounced by Veuillot as the kiss of Judas, and its publication ended the cordial relations between the Dictator and his Catholic subjects and Pio Nono, who never trusted him again. The gulf was widened by the Syllabus of Errors in 1864.

In the summer of 1859 Vieil-Castel recorded his impressions. 'Whoever endeavours to interpret him by what he says, even those with whom he is most intimate, will be gravely mistaken. There is a good deal of the conspirator about him with a preference for crooked methods. His coldness towards some people, even his show of affection towards others, means very little; as for esteem, he has none for anybody. He classifies people as useful and useless. The most honest of his followers, if not useful, is nothing to him.' Vieil-Castel was a shrewd observer, but he knew the Emperor too slightly to see the whole man. Very different is the verdict of Countess Tascher de la Pagerie, who had known him in early days at Arenenberg and held a post at Court: 'I love and admire him, but who can say he knows him? An eternal dreamer, his pale blue eyes conceal rather than reveal. He is an enigma. Grandeur and adulation do not dazzle him. He is always the same.' A Court functionary, driving with him in an open carriage through the streets of Paris, was amazed at his master's lack of response to the demonstrations which greeted him. Why was it? 'Because I know mankind,' was the reply.

At the close of the first decade of dictatorship clouds began to gather. All pretence of affection between husband and wife had disappeared; Prince Napoleon was a thorn in the flesh, and Princess Mathilde was rarely seen at Court. The death of Morny in 1865 was regarded by the British Ambassador as a great loss. Dictators are lonely men, and of his Ministers Persigny alone could be described as a friend. The prestige of the Empire received its first serious blow from the Mexican fiasco. Mexico, like other fragments of the Spanish Empire, had suffered a series of *pronunciamentos* since the Liberation, and in 1860 the vast country was convulsed by the rivalry of two Presidents, Miramon, champion of the landowners and the Church, and Juarez, standard-bearer of the workers and anti-clericals. French investors had backed the wrong horse, for the loans to the former were repudiated by the winner. The Emperor took up their cause, a French force was dispatched under Bazaine, and Archduke Maximilian, brother of Francis Joseph, accepted an invitation to found a Catholic Empire in the New World, only to discover that he had no local support. With the end of the Civil War in North America the Monroe Doctrine came into play and France withdrew her troops. The luckless Maximilian, refusing to leave with them, was executed by Juarez, and his Belgian widow went permanently out of her mind. The whole crazy structure had collapsed like a house of cards.

A second and hardly less spectacular loss of face occurred when Prussia thrust Austria out of the German Confederation in 1866 and unified the north under her rule. Fearing that the French schemer might at any moment demand territorial compensation for his neutrality, as he fully intended to do, Bismarck made peace on the morrow of Sadowa and secured all he needed at the moment. 'All we can do,' exclaimed Drouyn de Lhuys, 'is to shed tears.' Realizing that he had been outmanœuvred, the Emperor moaned '*c'est une déroute, une déroute*', and he never recovered his resilience. Duke Ernst of Coburg compared him to a sailing-ship which had lost its helm and was driven forward by winds which he could not control. In the words of the historian Lavisse, who saw him at close quarters while teaching the Prince Imperial, he ceased to believe in himself. Bismarck had taken his measure, and Austria, smarting under defeat, complained that French neutrality had amounted to complicity. He strove for compensation in Mainz, a portion of the left bank of the Rhine, Belgium and Luxemburg, but lacked the power to enforce a single demand. The hegemony of the Continent had passed to Berlin.

Though he fully understood the longing of Germans no less than Italians for a nation-state, the Emperor had no wish to see Prussia formidable enough to threaten the security of France. He hoped to limit the dimensions of her aggrandisement by cultivating the South German states and ending his feud with Vienna, but it was all in vain. Meanwhile domestic foes were growing in numbers and audacity. Since 1863 Thiers was back in the Chamber, Rochefort and Clemenceau were barking at his heels, and the young *méridional* Gambetta was thundering in the courts. Paris seemed to be tiring of the Second Empire as it had tired of the First, of the restored Bourbons and of the July Monarchy. Another major shock, it was widely felt, might destroy the *régime*, and common sense should have taught the ruler to play for safety. Convinced of the superiority of Prussian arms, confident of the military support of Saxony and the South German states, rightly counting on the neutrality of Russia, Austria and Italy, the Iron Chancellor steered towards a conflict which he openly confessed to be inevitable. From a distance, he declared, the Second Empire was something; seen at close quarters it was nothing. He had formed his impressions during his brief tenure of the Prussian Embassy in Paris. They were confirmed when he accompanied his master, King William, Crown Prince Frederick and Moltke, to the Exhibition in 1867, when a swarm of royalties from all over Europe witnessed the last flicker of the Empire and were impressed by the beauty of the Empress, the new boulevards, and the melting melodies of Offenbach. There was a chill in the air. In the words of the Austrian Ambassador, Sadowa was the Empire's Waterloo from which recovery was impossible. An exchange of visits in 1867 healed the breach between Paris and Vienna dating from the war of 1859, but failed to produce a military alliance. The Second Empire had no reliable friend in Europe.

Persigny, who understood and loved his master, almost broke his heart over the rapid decline, which he attributed to a congenital lack of toughness. Without the extreme kindliness which distinguished him, he writes in his Memoirs, a gentleness so attractive in a private citizen but so dangerous in a prince, he would not have had such Ministers or at any rate would not have let them abuse his consideration.

> So it all comes back to his character. It is impossible not to love and respect him, but he lacks a quality essential to great princes—severity, the faculty to punish as well as to reward. To see him at close quarters, as simple and modest in his brilliant fortune as the least of his subjects, the perfect gentleman without a shadow of personal pride or vanity, applying to every topic the greatest good sense, the most intrepid of men in moments of peril, it is impossible not to be charmed and conquered, and one understands the grandeurs of his reign. But if one looks deeper into his nature and witnesses the strife between his reason and his kindly heart, one pities this prince, so generous, so indulgent, for being unable to punish those who deserve punishment. How easily can this noble spirit be the victim of intrigue! Hence his errors, weakness and frustrations at home and abroad. With such a prince surrounded by men of sincerity and conviction dedicated to a great cause what lofty achievements would be possible we can judge by the beginning of the reign before intriguers discovered how far they could go with him and abuse his trust. So kindly a prince ceased to be feared and

selfish intriguers were assured of their victory in advance. He once said to me: Ah! Persigny, what a pity you are so angry! What a pity you are not! I replied. If you, like me, could not suppress your indignation against evil, injustice and intrigue, everyone would do his duty, which no one does now. Remember the wrath of Achilles. Why did not God give you this generous wrath which terrifies evildoers and rewards the good?

The harassed ruler found relief in studying the career of Julius Caesar and compiling a substantial biography with the aid of scholars and military experts, while Mérimée put the material into shape. The book had a political as well as an academic purpose, and the author's familiar ideology is reasserted in the Introduction. In times of crisis and confusion Men of Destiny—Caesar, Charlemagne, Napoleon—appear with a mandate to save society and restore the authority of the state. They are chosen by Providence to show the people their route, to stamp a new era with the seal of their genius, to accomplish in a few years the work of centuries. The ostracism of Napoleon by Europe had not prevented the revival of the Empire; but how far were they from the great questions solved, the passions appeased, the legitimate satisfactions given to the peoples by the First Empire! How much strife and blood and time would be needed, exclaimed the prisoner at St. Helena, for his designs to be realized! For such a formidable task the ruler requires a free hand, but he never forgets that success alone can justify the experiment to his conscience and posterity. The reader is invited to conclude that what was right in ancient Rome was equally right in 1851. The argument would have seemed more plausible had the volumes appeared when the Dictator's prestige was at its height, for by the middle sixties there was growing doubt whether the latest Saviour of Society was up to his job.

When Lord Lyons, an experienced observer, succeeded Lord Cowley in the British Embassy at the end of 1867 he pronounced that the Empire was in decline. 'The discontent is great and the distress among the working classes severe. There is no glitter at home or abroad to divert public attention, and the French have spent a good many years without the excitement of a change.' In the summer of 1868 he described the Emperor as much out of spirits, since, though the country districts were still on his side, all the towns were against him. 'Probably the wisest thing he could do would be to allow real Parliamentary government so as to give the Opposition hope of coming into office by less violent means than a revolution.' A year later he wrote: 'I have an instinct that they will drift into a republic before the year is over.' In the elections of May 1869 the votes for the Government were only in the proportion of four to three; the large cities, at no time very friendly, were growing rapidly hostile. Historians emphasize the ruler's waning health as a major factor in the decline and fall. The Liberal Empire with Ollivier as its standard-bearer was disapproved by the Empress, Rouher, Persigny and other authoritarians as a tacit admission that he had lost faith in himself. In 1866 Metternich reported that he could neither walk nor sleep nor hardly eat, and by 1870 he was always in pain. He had never rationed his dissipations, and the torturing stone in the bladder weakened his grip. The last time Mme Octave Feuillet saw him was at a reception at the house of Princess Mathilde shortly before the crisis of 1870. 'He sat sombre and silent. His wan expressionless eyes were fixed on the oriental carpet at his feet. The Empress appeared equally sombre. On the way out he whispered to her: Quick. I am in horrible pain.'

The acid test of his statesmanship occurred when Marshal Prim offered the throne of Spain to Leopold, younger son of Prince Antony, head of the South German branch of the Hohenzollerns. Carol, his elder brother, had been called to the Roumanian throne and proved an excellent ruler, and Leopold appeared a no less suitable choice. Scenting the outcry which the prospect of a Hohenzollern at Madrid was likely to provoke in France, and welcoming a pretext for the conflict which he believed inevitable, Bismarck secretly encouraged the candidature, for which King William manifested not the slightest enthusiasm. The Prince's acceptance provoked the anticipated explosion, which in turn led to the withdrawal of the candidate who, like his father, had no desire to set the world alight. Any ruler with a grain of sense would have been content with this diplomatic victory, but at this moment his sense of realities deserted him. While King William was taking the waters at Ems the French Ambassador was instructed to extract a promise that Prince Leopold would decline any renewed offer. The old monarch courteously refused a demand which seemed uncalled for, and when Benedetti asked for a second audience he was politely informed that he had nothing more to say. The calmly factual report to Bismarck by Abeken, the Foreign Office functionary on duty, known to all the world as the Ems telegram, was abridged—without altering a word—by the Chancellor in such a manner that it looked like an affront to France, all the more since it was promptly circulated to Prussia's representatives throughout Europe. In a moment of madness the French Government declared war, unleashing a conflict which the Emperor knew in his heart he could not win. The war had been forced on him, reported Lyons to Granville, principally by his own party in the Chamber, the Right and his Ministers; but that was no excuse for an autocracy.

Visiting him on 6 July at the opening of the crisis Metternich found him in the highest spirits.[1]

> *Emperor:* Do you think that after our very energetic protest Berlin can immediately yield?
> *Metternich:* I think so. If not at once, the efforts of Russia and England should prevail.
> *Emperor:* In any case we must be ready. The prize will go to whoever is ready first. Do you think we can count on Austria?
> *Metternich:* That would largely depend on the attitude of Russia and the time available for our preparations. You must tell us in good time of any warlike eventualities.
> *Emperor:* Of course, and you may be sure I shall only ask what I know is within your power.

The mood of optimism was brief and never returned.

In Paris crowds singing the 'Marseillaise' and shouting *à Berlin* surged along the boulevards. Among the voices raised in the Council for avenging a supposed insult was that of the Empress, whose influence had waxed as the health of the Emperor waned. She had acted as Regent during the war of 1859, represented France at the opening of the Suez Canal in 1869, and now in darker days she was to be Regent again. She always resented the charge that she was largely to blame for the catastrophe, indignantly denying that she had exclaimed '*c'est ma petite guerre*'; but there is not the slightest doubt about her bellicose attitude,

---

[1] '*Il avait l'air enchanté, je dirais même joyeusement monté.*'

and she never attempted to conceal it. 'Our army seemed to us invincible,' she explained to Paléologue many years later, 'and we counted on strong alliances.' If there was some slight excuse for her on the ground that she was not fully informed, there is none for the Emperor, who realized the unreadiness of France, the might of Prussia, and the improbability of help from Austria or Italy. One evening he sent a message from Paris that he would be late for dinner and that the Empress and the guests should begin. When he appeared at Saint-Cloud everyone stood up, the Generals raising their glasses of champagne and exclaiming *à Berlin!* '*Messieurs, de grâce,*' was his sombre reply. '*Priez plutôt Dieu de protéger Paris.*' 'You can't ride,' exclaimed Princess Mathilde with her usual frankness; 'how will you manage on the day of battle?' 'You exaggerate, my dear friend,' was the reply. 'Look in the glass,' she rejoined. 'You are right,' he confessed sadly, 'I don't look frisky.'

Ignoring Bismarck's maxim that politics are the art of the possible, he was doomed to pay the penalty. Francis Joseph had no stomach for a second round only four years after Sadowa, and why should Victor Emmanuel draw the sword for a ruler whose garrison barred the way to the Eternal City? Defeat followed defeat; MacMahon and Bazaine were no match for Moltke, and in little more than a month the stricken ruler, suffering agony when riding or driving, surrendered with 80,000 men. He had never lacked physical courage, and at Sedan he sought death by riding slowly along the line in the zone of fire. He passed the winter at the palace of Wilhelmshöhe near Cassel, once occupied by his frivolous uncle Jerome, King of Westphalia. To Lady Cowley, who visited him soon after his arrival, he complained that he had been deceived about the preparedness for war and the state of public opinion. He described the total demoralization of the troops at their first defeat. In describing the catastrophe of Sedan he completely broke down. He spoke most gratefully of the King of Prussia, and everything was done to spare his feelings. He looked ill and suffered from the cold, but had not lost all hope of a return to the throne.

When the news reached Paris a republic was proclaimed, for dictators never survive military defeat. The *régime* which had opened with a fanfare and had dazzled Europe for almost twenty years fell with a crash. The shattered Regent, in danger of her life, fled to Deauville in the carriage of the American dentist Dr. Evans and crossed the Channel, while General Trochu and Gambetta took over national defence. The crowning disaster was the surrender of Bazaine with his large army in beleaguered Metz, after which Paris was slowly starved and bombarded into surrender. The war was over but not the suffering of the capital. The Paris Commune seized control, burned the Tuileries, and was in turn mercilessly suppressed by the government of Thiers installed at Versailles. For two more years the fallen autocrat, now a mere shadow of his old self, lived quietly with his family at Chislehurst, visited by Queen Victoria and other old friends, watching with loving pride the growth to manhood of his devoted son, occasionally seeking a change at Torquay, Brighton or Cowes. 'I always found him simple and good, charitable and full of kindness,' declared Eugénie, now fully reconciled to her wayward partner. 'He endured contradiction and calumny with admirable equanimity, and when disaster overwhelmed us he carried his stoicism and meekness to the point of sublimity. If you could have seen him during his last years at Chislehurst! Never a word of complaint or recrimination!' Lord Malmesbury found him much more depressed by the sufferings of France than by his own misfortunes. 'His quiet and calm dignity and absence of all nerviness and irritability, were the grandest examples of moral courage than the severest stoic could have imagined. I confess I was never more moved.'

Robert Sencourt, the best of his biographers, describes him as 'the modern Emperor', and Emile Ollivier's colossal apologia argues that the Liberal Empire was a *bona fide* experiment which deserved to succeed. The weightiest verdict has been pronou ed in La Gorce's majestic *Histoire du Second Empire*. The reig he declares, was both brilliant and deadly, the ruler, liberal by n e, a blend of Don Quixote and Machiavelli, dreamer and conspi r, whom it is impossible to hate. He condemns the *coup* of 185 d as a Catholic he censures the Italian policy. In 1870, he ls, France deserved to be beaten, but Prussia did not deserve tc n. The demand for a guarantee against the renewal of the H n-zollern candidature was a fatal error. While rendering just to the generous ideas, the personal charm and the humanity he

Emperor, he paints a dark picture of his work, and a reviewer commented that the book ought to kill Bonapartism. When all allowances are made, he declares, it stood for autocracy and war. The system was wrong. 'Splendours and misery: in these two words lie the history of the Second Empire.' Thompson, his latest English biographer, credits him with 'the will to be great and the wish to do good; yet he was too small for the great things he set out to do.' Queen Victoria rightly pronounced him 'a very extraordinary man'. Such people—half idealists, half adventurers —rarely make satisfactory rulers, and dictators usually end by destroying themselves through military ambition or blind folly. In the words of Hübner, the Austrian Ambassador, he had only one principle and that a superstition—a belief in his star.

2

THE EMPRESS

IF the Empress Eugénie has been the subject of as many biographies as Marie Antoinette it is because she was something more than the wife of an Emperor and the best dressed woman in France. A personality in her own right, she combined womanly charm with an active brain, a determined will and an unsullied character. We come nearest to her in the two volumes of family letters published by the Duke of Alba in 1935. No crowned head in the nineteenth century received more adulation and none was less spoiled. Highly emotional, she sampled the joys and sorrows of life in a measure rarely granted to mortals. The Austrian Ambassador Prince Metternich, an intimate friend, described her as all fire and flame, and in his unconventional wife, Princess Pauline, she found a kindred spirit. Though not a maker of history like Elizabeth, Maria Theresa or Catherine the Great, she witnessed major transformations in the map of Europe and took some small part in the process. Though she declined repeated suggestions to write her memoirs, we learn her thoughts and feelings from her correspondence and from the testimony of a host of witnesses. Napoleon III was the most secretive of men, Eugénie one of the most uninhibited of women. Everyone knew what she thought of events and policies, whom she hated and whom she loved, for she often found it difficult to control her tongue. The publication in 1926 of the Austrian Ambassador's dispatches, from 1863 to the *débâcle*, depict her poring over the map of Europe, building castles in the air, and writing him long letters after their interviews. The least sensual of women was the most passionate of politicians, obsessed by considerations of national prestige and by dreams of territorial aggrandisement even though unobtainable without war.

Few would deny that her political judgment was weak and her influence at times detrimental to the interests of France.

Her father, Comte de Montijo, a grandee of Spain, had fought for Napoleon in the Peninsular War and died when she was a child, and her mother was the formative influence of her early life. Her maternal grandfather, William Kirkpatrick, a Scot who had settled in Malaga as a wine merchant, was appointed United States Consul and assumed American nationality. To this Nordic strain she owed the auburn hair which excited much admiration and differentiated her from the darker beauties of the south. In 1834 her mother took her two daughters to be educated at the Convent of the Sacré Coeur in Paris. The Countess had intellectual friends, among them Mérimée and Stendhal, the latter of whom regaled the little girls with breath-taking recollections of the Russian campaign of 1812. In 1836, at the age of ten, she caught the first glimpse of her future husband as he was brought to the Conciergerie after his *putsch* at Strasbourg, for the sisters were on friendly terms with the wife of the Governor and happened to be with her at the critical moment. The death of their father in 1839 left his widow a rich woman with a house in Madrid and a country estate. Before returning to Spain the daughters, who had learned some English from a governess, spent a year at school at Clifton. Back in Madrid at the age of fourteen, Eugénie witnessed the marriage of her elder sister to the Duke of Alba, the most illustrious of the grandees of Spain, descended not merely from the grim commander of Philip II but also from the Duke of Berwick, bastard of James II and Arabella Churchill. The younger girl's chance seemed to have arrived when a Marquis pretended to fall in love with her and she lost her heart to him. Her bliss turned to bitterness when she discovered that the suitor was employing her as a decoy to seduce her sister. In her despair she took poison, was with difficulty persuaded to swallow an antidote, and never recovered her faith in the constancy of men.

No one could live in Madrid society in the thirties without taking some interest in politics. 'I inherited my taste from my mother, in whose house I listened to talk of statesmen and diplomats, generals and journalists,' she told Paléologue half a century later. 'On my marriage I tried to understand the Emperor's problems, learning from him, from foreign diplomats, from books, and I filled notebooks with my reading.' The raid on Boulogne made headlines in the European press, and his escape from the fortress of Ham increased the interest of the Montijo family in the Bonapartist cause. Foreign travel enlarged her horizon. She was presented at Buckingham Palace, where she saw for the first time the Queen who was to befriend her in sunshine and storm for the next sixty years.

The Montijo family, with its tradition of Bonapartist sympathies, welcomed the election of the Prince to the Presidency. When Eugénie met him for the first time at the house of Princess Mathilde he was infatuated. She had neither need nor desire to practise the arts of coquetry: she had merely to be her natural self. Invitations to the Elysée followed the *coup* of 1851, and the final scene was staged at Compiègne after the proclamation of the Empire a year later. Rebuffed in his attempt to install the lovely Spaniard as a *maîtresse en titre*, he proposed to her in January 1853 and hurried on the ceremony in Notre Dame. His choice provoked the same amazement as the selection of the penniless Marie Leczinska for Louis XV, and in both cases it was widely felt that the ruler had let his country down. No one judged her more harshly and more unjustly than the newly installed British Ambassador Lord Cowley. The Emperor, he reported, had been captured by an adventuress.

> To hear the way men and women talk of their future Empress is astounding. Things have been repeated to me which the Emperor has said of her and others which have been said to him which it would be impossible to commit to paper. She has played her game so well that he can get her in no other way but marriage, and it is to gratify his passions that he married her. People are already speculating on their divorce. The marriage is a very false step. To put this *intrigante* on the throne is a lowering of the Imperial dignity with a vengeance.

After the ceremony the Ambassador returned to the charge. 'His foolish marriage has done him an infinity of harm in the country. It was of course ill-received in Paris, even by his friends, and it has set all the women against him. Church and army disapprove.' That the partnership was not a complete success was the fault of the fickle ruler, not of his wife, who was neither an *intrigante* nor a flirt.

In the course of a long life the Empress loved only two persons, her sister and her son, with all her heart, but for a brief space she believed herself to be in love with the Emperor. Her letters to the Duchess of Alba mirror her emotions during the brief interval between her engagement and the marriage ceremony. 'I must be the first to tell you of my marriage to the Emperor,' she wrote on 15 January 1853. 'He has been so noble and generous and has shown me such affection that I am still quite moved. He has fought and won.' She enclosed a formal letter to her mother. 'I have long loved your daughter and wish to make her my wife. I now ask you for her hand, for no one is better able to assure my happiness nor more worthy to wear a crown.' A week later she reported:

> I have just arrived at the Elysée, and I have not a moment to tell you my emotion. I bid farewell to my family and country. One must know him in his private life to realize his worth. I still feel frightened by the responsibility about to follow me, yet I fulfil my destiny. I tremble from fear not of assassination but from ranking in history below Blanche of Castile and Anne of Austria. Today they are crying *Vive l'Impératrice* for the first time. May God keep it so, but adversity will find me more firm and courageous than prosperity. Good and evil things will often be attributed to me. I have never been ambitious, though my destiny has led me to the crest of a slope whence a trifle can hurl me down; but I have not risen from so low a place as to feel giddy. Two things I hope will protect me, my faith in God and my immense desire to help the unfortunate classes who have nothing, not even work. If Providence has chosen me for such a lofty position it is that I may be the mediatress between those who suffer and those who can aid. So I have accepted this great position as a divine mission, and I thank God for having placed on my path a heart so noble and so devoted as that of the Emperor. I have known much suffering and my belief in happiness was almost gone, but now I believe in it. I was so little used to being loved. My life was a great desert. He is a man of irresistible strength of will though not obstinate, capable of sacrifices great and small. He always stakes his future on the throw of a card, and that is why he always wins.

For the next seventeen years she lived in the glare of the footlights. After a talk with her at a ball at Saint-Cloud soon after her marriage Mérimée, her oldest friend in France, reported to her mother in Madrid that she seemed in high spirits and looked prettier than ever. 'The more one looks at her,' was the verdict of Palmerston a year after her marriage, 'the prettier one thinks her.' That with such a destiny and such a face she never for a moment lost her head or her good name is a tribute to her strength of character. On the official visit of the Emperor and Empress to Windsor in 1855 she won the respect and affection of Queen Victoria who was not always easy to please. There was loss as well as gain, for she had left part of her heart in Madrid. She missed the bull-fights and, above all, her sister. 'I often look back,' she wrote in May 1853 after a miscarriage,

> and see all I have given up for ever and all the places I shall never revisit. In exchange I have gained a crown, which means I am the first slave of my kingdom, isolated, without a friend of either sex, never alone: an insupportable life unless compensated by a man at my side who loves me madly. He too is a slave who has no motive and no ambition except the good of his country, and God knows what his reward has been. Just now I thank God for the disappointment of a hope which filled me with joy, for I think with terror of the poor Dauphin Louis XVII, of Charles I, Mary Stuart and Marie Antoinette. Who knows what would have been the fate of my child? I should infinitely prefer a crown for my son less resplendent but more secure. Don't think I lack courage. You see my thoughts are not very gay, but remember that I have been lying up for three months and have pain in all my bones. Today I tried to stand but was too weak from loss of blood.

Another miscarriage in 1855 made people wonder whether there would ever be an heir. Pianori's pistol shot at the Emperor in May 1855 as he rode in the Bois de Boulogne was a shock for a highly strung woman. He continued his ride and on returning to the Tuileries he calmly remarked: 'Such attempts never succeed; to make sure it needs a dagger.' Hübner saw the Empress sobbing convulsively when she learned the news. 'It was terrible,' she confided to her sister; 'but thank God, the danger over, it is quickly forgotten; at any rate one tries to forget it, for to live in anxiety is no life. Well, God had so protected the Emperor this time that I trust He will continue to do so. This hope doubles my courage. Besides, a danger shared is less alarming.'

A year later, after three years of marriage and an agonizing confinement, Eugénie presented her husband with the heir so urgently needed to consolidate the *régime*. Henceforth the love which might have gone to a faithful husband was lavished on her only child. It was the proudest and happiest moment of her life. Her recovery, however, was very slow, and in moments of depression she wondered whether she would always remain an invalid. 'My little boy, thank God, is well,' she wrote to her sister; 'he is the only bright spot on my horizon. His eyes are superb, charming sky blue, with long dark eyelashes. He already smiles intelligently. But I must not go on with my description or I should never stop.'

Eugénie was such a solicitous hostess that some of her guests complained of an excess of zeal.

> The Empress [reported Lord Cowley from Compiègne in 1857] instead of letting people alone, torments herself and them by thinking she must provide constant amusement which suits some people and not others; but they are both so natural and unaffected, and there is so little ceremony and etiquette, that life is not disagreeable for a short time. Breakfast at half-past eleven, then either hunting or shooting or some other expedition. Horses and carriages are found for everybody who wants them, and nothing can be prettier than one of their cavalcades. Dinner about eight, which never lasts more than an hour. In the evening there is dancing to a band, or hand organ (a dreadful trial), or charades or cards. Now and then a theatrical company from Paris is invited.

Baron Hübner, the Austrian Ambassador, paints vivid pictures of the vivacious hostess in his journal after his many visits to the Tuileries, St. Cloud and Compiègne. 'Dinner passed like a moment,' he noted in 1855, 'as it always does when I meet this charming woman. In her youth I found her capricious and not very agreeable. She needed a throne to become serious and likeable. She sparkled, not exactly with intelligence, but with that Andalusian sprightliness which is one of her attractions.' Sitting next her at dinner at St. Cloud soon after her marriage, he delighted in her animation and lack of pose.

> She was Mlle de Montijo again. She has the tact and good sense never to play the Empress with people she knew intimately before she mounted the throne or, as she puts it, when she lived in the world. She remains what she had always been: a little more serious when she appears in public, she loves to let herself go in her private

circle. Queen Christina says she has found exactly the right position, not too high and not too low. I agree, but I should like a little more ballast, much more reading, more solid instruction, a more balanced mind, less inclined to marvels and more to serious things. At the moment she has thrown herself with all her Andalusian ardour into table-turning.

Modern spiritualism originated in the experiences of the Fox family in America in 1848 and reached Europe in 1852. *Séances* became the fashion, and Daniel Dunglas Home, a young Scot, took London by storm and though denounced by Browning as 'Mr. Sludge the Medium' he was never convicted of fraud or vulgar commercialism. In addition to the thrills of table-rapping and table-turning his performances raised the question of communication with the dead.

> I went to see a Mr. Home [reported Eugénie to her sister in 1857]. No words can give you an idea of his extraordinary doings. He is thin, pale, aged twenty-one, very sickly, and with a strange expression. He is a Scot and talks little. Asked what he is going to do, he replied: I don't know, I am merely an instrument. Little happened the first time, I mean little compared with other occasions. It began with a stamping of the table, on which he had one hand, his legs outside. I will tell you about the last *séance* because it was the most extraordinary.

At this point in her letter Eugénie drew the long table, the Emperor alone on one side, herself and a lady-in-waiting on the other, Home at one end and General Espinasse, *aide-de-camp* of the Emperor, at the other.

> Mme de Montebello had a bell in her hand, and so had I, the Emperor an accordion. When we all asked for something to happen the two bells were removed by invisible hands and mine was transferred to the hand of the General. He was very sceptical and was so upset that he thought he was about to be ill. The Emperor's instrument played some charming airs, and a footstool at the end of the room came to me as if propelled by an unknown force. And now occurred what would be beyond belief if one had not witnessed it. Afraid of seeing hands, I had put a cloth on the table, when suddenly the Emperor said: Look what is pushing the table-cloth towards me. Touch it, said Home. Yes, it was a hand which pressed his. The General saw it too and touched the little hand of a child.

I got up to look. Turning round, when my dress was grasped, we all saw my cushion seized by a hand. Summoning up my courage I said to it: I am not afraid and I wish you to press mine. The next moment the table-cloth is pushed towards me and a man's hand pressed mine. Then I tried to do the same, but there was nothing to press. All those present could confirm this and, strange to say, one was not afraid. I must see Mr. Home again and then perhaps we shall see even more.

She wrote to her sister on the death of a friend that if his mother could see Home it would do her good. 'She would feel the hand of her son pressing hers and he would tell her he is happy or needs prayers. She could have no doubt, for one recognizes the hand which always says or does something which indicates that it is the person you think.'

Eugénie's most remarkable experience occurred at a *séance* on 12 March, the anniversary of her father's death, though no one knew it but herself.

As we sat round the table a hand never ceased to press mine or to pull my dress in order to make me give it. Surprised by such importunity, I said to it: So you love me? The response was a very distinct pressure of my hand. Have I known you? Yes. Tell me your name on earth. Spelling the letters came the reply: Today is the anniversary of my death. Those present asked me who it was, and I replied: My father. Then the hand pressed mine with great affection and allowed me to press his. Then it made with a finger three signs of the cross on my hand and disappeared for ever. At a later *séance* he asked for certain prayers which we offered on the spot. He told us he was happy and going to heaven, and that was *adieu*. Unfortunately Mr. Home is not here, but he will return. I have the impression that death is not so sad as one thinks, and that sometimes they are near us, though invisible, till they return to heaven. Don't you agree, dear sister? Don't think this is imagination. It is reality and I hope to convince you.

The attraction of the medium for the sovereign was not shared by Princess Mathilde and her circle nor by Walewski, the Foreign Minister, who regarded him as a fraud and threatened to resign unless the *séances* in the Tuileries ceased. In 1858 anonymous accusations of evil conduct led to a brief imprisonment followed by expulsion from France without a trial which, it was feared, might lead to compromising revelations.

The Empress counted fewer friends than enemies, some of them shamelessly jealous of her amazing luck. Persigny resented the loss of his proud position as chief adviser, and Princess Mathilde deplored the loss of hers as the First Lady of the land. Prince Napoleon would have frowned on any woman who cut him out of the succession, hating her to the end of his life as much as she hated him, and his comments were sometimes unprintable. When he took the little Prince Imperial on his knee and caressed him, the Empress with her ladies and chamberlains watched him suspiciously, leading him to comment: 'She thinks I have arsenic in my pocket.' He pursued his vendetta after the collapse of the *régime*. 'In 1881,' records Maxime du Camp, 'he told me he believed that Nigra, the Piedmontest Ambassador, and a young officer were her lovers. He spoke with such deliberation that one felt sure he was lying.' Maxime du Camp himself, however, one of the few friends of the Emperor in the literary world, considered the marriage the gravest of his mistakes.

> Never did a futile creature bring to inordinate ambition a meaner intelligence. She pushed the country into adventures without counting the cost. She was a fatal influence, and her marvellous beauty does not absolve her. While the Emperor was indulgent she resorted to calumny when her *amour-propre* was involved, so she was not beloved. The Queen of Holland has spoken of her to me with contempt, and Hortense Cornu used to say 'She will ruin the Empire.'

He had known her as a frivolous girl, and in his opinion she never grew up.

> Superstitious and superficial, always preoccupied with the impression she made, parading her shoulders and bosom, her hair dyed, her face painted, her eyes shaded, her lips rouged. To be in her proper sphere she only lacked the music of the circus, the cantering, decorated horse, the hoop through which to jump and the kiss to the spectators. The balls at the Tuileries, the *soirées* at Compiègne and Fontainebleau, were staged for her glory. Frigid, without temperament, both miserly and extravagant, with no passion but vanity, she dreamed of playing the principal role, but was only a supernumerary, enveloped in a sovereignty which she did not know how to wear. I don't believe she ever had a serious idea about anything, but she

excelled with her dressmaker, and knew as much about precious stones as an old Jewish courtier.

Vieil-Castel, as usual, also found far more to blame than to praise. As a foreigner lacking the qualification of royal birth she could hardly expect to be popular, but in his opinion she scarcely tried.

The Empress has not made herself popular at Fontainebleau [he wrote in May 1857]. She has been most ungracious to the townspeople and garrison. When there were fireworks she had all the park gates closed despite the request that the public might be allowed to enjoy it. Unfortunately she confounds gravity with dignity, fearing she may not be thought sufficiently imperial. However democratic the French may be, they do not like upstart monarchs. She thinks that with her severe manner and Spanish genealogy she can keep the world at arm's length. She deceives herself, and perhaps will one day learn (we are far from wishing it) what a misfortune it is not to be loved.

'She does not approve of French society,' he added in 1858, 'though she was not so difficult to please before her elevation to the throne. She prefers the English and Spaniards.' He was incensed by her 'insane infatuation' for Orsini. 'She is losing her reason and talks of nothing else.' It was the more astonishing because she was no friend of Italian nationalism. In 1861 he renewed the attack. Prince Napoleon, he wrote in his journal, was not the Emperor's only family trouble, for the Empress did not appreciate her position, the obligations of France or the part she ought to play. 'She prefers the society of foreigners, from among whom she selects her intimate friends and invites them to Fontainebleau or Compiègne in preference to the French. Like Prince Napoleon she is avaricious; her only thought is to obtain and hoard securities.' His friend Princess Mathilde reported that at a recent *déjeuner*, where Dr. Conneau and herself were the only guests, the Empress spoke so bitterly of foreign policy that the Emperor rose from the table, remarking, 'Really, Eugénie, you seem to forget you are French and married to a Bonaparte.' She was aware of the hostility with which she was regarded in many quarters, and showed in her demeanour that she knew who were her enemies. Her sharpest critics were those who knew her least, and she was most esteemed by those who knew her best.

She was well aware of critical eyes and unfriendly talk, and on the last day of 1857 she poured out her heart to her sister.

> You know me well enough to think that if I am a victim of rash judgments I am not in the least to blame. Perhaps weary of struggling against destiny I have shut my eyes and let myself drift: that is my only offence. Those who can judge me at close quarters, I am sure, absolve me. I am so fed up with life; it is so empty in the past, so full of shoals in the present, and perhaps so short in the future (at any rate I hope so) that I often ask myself if the struggle is worth while. I lose courage, for these petty annoyances wear one out. You can imagine how many enemies I have, and I know not where to turn my gaze.

Two days later she wrote in the same sombre mood.

> A new year, and I am not sorry. Tonight I have a reception for the ladies—another great effort; I am surprised you know of my cough. I did not tell you nor mama in order not to alarm you. It is nothing and would not be worth mention if it were not so persistent. I have taken everything the doctors have given me, but without result. I am condemned to silence, but that is impossible, for at receptions I have to speak to everyone. What would the business world, the ladies and the girls say if I gave no balls? And if one gives a ball one must be there. I am like a soldier on the day of battle: one can't be ill. The world is my battlefield. But don't worry. God always gives the health required for one's duties.

The most shattering experience in her life was the scene outside the Opera House on 14 January 1858, when Orsini's three bombs killed and wounded scores of people and horses and wrecked the Imperial carriage. 'We are safe,' she reported to her mother next day, 'thanks to God who alone preserved us from this infernal plot. The Emperor and I got off, he with a scratch on the tip of his nose, myself with a tiny splinter in the eye, so slight that I can write perfectly. The Emperor's hat had a hole and the carriage was riddled with bits of iron. Don't worry. When God sends dangers He always gives one courage to bear them.' When her mother, shaken by the catastrophe, denounced the French, the Empress rejoined that the assassins were Italians. She told her sister that she had not shed a tear on the fateful night. Both had set a superb example of courage and self-control and the nerve-racking incident left no bitterness in her heart. To the disgust of the Austrian Ambassador she pleaded passionately but vainly for the lives of the conspirators, and showed practical sympathy to Orsini's widow and children.

The crime strengthened the Emperor's desire to help the cause of Italian unity and when he left for the front in the following year Eugénie was appointed Regent. 'It is a great responsibility for me,' she confided to her sister, 'for you know the Parisians were not always very easy to lead; but God, I hope, will give me all the knowledge I lack, for I have only the wish to do well and not to allow the slightest disorder. How strange is destiny! Life's happenings often follow each other in spite of ourselves. But I confess to a feeling of pride if by my presence I can help the morale of France.' Two months later she reported that Paris was very quiet and that the state of the country had never been more reassuring. 'So don't worry about us. I believe it is fortunate for the Emperor that the people should get accustomed to the Regency, for the assassins will be less inclined to try their hand when they see that even if they succeed they will not gain control.' Though her sympathies were with Pio Nono, not with Cavour and Garibaldi, she realized the significance of Solferino for the dynasty and rejoiced at the tumultuous welcome of the Emperor and herself in the fair land of Savoy which French arms had added to the dominions of France. It was the last happy phase of the Second Empire, marred only by the loss of her adored sister.

The radiant dawn of the romantic union was too good to last, and was followed by constant friction and stormy scenes. She knew too much of her husband's record to expect fidelity, accepting his *petits divertissements* as philosophically as possible though not always without anger and grief. 'Miss Howard' was bought off with cash and a title; but at the close of 1855 Countess Castiglione was dispatched by Victor Emmanuel and Cavour with written instructions to further the ambitions of the House of Savoy by seducing the Emperor, not a difficult task for such a beauty. No *liaison*, however, excited her wrath so hotly as that with the low born Marguerite Bellanger, and in 1866 the British Ambassador reported that he was starting a new flirtation with Countess Mercy d'Argenteau. 'There is no saying what influence such a woman might gain, and I shall look out for squalls on the other side of the *ménage*.' There was also scandal about the pretty Italian wife of his cousin Walewski.

As the health of the Emperor waned the influence of the Empress waxed. When Mme Baroche asked her husband which of the Ministers had most influence he replied, 'The Empress'. She took little interest in the Crimean War, but the Italian campaign of 1859 touched her closely, since she dreaded any threat to the territorial possessions of the Pope. 'I have never been a clerical', she explained to Paléologue in old age. 'Clericalism means the interference of the clergy in politics. Were there any priests in my entourage? Not one. There was no clericalism at the Tuileries. I am not an Ultramontane, indeed I was something of a Gallican.' She shared the opinion of most Catholics that territory was needed to secure the independence of the Pope, and that France was pledged to the Temporal Power which had been restored by French troops in 1849. When Paléologue long afterwards listed the mistakes of the Second Empire as he saw them, she replied that there had only been one. 'We ought not to have hoisted the flag of nationality; that alone was our error.' She had always detested Victor Emmanuel for his anti-Papal and anti-clerical policy, his coarse manners and his dissolute life.

In 1862 Lord Cowley reported her saying that if the Emperor withdrew the French garrison from Rome, and that as a result the Pope had to quit, she would follow him wherever he went. Her devoted friend, the Austrian Ambassador, reported an astonishing conversation with Nigra the able representative of Victor Emmanuel.

Empress: What do you want, M. Nigra?
Nigra: I wish Your Majesty would be a little less hostile to us and would persuade the Emperor to withdraw his troops from Rome.
Empress: I would rather drown myself than lend a hand to your brigandage. You are insatiable. You call the subjects of the King of Naples who have remained loyal to him brigands. How do you describe yourselves? You are the robbers and you want to make others your accomplices. Wait a bit. The day of vengeance will come. You will witness the triumph of your Mazzinis and Garibaldis. You will be hung and I assure you I shan't come to your rescue.

Nigra: Your Majesty is really too unjust. Is not the King of Italy doing today in Naples what the Emperor did in France yesterday?
Empress (furiously): Don't compare the Emperor to your highway robber. The Emperor deprived nobody of anything. He found France abandoned and the throne vacant, and saved her by destroying people like you.

Nigra made no reply and left the room.

The gravest error of her career was her ardent championship of a Catholic Empire in Mexico. The Emperor had taken a lively interest in the New World ever since his visit after the Strasbourg *putsch*, and had published a pamphlet on a Nicaragua canal. Her approach was from a different angle—to secure some spectacular compensation for the Vatican after the loss of the larger part of the Papal States and at the same time to enhance the prestige of the Empire. Knowing nothing of conditions in Central America, she swallowed the fairy-tale that an Emperor under French auspices would be welcomed. When the French troops obeyed the peremptory summons from Washington and left Maximilian to his fate, she found herself the object of bitter attack. 'The people are very severe on the Empress,' reported her old friend Mérimée to Panizzi, the eminent Librarian of the British Museum. Though she felt the humiliation like a blow in the face, she never lowered her flag. 'I am not ashamed of Mexico,' she told Paléologue; 'I deplore it but I do not blush for it. I suggested it at Biarritz in 1861 when some conservative and clerical *émigrés* urged intervention by France, Spain and Italy who had nationals there. We were misled about the resistance.' An even greater blow to the prestige of the Empire was struck when Austria was expelled from the German Confederation. 'The summer of 1866,' she remarked to Paléologue, 'sealed our fate.' She had urged mobilization to extort compensation and secured the Emperor's approval, but the arguments of the Council led him to change his mind. The Austrian Ambassador found her in tears over the physical and moral collapse of the Emperor and the humiliation of France. Had she had her way the Empire might have collapsed in 1866.

When the Empress and Rouher were in agreement it became increasingly difficult for the ailing and ageing ruler to resist. Despite her attachment to her husband, testifies Ollivier, she felt compelled occasionally to think about a Regency. In the event of trouble no one seemed to take Rouher's place at her side and help her in her difficult task. Some friends of the Emperor, disliking the concessions and alarmed by his decline, scarcely attempted to hide their view that alteration might soon be necessary and, like the Empress, believed Rouher would be indispensable at such a crisis. At this stage the support of the Empress was much more important to a politician than that of the Emperor. 'The Emperor yields to her in all,' reported the Queen of Holland to Lord Clarendon in 1867, 'and I was shocked by her unpopularity even among the Court people. I like her grace, her beauty, her sweetness.' She was no longer the pleasure-loving young woman, enjoying life and homage; she was now an ambitious and experienced consort with a taste for affairs. While the ruler was increasingly subject to whims, she had always possessed a strong will. Thus the 'Vice-Emperor' had nothing to fear from the Court or Parliament, no serious resistance in the exercise of the immense power the Emperor had just given him.

Though Ollivier was never a friend of the Empress, there is little exaggeration in his picture of the years between the crisis of 1866 and his appointment to high office in 1870.

Her growing influence was deplored by Persigny in a lengthy memorandum to the Emperor in 1869. In his opinion the failures in Poland and Denmark, Mexico and Germany, were mainly due to her presence at the meetings of the Council, which created a dualism in the State and gave rise to intrigues. Having tried in vain for a private audience with the Emperor, the candid friend felt it his duty to explain his views in writing, hoping that she would not learn of his intervention. By bad luck the document reached the ruler when he was ill in bed and was read by the Empress with his permission. Of course she should be prepared for the eventuality of a Regency, began Persigny, and she was a good learner. Everyone knew of her energetic discharge of her duties as sovereign, her courage in danger, her intelligence, her private virtues, the heroic resolution she would display in case of need. Her entourage knew how she had profited by the lessons of her august husband: in summoning her to the Council, however, he seemed to be going too far in thus identifying her with its decisions and exposing her to criticism if things went wrong. It was widely felt that she represented ideas for which the Bour-

THE EMPRESS EUGÉNIE

bons had been justly reproached, and the opinion was everywhere entertained in the army, the magistracy, even within the Government, that she had shaped policies which had failed. However unjustly, it was believed that she encouraged clerical pretensions, initiated the Mexico expedition, and sabotaged the policy of the Emperor after Sadowa by her zeal for Austria. People everywhere were saying that when she confined herself to court life the Empire, governed by a great prince, attained the height of power and glory, and that all this glory had been eclipsed by her. A revolting injustice! Whatever opinions she may have expressed, the responsibility rested with the Emperor; but all this talk showed the unwisdom of her presence in the Council. Differences with Ministers weakened the Government and encouraged the enemies of the State. Her attendance constituted a sort of division of power, always a source of weakness, and if the sovereigns differed it embarrassed the Ministers.

> The presence of the wife of a sovereign in the Council is a danger to the State, condemned by the theory and practice of all governments and contrary to the nature of things. I am criticizing not this or that policy but the principle. If she wishes to take part, any difference between the Emperor and the Empress should be composed before the Council meets. She gains nothing by her presence. If measures fail, she receives a share of the blame; if they succeed she deprives the Emperor of the honour. The wife of the sovereign should remain aloof in a calm, elevated sphere, inaccessible to the passions of politics. In the name of thirty years of faithful service I beg that this advice be not regarded as a crime. I hope that the great Prince whom I love, honour and admire, whose friendship has been the glory of my life, will not withdraw his affection.

No one but the *loyal Serviteur* would have dared to address the master of France in such peremptory terms.

The Emperor replied that the Empress had decided to cease attendance at the Council, a resolution which he disapproved since the future Regent ought to learn her trade. The mild tone of the letter (not preserved) suggested to Persigny that the writer shared his opinion more than he cared to show. The Empress followed in a letter of eight pages (not preserved) energetically denying her intervention in past events but accepting responsibility in order to relieve the Emperor. 'She believed I was the only person to hold that she influenced decisions and to disapprove her presence, but she would not be present again.' Evidently—and inevitably—she was deeply hurt. While welcoming her decision to withdraw, Persigny expressed surprise at her ignorance of what people were thinking and saying. 'It will be best for the Emperor, your son and yourself. Calm will be restored.' A few days later the ruler informed the audacious critic that he could not accept his wife's sacrifice, and desired her to continue attendance in order to avoid unfriendly comment if she were suddenly to disappear. Persigny replied that it was the principle, not the person, which was dangerous; he advised no sudden change but gradually decreasing attendance. This advice was followed and by 1869 she no longer appeared. 'I feel I rendered a real service to both sovereigns,' he wrote when compiling his Memoirs in 1869. 'Her anger is legitimate, but it is noble of her to have displayed so little resentment.' On the other hand there can be little doubt that the sharp criticism of the Empress—for such it was despite the sugar on the pill—was a factor in the estrangement of the ruler from his oldest and most devoted comrade.

With her authoritarian convictions Eugénie could hardly be expected to smile on the Liberal Empire, but the Austrian Ambassador, visiting her shortly after the appointment of Ollivier, found her very sensible. She deplored certain concessions, above all the cessation of official candidatures. The Government, she felt, should at any rate support citizens who stood for order, and universal suffrage should start at twenty-five. The Emperor, however, would give way on everything except the army and foreign policy: to yield on them would be to call a fiacre and be off. She distrusted what she called 'this Orleanist Cabinet' (except Ollivier a Republican) which at a crisis might call in the Duc d'Aumale. For the moment there was nothing to fear: if the Emperor were to die all friends of order who had anything to lose would rally round the Regent or the Prince Imperial, provided that within six hours of the catastrophe the public felt itself sustained by energy and force. A minute of hesitation and all would be lost. So long as she was alive there would be no wavering. The experienced Ambassador concluded his report with the words: 'I hope the Empress is not indulging in illusions.' Unfortunately her political insight was as limited as her spirit was high.

No chapter in Eugénie's political career has provoked such controversy and condemnation as her record in *l'année terrible*. 'She and she alone has been the cause of all France's misfortunes,' screamed Princess Mathilde; 'this woman has ruined the best and most generous of men and with him our poor country.' That she supported the fateful demand on the King of Prussia at Ems she admitted, while indignantly denying that she had exclaimed '*C'est ma petite guerre*'. Yet her intimates were aware that since the humiliation of 1866 she had dreamed of a triumphant conflict with Prussia. When someone remarked during the Exhibition of 1867 that the Germans—so impressively represented by the towering figure of Bismarck, the stately old King and his handsome son—were the race of the future, she exclaimed: 'We are not there yet.' On the gathering of the storm clouds she struck the Austrian Ambassador as looking ten years younger at the thought of a political triumph or a victorious campaign, 'Our army seemed to us invincible, and we counted on powerful alliances,' she subsequently explained to Paléologue. 'After Bismarck slapped our face we had to choose between war and dishonour. Better disaster than dishonour!' That she desired a showdown is clear. 'Neither the Emperor nor I wanted war,' testifies Ollivier, 'and only decided for it when Bismarck left us no option between war and dishonour. It was the Empress, spurred on by the Right and by the feeling of national greatness, who wished it even before it became inevitable.' On 6 July the Austrian Ambassador found her thirsting for war. 'It would be difficult for Bismarck to climb down,' she exclaimed, 'and if he did France would have no cause for gratitude. The chance of avenging 1866 seemed too good to be lost. The deepest motive for her intransigence was her conviction that the dynasty could not survive a further humiliation. That it could not survie defeat was beyond her limited range of vision.

The hour of destiny had struck and the Prince Imperial at fourteen was just old enough to play his part. 'Louis has written to you today and sent you a lock of his hair,' reported Eugénie to her mother on 27 July.

He is full of animation and courage, and so am I. Certain names carry obligations and his are heavy, so he must do his duty as I feel sure he will. You are lucky only to have daughters, for at times I feel like a wild animal longing to take my little one far away into the desert and rend anyone who tried to seize him there. Then I reflect and say to myself that I would rather see him dead than dishonoured, put my anxieties behind me, and leave him in God's hands.

That day he donned the uniform of a sub-lieutenant of artillery, and that evening at dinner the band played the 'Marseillaise,' disallowed since 1851.

When the Emperor and his son—the latter with an inscribed copy of *The Imitation of Christ* from his mother—left for the front next day, Eugénie performed her duties as Regent with courage and dignity. By the middle of August all the world had realized that the French army, instead of being ready 'to the last gaiter button', was unfit for a major war. 'I have suffered everything it is possible to suffer,' she reported to her niece in Spain on 18 August. 'My health is fairly good, except that I can no longer eat nor sleep. My morale is intact, and my trust in God equals my resignation to His decrees.' To her mother she wrote that there was nothing for it but resignation. 'I have often thought of past days, and I wonder how one can stand up to all these cruel heartbreaking emotions. One can wish for everything except a crown. One surrenders everything, rest, happiness, tenderness, and often meets nothing but failings and sometimes worse. But I have found sure and devoted friends in these testing days.' An offer by her mother to provide a place of safety for her grandson was gratefully declined.

> My cruellest affliction is to see Louis exposed to all kinds of dangers, but I can't change his destiny. He must remain in his country so long as it wants us. One can't think of oneself in moments of danger and then turn up again when it is over. Our fate is in the hand of God. We will do our duty, each of us. Believe me, it is not the crown I am defending, it is honour. If, after the war, when there is no longer a Prussian on French soil, the country no longer wishes for us, then perhaps, far from noise and people, I may perhaps forget that I have suffered so much. I can't speak of Louis, it is too painful. You wept for my sister; ought not one rather to weep for the living? Forgive this sad letter. I try to believe, but my heart overflows

when I think of this poor child of fourteen exposed to such trials. Don't imagine my morale is gone. I am still hopeful.

Two days later she told her nieces that she had had no news of the Emperor and their son for three days. 'If this goes on I fear my head won't stand it. We are preparing for a siege, determined to hold out as long as possible; if the city gives way, we shall continue the war elsewhere while a single Prussian remains on French soil.'

On the crushing news of Sedan Eugénie refused to resign the Regency, but the tidal wave of revolution surged over her head. Hearing the hoarse cries of the mob outside the Tuileries: '*Vive la République!*', '*À bas l'Espagnole!*', she felt that—as she had always expected—she was about to suffer the fate of Marie Antoinette. Fleeing through the galleries of the Louvre, accompanied by her faithful friend the Austrian Ambassador, she hailed a passing fiacre, sought refuge in the house of Dr. Evans, the American dentist, drove with him and her sole attendant the Duchesse de Monchy to Deauville with a false passport, and almost perished in a stormy crossing in an English yacht which happened to be there. 'I took her on board,' reported Sir John Burgoyne from Ryde to Lord Granville, 'and the only remark she made was "I know I am safe now under the protection of an Englishman." She said "*Pauvre France*", and became very hysterical for a time.' The Foreign Secretary congratulated him on having had the opportunity of being of service. If he still saw her, he should inform her 'how much honoured I should be if I could be of any possible use to her Majesty, and what a deep recollection I have of her Majesty's kindness'. To the Queen's Private Secretary, Sir Henry Ponsonby, he wrote a week later: 'Her misfortune is great, although it is much owing to herself: Mexico, Rome, war with Prussia.' He spoke for England, which had always liked the Imperial couple more than their doings.

From the Marine Hotel, Hastings, the fugitive wrote to her mother that she had only left after the proclamation of the Republic and the invasion of the Tuileries: she had not deserted her post. 'I can't tell you at present of my plans. If I am allowed I expect to rejoin the Emperor. I have not the courage to tell you about us; we are very unhappy; Providence is crushing us, but its will be done.' The only ray of light was to find the Prince Imperial who had reached the hotel two days earlier. A few days later mother and son settled in at Chislehurst, which remained their home till the death of the Prince Imperial in 1879.

The *débâcle* caused a resurgence of affection between the long estranged sovereigns. 'I am heartbroken to see by your letters how you are suffering,' wrote the Emperor from Wilhelmshöhe on 6 October. 'Is there a little place in your heart for me?' 'Nothing remains of past grandeurs to separate us,' she replied. 'We are united, a hundred times more united, because our sufferings and our hopes meet on this dear little head of Louis. The darker the prospect, the more we feel the need to lean on each other.' Complete harmony was restored during a two days' visit to the captive, whom she found calm and resigned.

> Dear friend [she wrote on 31 January 1871], today is the anniversary of our marriage. It will be sad so far from each other, but at any rate I can tell you I am deeply attached to you. In the good days the ties were loosened and I thought broken: it needed a storm to prove their solidity. More than ever I have in mind the words of the Gospel: the wife will follow her husband everywhere, in health and in sickness, in happiness and sorrow. You and Louis are everything to me and take the place of my family and country. The misfortunes of France affect me profoundly, but not for a moment do I regret the glamour of the past. To be reunited is my sole wish. Poor dear friend, may my devotion make you forget for a moment the trials through which your great soul has passed. Your adorable resignation makes me think of Our Lord. Believe me, the day will come when justice is done to you. Meanwhile Louis and I embrace you with all our heart.

When the conflict was over, the fallen ruler joined his family at Chislehurst, adapting himself to his new surroundings with far less difficulty than the woman of forty-five and the lad of fourteen. The burden of boredom and frustration lay heavy on the household, and the winter fogs were hard to bear. The Empress fretted like a caged bird: at times, she exclaimed to Filon, they felt inclined to gobble each other up. 'I find England very dismal,' complained the Prince to Princess Mathilde on the last day of 1870; 'the grey skies make me long for France more than ever. I hope 1871 will be happier; it cannot be worse.' The Emperor, now an invalid and always something of a fatalist, accepted his doom with composure. Since he possessed £60,000 and Eugénie sold her jewels for £150,000 there was no immediate financial anxiety. The unchanging friendship of the Queen was a comfort, and the two mothers discussed a possible marriage of Princess Beatrice to the Prince Imperial. The intelligent, high-spirited, industrious and affectionate youth was the light of his parents' eyes. The faithful Dr. Conneau was at their side, his son the companion of their boy, and Filon, his beloved tutor and biographer, helped to dispel the gloom by his cheerful temperament. Bonapartists came and went, but the most highly placed of them, Prince Napoleon, was an irritant, not a consolation. Having frequently been a nuisance throughout the Empire, he aroused the fury of Eugénie after the Emperor's death by demanding the sole care of the heir during his minority. Occasionally she sought relief in travel, visiting her mother in Spain and taking her son to Scotland, Switzerland and Italy. Mother and son lived for the future and refused to abandon hope of a restoration. Longing to make himself known to France by some dramatic achievement, he secured the reluctant permission of the Queen and the Prime Minister to join the campaign in Zululand in 1879 where he met his death in an ambush. 'Everything that happens is indifferent to me,' cried his distracted mother. 'I have only one wish—to join him.'

Dividing her time between her new home at Farnborough and Cap Martin, Eugénie survived for another forty years. Sometimes she complained that she could not die. A pilgrimage to the scene of her son's death brought mingled emotions of grief and pride, for on all sides she heard of the affectionate respect he had inspired. She followed every move on the European chessboard with eager interest, and survived to salute the recovery of Alsace and Lorraine. In the following year, 1920, she passed away on a visit to Spain in her ninety-fourth year. Father, mother and son lie together in the shrine she erected at Farnborough. None of her contemporaries except Francis Joseph could look back on such length of days and such varied experiences. When asked how she could bear to stay in the Hôtel Continental overlooking the Tuileries gardens, she used to reply: 'The Empress died in 1870.' Which were her most radiant memories? inquired Paléologue in

1901. She replied: 'The christening of the Prince Imperial in Notre Dame in 1856, the Te Deum in Notre Dame for the victory at Solferino in 1859, the regatta on the lake of Annecy after the annexation of Savoy in 1860, and the inauguration of the Suez Canal in 1869.' Among the women of high estate in the nineteenth century Victoria and Eugénie are the least likely to fall into oblivion.

3

'CHERCHEZ LA FEMME'

NAPOLEON III, like his uncle, was *grand coureur de femmes*, but, unlike the mighty Emperor, he sought to excuse himself. 'As a rule the man attacks. I am on the defensive and sometimes I capitulate.' Bacciochi, his Chamberlain, described him as the most faithful of friends and the most inconstant of lovers. No one has ever attempted to calculate the number of his flames, and his appetite was insatiable. During the five and a half weary years in the grim fortress at Ham he became the father of two sons by *La Belle Sabotière*, daughter of the village cobbler, who looked after his linen and brought up his meals. Later he married her to her foster-brother for whom he found employment, and he took care that the lads Eugène and Louis should have their chance. The elder entered the Foreign Office, serving as Secretary of the Embassy at St. Petersburg and later as Consul in Zanzibar. The younger occupied a post in the Ministry of Finance. Both became Counts of the Empire.

Reaching London in May 1846, the Prince found all doors open to him and made the acquaintance of 'Miss Howard'. Beauty, intelligence and charm had enabled Elizabeth Haryett, daughter of a Brighton bootmaker, to make her way on the stage in the capital at the price of her virtue. Her earliest patron was James Mason, the prodigal son of a wealthy merchant. Since, however, there was no pretence of love on either side, she transferred her favours to Francis Martyn, a rich major in the Life Guards. Though he could not marry her, since he had an invalid wife in the country, he offered her the position not of a kept woman lurking in the shadows but of his 'hostess' in St. John's Wood where she helped to entertain his friends. As a pledge of his good faith he handed over house property and valuable building land with instructions to her trustees to pay the interest to her for life. Henceforth she was a rich woman. A year later, in 1842, at the age of nineteen, she presented him with a son. Anxious to spare her child the brand of bastardy, she registered it as her brother, the legitimate son of her parents, hoping that the perjury would never reach their ears, for she had broken with them when they opposed her determination to enter the theatrical world. Having no hope of legitimate offspring, the father settled a large sum on 'Martin Constantin Haryett'.

A more exciting chapter opened when he took his pretty mistress to a reception at the house of his cousin by marriage, Lady Blessington, in June 1846, and Count d'Orsay, the lover of the hostess, presented her to Prince Louis Napoleon. She was advised to make a low curtsy to the man of thirty-eight of whom d'Orsay spoke as Monseigneur and Son Altesse Impériale. Listening enraptured to the story of his recent escape as the guests crowded round him, she felt a strange attraction and the Prince was struck by her obvious interest in his fate. After further meetings she confessed to an illegitimate son. He blandly replied, 'I have two, the fruits of captivity.' When she informed the father of her son that she had never loved him and was in love with the Prince, he accepted the situation and allowed her to take the child. Since the Prince had debts, she rented a small house where they lived till the fall of the Monarchy two years later. For the first and last time her heart was engaged. Ambition doubtless played a part, not merely because she shared his political expectations but because she may have dreamed that as a reward for her devotion and timely aid she might some day become his wife. The researches of Mme André-Maurois have revealed her, not as a greedy courtesan but as a woman of heart and conscience anxious to escape from the position into which she had drifted. Desiring to improve her education, she took lessons in history from A. W. Kinglake, who proceeded to beg for her favours. Since she thought of herself as a morganatic wife, she repulsed her suitor, who revenged himself many years later by a savage attack on the Emperor in his *History of the War in the Crimea*.

When the Prince crossed the Channel on his election to the Chamber in June 1848 he took rooms in a hotel in the Place

Vendôme, while she lived in another hotel close by. There was no attempt either to advertise or to conceal the *liaison*. They rode together and she listened to the talks with his supporters. When the new President moved into the Elysée she rented a small house accessible from the garden without exposure to observation. Persigny the *loyal serviteur*, General Fleury the equerry, Mocquard the Political Secretary, Bacciochi the Chamberlain, and a few other Bonapartists occasionally met at her table for dinner. The Marquis of Hertford, who preferred Paris to London, and his illegitimate son Richard Wallace became her friends, and Lord Normanby opened the doors of the British Embassy. The anglophobe Princess Mathilde, on the other hand, while living openly with a lover, ostentatiously ignored 'that creature'. When she accompanied the President on a visit to Tours in 1849 and was billeted in the home of a high official, the latter complained to Odilon Barrot, President of the Council. The letter was forwarded to the Prince, who replied with a defence of his mistress and himself. 'How many women are a hundred times less pure, less devoted, less excusable? I detest this pedantic rigour. True religion is not intolerant. I confess to seeking in illegitimate relations the affection my heart demands. Since my position has prevented me from marrying, and since amid the cares of government I have alas! neither intimate friends, nor old acquaintances, nor relatives who provide the sweetness of family life, I think I may be forgiven an affection which injures no one and which I do not parade.' A suite was assigned to her at Saint-Cloud, and she assumed the role of a mother to the President's bastards, whom she described as her beloved boys and who were brought up with her son. She manifested her gratitude in selling property, pawning her jewels, paying the President's debts, and supplying 200,000 francs in cash on the eve of the *coup d'état*. Lord Normanby and other observers believed that she would soon become the wife of the new master of France. One evening at Saint-Cloud he swore to her what she described as 'the holy oath' and which she always recorded as a promise of marriage, though he interpreted his words in a more limited sense.

His triumph was her undoing and she must have realized that a mistress would be impossible as an Empress. To adorn a court, to found a dynasty, to disarm an unsmiling Europe he needed a woman of good birth and unblemished record. Eugénie fulfilled the necessary conditions and a painful interview followed. 'His Majesty was here last night,' she wrote to a friend, 'offering to pay me off: yes, an earldom in my own right, a castle, and a decent French husband into the bargain. Oh! the pity of it all. I could put up with a dose of laudanum. The lord almighty spent two hours arguing with me.' A few days later he requested her to cross the Channel on a confidential mission to deal with a threat of blackmail, but *en route* at Havre she read in a paper that he had formally announced his engagement. Resenting what appeared to be a ruse, she drove straight back, only to find that her apartments had been ransacked by order of the Prefect of Police in search of letters which might compromise the ruler.

At a painful interview, terms for a separation were arranged. She was to become Comtesse Beauregard; her son was to inherit her dignities and property and to be provided with a career; and the Emperor's bastards were to remain with her till they grew up. She was not in need of a home, for she had purchased the fine estate of Beauregard to the west of the capital shortly before the proclamation of the Empire. The romance was over but affection remained. They continued to meet from time to time, and she was noticed in an open carriage at a military review. It was rumoured that they had resumed their intimacy, that the jealous Empress had threatened to leave France, and that the ruler had promised to break off correspondence. He reluctantly requested her to cease writing to him, adding that any news of importance could be transmitted through his secretary Mocquard. She was requested to keep away from Paris and to leave the country for a time. Taking her three little boys she revisited London where, in May 1854, 'Elizabeth Ann Haryett, spinster', married Clarence Trelawny, whom she had met in Florence while a guest of her old friend Lord Normanby, British Minister to Tuscany. She had been looking round for a husband of good family and of reputable character in accordance with the Emperor's wish.

Though she had little expectation of happiness, her experiences were even more distressing than she had feared. There was no pretence of affection on either side. The impecunious Trelawny, who cared for little but sport, needed a rich wife, she a recognized position in society. Her hope was disappointed, for it proved impossible to live down her past. She was ignored by her husband's relatives and friends who made no attempt to ease her position. When her son and the Emperor's bastards, to whom she had been a devoted second mother, reached adolescence and discovered their family backgrounds the affectionate ties were broken. Death came to the lonely woman in 1865 at the age of forty-two and was not unwelcome. She had known little happiness except during the six years with the only man who really loved her and the only man she ever loved.

The English temptress was gone, but the Empress could not expect fidelity. 'I was faithful to her for six months,' he confided to Princess Mathilde, 'but I need little distractions and I always return to her with pleasure.' Three years later the most glamorous of his mistresses flashed like a meteor across the sky. In *La Castiglione, le Coeur de l'Europe*, published in 1953, Alain Decaux, the latest and best of her biographers, has reconstructed the thrilling drama with the aid of her diaries and correspondence. Virginia, daughter of the Marquis Oldoini, member of an old Piedmont family and cousin of Cavour, was married at the age of sixteen to Count Castiglione, but after the birth of a son she started on a series of *liaisons*. Never had the moral standard of society been so low at the Court of Turin as during the reign of Victor Emmanuel, who boasted with a laugh of his easy conquests and was credited with a score of illegitimates. When her husband charged her with being the mistress of one of the Doria brothers, she calmly continued to write and made no reply. Every incident was recorded in her journal. Besieged by a host of hot-blooded young Italians, and unfettered by scruples of conscience, the most celebrated courtesan of her time except Lola Montez was ready for any adventure at home or abroad.

Her hour struck when the King and Cavour decided to employ her pretty face for their political designs. The defeat of Charles Albert at Custozza in 1849 had demonstrated the inability of the House of Savoy to expel Austria from Italy without an ally, and where could they hope to find one except in France? The Emperor's views on nationality and his early contacts with the Carbonari were known throughout Europe, but more was needed to transform sympathy into a military alliance. In the winter of

1855 the Crimean war, to which Piedmont had sent a token force, was nearing its close, and it was time for Cavour and his master to think ahead. On the evening of 16 November, during the absence of her husband, Victor Emmanuel entered the drawing-room of the Countess unescorted. He had seen her at Court festivities, but they were now alone for the first time. 'The King,' she noted in her diary, 'talked about people, his misfortunes, his anxieties, the war.' A month later, accompanied by her husband and son, she started for Paris. On the evening before leaving home her journal records that IL (with a capital letter) visited her for the second time and stayed till eleven. An illegible entry is interpreted by her biographer as an indication that the royal Don Juan had added another fair sinner to his list.

Installed in rooms within sight of the Tuileries in January 1856, she watched the carriages heading for the Tuileries. Her father, Secretary of the Piedmont Legation, opened all doors, and the daughter, still under nineteen made her *début* at a party given by Princess Mathilde, a friend of Italy, since her early days. When the Emperor was announced her usual self-assurance momentarily deserted her, and when he addressed her she remained silent. '*Elle est belle*,' he remarked to Comte de Reiset who records the incident, '*mais elle paraît être sans esprit.*' They met again a few days later at a reception at the Palais Royal and she noted in her diary: 'Went at midnight to the ball of Prince Jerome. Met the Emperor on the staircase. Said I arrived rather late.' After the introduction to the host, whom she had known as a child in Florence, she was presented to Morny, with whom she talked till two in the morning. A third contact took place on 29 January at a ball at the Tuileries. By this time she had regained her self-possession and received her reward. 'The Emperor came and talked to me. Then everyone looked at me. I laughed.' She had just received marching orders from Cavour containing the peremptory words: 'Succeed, my cousin, by any means you like, but succeed.' That night she may well have felt that the glittering prize was within her grasp.

During the following days the journal records several other meetings. 'February 2. A small ball at the Tuileries at nine. Stayed till two. Talked at supper with the Emperor who gave me oranges. February 5. To the costume ball of M. Le Hon where

I talked with the masked Emperor. February 21. To the concert at the Tuileries where there were only diplomats. Dined, talked with the Emperor.' Cavour now arrived for the opening of the Peace Congress and had frequent talks with his fair decoy. On 25 February he reported to the acting Foreign Minister at Turin that he had engaged a very beautiful Countess XXX and invited her to conquer and, if opportunity occurred, to seduce the Emperor. 'She has begun her mission discreetly at the Tuileries yesterday.' To Ratazzi, a Cabinet colleague, he wrote: 'If I do not succeed it will not be for want of zeal. I have even tried to stimulate the patriotism of the very beautiful Castiglione in order that she may seduce the Emperor.' Well might Italy's greatest statesman exclaim: 'If we did for ourselves what we do for our country, what rascals we should be!' Since the Dictator had smiled on her she was at all the balls and diplomatic receptions incidental to the greatest gathering of celebrities since the Congress of Vienna. The absence of the Empress from the festivities due to her advanced pregnancy left the field open, and the Countess sailed into the front line. Her days were spent with the dressmakers, her nights amid the gilded throng. Success went to her head. She gave herself airs, neglected her son, and treated her husband with contemptuous indifference while ignoring his appeals to curb her extravagance.

How much Eugénie had heard of her husband's latest flame we do not know, but at the end of June the Countess was invited to an evening party at St. Cloud. Robed in transparent muslin, her hat trimmed with white flowers and her hair falling over her shoulders, the sorceress looked at her best. Like an apparition, records Countess Tascher de la Pagerie: 'What virtue would have been required to resist her, and virtue was not a quality on which the men at such gatherings could pride themselves. Everyone expressed admiration.' She seemed perfectly at ease, steering straight towards her goal. Illuminated boats stood ready on the lake in the warm summer night, and the host smilingly invited her to join him in his own. In his gossipy journal Vieil-Castel noted that they spent some considerable time on a little islet, that she returned looking a little flustered, and that the Empress showed signs of annoyance. 'I have inquired of several Piedmontese about the resources of the Castigliones. I find they have only 18,000 francs a year left, and their mode of life needs at least sixty or eighty thousand. The Countess has been the mistress of the King of Piedmont, and I strongly suspect her of intimacy with Nieuwerkerke.' The lady described the occasion in a letter to her Polish friend Prince Poniatowski, who replied that the Empress was fundamentally good-natured and that her attitude was natural to a woman.

At what stage did they become lovers? The answer may have been enshrined in the missing pages of the diary which we may assume were deliberately removed. Shortly after the fête at St. Cloud the Emperor left for the waters of Plombières and the sea breezes of Biarritz, and there was no further meeting till the fair Italian was invited in the autumn at Compiègne. 'A miracle of beauty, like a classical statue,' commented Princess Metternich, 'Venus descended from Mount Olympus; I have never seen such beauty and I never shall.' That she was disliked for her arrogance and, in the opinion of another guest, possessed neither heart nor soul, troubled her not at all. One evening when she left a theatrical performance explaining that she felt unwell, the Emperor employed the first interval to inquire what was wrong.

'Yesterday evening,' recorded Vieil-Castel on 18 February 1857,

> there was a delightful fancy dress ball at the Foreign Office: the Emperor wore a domino and amused himself vastly by mixing with the guests, but his slow sidling walk and habit of twirling his moustache betrayed him. The Countess de Castiglione, who is said to be on the most intimate terms with him, wore a fantastic dress. Her marvellous hair rippled about her forehead and fell in waves on her neck. Her whole costume, which glistened with gold, was magnificent. Men thought, if they did not say, that they would have gladly changed places with the Emperor. She carried her beauty with insolence and displayed her charms with effrontery. Her neck is truly magnificent, without a wrinkle or blemish, and she carries it erect with the proud consciousness of some Moorish beauty. She is as much a courtesan as Aspasia. The Countess was the feature of the ball. The Emperor imagines he reigns supreme in her heart. Poor dupe!

On 24 March the Duchesse de Dino recorded in her journal that he had given her an emerald worth 100,000 francs. A few weeks later Nassau Senior met her and her husband at a dinner party in Paris given by Lord Holland. 'I thought her wonderfully beautiful, more so than when I saw her last year at Holland House. She is a Louis Quinze beauty, tall, round, well formed, with large dark eyes, straight eyebrows, a clear white complexion, and a mouth which, as I saw it always smiling, was charming. She sat in the evening, filling with her crinoline a whole sofa, to receive and certainly to enjoy the homage of all around her.'

In April *tout Paris* was talking about an attempt on the Emperor when he emerged at three in the morning unescorted from the residence of the Castigliones. After he entered his carriage three men darted from the shadows and tried to seize the horses' heads. The coachman whipped up his steeds, knocking down one of the assailants, and drove rapidly away. That the conspirators had chosen that place and time indicated that it was not the ruler's first visit. In the ensuing trial of the Italian malefactors the name and address of the Countess were suppressed in the papers.

A month later, on 3 May, Vieil-Castel records another ball, at the Ministry of Marine during a visit of the Grand Duke Constantine, where the Countess appeared more prominently than ever, though people were saying she was out of favour. 'The Minister had refused to send her an invitation, and she only procured it at the special request of Princess Mathilde. When the Princess toured the rooms with the Grand Duke, the Countess came next on the arm of a Russian gentleman. In the small drawing-room reserved for Princes of the blood, except the Minister of Marine and the ladies in attendance on Princess Mathilde no one was admitted but the Countess Castiglione.' Soon afterwards the Emperor left for Plombières, and the Countess visited London at the invitation of Lord and Lady Holland. In the autumn she was a guest at Compiègne for the second time, and at the end of her life she included in her will the tell-tale injunction to bury her in 'the nightdress of Compiègne, 1857'. At this moment of triumph the sky suddenly darkened and she resolved to return to Italy. What had happened? The answer has been recently found in a letter to her from her friend Prince Poniatowski recording a conversation with the Emperor, who, after paying tribute to her intelligence, charm and beauty, added that he regretted her lack of discretion. 'I never said a word to anyone,' he continued. 'Even Mocquard

F

knows nothing. If there has been talk it is because her friends found her in bed with sheets and lace of great value.'

The fall was even more rapid than her ascent. The romance had lasted two years. The blow was to her pride, not to her heart, for love had played no part in the thrilling drama. Living in the country, alone with her son, she consoled herself with the thought that *Notre Dame de Cavour* had done her work, since she had strengthened the Emperor's sympathy with Italian aspirations. Her fantastically exaggerated claim that she made Italy and saved the Papacy, mirrors her pathological vanity. Long afterwards she wrote to a friend that, if she had been dispatched to France a few years earlier, an Italian would have reigned in the Tuileries. 'I would not have gone to Mexico like the Spaniard who caused the defeat at Sedan, the destruction of the Empire, and the dismemberment of France.' Moreover, she had not given up all hope that the clouds would clear away. Poniatowski, now naturalized and a Senator, did his best for her in Paris; but the Emperor had lost all interest in her, he reported at the end of 1858, and believed that she was the mistress of Victor Emmanuel. She must be patient.

She had not long to wait, for in April 1859 the Emperor hurried across the Alps to join Victor Emmanuel in the plains of Lombardy. Her husband, now legally separated but still retaining some slight affection for his unloving partner, reported the progress of the brief campaign from the front. The first step towards the unification of Italy had been taken, and she flattered herself that she had played a vital part in the process. Meanwhile she consoled herself with the new French Ambassador at Turin, Prince Henri de la Tour d'Auvergne, whom she had met in Paris. As usual, all the passion was on one side, for her lovers, like her husband, complained of a certain reserve even in the most intimate relations. 'Beautiful from head to foot,' commented Countess Tascher de la Pagerie, 'but a beauty of the flesh, not of the soul. She reminds me of an *objet d'art*, just right as the ornament of a drawing-room and the entertainment of lazy folk but with little capability of holding the heart. She seemed quite self-possessed and cold, her eyes fixed on her goal. Her real satisfactions were those of her *amour propre*.'

Bored by her seclusion, the Countess returned to Paris with

her son in the autumn of 1860 and settled at Passy. She received a few friends, but Vieil-Castel noted two months later that no one talked about her. Despite her poor health she retained her attraction, accepting Poniatowski as her lover from fear of losing his friendship. The prospect seemed bleak enough, but she still hoped. On 28 January 1862 she was thrilled by a letter from Count Bacciochi announcing that she would be invited to a ball at the Tuileries on 9 February. 'I did not see a single pretty woman,' she recorded scornfully in her diary. 'They were all furious to see me so pretty and admired, and their faces were a sight. Met the Emperor, who was very embarrassed in talking to me. He asked for news and wanted to say more, but everyone was staring at us. I was very calm.' Paris was once again talking of her, and criticisms of her dress in an Italian paper stirred her husband to angry remonstrance. She appealed to Eugénie to stop the calumnies, and on receiving a friendly reply (not preserved) she asked Persigny, Minister of the Interior, to announce that the offending journal would be excluded from France by order of the Empress. A *communiqué*, replied Persigny, would appear, but the authority of the Empress could not be invoked. He suggested they should talk it over, signing himself 'your most devoted admirer'.

The ball at the Tuileries proved to be a false dawn, for she never met the Emperor again. Her failure to recover his friendship or his interest throws light on one of the disputed problems of the Second Empire. That the dentist, Dr. Hugenschmidt, was a son of the Emperor has been generally concluded from the fact that he was often the playmate of the Prince Imperial, to whom he bore a striking resemblance; that he was entrusted to Dr. Evans, the family dentist, who taught him his trade; that he visited the fallen ruler at Chislehurst and kept in touch with Eugénie till her death; and that he was a close friend of Prince Victor, eldest son of Prince Napoleon. His executor, on the contrary, affirms that he was the legitimate son of Hugenschmidt, major-domo of the Court. He himself apparently believed not merely that he was the son of the Emperor but that the Countess Castiglione was his mother. Walking with a friend one day along the Rue Cambon, he pointed to a house and remarked: 'That is where my mother died.' 'Your mother?' queried his companion.

'Yes, the Countess de Castiglione.' Another witness testifies to having seen her portrait above his bed. Her surviving diaries and correspondence, on the other hand, contain no reference to Hugenschmidt, and her latest biographer rejects any connection on the ground that in her efforts to regain favour she would have played her trump card had she held one in her hand.

Resuming her shattered life at Passy she consoled herself with a Jewish banker named Bauer, who was followed by other admirers, French and Italian, for her *liaisons* rarely lasted long. Except for Prince Napoleon no member of the Bonaparte family took notice of her. Countess Tascher de la Pagerie was astonished to see her in 1866 at a ball at the Russian Embassy. 'They look at her and admire her and she returns home with her success and convinced that she was queen of the ball, like a divinity who manifests herself for a moment to her worshippers and immediately disappears. Much good may it do her if that amuses her.' On the death of her husband in 1867 she returned to Italy, and was welcomed by the King, who granted her a pension; but he too gradually wearied of her requests for money. Reminding him that he was the father of a child 'of whom I am the mother', she begged not only for cash but for recognition of their son. Whether the King acknowledged his paternity, and indeed whether she invented the story, we do not know. Her last appearance on the European stage occurred after Sedan when she assisted Thiers in his futile efforts to bring Italy into the war. Returning to Paris after the *débâcle* she lingered on till the close of the century, poor and lonely, fat and slovenly, frustrated and forgotten. Dreading the cold scrutiny of the world when her beauty was gone, she emerged after dusk with her dogs, wandering among the scenes of her former triumphs and gazing at the vacant space where the Tuileries had stood. Certain coveted prizes she had secured, not by heart nor brain, but by her pretty face. Worthier rewards—the love and respect of her fellows—she never strove to win.

The fourth *maîtresse en titre* gave the greatest offence to the Empress and to all who cared for the prestige of the Empire. When the low-born *cocotte* Marguerite Bellanger, a du Barry without her charms, was expecting a child in 1864 she was installed in a villa in the grounds at Saint-Cloud. By this time Eugénie had lost whatever affection for her husband she had ever had, and at times she talked of escaping from her golden cage. 'Don't imagine I haven't always known of his infidelities,' she exclaimed to Walewski and his wife. 'I have even tried to make him jealous, but it was no good. Now that he has sunk to this debauchery I can stand it no longer.' One day he fainted during a visit to the woman she described as the scum of the earth and 'this female devil'. The injured wife hurried to the scene, taking with her the family lawyer. 'Mademoiselle,' she wrathfully exclaimed, 'you are killing the Emperor. This must stop. I will pay. Off you go. Leave this house tomorrow morning. I repeat, I will pay you.' The offer was reported by Lord Cowley to his chief. 'I never heard of such imprudence,' replied Lord Clarendon. 'It was asking for a rebuff, as the wench knew she could get more money out of the husband than from the wife.' The ageing profligate kept his mistress, but since his health was failing his injured consort built castles in the air and dreamed of a Regency for her adored son. Was the Emperor also, as many believed, the lover of Mme Walewski? 'As for getting Walewski away from Fontainebleau,' reported the British Ambassador in 1858, 'and leaving Madame behind, it is out of the question. He is always thinking whether His Imperial Majesty is not cuckolding him, which he may be sure he is.'

After sojourning in this murky atmosphere it is like a breath of fresh air to meet a woman who wanted nothing from Louis Napoleon beyond his friendship. The publication in 1937 of his correspondence with Hortense Cornu revealed a noble personality. The daughter of Queen Hortense's lady-in-waiting grew up with the future Dictator, and their mutual affection—despite differences in their political ideology—continued till his death. 'I loved and cared for him as my child when he was a prisoner,' she wrote. 'I was never in love with him. The idea never crossed my mind and I loved him as a brother.' After her marriage to Cornu, a little-known artist, in 1837, they met only at intervals, and there are long gaps in their correspondence; but enough remains to make us think more gently of the lonely ruler who showed himself capable of disinterested friendship with good women. 'My feeling for you is better than love,' he wrote to her from Ham in 1842, 'more durable, and better than friendship, more tender.' 'I am very lucky to have a friend like you,' he added in 1844, 'whose enlightened solicitude and tender devotion are at once a guide, a consolation, a powerful stimulus for me. How kind you are! What I love I love so much, and I love everyone who loves me. It is so rare to find someone who identifies herself so intimately with all one's thoughts and feelings. You are now indispensable to me. My tender and unalterable affection.' Their platonic relationship was doubtless fostered by the fact that she was an ugly hunchback with a harsh voice, so physically unalluring that she reminded Émile Ollivier of one of the witches in *Macbeth*.

The friendship of childhood blossomed into intellectual *camaraderie* when the Boulogne fiasco consigned the Pretender to the fortress of Ham. The company of Montholon, the Napoleonic veteran, and Conneau, the faithful doctor, was a consolation, but the frustrated captive needed an outlet for his energies even more than sympathy. He was allowed occasional visitors, among them Dumas and Louis Blanc, but he could scarcely expect such celebrities to aid him in his historical studies. Now was the time for Hortense to show her friendship in a practical way, all the more since she shared some of his interests. During his five and a half years in the gloomy fortress she visited him seven times, raised money by selling some of his *objets d'art*, and above all procured the books he needed. His earliest plan was a life of Charlemagne, the most commanding figure on the European stage between his two heroes Caesar and Napoleon. As she occasionally travelled in Germany she was requested to get in touch with German scholars and to purchase their works. The project never materialized, for his active mind turned to contemporary themes; but his letters reveal something more than the passing fancy of a *dilettante*.

Two years after his escape he was back in France, first as a member of the Chamber and soon as President of the Second Republic. When he migrated from his hotel to the Elysée she dispatched a long letter concluding with an offer of further services. 'Don't forget your promise to see me from time to time. I undertake to bring you a faithful report of the thermometer. If when you visit public institutions or receive scientific and literary bodies and need information I will send you brief notes.' Though henceforth they lived in the same city their contacts became less frequent, for he was a very busy man. As an uncompromising lifelong republican and anti-clerical and a friend of Mazzini, she frowned on the expedition to Rome which secured the return of Pio Nono. Though the dispatch of troops would have taken place under any other President, she wrote to protest and declined further invitations to the Elysée.

A far graver offence, and one for which he bore undivided responsibility, was the *coup d'état*. 'He has sown blood and will reap blood,' she wrote indignantly. 'He has betrayed and will be betrayed.' Her passions and her pen ran away with her as she denounced her old friend as 'a perjured assassin, an ungrateful egoist, completely without scruples, a mediocrity without artistic sense or originality, undecided and obstinate, now apathetic, now ferocious.' The mood was too hot to last, and she sent a present to the Empress on the birth of an heir. Despite attempts by the Dictator to rebuild the bridges, she broke off all contact and openly subscribed to the funds for the support of the Orsini family. A *détente* began in 1860, when the Emperor requested her aid in his project of a life of Caesar on the ground that she sometimes visited Germany. She promptly concurred, though not yet ready for a meeting. Two years later she sent congratulations on the seventh birthday of the Prince Imperial. 'The signs of your friendship are always very precious,' replied the Emperor, 'and I should like you to see this dear child.' On the same day Count Walewski brought her to the Tuileries. When the old friends met after many years of estrangement the iron curtain was rolled away. The Empress seized her hands and the Emperor clasped her in his arms. '*Méchante femme*,' he exclaimed, 'you have kept me at arm's length.' She embraced them both and all three shed tears. When the young heir was fetched the reconciliation was complete. Henceforth she was often to be seen at the Tuileries, not at the crowded receptions, for which she had no taste, but when the busy ruler snatched an hour for his life of Caesar. One day she found him to her surprise reading *Hernani*, the work of his bitterest foe, and exclaiming '*Que c'est beau!*'

Scorning to ask anything for herself, she declined the offer of a substantial sum to open a large-scale salon necessitating extensive hospitality. No, she explained, 'I wish to be free to retain the right, which is mine alone, to tell you the truth.' Her drawing-room—frequented by authors, artists and scholars, among them Renan, George Sand, Gautier, Dumas and Duruy, the scholarly Minister of Education—was all she needed. Yet she never hesitated to plead for her friends or those in distress. She was equally *persona grata* with the Empress, who often discussed with her such topics as the improvement of hospitals and asylums. The *débâcle* brought the friends even nearer. The captive Emperor wrote from Wilhelmshöhe to sympathize on the death of her husband, and affectionate letters on family matters and health passed between Paris and Chislehurst before and after the death of the ailing exile. Though the personal reconciliation had been complete, Hortense had never changed nor concealed her republican ideology. Her affection was for the man and the woman, not for the Empire with its tinsel glories.

4

THE MEXICAN FIASCO

THE Empress took little interest in the Crimean War and detested her husband's Italian policy, but the Mexican gamble commanded the enthusiasm of both. Had it prospered they would have shared the glory; since it failed they shared the disgrace. Wishful thinking, inexcusable miscalculation, above all the flouting of the Monroe Doctrine, indicate that the spirit of the gaming-table remained in the Man of Destiny. The whole poignant story was told for the first time by Count Egon Corti in 1923 with the aid of the correspondence of the luckless Emperor Maximilian and the Empress Charlotte.

The rise and fall of military dictatorships drove the losers in the latest round of the boxing-match to seek refuge in Europe, where they quarrelled with each other and sought support for their competing schemes. Both Emperor and Empress had long been interested in Central America, the former advocating a Nicaragua Canal, the latter listening to the talk of Hidalgo, a young Mexican diplomatist, in her mother's salon in Spain. Numerous investors in England, France and Spain had material reasons for concerning themselves with the fate of the country, and for desiring an end to the chronic anarchy which was ruinous to its inhabitants and its creditors alike. In this atmosphere of chronic frustration certain *émigrés* dreamed of importing a *deus ex machina* from the Old World; no European Prince, however, could be expected to undertake such a perilous task without the backing of one or more of the Great Powers.

In 1856 the Archduke Maximilian, younger brother of the Emperor Francis Joseph, arrived in Paris to report on the ruler and his entourage. It was the sunniest phase of the Second

Empire, for French arms had restored their prestige in the Crimean War and an heir to the throne had been born. 'The Emperor, who received me at Saint-Cloud, was ill at ease,' reported the visitor. 'His short, unimpressive stature, his exterior which is utterly lacking in nobility, his shuffling gait, his ugly hands, the sly inquiring glance of his lustreless eyes: all this was not calculated to correct my first unfavourable impression. The Empress, still weak from her confinement, appeared no less embarrassed, though she took great pains to please. Her undeniable beauty, aided considerably by art, shows no trace of the Spanish type. She is of good family, but lacks the august quality of an empress. The dinner was badly served, the Emperor restless, the conversation dull.' A state banquet next day was equally unimpressive.

> The Emperor's embarrassment was obvious. Probably he felt uncomfortable in the presence of a prince of older lineage. When he overcomes this restraint he displays great frankness. The more I know him, the greater seems his confidence in me. There is a laudable intention to create a suitable Court, but the whole machinery does not yet work smoothly. The stamp of the *parvenu* is on everything. He seems respected by many but beloved by none. I try to be very agreeable and to conceal my unpleasant impressions. His transformation of Paris is almost incredible—all very brilliant but evidently intended for the moment alone. He lives in great retirement. He and the Empress are hardly greeted in the street except by members of the Court. He does not accompany me when I move about: perhaps it would upset him to have me witness this universal indifference. I lunch daily with the Emperor and Empress. His personality is unattractive at first sight, but ultimately creates a favourable impression by his great calm and noble simplicity of character. The Empress's gaiety and naïve vivacity do not always seem to please him. The whole impression is that of a make-believe Court, the posts filled by courtiers not very sure of their part. This Court is absolutely lacking in tone.

As the days passed the ruler overcame his embarrassment, talked freely about international problems, and displayed marked amiability. 'I was far better pleased with his manner during the closing days of my visit than at first I could have expected. Yet my regret at leaving Paris was small, indeed I blessed the day when I left the centre of civilization.' His hosts, on the other hand, had been greatly attracted to their visitor.

A year later Hidalgo visited the Empress at Biarritz, described the misery of his country, and suggested the establishment of a Catholic Monarchy in Central America. Fascinated by the idea, she promised to speak to her husband. She knew nothing of the United States and liked republics as little as Queen Victoria. Sooner or later, she exclaimed in 1853, war must be declared against them, a frothy utterance gently rebuked by the Emperor. At her wish Hidalgo was invited to Compiègne in the autumn of 1858, and now for the first time the Emperor inquired about Mexico.

> *Hidalgo:* The news is very bad and the country faces ruin unless Your Majesty helps us.
> *Emperor:* Nothing can be done without England. We told Palmerston on a recent visit to Compiègne that an army and vast sums would be needed, as well as a prince.
> *Hidalgo:* Your Majesty knows that Don Juan has been mentioned.
> *Emperor:* We thought of the Duc d'Aumale, but he declines.

Delighted to learn that the Dictator had been thinking about his country, Hidalgo stressed the danger of Latin America falling under the influence of the United States, if no action were taken. He continued to visit the Emperor and Empress, making little progress with the former who kept repeating that he would gladly act, but how could he without England? The impulsive Empress, on the other hand, never interested in the prosaic details which make or mar great enterprises, became ever more obsessed by the project, and the repudiation in 1861 by Juarez of debts incurred by his predecessor brought intervention within the sphere of practical politics. Though the new radical and anti-clerical Dictator Juarez had ousted his conservative rival Miramon, he failed to maintain order or to win popularity and the search for a ruler went on.

When England and Spain seemed inclined to champion the interests of their nationals the Emperor prepared to bestir himself. The French Minister in Mexico favoured action. Thouvenel, the Foreign Minister, approved, and Morny was in touch with Jecker, a Swiss financier who had lent large sums to Miramon.

Various candidates were discussed by the *émigrés* and, with the approval of Napoleon III, Maximilian was approached in his fairy palace of Miramar. The Archduke and Charlotte, his ambitious Belgian wife, were longing for a crown, and Francis Joseph welcomed the opportunity of a dazzling career for his brother. Two conditions he required—the active support of England and France and a definite invitation from Mexico; but since the House of Hapsburg must not be exposed to a spectacular failure, no material support could be supplied. Assured of conditional approval in Vienna, Napoleon III instructed his Ambassador in London to interest Palmerston in the scheme to prevent further encroachments by the United States and to open up a valuable market. With the Civil War waging to the north, he added, there was no fear of intervention, and Maximilian was a suitable candidate. King Leopold was begged to support the French *démarche* in London. Though neither England nor Spain displayed ardour, the three Powers signed the London Convention in October 1861, undertaking to send ships and troops, renouncing in advance territorial advantages, and recognizing the right of Mexicans to choose their government. Each signatory was to appoint Commissioners to assess claims and conduct negotiations. There was little optimism except among the refugees, and warnings reached the Archduke from various capitals. 'What a lot of cannon shots it will take to set up an Emperor in Mexico,' commented Metternich in Paris, 'and what a lot more to keep him there!' Lord Russell, the British Foreign Secretary, was sceptical from the first, and Palmerston was much more interested in the old world, while Queen Isabella and her advisers would have preferred a Bourbon to a Hapsburg candidate.

The Archduke, with the steady encouragement of his wife, declared himself ready for all risks and sacrifices. His most ardent champion was Eugénie, who, annoyed by the caution of the English and the inertia of Spain, declared that if necessary France would shoulder the whole burden. Living in a world of illusions, the two couples took no account of the yellow fever on the coast, the toughness of Juarez, the absence of a Monarchist party and the frowns of Washington. A repulse at Puebla, on the road to the capital, caused consternation in Paris, but the dreamers of Miramar refused to despair. Reinforcements were dispatched, and the commander proclaimed that he was making war on the Government, not on the people of Mexico. Warnings continued to pour in from many quarters, and when the Greek throne became vacant Russell advised King Leopold to sound his son-in-law, who contemptuously declined. When Puebla was taken in May 1863 and Bazaine marched into Mexico City without opposition, the French Emperor, reported Metternich, wept for joy. Though Juarez remained full of fight and the country was far too large to corner him, the goal seemed within sight.

'I hope the whole of Mexico will soon follow the example of the capital,' telegraphed the Emperor, 'and summon you to regenerate the country. The Empress joins in congratulations.' His enthusiasm stood out in sharp contrast to the reserve of Austria and England, where no desire was felt for an extension of French influence in the New World. Without a shred of evidence the Emperor continued to believe the assurances of Mexican exiles that the people would welcome a liberator, and at the end of 1863 he urged the Archduke to cross the water without waiting for solid guarantees of local support. He had no desire to lock up French troops in Mexico, now increased to 40,000, and hoped to withdraw the larger number as soon as the new ruler had created a native force. He had never been quite so enthusiastic as the Empress, and his fear of trouble with Washington increased as the chances of a victory for the North improved in the Civil War.

In January 1864 the Archduke announced that he was only waiting for the Emperor's consent to start for Paris, for the time had come to learn precisely to what extent France would pledge her aid. Arriving in March, they found him in excellent spirits on the strength of dispatches from Bazaine. A new convention promised that 25,000 French troops would remain till local forces were available and the Foreign Legion would stay on for eight years. Onerous demands for the payment of expenses and the repayment of a loan were accepted, since funds could be found nowhere else. A secret article, insisted on by the Archduke, provided that French assistance should never fail whatever might occur in Europe. A Commission was established in Paris of French, British and Mexicans to represent the foreign creditors of the state. Once again Maximilian and his wife made the best impression on their hosts, and on parting Eugénie gave him a gold medallion with an image of the Madonna, adding 'this will bring you luck'. The Austrian Ambassador remained a pessimist. Even the Empress, he reported, was a prey to feverish excitement owing to the feeling of responsibility she had incurred. In reply to the guests' parting letter of gratitude the Emperor renewed the assurance that his support would never fail. Crossing the Channel on a courtesy visit the travellers found a more realistic atmosphere. Palmerston foretold that the burden would prove too heavy, and Charlotte's grandmother, Queen Amélie, exiled widow of Louis Philippe, exclaimed to the Archduke, 'They will murder you.'

Duke Ernst of Coburg describes in his Memoirs a visit to Paris in March 1864. While the Empress assured him that the Archduke would without fail soon become one of the most powerful rulers in the world, the Emperor repeated several times: *'Une très mauvaise affaire; moi à sa place, je n'aurais jamais accepté.'*

In April 1864, after three years of discussion, a Mexican deputation bringing certain documents of adhesion arrived at Miramar, assuring the Archduke of 'the unending love and unshakeable fidelity of a Catholic and monarchical people'. When the host announced that he was ready to accept the crown there were cries 'Long live the Emperor Maximilian. Long live the Empress Charlotte.' A telegram was received from Paris once more pledging friendship and support. The strain had been too much for the sensitive Archduke, who left Miramar in tears while his stout-hearted consort maintained her dignity and calm. A brief visit was paid to Rome to receive the blessings of the Pope.

Maximilian quickly recovered his spirits. If Mexico was to have a ruler from Europe no better choice could have been made. To his sense of duty and pride in his Hapsburg birth was added a romantic idealism, a thirst for adventure, the conviction that the task of serving and civilizing a backward country was well worth while. The reception on landing was chilly enough, but on hearing a promising report from Bazaine he remarked: 'The present is gloomy, but the future is splendid.'

The French Emperor plied the inexperienced ruler with advice, based on his own experience.

You must keep absolute power in your own hands for a long time. But it would be a great advantage, particularly in European eyes, if, after completing the organization of the country and settling all great outstanding problems, you were to summon a Congress for a day or two, the members to be nominated by you from elected municipal councillors. Tell them that after the full participation of the country you would work towards a constitution, and ask them to give you dictatorial powers for a few years. You have already achieved much good, and I rejoice that the whole world does you justice.

King Leopold was equally lavish with advice, above all to look after the finances. Charlotte described the appalling situation to Eugénie.

From all I have seen there is room for a Monarchy and it meets the needs of the population; but it remains a gigantic experiment, for we have to struggle against the desert, the distance, the roads and the utter chaos. Everything calls for reconstruction. There is nothing, physical or moral, except what nature provides. Things will develop if Your Majesties stand by us, but the appalling task does not alarm us. We have dedicated ourselves to the task in full knowledge of what we are doing, and I was only surprised at the roads. Everything else I found better than I expected.

Difficulties increased rather than diminished. There was friction with Bazaine and the Church, and Maximilian's health began to deteriorate. Juarez was as active and mobile as ever. The end of the American Civil War, in which the Emperor had sympathized with the South, threatened irresistible pressure from the North. Charlotte stood the strain best, but they were fighting a losing battle and they knew it. Conscious of the growing unpopularity in France of the Mexican experiment, Napoleon III became impatient with the slow progress in the formation of a Mexican army, since he had merely intended to give the *régime* a good start. The death of King Leopold deprived his daughter and son-in-law of a fatherly friend and a wise counsellor. By the autumn of 1865 Louis Napoleon realized that, in Morny's phrase, he had put his hand into a hornet's nest and would have to cut his losses. 'The Emperor Maximilian,' he wrote to Bazaine, 'must understand that we cannot stay in Mexico for ever, and a national army should be formed as soon as possible.' He further complained that his protégé had done nothing to enable him to live on his own financial resources. Since a conflict with the United States was unthinkable, he proposed that Austrian troops should replace the French. The letter was a shock to Maximilian, not only because the proposal was impracticable but because it revealed that his patron was preparing to break his promises. To withdraw the troops, he replied, would not merely undo the results already achieved and shatter public confidence but tarnish the honour of France. 'Time is indispensable for restoring a nation that has been shattered for half a century. The Mexican nation does not despair, relying on Your Majesty's formal declaration that your troops would not leave till their Commander-in-Chief pacified the country and crushed all opposition.' The reproach wounded the French Emperor like an arrow in his heart but without weakening his resolve to throw in his hand.

If the patron flinched, the protégé declined to haul down the flag. 'For nothing in the world,' he confided to a friend, 'would I give up my position and return to the old life. I am struggling with difficulties, but fighting is my element and the life of Mexico is worth a struggle. Here, my work has reaped gratitude and recognition, which I never knew in Europe. Both the country and the people are far better than their reputation.' Idealism and heroism were not enough, for at the close of 1865 the United States demanded the withdrawal of French troops without softening the blow by any promise of recognition for Maximilian; Washington objected not merely to foreign troops but to foreign rulers. Hardly less decisive a factor was the refusal of Fould, French Minister of Finance, to find more money. The fateful announcement was conveyed in a letter from Napoleon III in January 1866. Since the Corps Législatif would no longer pay for the French troops and Mexico was unable to do so, a gradual withdrawal as soon as possible was unavoidable. This would remove all pretext for American intervention. The Foreign Legion would remain for a few years. 'I do not believe that Your Majesty's power can be shattered by a measure imposed on me by circumstances.' The decision was announced at the opening of the Chamber. Austria could do nothing, for a struggle with Prussia was at hand.

When Maximilian realized that the game was up, Charlotte

volunteered to visit Europe. She reached Paris when the Emperor's prestige had been shattered by his role in the Austro-Prussian War. Since France seemed in danger, her resources were needed at home and Maximilian would have to fend for himself. Moreover, the Emperor was weary, in constant pain, and depressed. Even the Empress had lost faith in the adventure. Charlotte's unheralded arrival was extremely unwelcome. While the Emperor wrote that he was ill in bed, the Empress called at the Grand Hotel, listened with sympathy to the story of disillusion and the renewed appeal for help, but could offer no consolation.

Charlotte: And the Emperor? Shall I not be able to see him?
Eugénie: He is unwell.
Charlotte: I must see him. Otherwise I shall break in.

In reporting the interview to her husband Charlotte reported that she knew more about China than 'these people' about Mexico. She thought the Empress had lost much of her youth. 'Amid all their greatness any sort of pressure is irksome to them and they can endure no longer.' Next day she was received at Saint-Cloud and reiterated the demand for the continuance of financial support and the use of French troops till the whole country was pacified. As she described the desperate plight of her adopted country, reminded her host of his promises, and appealed to his sense of honour, tears rolled down his cheeks. At last he replied that he could do nothing more. After further talk Charlotte exclaimed that she would see the Ministers who were holding their master back, and the host undertook to consult them once again. The agitating interview had lasted an hour and a half. After interviewing the Ministers of Foreign Affairs, War, and Finance, and the Austrian Ambassador, she returned to Saint-Cloud next day, where a Ministerial Council unanimously decided to liquidate the adventure in view of the threat of war from the United States and the danger to the dynasty from the unpopularity of the enterprise. The Emperor, reported Charlotte to her husband, had been degenerating physically and morally for the last two years; the Empress was incapable of directing affairs and did more harm than good. They were getting old and childish and were often in tears. Even now she refused to despair. A third interview took place when the Emperor called at her hotel. She implored

G

him to summon the Chamber, dissolve it if it refused supplies, and issue a direct appeal to the country. It was all in vain.

> *Emperor:* You must not indulge in illusions.
> *Charlotte:* Your Majesty is directly concerned in this affair and should also not indulge in any.

At this point he rose, bowed, and left the room. Two days later she was officially informed that no further aid was possible. Overwrought in mind and body she compared the Emperor to the devil and his entourage to hell. On the eve of leaving Paris she reported the bad news to her husband.

> I have given you a moral triumph, but he has hell on his side. It is not the Opposition, for he chooses the Chambers, still less anxiety about the United States. He intends a long premeditated crime, not out of cowardice or discouragement or any reason but because he is the evil principle on earth. To me he is the devil in person. He has never loved you, for he is incapable of loving. When I said goodbye yesterday he even kissed my hand, but it is play-acting. The reign is nearing its end and then we shall be able to breathe again.

The first symptoms of mental derangement now appeared, including a suspicion that an attempt to poison her with a glass of orangeade had been made at Saint-Cloud.

> We had great pleasure in receiving the Empress Charlotte [reported the Emperor to Maximilian on 29 August 1866], but it was very painful to me to be unable to accede to her requests. Henceforward it is *impossible* for me to give Mexico another *écu* or another man. Can you maintain yourself or will you have to abdicate? If the former, my troops will remain as agreed till 1867; if the latter, other measures will be needed. You should issue a manifesto explaining the noble ambition which led to your acceptance of the mandate offered by a large part of the Mexican people, and set forth the insurmountable obstacles which have forced you to renounce your task. Then summon a representative assembly and have a government elected. Your Majesty will understand how painful it is for me to enter into such details, but it is no longer possible to lull ourselves with illusions, and the Mexican question, so far as it concerns France, must be settled once for all.

Maximilian replied that he needed time to decide his future action. Charlotte's only remaining hope was the Pope, and the Emperor supplied a special train to the Italian frontier; but by the time she reached the Vatican, after a brief visit to Miramar, she had developed persecution mania in acute form. She believed that the members of her entourage were in league to poison her and, for a brief space, that even her adored husband was in the plot. Overcome by emotion during her audience with the Pope and by his inability to help, she refused to leave the Vatican and a bed was made up for her in the Library. Convinced that she was about to be poisoned, she made her will and wrote a brief farewell to Maximilian.

The news that no aid could be expected from Europe reached Maximilian at the same time as the shattering blow of his wife's illness. Should he now leave with the French troops? After a phase of vacillation he decided to stay. The whole country was now in the hands of Juarez except Vera Cruz, Mexico City, Pueblo, and Queretaro. There was no money to pay the troops and the Generals quarrelled about strategy. The doomed ruler and Miramon, former Conservative President, transferred their headquarters to Queretaro, where they were promptly besieged. Three months later, after a series of unsuccessful sorties, the town was captured and they were taken prisoner. Appeals for clemency from the European Courts and Washington were ignored, and on 19 June 1867 the Prince, fearless and dignified to the last, was shot with two Generals at his side. The news reached Paris as the Great Exhibition was closing, and there was a fierce outcry against the Emperor who was doubly responsible, first for initiating the enterprise and then for abandoning his protégé. 'He will never recover from this curse,' exclaimed Thiers; 'this outrage will overwhelm him with the contempt of France.' 'The grief of the Empress is profound,' telegraphed Metternich to Vienna. 'I have seen them crying over the result which to some extent involves their responsibility. It is touching to see the Emperor so despised for his share in the horrible result in urging the Emperor Maximilian to accept this crown of thorns. It is hardly to be imagined what a deep impression the news has produced here.' No one reproached him more bitterly than he reproached himself. 'The appalling news has plunged us into the deepest grief,' he telegraphed to Francis Joseph. 'I both deplore and admire the Emperor's energy in fighting single-handed against a party which has only triumphed by treachery. I am inconsolable at having with the best intentions contributed towards such a lamentable result. Will Your Majesty accept the expression of sincerest and deepest regard?' The heart-broken widow lingered for another sixty years without regaining her reason. The whole enterprise had proved an unmitigated disaster: not a stick was saved from the wreck. French soldiers had died, French money had been poured out, French investments had been lost, and the prestige of France had sunk to its lowest ebb since Waterloo. In the pregnant phrase of Metternich it was the Moscow of the Second Empire.

5

DUC DE MORNY, THE HALF-BROTHER

NEXT to the sovereigns the Duc de Morny is the most arresting personality of the Second Empire. That he was a close relative of the Dictator gave him a good start, but he owed more to his abilities than to his birth. He combined charm, culture, tact, ambition and a flair for business with a steely determination to drain the cup of life to the last drop. We meet this sceptical dandy at every turn—in the Corps Législatif, in diplomacy, in the world of industry, on the Bourse, on the racecourse, in literary and artistic circles. Morals he had none and not much heart, and marriage made little difference to his amours. The Emperor, who detested corruption, complained to Hortense Cornu that Morny would be the disgrace of his reign. Though the relations of the half-brothers were never genuinely affectionate they needed one another, and when he died at the age of fifty-three the *régime* lost its stoutest support.

Morny was the illegitimate son of an illegitimate father. When Hortense and Louis Bonaparte parted company after quitting the throne of Holland, the former gave her heart to Comte de Flahaut, a dashing young cavalry officer who had accompanied Napoleon on his later campaigns and rode away at his side from the stricken field of Waterloo. Though he bore the name of his mother's elderly husband, General Comte de Flahaut, Superintendent of the Jardin des Plantes, everyone knew that he was the child of Talleyrand, Abbé de Périgord and later Bishop of Autun, the principal ornament of his mother's salon. The erring wife was a devoted mother and showed her mettle when the storm broke over her head. When her husband died on the scaffold she escaped to England and thence to Hamburg to earn a living for herself and her child by writing novels. Exile ended with the appointment of Talleyrand as Foreign Minister, and financial anxiety with her marriage to de Souza, the wealthy Portuguese Minister in Paris, and with the launching of her son on a military career.

The *liaison* of 'le beau Flahaut', a General at twenty-six, with Hortense resulted in 1814 in the birth of a son, who was registered under the name of Auguste Demorny, a retired officer who received an annuity in return for his aid in keeping the secret. Since his mother, an ornament of the Court, felt unable to recognize him, he was brought up by his grandmother, Mme de Souza, who took him to her heart and fostered his career. Hortense sent money every quarter through her banker and was kept informed of his progress. After the collapse of the Empire Flahaut married a Scottish heiress and made his home beyond the Channel. The son of Napoleon's *aide-de-camp* could hardly expect smiles from the restored Bourbons, but on the accession of Louis Philipppe the clouds rolled away. Boycotted by the Loyalists of the Faubourg Saint-Germain, *le roi des barricades*, as they contemptuously described the new ruler, welcomed Bonapartists at the Tuileries. Demorny now changed his name to de Morny, adding the title of Count, to which he had not the slightest claim. So far as we know he saw his mother for the first time when his father met Hortense at Aachen in 1829, though apparently without suspecting their relationship. The secret, however, was impossible to keep, and Maxime du Camp records that they remained in touch, though we possess no details. In an age of easy morals the handsome young man displayed no embarrassment over his irregular background, which in days to come was to prove a priceless asset. That he was the son of Flahaut was no longer concealed when the latter installed him in the house he purchased in Paris after his return to France in 1830, and where he was treated as one of the family when Flahaut's wife and their five daughters were in residence. '*Auguste me parait fort occupé des femmes*', wrote his adoring and indulgent grandmother in 1831, and so he remained to the end; but he was never a mere playboy. Since the army seemed his obvious destiny, his father procured him a commission for the Algerian campaign, where bravery in saving his commander's life won him the Legion of Honour.

Among his fellow officers were Saint-Arnaud, his future accomplice in the *coup d'état*, and Changarnier, whom he was to arrest on that fateful December day. The slow promotion which was all he could expect, and the physical hardships of campaigning, offered no temptations to the ambitious young man, who was proudly aware of his abilities and his influential connections. The path to fame and fortune led through the capital, not through the battlefields of North Africa where he had nearly died of dysentery.

Paris under the Bourgeois Monarchy offered ample opportunities in half-a-dozen fields—journalism and politics, business and society, literature and the arts. While less versatile aspirants had to select their sphere of action, Morny took them all in his stride. Securely anchored in the house of his father, whom the revolution of 1830 had restored to his position as Lieutenant-General and a member of the House of Peers, *Monsieur Frère* found all doors open to him, including the Tuileries, where he made friends with the young princes and the diplomatic corps. He was received with particular favour in the salon of the Countess Le Hon, daughter of a rich Belgian banker, wife of the Belgian Ambassador, twice her age, and a friend of the Brabant family of Queen Hortense. Living in a spacious mansion filled with *objets d'art*, the beautiful hostess, who was likened by an admirer to the Venus of Botticelli, became a queen of society, equally welcome in the Faubourg Saint-Germain and the Tuileries. The heir to the throne, the short-lived Duke of Orleans, was among the limited number of friends who were privileged to visit her whenever they liked. Saluted by Balzac as 'Iris of the blue eyes' and by Théophile Gautier as 'the Ambassadress with the golden hair', she was the chief political asset in France of the newly established Belgian Monarchy.

When Mme le Hon and Morny met for the first time at the Chantilly races the attraction was mutual. She was always charming, and he could fascinate if he thought it worth while. After his election to the Chamber in 1842 her salon was enlarged by leading celebrities from the world of politics and finance. Their friendship ripened into a *liaison*, and the indulgent husband, mindful of the interests of his country, made no fuss. That she helped to finance his sugar enterprise in his constituency of Clermont Ferrand was revealed many years later on the collapse of the partnership owing to his marriage. When the Ambassador returned to Belgium at the close of his official career he obtained a legal separation, leaving the field clear to Morny who took a large house close to that of his mistress. Every Saturday she gave a dinner for forty guests in which he was the host in all but name. Though she could boast of no literary lion of the stature of Chateaubriand who adorned the drawing-room of Mme Récamier, her salon was the most brilliant in the capital. That Princess Louise Poniatowski was their daughter was generally believed. In the Chamber he spoke mainly on financial and commercial topics. Even in an age of *nouveaux riches* he astonished his acquaintances by the style in which he lived, the last word in sartorial elegance, owning racehorses, and spending large sums on pictures and at cards. Staying with him in his country home Ludovic Halévy reported to his mother that she could not conceive of the extravagances of the *cuisine*, *déjeuner* and dinner alike insensate. 'Everything is exquisite, marvellous, impossible.' Unlike the Emperor, who took no interest in the pleasures of the table, Morny was an epicure. Though fairly satisfied with the constitutional monarchy he vainly urged Guizot to disarm its foes by extending the franchise.

On the outbreak of the revolution of 1848 the timid old King fled to England, leaving Legitimists, Orleanists, Republicans, Bonapartists, and Socialists to compete for the succession. Morny had identified himself with one of them, but when his half-brother, whom he had scarcely ever met, was elected to the Presidency he called at the Elysée. 'Neither of us liked the other,' he wrote, but the utility of collaboration was obvious. The returning exile knew scarcely anyone in the political, social, or business world in which Morny had long been a prominent figure. 'I see the President every day, mostly twice a day,' he reported to his mother-in-law Lady Flahaut in May 1849; 'he discusses everything with me, both persons and events.' Neither believed that the Republic had come to stay, not merely because it could boast of few convinced supporters, but because its handling of the *ateliers nationaux* revealed its incompetence. When the crazy experiment which was ruining the country's finances had to be called off, the indignant workers threw up barricades and were shot down by General Cavaignac. Like other industrialists whose interests had suffered in the financial panic, Morny dreaded social anarchy and calculated that an autocrat would be a better guarantee of order than another blundering Bourbon or another Orleans prince. 'Only the Empire can save us,' he confided to Lady Flahaut in May 1849; 'the Prince has scruples, but there will soon be great events.' Flahaut told the same story in the following November in a letter to his wife. 'The President is determined to take every means, both as to measures and men, for the establishment of order. It was evident when I saw him that his mind was made up to escape from his present position. It appears that, though very quiet and gentle, nothing has any effect on him when his decision is taken. Though under the constitution he had no more right to dissolve the Chamber than had the Chamber to evict the President, he justified his action by the plausible formula that he had flouted legality in order to defend the law.

During the first two years Louis Napoleon built up his power by official tours, and cries of *Vive l'Empereur* confirmed his belief that his hour was at hand. It was clear that the constitutional obstacle in his path—the time limit of the Presidential term—could only be removed by illegal action, and he and the Chamber eyed each other suspiciously while the world wondered who would strike first. Meeting the Austrian Ambassador in the Tuileries Gardens on 12 October 1850, General Changarnier exclaimed: 'I am building up my strength to counterwork the *coup d'état*.' The ground was prepared by the appointment of Saint-Arnaud as Minister of War, Maupas as Superintendent of Police, and Magnan as Commander of the troops in Paris, and by discussions with Morny and Persigny. Danger to the President threatened not from the Chamber, where the parties were too divided for effective action, but from three Generals, Cavaignac, Lamoricière, and Changarnier. When the latter spoke openly of arresting the President he was dismissed at the opening of 1851. The *coup* was planned for September, but Morny advised postponement till the Chamber was in session. Walking in the Elysée garden in the summer he observed: 'I see the only course for your interest and that of the country is a *coup*.' 'I agree,' was the reply, 'and I am seriously thinking of it.' When the President inquired who would deal with the Chamber at the critical moment

Morny offered his services. 'I would not expose you to such dangers,' was the reply; but Morny had no fears. 'Without me,' he declared when it was all over, 'there would have been no *coup*. I found the President surrounded by ninnies, incapable of tendering good advice.' The claim was justified, for the kind-hearted Man of Destiny shrank from bloodshed. Morny, denounced by Victor Hugo as 'this malefactor', had told Thiers as long ago as the end of 1849 that a *coup* would be easy enough. 'Was not the President elected by a vast majority? If he appealed to the people again they would support him.' In resolving to strike he believed that he would be fulfilling the wish of the nation, and the events of the next two years confirmed his conviction. 'Since the establishment of the Presidency,' he wrote in February 1851, 'the Republic exists only in name.' It had never been popular, and what little prestige it once possessed had disappeared.

The night of 1–2 December 1851 was the decisive moment in Morny's career, for within the space of a few hours he made history and became the second political personage in France. That he performed the surgical operation with cool efficiency is attested by friend and foe. The secret had been well kept: only the President and his Secretary Mocquard, Saint-Arnaud, Morny, Maupas, and Persigny knew what was coming. General Magnan had promised support but preferred to remain aloof till he received the order to march. Morny spent the evening at the theatre in order to dispel suspicions, before going to the Elysée after the guests at the usual Monday reception had left. Cavaignac and Lamoricière, whom he was to arrest a few hours later, were also at the theatre. The conspirators were well aware what was at stake. 'We realize we are risking our skins,' remarked Morny. 'I count on success,' replied the President; 'I always wear my mother's ring with the word *Espère* on it.' The necessary proclamations were sent to the State printing office and were posted up in the principal streets. While the troops took up their stations before daybreak, Morny entered the bedroom of the Minister of the Interior at 7.15 and delivered his message. 'You are dismissed and I am your successor.' The new chief promptly issued instructions to clear the Chamber, close the Conseil d'Etat, arrest the leaders of the Opposition parties, and muzzle the press. A few hours earlier Lamoricière had been talking in his home circle of the explosive situation, the suspicions of the Chamber, and the urgent need to stop the President if necessary by imprisonment. 'But if he gets his blow in first?' queried a member of the family. 'Impossible,' replied the General; 'the army would not follow him. I should only have to show myself to prevent any action.' 'But if he were to strike in the night with civilians, not soldiers, and arrest the deputies in their homes?' 'In that case I have always two pistols under my pillow. I would blow out the brains of anyone who tried to lay hands on me.' A few hours later two agents of police entered his bedroom.

Lamoricière: Gentlemen, this is illegal.
Police: General, this is the *coup d'état*.

There was no resistance. France, it has been said, went to sleep in the arms of her master.

In his capacity as Minister of the Interior and fortified by the confidence of the Dictator, Morny was for a short period the virtual Premier. While Louis Napoleon was to look back on the December days with remorse at the blood shed, Morny, with his thicker skin, prided himself on saving the country from anarchy. 'Auguste has been heroic,' wrote Flahaut to his wife; 'his courage, resolution, good sense, prudence, severity, good humour, *sangfroid* have been unequalled, and one may say the same of his modesty. Those who love him can be proud of him.' The old General, who had been initiated into the plot, witnessed its execution but took no part. 'The chances of conciliation had been exhausted,' testified Rouher on Morny's death fourteen years later.

> Before December France was torn by dissensions and almost reproached Prince Louis Napoleon for not saving her. The Emperor took his decision and entrusted its execution to M. de Morny. Penetrated by the importance of the service he was to render, he accepted this formidable responsibility with a kind of gaiety and courageous delight. We all know with what coolness, moderation and serene firmness he fulfilled his memorable and perilous task. He was the General Monck of nineteenth-century France.

The Minister of the Interior only retained his post for a few weeks, for the first important act of the new Dictator, the confiscation of part of the Orleans property, was a shock. That the decree pronounced the grant illegal and that the money was used for social betterment failed to remove widespread regret. Morny, who had received nothing but kindness from the House of Orleans, resigned and no attempt was made to keep him.

> Since the second of December [he wrote in anger to his father], I have come to understand his character still better. He has no real friendship for anyone. He is suspicious and ungrateful, and only likes those who obey him slavishly and flatter him. He could not find anyone else for the second of December, so he made use of me. I risked my life and accomplished my task, but what matter? I am in the way. I am neither a slave nor a sycophant, so I am cast off as useless. I would prefer to have nothing more to do with this government. I feel affection for the man himself but contempt for his government and his entourage. I have done everything in the world and gone so far as to risk the loss of his confidence. It is because I find that loyalty and devotion when accompanied by candour are not always appreciated that I do not wish to remain longer. This will become a government of nonentities. There will never be room for a man of character and independence. I cannot tell you how all this distresses me.

The half-brothers, however, occasionally saw one another, and he knew that his services would be required again.

Apart from the Orleans issue, there had been a slight cooling off when *Comte Hortensia*, as he was sometimes called, began to parade his relationship and introduced Flahaut on his visits to Paris as *mon père*. He retained his seat in the Chamber, while never opposing the measures of the Government. For the next two years he held aloof from politics, devoting himself mainly to his business interests and the charms of society. Industrialists sought his permission to whisper the magic formula: *Morny est dans l'affaire*. He was no less enterprising and no less successful in love than in commerce and finance. He was too able to be long ignored by the Emperor, who appointed him President of the Chamber when the post fell vacant in 1854. The work suited him better than that of a Minister with little time to enjoy himself, and he filled the post with a dignity which won general recognition. Since the power of the Chamber was strictly limited and no interpellations were allowed, the atmosphere was calm and the members of the Opposition could be counted on the fingers of one hand. Beyond the fact that he was a pillar and a beneficiary of the *régime*, Morny was not by nature a politician and cared little for the party game.

When the Crimean War was over the Emperor strove to restore friendly relations with Russia. The frowning Nicholas was dead, and the coronation of Alexander II provided the opportunity for a fresh start. That the most influential figure in France after the ruler should represent his country, was to pay the new Tsar a compliment, but the success of his mission was due as much to his personal distinction as to his rank. The new ties were strengthened by his marriage with Sophie Troubetzkoi, maid-of-honour to the Empress and a member of one of the highest families in the land. Meeting at a ball at the Winter Palace they were attracted to each other and were promptly married, the Tsar providing a dowry of 500,000 francs. His friends were amazed at the news of the marriage of the bald and dissipated bachelor of forty-five to a girl less than half his age, and Mme le Hon, the friend of twenty years, was deeply hurt. She knew him better than anyone but not well enough; surfeited with transient amours, he wanted to settle down. 'Happy man,' he exclaimed to Count Fleury, 'I should like to follow your example. Marriage seems to me like a paradise compared with the life I lead; no hearth, no child; it is horrible.'

The chilly terms in which he announced to Mme le Hon the termination of their *liaison* added insult to injury. 'I am going to be married. The Emperor desires it, and so does France. I hope my wife will have no better friend than you and that you will continue to find your way to our home.' The angry woman went straight to the Emperor to implore his veto; but Morny had as much right to choose a wife as anyone else, and the ruler contented himself with a reprimand. The bridegroom retaliated with a sharp letter to his old flame, who counter-attacked in the same heated tone. The quarrel was complicated by the fact that she had lent him large sums. Fearing a first-class scandal if, as she threatened, the dispute came before the courts, the Emperor asked Rouher to report on her contention that a considerable part of her fortune had passed into Morny's hands. After prolonged examination, Rouher decided that he was indebted for $3\frac{1}{2}$ million francs and must repay it. The award pleased neither party, the lady protesting that the debt amounted to six millions, the debtor complaining of the size of the estimate. The Emperor, not usually inclined to strong language, described his half-brother as a *faquin*, and for a moment thought of depriving him of the Presidency of the Chamber; but the storm blew over. Mme le Hon was reimbursed from the Emperor's Privy Purse, and Morny consoled himself for the loss of his best friend with *liaisons* from the opera. The aggrieved lady had the satisfaction of the last word. 'Such ingratitude! I found him a sub-lieutenant and left him an Ambassador.' Though he was the main architect of his colourful career she had at any rate assisted him to climb. Vieil-Castel declined to believe in the sincerity of her anger on the ground that she had found a new lover in Rouher; but the diarist had a disagreeable habit of accepting and circulating scandalous gossip as fact. Morny's wife scarcely expected marital fidelity from such a notorious libertine. Returning one day earlier than expected she found her husband with one of her ladies, dismissed her, and forgave her erring partner. She made no effort to perform her duties as the hostess of the President of the Chamber, taking little interest in politics, despising politicians, and sometimes failing to appear at dinner parties in her own home; but there were four children of the marriage and a mild affection persisted to the end.

The eight years between Morny's return from Russia and his death in 1865 were the most brilliant phase of his career. His services were rewarded in 1862 by the title of Duke, his favour sharply contrasting with the jealous hostility of Prince Napoleon. He loved the theatre, launched Sarah Bernhardt on her dazzling career, and wrote light comedies under the pseudonym M. de Saint-Rémy, one of which *Monsieur Choufleury restera chez lui* still holds the stage. The secret leaked out or may have been let out, and flatterers extolled the work which Rochefort denounced in the *Figaro* as trash. His only intimate in the literary world was Ludovic Halévy, dramatist and novelist, whom he invited to help him with his vaudevilles, for one of which Offenbach composed the music. Though Daudet was one of his secretaries he never realized his abilities, little guessing that the observant young *méridional* would immortalize him as the Duc de Mora in *Le Nabob*. Among writers who attended his receptions were Emile Augier, Edmond About, Octave Feuillet, Arsène Houssaye, and Labiche —none of them stars of the first magnitude but popular enough in their day. He was a better judge of pictures than of literature, patronizing the young Impressionists as well as collecting Old Masters. His most enduring monument is Deauville.

As President of the Chamber Morny had far better opportunities of judging political trends than the Emperor, who hardly knew the names of the speakers when he read the carefully edited reports of the debates. While neither of them had the slightest intention of permitting Parliamentary control of the Executive, Morny came to realize that the *régime* might well be strengthened by minor concessions. After a decade of internal peace the dread of social revolution had disappeared and the muzzling of the press was particularly resented. Though only five deputies ventured on systematic criticism, *Les Cinq* represented a growing body of opinion. The first relaxation of autocracy in 1860 permitted a debate on the Speech from the Throne at the opening of the session and a full report of speeches in the Chamber. Impressed by the eloquence and sincerity of Émile Ollivier, the most prominent member of *Les Cinq*, Morny introduced him to the Emperor and sounded him about accepting office. 'I have always been both Conservative and Liberal,' he declared; but the young lawyer desired more scope than either the Emperor or Morny was prepared at that moment to grant. Though the Liberal Empire only began to take shape after Morny's death he prepared the way.

The election of 1863 revealed diminishing support in the large cities and reinforced both Republicans and Monarchists in the Chamber with formidable recruits, among them Berryer and Thiers. The Emperor greeted the new Assembly with a few polite words. 'Welcome! Despite some partial disagreements I can only applaud the result.' On the following day the President of the Chamber went much further to meet the new spirit. 'The elections have revealed aspirations which have slumbered in recent years. The word liberty has often been uttered and will be heard again. The Government is not alarmed. Liberty can be peacefully established only by concord between a liberal sovereign and a moderate Chamber.' With the veterans Thiers and Berryer in mind he continued: 'The vote of the people has restored to our midst former ornaments of Parliament. For myself I venture to rejoice.' These carefully considered phrases were designed not merely as a *beau geste* to the new Chamber but also as a hint to the Emperor to initiate reforms instead of being forced to grant them. It was Morny's finest hour, for it required courage and it was not without result. On reading the report the Emperor gently complained that 'rejoice' was rather a strange word to use in regard to Thiers. Morny was impenitent, and on being described by a member as an enemy of liberty he nailed his colours to the mast. 'You do me an injustice. I know that the Empire cannot live without it, and if it develops some day the country will owe it to me.' With the concession of the right of interpellation the debates became more lively and the Chamber more representative.

Among the crowding business interests of Morny's later years was the development of Mexico. The Swiss banker, Jecker, who had obtained French nationality, supplied 75 million francs to Miramon, the right-wing competitor for power in that land of revolutions, to be repaid with interest after his expected victory. Well aware of the highly speculative character of his investment, he approached Morny, who promised to secure high priority among French claims on the Mexican state. When Juarez won he repudiated the loans of his rival, and as a last resource Jecker, hard pressed by creditors, turned to the Emperor to help. 'You will have heard of my loan,' he wrote in 1869, two years after the execution of the Emperor Maximilian wound up the Mexican adventure. 'I feel the Government is too indifferent, and it may injure the Emperor if nothing is done. You are doubtless unaware that the Duc de Morny was my associate and was to receive 20 per cent. of the profits in return for securing payment of the claim.' Since Morny's death, he added, the Government had taken no action. This long letter, with its veiled threat of exposure, was published in 1871 with scores of other secret documents found in the Tuileries in order to discredit the fallen *régime*. A note attached by the Emperor's secretary records that the writer brought the letter himself, was informed that he was rendering himself liable to prosecution for blackmail, and was shown the door. How deeply was Morny involved? While his first serious biographer Boulenger argues that Jecker exaggerated his involvement, the latest contends that the financier's statement should be accepted. The matter is of minor historical interest as the Jecker loan played no part in the shaping of policy.

DUC DE MORNY

The most engaging portrait of Morny in his closing years was painted by Ludovic Halévy, author of *L'Abbé Constantin* and, with Meilhac, of *Frou Frou* and other popular favourites. Requiring help in the completion of his most successful farce *M. Champfleury restera chez lui*, the Duke invited the young writer to his official residence at the Palais Bourbon in 1860. The two men liked each other from the first, and Halévy was appointed to prepare the report of the debates in the Chamber for the *Moniteur*. 'What it means to me,' he wrote on the death of his friend five years later, 'is beyond words. I have never known such desire to please, to do a service, to ignore the difference of rank. His home became mine, and I felt a void on the days we did not meet. Such a mind, such grace, such charm! He would have done more for me if I had wished, but my only desire was to pursue my career at his side and never to leave him.' The dandy often dismissed as a cynic must have had a heart to inspire such affection. Daudet, on the other hand, confesses that he never felt at ease with him, 'any more than one is at ease with a lion or a panther with velvet paws. It is no good saying: "Don't be afraid, he won't hurt you."'

Declining health after his fiftieth year was aggravated by his addiction to drugs, one of which contained arsenic, a powerful stimulant followed by an equally powerful reaction described in Daudet's novel as 'Dr. Jenkins' pills'. Even a wiser physician could scarcely have lengthened the days of a man who had worn himself out by sensual indulgence, late hours, and the burdens of office. The last order of the dying Duke, who had warmed both hands before the fire of life, was to burn a drawer-full of scented love-letters. The Emperor and Empress visited him a few hours before the end, the former leaving the bedroom of his partially conscious half-brother in tears. Though an unbeliever like his half-brother, he summoned the Archbishop of Paris to his bedside and he was honoured by a State funeral on a grand scale. 'His Elegance' was spared the sorrow of witnessing the collapse of the Second Empire, of which he had been one of the principal architects and ornaments. He used his influence to fill his pockets, complained Prince Napoleon, who disliked and despised almost every member of the Emperor's entourage. A more impartial verdict was delivered by Lord Cowley, the British Ambassador. 'In critical moments he had great calmness and firmness, and even his enemies admit that his judgment in political affairs, when not warped by his own interests, was sound. He was a very good and impartial President of the Legislative Body and, I believe, desired the Emperor to give them greater liberty of discussion. He had it in him, if he had been honest, to be a very great man.' No one doubted his ability, but there was a chorus of complaint that he had not put it to better use.

6

PRINCE NAPOLEON
L'ENFANT TERRIBLE

THE publication in 1925 of the correspondence between Napoleon III and his cousin Prince Jerome Napoleon supplies the key to the career of the *enfant terrible* of the Second Empire. When he reproached the Emperor for having nothing of his uncle, he received the crushing reply: 'I have the faith.' 'He is as much a republican as myself,' declared Jules Favre on the day of the *coup d'état*, and he had no use for the Church or its faith. Never did he forget that he was the nephew of the greatest of mortal men (whom in his *Napoléon et ses Détracteurs* he defended with passionate conviction), and when the new Man of Destiny became the master of France he expected to play a part commensurate with his talents and his birth. That he remained 'on the fringe of the Empire', to quote his resentful words, soured him, though it was largely his own fault. The good fairies had lavished their gifts, among them a facial resemblance to *le petit Caporal*, but had withheld a capacity for teamwork and an ability to hold his tongue. That he was no courtier was to his credit, but Jérome Égalité, as he was sometimes called, was unpredictable, and his outbursts embarrassed the Dictator again and again. He despised his cousin and the ruler knew it. Too patriotic to be dismissed as a mere *frondeur*, he was certainly a *mauvais coucheur*. Yet in this complex personality there were a few grains of gold amid the dross. Physically and politically fearless, industrious and incorruptible, he was capable of generous actions, a man neither to be greatly admired nor wholly despised. 'I loved him deeply,' testified Renan, and Ollivier saluted him as a faithful friend.

Born at Trieste in 1822, the son of Jerome Bonaparte and Catherine of Wurttemberg, Plonplon—an infantile attempt to pronounce his name—spent his childhood in Rome, where his grandmother Madame Mère, his uncle Lucien, and other members of the clan kept the fires burning. Every winter his aunt Hortense descended from Arenenberg with her younger son Louis to meet her elder son who lived with his disgruntled father in Florence. From his earliest days the precocious lad detested discipline, and his sister Mathilde had to remove his hat when he refused or forgot to comply with the customs of society. The family migrated to Florence after the Carbonari revolt in the Papal states in 1831, moving later to Lausanne, where he attended a French school. On the death of his mother his cousin Louis invited him to Arenenberg and taught him Latin and mathematics. Though Hortense disapproved his constant exclamations of 'stupid' and 'ridiculous', she liked him and left him 20,000 francs. The Arenenberg idyll, which lasted for a year, ended with the *putsch* at Strasbourg in 1836 and the return of the boy to Lausanne. The cousins were not to meet again for ten years, but they kept in friendly touch by correspondence.

At fifteen Jerome entered a military school in Wurttemberg at the wish of his uncle King William. 'Plonplon is working and his masters praise him,' reported his elder brother, an officer in the Wurttemberg army, 'but it is very difficult to inculcate military discipline. Though he is not directly disobedient, he thinks it silly, contrary to the rights of man, and offensive to his democratic principles.' Despite his rebellious spirit he enjoyed military life. 'I think you are working well,' wrote Louis Napoleon in 1838 after returning from his American exile, 'and you will soon be a first-rate officer. You know I love you as a brother. I almost envy you. It forms the heart and mind.' After three years of study he received a commission in the Wurttemberg army and served on the staff; that he had learned his trade he was to reveal in the Crimean War. While the Boulogne escapade was frowned on by the ageing uncles, he expressed his sympathy. 'Louis has had bad luck,' he wrote to his sister, 'and he may lose his life. His error is not so grave as people think. I am deeply distressed at this unhappy adventure. He has been my friend since childhood.' Writing from Ham the prisoner informed his cousin that before starting from Boulogne he had made him his sole heir, and the letters from the fortress breathe genuine affection. When the Prince proposed a visit the prisoner replied that it would probably be vetoed, though another first cousin Lucien Murat had been admitted. After several applications for leave to enter France he was granted a passport for 'Count Starberg' in 1845, and on reaching Paris requested permission to visit Ham. That was for the King to decide, replied the Minister of the Interior. Receiving him at the Tuileries, Louis Philippe declared that he had no objection but that the Ministers must decide. Their adverse decision was a blow to both, and the prisoner expressed his gratitude for the attempt. 'You are the only member of my family whom I love as a brother, the only one worthy of the great name we bear, as I have tried to be.' A protest, firm but in moderate terms, should be made in the press. 'That is indispensable, for you as for me: for me so that it be not thought I am abandoned by all my relatives, for you so it cannot be said that you have merely frequented the salons of our contemptible rulers.' Conscious of its declining popularity, the Government grew uneasy at the news that the visitor was meeting left-wing politicians, and after four months ordered him out of France. 'Everyone,' reported Thiers to his father Jerome, 'was struck by his resemblance to the most popular figure of modern times, and also, more important, by his intelligence, tact and correct attitude.'

Though the object of his journey was unfulfilled it had not been wholly in vain. The escape from Ham made governments more suspicious of Bonapartist activities. 'We have had to veto the entry of Prince Louis,' declared the Foreign Minister of Tuscany, 'all the more because we already have his cousin Prince Napoleon who aspired to a political role.' Jerome joined Louis in London, where a meeting with Mazzini increased his sympathy with Italian nationalism. Louis was struck by the complexity and contradictions in the cousin whom he had last seen as a lad of fourteen. 'My chief complaint is his unintelligible character, sometimes frank and loyal, sometimes embarrassed and dissimulating. At one moment his heart seems to speak of glory, to sympathize with all that is great and generous; at another it is empty, arid, deceitful.'

When the fall of the Monarchy opened the way for the return

of the Bonapartes to France three of them, Jerome, a son of Lucien, and a son of Murat, entered the Chamber. Jerome took his seat on the Left as member for Corsica among the moderate Republicans, and was sometimes described as the Red Prince. Proclaiming himself a son of the Revolution, he shared his cousin's interest in social questions and cultivated advanced thinkers, among them Proudhon and Pierre Leroux, Lamennais and George Sand. An ardent nationalist, he sought out the Polish *émigrés* and dreamed of the liberation of their country from the embrace of the Russian bear. The triumphant victory of Louis Napoleon in the plebiscite in December 1848 brought the family of the ex-King of Westphalia to the centre of the stage. Old Jerome was appointed Governor of the Invalides, Mathilde became hostess of the Elysée, and Prince Napoleon was packed off as Ambassador to Madrid at his own request. Incapable of controlling his tongue, he complained at Bordeaux on his way south that the President was dominated by reactionaries and could not follow his own course; in consequence in the coming elections opponents of the Government should be returned in order to strengthen his hands.

The petulant utterance brought a well-merited reproof.

> You know I shall never submit to any ascendancy [wrote the President]. I shall always endeavour to govern in the interests of the masses, not of a party. I honour the men who by their capacity and experience can give me good advice. Every day I receive conflicting counsels, but I obey only the promptings of my reason and my heart. You were the last person to blame a wise policy, you who disapproved any manifesto because it was not wholly to the satisfaction of the chiefs of the moderate party. This manifesto contains the conscientious expression of my opinions. The first duty is to reassure the country. Each day has its task; first security, then ameliorations. The coming elections, I do not doubt, will be the time for reforms and for strengthening the Republic by order and moderation. To reconcile all the old parties—that should be our aim and such is the mission attached to the great name we bear. It would fail if it divided instead of rallying the supporters of the government. For all these reasons I could not approve your standing in twenty Departments. Under the shelter of your name candidates hostile to the government would be returned, its loyal supporters discouraged, and the people wearied by the many by-elections which

would be required. So I hope you will be extremely careful to explain my real intentions to your friends, and not by any unconsidered words encourage the absurd calumny that my policy is dominated by sordid interests. Nothing, I repeat nothing, will disturb the serenity of my judgment nor weaken my resolve. Free from all moral pressure, I shall go forward on the road of honour with conscience as my guide, and when I step down, if they reproach me for unavoidable mistakes, I shall have done what I sincerely believe was my duty.

No one was less fitted by temperament for the profession of a diplomat, whose first task is to become *persona grata* wherever he is sent, for he was soon on such bad terms with Queen Isabella that she asked for his recall. Anticipating an unpleasant interview with the President, Drouyn de Lhuys, the Foreign Minister, began to explain the situation in soft words when his embarrassment was relieved in an unexpected manner. 'I see what you are driving at. I know my cousin well. He is a monster.' The verdict was delivered in quiet tones but with deep conviction. The Minister reported that on his way south the Ambassador had visited the prison at Bordeaux, shaken hands with political prisoners, promised them early liberation, and indulged in diatribes against his cousin. Installed in Madrid, he had established contact with enemies of the Spanish Government, openly declaring that the Bourbon dynasty should be expelled, if necessary by force, from the countries where it still ruled. Since he had already returned to Paris without instructions, his action was treated as a resignation and he was relieved of his post. 'He is a terrible scoundrel,' wrote Vieil-Castel in his journal in August 1851, 'he acts the same part towards the President as Philippe Egalité towards Louis XVI. He is a braggart and a coward, quarrelsome and dissolute, the embodiment of every evil quality. His father was a mischievous rascal but he is even worse.'

No longer in the confidence of his cousin, he was excluded from the preparations for the *coup*, which he never approved. If we may trust the testimony of Victor Hugo, the Prince came to him in a fury on 2 December and poured forth a stream of abuse. 'This miserable Louis is a disgrace to the family—if indeed he belongs to it, the dirty bastard. I expect he will get shot, which would be a great relief to everybody including myself.' The Prince degraded himself by giving credence to the baseless legend that the new master of France was the son of Admiral Vertruell, the Dutch Minister at Paris during the brief reign of King Louis Bonaparte. Holding aloof from public life for many months, he took the first step towards a reconciliation when he learned of a plot against the life of the President during a visit to Marseilles in September 1852. 'My dear Louis, All my old feelings of brotherly friendship revive as keenly as ever. I feel that if politics have estranged us, my devotion to your person is unchanged. My heart goes out to you in the danger to which you were exposed.' On the proclamation of the Empire a few weeks later he was restored to favour, appointed a Senator, a member of the Council of State, and a General of Division, with a residence in the Palais Royal and a country estate at Meudon. His work as President of the Commission to prepare for the Exhibition of 1855 earned his election to the Académie des Beaux Arts. He was seen at his worst on the occasion of the birth of the Prince Imperial. While the delighted Emperor hurried through the corridors of the Tuileries exclaiming '*C'est uns fil, c'est un fils, je suis bien heureux,*' and embraced everyone he met, the Prince sulked in his tent as his dream of the succession faded into thin air. When the Ministers invited him as first Prince of the Blood to sign the birth certificate he turned them roughly away. Fresh efforts were equally unsuccessful till, five hours later, his sister intervened. 'I have been here for twenty-seven hours,' she complained; 'are you going to keep us here longer? What is the point of refusing to sign? You will not prevent the attestation, and your ill-humour will harm no one but yourself.' He yielded at last with a bad grace, and his exhibition of selfishness and jealousy increased the general rejoicing that he would never become the ruler of France. 'He has heaps of brains,' declared the Empress, 'but he makes detestable use of them. But what can we do? We are not living in the MiddleAges and the time is past when inconvenient cousins could be removed.'

On the outbreak of the Crimean War the Prince requested and received the command of the Third Division. Caring for his men in sickness and in health, and displaying conspicuous bravery in the battles of the Alma and Inkermann, he was acclaimed by Saint-Arnaud as worthy of the name he bore. A rumour that his return to France was due to cowardice was a libel, for he was sorely stricken by dysentery. No member of the family excited such vehement hostility. 'He is a bad man,' wrote Vieil-Castel in his journal at this moment, 'cunning, cowardly, lacking gratitude or generosity. He has intelligence, but of a low order. His dissolute life makes him look years older than he is. If he should ever come to the throne, which God forbid, France will have a bad time.'

After his first and last smell of powder important civilian tasks awaited him. He was dispatched on a mission to Berlin to persuade the King of Prussia to abandon his claim to Neuchâtel, and in 1858 he was appointed Minister for Algeria and the Colonies. Though he was difficult to work with, the Emperor valued his services. 'My cousin', he remarked, 'has often annoyed me. He loves contradiction and criticism, but he is clever and has a good heart.' His most conspicuous service to the Empire was his marriage to Clotilde, the sixteen-year-old daughter of King Victor Emmanuel, as part of the plan to drive the Hapsburgs from Italy. 'He is clever,' reported Cavour to his master. 'Thrown in early life into the turmoil of revolutions he developed extreme opinions which brought him many enemies. Now he has grown more moderate. Greatly to his honour he has remained faithful to the liberal principles of his youth. He has always been a good son and has loved his cousin. If he has sometimes incurred his displeasure he has always remained loyal and affectionate.' The Emperor warned the Savoy monarch that a refusal of his daughter's hand would arouse the enmity of the most Corsican of the Bonapartes. Lord Cowley, on the other hand, was horrified by the bargain. 'The bride looks a mere child,' he reported after a dinner at the Tuileries. 'When one sees this child sacrificed, for it is nothing else, to the ambition of her father and Cavour, what can be thought of such men? It is positively horrible to see that poor little frail creature by the side of that brute (I can call him nothing else) to whom she has been immolated.' He had been hissed in the streets of Turin where the marriage had taken place, and on their entry into Paris there was not a cheer. Her first act on entering the Palais Royal was to sprinkle her apartments with holy water brought from Turin.

> She was not pretty [testifies Maxime du Camp], but she was gentle absolutely virtuous, and devoted to her husband. Blond and clumsy, with big lips and a vague expression, her piety was excessive. Her

certainty of an eternity of bliss inspired wide charity and unfailing kindness. She is the most saintly woman I ever knew. The Empress complained that she was insufficiently *décolletée*, and her husband said she aspired to beatification. She never complained, never reproached. She admired his ability and delighted to hear him talk in the evening with his friends. Such a woman, respected by all and adored by her staff and her beneficiaries, should have reformed the Prince, but he remained a shameless Bohemian, frequenting the theatre with his many mistresses.

The Austrian Ambassador thought no better of him, though everyone recognized his ability. 'He is reputed to have liberal ideas,' he reported in 1859. 'He has *esprit*, plenty of it, perhaps too much initiative, an iron will which disdains scruples, but he lacks consistency in his ideas.' In addition he was such a notorious Austrophobe that his marriage to a princess of the House of Savoy caused people to talk of war.

Since the war in Italy was timed for the summer of 1859 the Prince resigned the Ministry of the Colonies and was dispatched to sound the Tsar. A further assignment was to encourage exiles in Italy to form a Hungarian Legion, but Kossuth's offer of the crown of St. Stephen if Hungary threw off the Hapsburg yoke was declined. When the storm broke he was appointed to command the fifth army corps and dispatched to Genoa to await the arrival of troops from Africa. Then he was ordered to Florence with instructions to hold Tuscany to the French alliance, to add the Tuscan forces to his own, and to prepare against an Austrian attack. The brief campaign was over before he could reach the front, but a further responsible task was assigned to him. After the preliminary meeting of the Emperors at Villafranca he was sent to work out the details of the settlement with Francis Joseph at Verona, and was rewarded by a letter commending him for his zeal and skill.

While the cousins were in full agreement about enlarging the dominions of the House of Savoy, they differed sharply in regard to the Temporal Power of the Pope. In 1861, in a three hours' oration in the Senate, the Prince argued that Rome should become the capital of the new Italian kingdom.

> I do not pretend to be a fervent Catholic [he began], but I was born in the Catholic religion and have as much right to talk Catholi-

cism as you. We wish the priest to remain an object of veneration without needing a gendarme to aid him in spiritual things as has been the case in Rome. When he does something unworthy and the *exaltés* indulge in ridiculous demonstrations, his name is coupled with it. That is a pity. I shall utter no disrespectful word about his spiritual power, for I have the greatest respect for the chief of the Catholic world.

After this exordium he suggested a possible compromise between the Vatican and the Monarchy: let them divide the city between them with the river as a boundary, and let the Powers guarantee the independence of the Papal zone. 'Then you would have a completely independent oasis of Catholicism in a stormy world; Catholics would provide a budget sufficient for the dignity of religion and the payment of a garrison.' This striking anticipation of the Lateran Treaty of 1929 earned congratulations from the Tuileries. 'Though I do not agree in every point, I congratulate you on your nobly patriotic sentiments so eloquently expressed and on your immense oratorical success.' Since neither Pio Nono nor Victor Emmanuel, who wrote to thank his son-in-law, was in a mood for compromise, the speech produced no effect, and—to the Prince's regret—the Emperor dispatched a brigade to reinforce the Pontifical volunteers. 'Unfortunately my advice has no chance of acceptance,' he reported to Ricasoli, the heir of Cavour. 'Despite his keen desire not to thwart the wishes of the Italian people, he will only withdraw his troops when he can do so without breaking his promises.'

In referring to the recent overthrow of the Bourbons in Naples and Sicily the Prince spoke with contempt of 'that family which everywhere and at all times, in every country where it has reigned, has given us the scandalous example of struggles and domestic treacheries. We represent not reaction but modern society. Sympathy has been expressed for Francis I. Do not confound sympathy with pity. Our sympathy is reserved for the glorious Italian cause; for the ex-King of Sicily we have only pity.' Contrasting the divisions in the Bourbon family with the unity of the Bonapartes, he continued: 'If bad times come, history will not tell of treason among the Bonapartes as among the Bourbons, for they would all be united in face of danger.' What had happened in Naples was only the prelude. Now that the Bourbons had gone the Pope as a temporal ruler must go too, returning to the primitive simplicity of the apostles, handing Rome to Victor Emmanuel, and withdrawing into an honorable retreat whence he would rule without dependence on anyone. The speech was as rapturously received in Italy as had been England's blessing on Italian unity in Lord John Russell's celebrated dispatch to Sir James Hudson, and it appeared as a brochure in Italian dress.

> Your speech is for the power of the Pope [wrote Cavour], what Solferino was for Austrian rule. Your help will not fail us. After making such a large break in the walls of the Eternal City, your shoulder will give a further push towards the entrance. That will be a great day for Italy, for France, for the universe. The destruction of the Temporal Power will be one of the most glorious and fruitful events in the history of mankind, and your name will always be associated with it.

The speech equally delighted Persigny, Minister of the Interior, who placarded it throughout France and published it in the *Moniteur des Provinces*, but it was generally deplored as an unprovoked and ungenerous outburst. The Duc d'Aumale, the youngest and most distinguished son of Louis Philippe, replied from his exile in Twickenham in a brochure entitled *Lettre sur l'histoire de France*, which defended the Bourbon record, recalled the leniency of Louis Philippe, and carried the war into the Bonaparte camp. The manuscript was sent to the Orleanist Comte d'Haussonville who undertook to get it printed in Paris. Though no name appeared on the cover it was signed Henri d'Orléans. Copies were seized by the police, but large numbers were distributed by trusty hands and extracts appeared in the European press. Though the publisher and printer were sentenced, a blow had been struck at the *régime*. In a land where affairs of honour were commonly settled by sword or pistol, the author expected a challenge and chose his seconds, but the aggressor made no move. 'As for Prince Napoleon,' reported Lord Cowley, 'he is lost. He seems resolved not to fight. Man, woman and child look upon him as completely dishonoured. The Emperor is more upset than by anything since he has been chief of state. The Empress exclaims: "If my son were in his place I would conduct him to the field of honour and place in his hand the sword or pistol to avenge the slur on his name." ' Meeting him in the Tuileries she was believed to have greeted him with the cutting words: 'I thought you were in London.' Vieil-Castel noted that he had fallen into universal contempt.

When the Poles rose against their Russian masters in 1863 the Prince dispatched a lengthy memorandum to the Emperor advocating intervention. 'The restoration of Poland is an axiom of our policy which needs no discussion. The support of the insurgents by the Church ensures the support of the Catholics in France. The Emperor declares that the restoration of Poland is no longer a dream. Let us go forward to fulfil the greatest idea and repair the greatest crime of modern times. That would evoke unparalleled enthusiasm.' The first duty was to encourage the insurgents to hold out by the prospect of foreign aid, the second to summon Prussia to stand aloof. As if this playing with fire were not enough, the author proceeded to redraw the map of Europe. The Emperor replied that the dream might perhaps be realized some day but that great prudence was needed. 'I desire no demonstrations or provocations. I count on you to assist me instead of embarrassing me.'

The appeal was ignored, and a speech in the Senate declaring that he had a Polish heart and denouncing Russian repressive methods incurred public reproof. Billault, who followed in debate, repudiated the incautious utterance and explained the attitude of the Government: and the Prince was deeply hurt to read in the *Moniteur* a letter from the Emperor congratulating the Minister on his intervention. 'Your words were in every respect in accord with my ideas and I repudiate any other interpretation.' 'He can't resist the pleasure of playing tricks,' wrote Mérimée to Panizzi. 'No one is a more eloquent or a wittier speaker, but his lack of tact is incredible in such a clever man. He lost the Poles about forty votes. I am not sure if he wanted to help them. He is *blasé*, out to amuse himself. He thinks of the effect he will produce, nothing more.'

An aggrieved letter from the thin-skinned Prince provoked a severe and detailed indictment from the Emperor of his conduct throughout the years.

> Since my election as President you have never ceased in word and deed to combat my policy. How have I retaliated? By striving on all occasions to bring you forward, to give you a position worthy

of your rank and scope for your brilliant qualities. Your speeches in the Senate are always a serious embarrassment. People wonder that I tolerate such sustained opposition. I have a right to ask that you should conceal any divergence of opinion. Your last speech was outrageous. You must choose between supporting my government and giving rein to your violent opinions, in which case I must announce my dissatisfaction. I deeply regret that your good sense and good heart have not controlled your passions.

The Prince asked permission to visit Egypt with his wife and thereby to prove that he would give no further trouble. He had only one request—a command in the event of war. The offender, now in a somewhat chastened mood, explained to the Russian Ambassador that he had not preached rebellion, that he merely desired a better life for the Polish people, and that he was mindful of his relationship with the Tsar. Some of the insurgents expressed their gratitude to their champion by offering him the crown of Poland if independence were achieved.

On his return from Egypt the Prince resumed friendly relations with his cousin, who appointed him President of the Commission for the publication of the correspondence of Napoleon of which fifteen volumes had appeared, and the enterprise was completed under his direction. Conscious of his abilities he fretted at inaction. 'My position looks very agreeable,' he complained to the Emperor, 'but it does not satisfy me because I am not fulfilling my destiny. I can do nothing to earn glory and a place in history. What humiliates me is to be out of touch with the Government.' 'You are very clever and well informed,' replied the Emperor, 'but you have too little tact in your conduct and too little measure in your words.' The reproof was fully justified. How little tact he possessed—or even good manners—was illustrated at Compiègne in 1863.

At dinner on November 15 [reported Mérimée to Panizzi], he declined to propose a toast to the Empress, at whose right he was sitting as usual. When the Emperor asked him to speak he made a grimace. 'I am not keen on it,' remarked the hostess, 'you are very eloquent, but your speeches sometimes rather frighten me.' The Emperor now made a second attempt.

Prince Napoleon: I can't speak in public.
Emperor: You won't propose the health of the Empress?
Prince Napoleon: If Your Majesty will excuse me.

The host and hostess maintained their self-control, and the latter gave him her arm as they moved into the drawing-room. There everyone cold-shouldered him as he stood with a sulky expression which made him look very like Vitellius.

> I wouldn't have stood such a performance [added Mérimée], but you know the magnanimity of the Emperor who regards him as a child and overlooks his tantrums. It is very sad that the Bonapartes do not rally round the head of the family. He makes himself detested by his bad manners: wanting to play a political role, he flatters the Reds and believes he would be spared in the event of a revolution, forgetful of the fate of Philippe Egalité.

In May 1864 the dissatisfied Prince begged for a conversation with his cousin

> not about politics, as I see you do not wish to discuss them with me, nor about money. I desire your advice about my future. I am forty-two, in poor health. I have a child and am expecting a second. With my name, my position and my limited capacity I should try to render services to my country, to leave some trace of my life, in a word to find my duty and to do it. I cannot continue to live from hand to mouth. Before deciding my course I have a right to consult you as head of the family. My ambition is neither culpable nor unreasonable, and everything depends on what you will say to me.

If there was a reply it has not survived. The Prince was incorrigible. Representing the Government at the unveiling of a monument in Ajaccio to Napoleon and his brothers in 1865 he renewed his attack on the Temporal Power. The fresh outburst provoked the most wounding reprimand he ever received, for, on this occasion, it was published in the *Moniteur*. 'I must inform you of my painful impression on reading your speech at Ajaccio. Your programme can only serve the foes of my government. To prevent confusion in public opinion the Emperor established—first in the family and then in the government—the severe discipline which admitted only a single will and unity of action. From this line of conduct I cannot depart.' The publicity was even harder to endure than the rebuke. The culprit promptly resigned his post as Vice-President of the Privy Council and the President of the Exhibition planned for 1867.

At the opening of 1866 the frustrated Prince poured out his

heart to Queen Sophie of the Netherlands. 'I am being very badly treated and have no illusions. To love liberty is an unpardonable offence. Darkness prevails here; it can't go on like this. I am very sad. Nothing is done, no one is listened to. We are heading to disaster.' Retiring to his residence in Switzerland, he waited for the Emperor's wrath to cool and a month later he was summoned to the Tuileries.

> *The Emperor:* I am grieved but I had to do it. I am not angry with you, but I have long been annoyed by the embarrassments you cause me. I do not want people to think I have two policies, one official, one secret of which you are the mouthpiece. My letter was written to disassociate myself from what you said.
>
> *The Prince:* It might have been done in a less wounding manner. I do not recall any similar publication. Our uncle wrote sternly about your father and Murat but never published his letters. I am deeply hurt. What have you against me?
>
> *The Emperor:* I am not criticizing this or that passage but the whole thing. No one but myself should put forward a programme, even a good one. We cannot have two heads under one hat.
>
> *The Prince:* Knowing my opinions and my record, why did you appoint me to the Privy Council?
>
> *The Emperor:* It is easy to blame my policy if one is not in power.
>
> *The Prince:* There is no liberty. I cannot believe it suits France in the long run. Our great uncle understood this. Your government is badly organized and there is a lot of friction. You cannot even do good. The country is oppressed. You know I have always thought the same. You no longer care for me. You only made me Vice-President of the Privy Council owing to the solicitations of Walewski, Magne and Persigny who wanted thereby to enhance its prestige, and now you regret it.
>
> *The Emperor:* No sentiment, please.
>
> *The Prince:* If the Empire and liberty prove incompatible it will be a bad day for our dynasty. If you do not regret your letter, I do not regret my speech.
>
> *The Emperor:* You consort with all the enemies of my government.
>
> *The Prince:* I never drop my old friends. I see very few people, and of these very few are your enemies. No word is uttered under my roof which you should not hear.

On the eve of the Austro-Prussian conflict in 1866 the Prince requested a command if France were involved; his desire was granted and harmony was restored. The Seven Weeks War ended as suddenly as the campaign of 1859, and his sole assignment was to persuade his father-in-law to conclude an armistice with Austria. Since France had come so close to the precipice and doubts had been expressed as to her readiness, a mixed commission of soldiers and civilians, including the Prince, was appointed to reorganize the army; but its recommendation of compulsory service was rejected by the Chamber. 'You wish to turn France into a vast barracks,' exclaimed Jules Favre. 'Take care not to make her a vast cemetery,' retorted Marshal Niel, the Minister of War.

The Prince's anxieties were increased by a visit to Germany in 1868 when Bismarck frankly revealed his plans for South Germany and described France as the only obstacle.

> *Bismarck:* What do you want?
> *The Prince:* The Rhine frontier.
> *Bismarck:* Impossible. Belgium?
> *The Prince:* That would need a treaty.
> *Bismarck:* Why? If it did not suit me I should break it.

Still more alarming was the impression of military efficiency derived from visits to Prussian barracks in the company of Colonel Stoffel, Military Attaché at the Embassy in Berlin.

The first phase of the inauguration of the Liberal Empire in 1867 gave the Prince the keenest pleasure.

> Your *Acte Additionel* in favour of liberty is an immense event [he wrote to the Emperor]. It is good for you, for your son, for France. It will make an enormous impression in Europe and restore our great prestige if loyally and skilfully implemented. The French people have always understood you when you had confidence in them. Good laws on the press and the right of association will be useful and glorious reforms due to your unforced initiative. You know my old convictions. Partly trained by you I have only two passions—the glory and liberty of our country under our family. Persevere. Do not let yourself be hindered by selfish and narrow-minded men. When history can say that after restoring order and bringing glory to France you initiated real liberty you will have little cause to envy the greatest sovereigns. That is the first utterance of my heart.

'I am very touched by your comment on the new phase,' replied the Emperor.

The friendly letter emboldened the Prince once again to proffer advice. 'Your liberal programme has caused the more satisfaction since it came as a surprise. The press, most of it hostile, found it difficult to conceal its embarrassment, and our enemies have been put out of countenance. A great effect was being produced, but the announcement of your new Ministry has changed the feeling and everyone is saying "this is not serious".' Thiers exclaimed:

> This is a trick, but we can turn it to our account. The benefits conferred by the Emperor, it is said, are being whittled away. Distrust is rife. If this goes on the reaction will be serious and your generous initiative will weaken instead of strengthening you. You change your technical Ministers and retain the politicians. You even keep the silent ones who cannot appear in the Chamber. As Minister of State, the sole effective organ of government, Rouher was already too omnipotent and now you add the Ministry of Finance. He is a man of great talent and real worth and has rendered you too great services to retire. To make him Minister of Finance seems to me excellent, but ought he to remain spokesman of the new domestic policy? New situations require new men. What confidence would a Minister inspire who proceeds to praise what he condemned a year ago? The malady of our time is flabbiness of character, the enfeebling of conscience, the spectacle of Ministers defending the policy they have opposed, retaining their post in order to ensure its failure. That is not the way to raise the *morale* of a nation. My sole motive is my desire for the success of a policy which I warmly approve, and which I regret to see compromised by feebleness in its application.

The Emperor replied that such criticisms would only be justified under a Parliamentary *régime* like that of Louis Philippe. 'I am to a certain point responsible for all that the Ministers have said or done, and if I take the initiative that is no condemnation of past actions. Moreover, since neither the Minister of the Interior nor the Foreign Minister is an adroit speaker, I had to retain Rouher as spokesman on all questions. I am glad to give you these explanations.'

No sooner was one crisis over than the clouds rolled up again. After the war of 1866, which added Venetia to the Italian kingdom, the French garrison was withdrawn from Rome. In the following year Pio Nono, menaced once more by Garibaldi, appealed to the Emperor, who promised its return. 'You can imagine the effect in Italy,' telegraphed the King to his son-in-law. 'The consequences will be terrible for both nations. Do what you can to prevent this misfortune.' The Prince replied that he knew nothing about affairs and had not seen the Emperor for a long time. Despite the defeat of the Garibaldians at Mentana by the Papal troops, the French garrison returned to Rome. The Prince drafted a protest, but its publication was vetoed by the Emperor and an interview failed to calm the troubled waters.

> The more I reflect on our talk [wrote the Emperor], the more I want to convince you how regrettable it would be if you appear to be separating from me. It is bad enough at ordinary times to display division in a family, but now any publication opposed to my policy would constitute a hostile act. The situation is grave. I am attacked on all sides, and your opposition would be regarded as a sign of weakness. Despite my friendship I must repeat that if you wish to go your own way I shall be obliged to announce a dramatic rupture.

The offender cancelled publication and wrote an aggrieved letter of submission. 'You deprive me of the rights of the humblest citizen and relegate me to the position of a suspect and a pariah in my own country.'

At the opening of 1869 the Prince unbosomed himself to Maxime du Camp.

> The old man is failing rapidly; he is more weary than people realize. There is no controlling hand. The Empress is a fool, incapable of governing except among the dressmakers, and yet she aspires to reign. She awaits with impatience the death of the Emperor in order to become Regent. If he dies there will be a revolution, and then my hour will come. France will never accept the rule of a woman and a minor. The country loves the Bonapartes, of whom I am one, as you see if you look at me. The old man is worried. Recently he showed me a portrait of the Prince Imperial and remarked: What will his destiny be?

After a year of sulky silence the Prince felt so alarmed at the foreign and domestic situation that he meditated a resounding declaration in the Senate. On second thoughts he addressed a memorandum to the Emperor who briefly replied that they were not in agreement. 'At home we need firmness; abroad we must await events. I am always glad to receive your views.' A second memorandum was dispatched a month later analysing the elections of May 1869, in which the Government won only two-thirds of the seats.

> Thus the Emperor is once again the master of the destinies of France. If by a change of men and system he pursues a liberal and constitutional course, if he sacrifices part of his power, he will receive the support of the Chamber and increase his popularity. If, on the other hand, he favours a reactionary clerical policy, and continues to employ the discredited personnel of the present government, he will strengthen the republican, socialist and revolutionary Opposition which would erupt in a terrible manner in the event of domestic or external complications. The Empire has plenty of strength but its adherents are dispersed, while its opponents are disciplined and concentrated in the great cities, above all in Paris. To live in an immense capital where the large majority of the inhabitants dream of upsetting a régime is a most difficult problem. Insurrection can be suppressed by force once, twice, thrice, but to hold Paris by force indefinitely is impossible. It must be averted by a wise policy. The situation is grave; the democratic flood is mounting. It must be canalized, not resisted. The men identified with the old system must go and liberal concessions be made. There must be a holocaust to save the Emperor, the dynasty and the Empire, and new Ministers, such as Ollivier, must inspire confidence.

The writer concluded with a list of urgent reforms, above all ministerial responsibility. When the Senate resumed after the summer recess he renewed his demand for a clean break with the past. 'I should like to see the authoritarian Empire burn its boats. The art of government is to yield at the right moment. Do not be afraid of opposition: it is the salt of politics.' The last of the Prince's lengthy memoranda reached the Emperor in February 1870, after Ollivier was called to the helm. A plebiscite, he argued, was essential to ratify the new system. The last plebiscite of the reign, in April 1870, brought a majority of $7\frac{1}{2}$ to $1\frac{1}{2}$ millions, but the abstention of 2 million voters was ominous. Though he had welcomed the Liberal Empire he felt that the advance was too cautious.

The Prince was yachting in Norway when the storm burst. Hurrying back to Paris he accompanied the Emperor to Metz, whence he was dispatched with an appeal to his father-in-law. The mission was fruitless, for a French garrison blocked the road to Rome. When the news of Sedan reached him in Italy the old resentments melted away. 'I ask to join you. Misfortune can only strengthen the ties which bind me to you since childhood.' 'I am touched by your offer to share my captivity,' replied the fallen ruler; 'but I desire to remain alone with the few who followed me, and I have begged the Empress not to come.' The stormy petrel of the Second Empire, '*le solitaire de Prangins*', jealous of the Prince Imperial, and detested by the ex-Empress, lived for another twenty years, writing, travelling and quarrelling with his family, but he had ceased to count. While Morny had fulfilled himself, Plonpon had always been his own worst enemy.

Despite his grave failings Plonplon possessed faithful friends, among them Maxime du Camp.

> He was the most calumniated man I ever knew. Parties which dared not make a frontal attack on the Emperor traduced him with fury, knowing that he would never take proceedings. No one was so insulted, but he never flinched. His bitterest foes in the capital were the Orleanists who circulated all sorts of gossip with which the enemies of the régime fed their rancour. The legend of his cowardice was an Orleanist fabrication and the Empress encouraged slander. I often dined with him at a restaurant in the company of George Sand and Flaubet, whom he greatly liked. Politics were never discussed, and everyone was perfectly at ease. His greatest fault was intemperance of language, which in a statesman may amount to a crime. A strange man misjudged and misunderstood. Liberal—by conviction? by interest? by the spirit of contradiction? by ambition? I cannot tell. In this sphere he remains a sphinx, but I believe that he would have ruled with a heavy hand. Once I said to him with a smile: God preserve me from living under your sceptre! I am not sure what I should be, he replied, but I would certainly not tolerate discussion of myself.

The best testimonial to his worth is to be found in the friendship of George Sand, who shared his desire for the liberalization of the *régime*, his sympathy with nationalities, and his dislike of the Church. He was a welcome guest at Nohant, where he won the heart of the whole family. 'I shall teach the people of my Berry that they may love you as I do,' she wrote shortly after the *coup d'état*. His good offices were enlisted for its victims and whenever she hoped they might be of use. 'Herewith the position of a poor old soldier of the Empire. Having to pass through the Prefecture, which here as elsewhere pays no attention to simple folk, it has not yet reached the Minister.' 'May you be blessed for what you have done,' she wrote in 1858 after a similar appeal had borne fruit. 'I believe I love you more than ever if that be possible.' 'You alone are young and generous,' she added in 1863. 'You alone love truth for its own sake. Among the men of genius today you are the only one whose genius springs from the heart. I esteem and love you more and more.' There is no reason to doubt her sincerity; though she had often loved she had never flattered. He sent her reports of his key speeches, and she sympathized with his feeling of frustration. After a visit to Nohant in 1868 he received a letter signed by the hostess, her son, and her daughter-in-law which must have warmed his heart. 'Thanks once more from myself, my children, grandchildren and all our friends whose hearts you have captivated. Since you left we have all been exclaiming: How handsome he is! How kind! How well he talks! How unpretentious, young and amiable! As you well guess, we fully agree and love the more those who love you. You will come again, won't you?'

7

PRINCESS MATHILDE,
NOTRE DAME DES ARTS

THE daughter of Jerome, King of Westphalia, niece of the mighty Emperor and first cousin of Napoleon III, was connected through her mother with several historic dynasties. Catherine was the daughter of King Frederick of Wurttemberg, sister of his successor King William, and niece of Marie who had married the unlucky Tsar Paul and became the mother of Alexander and Nicholas. To complete the family background her mother was a niece of George III.

Mathilde was unlucky in her parents, in her husband, and in the inconstant lovers who partially filled the vacuum left by a commercial marriage. The youngest of the Bonaparte brothers was the most contemptible of the brood. 'My father,' she testifies in her Memoirs, 'was the most amiable of men and pushed gallantry to imprudence.' An unfaithful husband and an unloving parent, his extravagant habits kept him perpetually in debt and drove him to cadge shamelessly from every available source. Having occupied a throne till the battle of Leipzig drove him into the wilderness, he expected to be supported and treated as a royalty for the rest of his life. The most honourable incident in his career was a wound at Waterloo. Excluded from France with the rest of the Bonapartes, he lived in exile as Prince de Montfort till his nephew nearly forty years later brought him back in honour and affluence. The lack of a father whom Mathilde could love and respect was not compensated by the affection of her mother, who declared that she would give her children for her husband's little finger and lived on friendly terms with his Italian mistress. The only warmth in the girl's early years was supplied by a Swiss widow, Baroness Reding, lady-in-waiting to her mother. 'She loved me as her child. I loved her more than my mother, whom I scarcely knew. I consulted her about everything; she never left me and she died in my arms.'

Mathilde was born in Trieste in 1820. Three years later the family migrated to Rome, where the thrifty old Mme Mère formed a rallying-point for her large family. Weekly visits to the gloomy palace of her grandmother were a trial, but in her own home there was plenty of company. Jerome visited his mother every day and paid a formal visit to the Pope once a year, on one occasion taking his daughter with him. The Roman phase ended abruptly when her cousins, the sons of Louis and Hortense, joined the revolt in the Papal states in 1831. Jerome was expelled and settled in Florence, the capital of the Grand Duchy of Tuscany, which her Memoirs describe as a happy place. The neglected wife of Joseph Bonaparte, who preferred the company of a mistress, lived in Florence and became almost a second mother. Louis Bonaparte, who migrated to Tuscany after the fall of the Empire, is portrayed as a morose and miserly invalid, eternally grumbling about his wife. To know him was to sympathize with Hortense, who became a valued friend and invited Mathilde to spend the winter at Arenenberg after the death of her mother in 1835. Though there was a difference of twelve years between the son of Hortense and the daughter of Jerome the idea of a union occurred independently to the respective parents. One night when she was believed to be asleep Mathilde overheard Baroness Reding talking to Jerome about her marriage and discovered that the mind of Hortense was travelling in the same direction. Louis Napoleon had always been like a brother, she writes, and kisses were exchanged. Her father approved, and his father after some hesitation gave his assent. The project was ruined by the *coup* at Strasbourg and the exile of the conspirator, who, amid the attractions of New York, soon forgot his first romance. There was no heartbreak on either side, for there had been attraction but never love. They would scarcely have been happy together for their temperaments were as different as their interests, and both were too self-centred to make any partnership a success. 'He is never angry,' she complained; 'his strongest expression is "Absurd." If I had married him I should have broken his head open to see what was inside.'

After this fiasco, thoughts of marriage were never far from the girl's mind. Though penniless, for the family was financed by the King of Wurttemberg, she was vivacious, intelligent, and well-educated with a taste for painting. Longing to escape from an uncongenial home and having seen too much of the world to dream of a love match, she asked little more than a wealthy husband. She met her future husband for the first time in Florence in 1838 and saw her chance. Anatole Demidoff, a coarse Russian millionaire, derived his fabulous income from mines and factories, and his father had built a house near Florence where he had established a silk factory. The son, who had a liking for the arts and travel, visited the Jerome family in company with Jules Janin, the French author, who first suggested to his patron the idea of marriage.

> People spoke of it to me [records Mathilde]. The man did not displease me. I found him *distingué*. He lived in Paris, an important factor in my decision. My aunt Julie approved, and my father too, though he wanted to make conditions which were rejected. I was much annoyed, but Demidoff told me it was only postponed. I looked forward to the marriage because it meant escape from a false situation. Imagine a girl of eighteen alone with a father who paid no attention to her, was enslaved by a love of pleasure, and lived only for his passions.

Negotiations dragged on till 1840, when Demidoff consented to pay some of Jerome's debts. That he was a notorious *roué* with a *maîtresse en titre* was a trifle. 'Nothing viler could be imagined,' commented Vieil-Castel, 'false, cowardly and vicious, without a single good quality.' For once the ill-natured diarist was justified in his scorn.

A more serious obstacle was that the bridegroom belonged to the Greek Orthodox Church and required the consent of the Tsar. The Grand Duke of Tuscany strove to ease the situation by conferring on him the title of Prince of San Donato, and the girl's eagerness increased as the ceremony approached. 'I was very satisfied. He pleased me in every way. I wanted to bring into his life a serenity and regularity which he had never enjoyed and which he seemed to crave.' She was deceiving herself, for he loved her even less than she loved him. Each wanted something the other could supply—she a sumptuous establishment, he social prestige by marrying the daughter of a former king. He had never been accepted by the old Russian nobility, and he retained the mentality and manners of a *parvenu*. Those who knew him best liked him least. Rarely has a marriage started under less favourable auspices.

The ceremony took place at Florence in November 1840, first according to the Greek Orthodox rite, then in the sacristy of the Duomo. 'He seemed very fond and proud of me,' she writes; 'his vanity was for the moment wholly satisfied.' It was a false dawn, for an altercation between him and the Russian Ambassador in Rome resulted in a summons to St. Petersburg. It was a blow to the bride, who had counted on a visit to Paris, which she had never seen, and the winter drive to the Russian capital was rendered still more disagreeable by the sombre mood of her husband. The Tsar's friendliness to Mathilde, due partly to family ties, partly to her intelligence and charm, contrasted sharply with his studied coolness to Demidoff. In granting them permission to leave the country he warned her that she had made a bad choice. 'You do not know what a scoundrel you have married. He is a contemptible fellow and you will never be happy with him, but I will always be your friend.' She carried away an abiding memory of the kindliness of the ruler and the squalor of his dominions. As the ill-matched pair drove slowly westward she consoled herself by the thought of social triumphs and intellectual contacts in the city of her dreams.

Her first excursion was to the Invalides, for devotion to her uncle coloured the whole of her life, and she vainly sought permission to visit her cousin at Ham. Though her family loyalties were unconcealed she was soon on excellent terms with Louis Philippe and the motherly Queen. Guests flocked to her receptions and musical parties, among them Thiers, who divided his time between politics and the narrative of the Napoleonic saga. When the couple returned to Italy in 1843 she was known as 'the great lady of Florence'. Though she lived in semi-regal splendour the marriage had broken down, for her husband's irritability was aggravated by poor health. When he entered her salon during a reception with his latest mistress on his arm she decided to go her own way. Craving for love, she believed she had found it in Nieuwerkerke, the son of a Dutch officer, who was passing through Florence in company with the Comte de Chambord in the course of a tour in Italy. Unable to bear the yoke any longer she sought temporary refuge in a nunnery, but she was not made for the cloister. The day of deliverance dawned when the Tsar, after summoning Demidoff to Russia, permitted a separation while retaining most of her jewels and securing her an allowance of 200,000 francs a year. The husband was forbidden to return to Paris and they never met again. For the first time she was a rich woman on her own and looked forward to a happy *liaison de convenance*.

The political scene was transformed by the proclamation of the Second Republic and the election of Louis Napoleon in five Departments. At this point Mathilde emerges on the political stage, supporting him with her money and influence. The simultaneous election of her brother to the Chamber provided a further reason for identifying herself with the Man of Destiny. When he was elected President and moved into the Elysée, she acted as his hostess. Friend and foe foretold a Second Empire, and the expectation that the cousins would marry was almost equally prevalent. That a divorce from Demidoff would be needed was a trifle: a graver obstacle was her *liaison* with the Dutch sculptor Nieuwerkerke, formerly page to Charles X, residing in Paris since his youth. He had given her painting lessons during a visit to Florence. Now *le bel Emilien* was *persona grata* at the Tuileries, with a residence in the Louvre. Her salon was the most brilliant in Paris, and with a bachelor President she was recognized as the first lady in the land. Her position seemed still more assured when he moved into the Tuileries and Jerome was appointed President of the Senate with a dignified residence in the Invalides. Father and daughter had never loved one another, and the stopping of her allowance to him of 40,000 francs created a final breach. Rich though she was, the Emperor allowed her 200,000 francs a year (later increased to 500,000) which enabled her to buy a country home at Saint-Gratien within easy reach of her house in the capital. Her only political regret was the appropriation of part of the Orleans property for the State, a measure against which she protested in vain.

Though well aware that Napoleon III needed an heir, she dreaded the moment when she would have to step down. She liked Eugénie at first and encouraged her meetings with the President, never dreaming of anything beyond a *liaison*. When he announced his decision no one was more surprised, and his appeal to her for kindness to the woman of his choice fell on deaf ears. Henceforth her attitude to *Elle*, as she always called her, was chilly and soon degenerated into unconcealed hostility, while the Empress resented the opening of her salon to men who were never seen and never wanted to be seen at the Tuileries. She had never possessed much influence over her cousin and henceforth she had none. Though they remained on friendly terms and she paid him a duty visit every autumn at Compiègne, she was rarely seen at the Court. The estrangement was sharpened by occasional political differences; while he was Anglophil she was Anglophobe. Mindful of the kindness of the Tsar, she disapproved the Crimean war. The Italian policy, on the other hand, commanded her approval as strongly as it shocked the Empress; and Nigra, Cavour's trusted Ambassador, was a welcome guest. Neither a *dévote* nor an anticlerical, she was proud of the laurels of Solferino.

After the Emperor's marriage her salon became the main occupation and pride of her life. Nieuwerkerke, like Demidoff before him, had never loved her, but the *liaison* lasted till 1870. Since neither Emperor nor Empress cared for literature and the arts Mathilde became the queen of the literary and artistic world —*Notre Dame des Arts*, a Marguerite of Navarre in the skin of a Napoleon, as the Goncourt brothers described her. With the exception of Victor Hugo, sulking in Guernsey, and George Sand, who in later life preferred her country home to the racket of the capital, almost every writer and artist of note frequented her dinners and receptions. Among the former were Dumas *père* and *fils*, Sainte-Beuve, Gautier, Mérimée, Flaubert, Feuillet, About, Labiche, the de Goncourt brothers, Arsène Housseye, Director of the Comedie Francaise, Taine, Renan, Littré; among the latter Meissonnier, Gavarni, Carpeaux and Viollet-le-Duc. 'Her guests are not announced,' records an *habitué*. 'What need is there to announce Émile Augier and Meissonier, Ingres and Émile de Girardin, the blond beard of Arsène Houssaye, the high life of M. de Morny and M. de Nieuwerkerke? Who does not recognize Viollet-le-Duc, Vernet, Gounod, the majestic Théophile Gautier?' The latter she described as *mon poète*, and he classified their happy relationship as *amitié voluptueuse*. As the Bohemian journalist with his expensive tastes was often in financial straits she created for him the sinecure post of her librarian. Their letters breathe genuine affection without a trace of anything more. When after *l'année terrible* he was too ill to resume his visits to her salon he wrote: 'I do not forget you. No one has taken your place. I love you with all my heart, and my heart has not yet grown old.'

Her two houses were crammed with pictures, furniture and *bric-à-brac* which she loved to show to her guests. A bust of her adored uncle adorned her drawing-room. She had only one pleasure, she told the de Goncourt brothers in 1867, namely, to have company, to live surrounded by people she liked. The talk was completely unrestrained. The leading lion was Sainte-Beuve, whom she saw every week and consulted on her private affairs and with whom she exchanged hundreds of letters. To love him was impossible, but she delighted in his conversation. In 1862 he contributed a vivid sketch to a symposium entitled *Galérie Bonaparte*.

> Her brow is lofty and proud, her features clearly and boldly defined with no trace of indecision. Despite the classical purity of the lines she is more than a mere type. Her deep-set brown eyes shine with the affection or the idea of the moment, incapable of feigning or concealing her thought. Her glance is lively and piercing. Her whole countenance breathes nobility, dignity, when animated a blend of grace and power, the joy of a healthy nature, frankness and kindliness, sometimes fire and ardour too. Her cheeks colour in righteous anger. Her head rises in dignity above a dazzling and magnificent bust and the shoulders are like marble. She has the lovely hands of the Bonaparte family. There is something sovereign about her, a woman in the full flush of life.

The prince of critics found as much to admire in her character as in her looks.

> She is uncomplicated and straightforward; nothing is left in shadow. Duplicity, subterfuge, intrigue, cunning, perfidy, she abhors. Her friendships are faithful and durable. She needs to believe in people. Though her first reaction is sometimes impetuous and may carry her too far, she holds herself in if warned. Her mind resembles her character, combining elevation with simplicity. Here, as everywhere else, there is sincerity. Do not talk to her of complexities or

ambiguities; she has no use for nuances and half-tones. She dislikes all that is vague and goes straight ahead. In her and her brother there is something of their uncle the Emperor.

In gratitude for his friendship she procured him an invitation to Compiègne and a nomination to the Senate with its welcome salary. The pleasant comradeship ended abruptly when in the last year of his life he committed the offence of contributing literary articles to the *Temps*, an opposition journal. Driving unannounced to his house she furiously reproached 'the vassal of the Emperor' with treachery, shook her muff at him, and renounced his friendship. They never met again. In crediting her with durable friendships he had overlooked the fact that the cult of the Bonaparte family meant more to her than any personal tie. Though not flirtatious, she preferred male to female company and had few women friends. She disliked Pauline Metternich almost as much as the Empress herself.

Her portrait by another *habitué*, Vieil-Castel, as we might expect, is less brightly tinted. With the exception of the President and Princess Mathilde, he wrote in 1851, all the Bonaparte family were good for nothing.

> I go every Wednesday and Saturday to St. Gratien where I meet all sorts of people. The Princess ignores the aristocracy, the influence of birth and family traditions, except such as belong to the Bonapartes. All is to be forgotten except that great man whose acts are beyond dispute and in whose record it is treason to find a blot. France is nothing without the glory of the Bonapartes; the monarchy deserves scarcely a thought; it is almost a crime to compare Napoleon with Charlemagne.

Though he enjoyed her company as much as such a misanthrope could enjoy anything, he was well aware of her failings. 'She pretends to be liberal in her views and to encourage discussion, but she detests anyone who does not agree with her. She pretends to have some knowledge of pictures and of art generally, but she has not, though she paints with some success. Her major-domo gives her guests most detestable dinners and poisons us with nasty wines. Her surroundings have become intolerable,' he noted in 1857, 'composed as they are of enemies in disguise, courtiers, of the vilest kind, or simple buffoons. But if she remains for a time under the malign influence of her entourage, she soon returns to herself and her charming, intelligent nature reasserts itself.' In 1863, the last year of his life, Vieil-Castel was dismissed from his post in the Louvre by his chief, Nieuwerkerke, on the ground that he had criticized an exhibition, but in fact because he was associated with a new paper which the autocratic Princess disapproved. He regretted the loss of his post more than the termination of her friendship, for he had found her circle increasingly distasteful and the hostess less and less attractive. After the rupture his jottings became definitely hostile. 'Poor Princess Mathilde thinks she has a salon, whereas it is only a sort of bazaar with flatterers and sycophants. She is beginning to adopt the vulgar tone and language of her associates and has come to think that the commonest familiarity denotes majestic ease.' But Vieil-Castel should never be taken too seriously. 'His little guillotine,' she told him, 'was always kept greased for action.'

When the news of Sedan reached Paris Mathilde was advised to leave home, but her offer to visit the captive at Wilhelmshöhe was politely declined. 'I regret to be still alive,' she wrote to Dumas *fils*. 'Is it fair that I should suffer so much? I have never been ambitious and only wanted to be loved for myself. I have tried to help people who sought my aid, and I thought if I were ever to need help I should get it. Though I never expected gratitude this injustice is a trial.' She met the fallen Emperor for the last time when he passed through Belgium *en route* for Chislehurst, bursting into tears as she embraced him, while he remained calm and cool. She attributed the *débâcle* to the Empress and the Ministers, but found few to agree.

Returning to Paris in her fiftieth year she strove to rebuild her life as a private citizen. She told Thiers, now head of the state, that she would stand aloof from politics, and she kept her word. The death of Demidoff in 1870 left her free to remarry, but she preferred a new *liaison*. When Nieuwerkerke fled to Italy without saying farewell, his place was filled by Popelin, artist and poet, whom she loved much more than he loved her. Her painting and embroidery remained a great resource. She resumed her weekly dinners for writers and artists, but the surviving Goncourt noted in his journal that she was sometimes very depressed. Though she secured some brilliant young recruits, among them

Maupassant and Coppée, Paul Bourget and Anatole France, Barrès and Proust, she lost one of her oldest friends when Taine's criticism of Napoleon and his family excited her wrath. Meeting him later at an Academy election she turned her back on him, exclaiming to a friend: 'That beast!' When the friend urged her to let bygones be bygones she exclaimed: 'Never!' The same fate befell Sardou whose picture of her adored uncle in *Mme Sans-Gêne* caused her to leave the theatre, loudly and repeatedly exclaiming '*Quelle indignité!*' The least amiable feature of her character was her readiness to sacrifice friendships to differences of opinion. On the death of the Prince Imperial she lost all hope of a restoration. The *liaison* with Popelin ended with a discovery that he was in love with a young member of her household. The death of her brother in 1891 severed the last link with the past and, like him, she had no expectation of an after life. Dying at the age of eighty-four, she left her possessions to her nephew, Prince Louis, who had taken service in the Russian army. Like her old rival Eugénie she lived too long.

8

COUNT WALEWSKI, THE POLISH COUSIN

THERE is a close resemblance between the careers of the illegitimate half-brother and the illegitimate first cousin of Napoleon III. Both were men of literary tastes and wrote plays; both adopted and abandoned a military career; both were virtually unknown to their relative until 1848; both held high posts and served him with unvarying fidelity. Though there was little affection, the Dictator was grateful for their support and regarded their death as a blow to the *régime*.

Every student of the Napoleonic saga is familiar with the story of the beautiful young wife of the elderly Count Walewski employed by Prince Joseph Poniatowski to interest the master of the Continent in the cause of Poland, as Cavour dispatched Countess Castiglione to capture Napoleon III for the cause of Italy. Her indulgent husband assumed the paternity of Alexandre, whom she took with her on a two days' visit to Elba a year later. His parents met once more at Malmaison after Waterloo, a scene of which he retained vivid childish memories. On the death of Count Walewski the widow married General d'Ornano, and on her death two years after the fall of the Empire Alexandre was brought up in Poland by her brother. After studying in Warsaw and Geneva he settled with his kindly stepfather in Paris, but his devotion to the land of his birth never waned. Returning to play his part in the rebellion of 1831 he had his horse killed under him. He served his apprenticeship in diplomacy when the French Government dispatched him to consult with Talleyrand, French Ambassador in London, and to plead with Palmerston for aid to the suffering Poles.

Though the mission was a failure, Walewski's sojourn in

England proved the foundation of his fortunes. Moving freely in London society he met and married a daughter of the Earl of Sandwich and became an ardent Anglophil. Polish patriots, with Mickiewicz at their head, were welcomed in Paris after the suppression of the rebellion, and Walewski attended the New Year reception at the Tuileries in 1832 in Polish uniform. Since there was no place for him in Poland he had to make his career in France, fulfilling his father's testamentary desire that he should serve in the French army. He joined the Foreign Legion, for he was still a Polish subject, and took part in the Algerian campaign; but the military routine satisfied him as little as it satisfied Morny. Retiring from the army he became a French subject and threw himself into the political and social life of the capital. He published a brochure urging France to cultivate the Arabs and advocating an English alliance. Though an evening paper which he bought failed, and his comedy *L'école du Monde* achieved only limited success, he found his feet in the literary world.

Thiers, the leading figure on the political stage in the thirties, thought him exceptionally fitted for a diplomatic career, and during the eastern crisis of 1840 dispatched him on a mission to Mehemet Ali in Cairo. 'I am sending a young Frenchman,' wrote the Prime Minister to the French Consul at Alexandria, 'a clever, tactful and well-informed young man whom I have seen succeed in more than one difficult situation. He is a special friend of mine and knows my views.' His task was to persuade the ambitious Viceroy to accept the protection of Louis Philippe in his challenge to the Sultan. Thiers' adventurous policy cost him his place, but his protégé emerged unscathed. 'The King thought he could frighten Europe with his armaments,' wrote the fallen Minister; 'when he saw his mistake he drew back and I resigned. I will see that your reputation does not suffer.' He had been very pleased with him, he added, and the King was very satisfied. The new Ministry under Guizot added its plaudits.

Walewski's English wife was dead when his mistress introduced him to her friend Rachel, queen of the European stage, and for three years he enjoyed her coveted favours. She who had never loved so deeply was also his first real love, and the birth of a child brought happiness to both. He was the first of her lovers to polish the Jewish girl, who had never been to school nor learned to spell. When the *liaison* ended in 1846 he married the daughter of a Poniatowski who had settled in Florence. Thiers regretted that she was not rich enough to assist his career. 'You know how fond I am of you, and I do not want you to be financially dependent on politics. You have an excellent political brain and you will make an excellent diplomat.' That his choice was wise, society in various capitals was soon to realize. Though Thiers and Guizot were political rivals, Walewski, with the approval of the former, offered his services to the new Foreign Minister, who dispatched him for a brief spell to Argentina. Visiting his wife in Florence when the Monarchy collapsed in 1848, he volunteered to serve the Republic as Minister to Tuscany on the ground of his family connections, and the offer was accepted.

Walewski, like Morny, had never aided the Bonapartist cause, and the new master of France showed no desire for his services. 'Sometimes I feel a little hurt', he confided to his former mother-in-law Lady Sandwich, 'that the nephew of the Emperor forgets me in looking round for men to share his task. I cannot push myself and stake my fortunes in a game where the players do not seem to want me.' He complained too soon, for he was promoted from Florence to the more important post at Naples, was raised to the rank of Ambassador, and was appointed Commander of the Legion of Honour. The tide of fortune had turned and he received the highest mark of favour by his appointment to London. 'An old *roué* without ability,' commented Vieil-Castel. 'He is one of those favourites of fortune who build on sand and leave nothing to mark their past greatness.' The diarist was unfair as usual, for Walewski was well suited to his task. Frowned on by those pillars of legitimacy, Tsar Nicholas and Frederick William IV of Prussia, Louis Napoleon coveted the friendship of England and believed that his cousin was the fittest agent to secure it. 'I want your Embassy to resemble Paris,' he explained to Mme Walewski, 'a centre of perfect taste, elegance and *bon ton*, so that all your guests should repeat the flattering yet truthful phrase: Everyone has two countries, his own and France.' Their reception was all that could be desired when they arrived in the summer of 1851. 'All the press is with you,' reported the Ambassador. 'Opinion here, with its traditions of loyalty, absolves you in advance for all that your uprightness, energy and patriotism may lead you to undertake against the factions and in the interests of France.'

When the long-expected *coup* took place, Walewski explained it to Palmerston as a measure to save the country from a revolution which would affect the whole of Europe, since England and Europe were directly interested in the stability of France. If, as might be expected, the President succeeded, he would have accomplished one of the most useful tasks of the time. The Foreign Minister needed no conversion, but his prompt approval of the *coup*, unauthorized by the Prime Minister Lord John Russell and the Queen, was punished by dismissal. The popularity of the Ambassador was unaffected. Lord John and Granville, the new Foreign Secretary, showed themselves in his company, the Queen invited him and his wife to Windsor, and Lord Normanby, the British Ambassador in Paris, whose hostility to the new *régime* was unconcealed, was replaced by Lord Cowley. The greatest social triumph was the presence of the octogenarian Wellington at a dinner in the Embassy when he drank a toast to 'Your Prince, to the memory of the greatest genius of the century.' Three months later the Ambassador followed the coffin of the Iron Duke to St. Paul's. Having always dreamed of an Anglo-French *entente* he fully earned the Emperor's expression of gratitude, and henceforth was regarded as a pillar of the *régime*. The brotherhood in arms during the Crimean war strengthened the ties. In May 1854 the Queen, the Prince Consort and the Ministers attended a costume ball at the Embassy; in the following spring the Emperor and Empress paid a state visit to Windsor, and Walewski accompanied the Queen when she returned the compliment by a state visit to Paris. Greville dismissed him as 'an adventurer, a ready speculator, without honour, conscience or truth, utterly unfit, both by character and capacity for high office of any kind'; but the British diarist was almost as ill-natured as Vieil-Castel in France. His Embassy had been a success in the Emperor's eyes and he had not long to wait for his reward.

When disagreement with the Emperor on the terms of the settlement of the Russian conflict caused the resignation of the Foreign Minister, Drouyn de Lhuys, the vacancy was filled by Walewski, whose first duty was to preside over the Congress of Paris. He had reached the summit of his career. For the next two years the cousins worked in unbroken harmony, but differences emerged when the ruler decided to take a hand in Italian politics. The Russophobe Walewski wished to retain the friendship of Austria which the Emperor was prepared to sacrifice on the altar of Italian nationalism. He was not informed of the plan for Cavour's visit to Plombières. When that fateful meeting occurred he offered his resignation, complaining that he had not been consulted in regard to several important decisions and declarations, negotiations with the Piedmontese Ambassador, and the publication of articles and pamphlets inspired by the Emperor himself. 'I say without bitterness that it was not treating me as a Minister or a friend. I hope Your Majesty respects me too much to believe I could serve under such conditions. I could only continue if I felt certain I was useful, but now unfortunately I am assured of the contrary.' 'I have full confidence in your ability and devotion,' replied the Emperor. 'Would not your resignation give rise to absurd notions, and would not people conclude that the change of Ministers meant a change of policy? That would be a real misfortune for me, both as man and sovereign.' 'You speak of your regret and that settles it,' rejoined Walewski. But he was no rubber stamp and he continued to strive for the maintenance of Austrian friendship. The alternative to war was a Congress of the Great Powers, but Austria was resolved to teach Victor Emmanuel a lesson as she had taught his father in 1849. Since Francis Joseph, Victor Emmanuel and Napoleon III were equally resolved on war the Foreign Minister was powerless.

The sovereign continued to keep all negotiations in his own hands, and Walewski offered his resignation for a second time, stressing the dangers of the principle of nationalities. The Emperor replied in a long and friendly letter on the eve of the campaign. Walewski's conversations, he complained, had not always reflected official policy.

> You disapproved the Guerronière brochure and I disapprove *Le Pays* which you inspire and which takes a line directly opposed to my ideas. You declare that without universal suffrage the Chambers do not represent public opinion. If I do not represent the French Revolution I represent nothing, and Henri V (the Comte de Chambord) should be in my place. Mine is a representative government with a freely elected Chamber voting laws and taxes. I am a sovereign

possessing a Civil List and I do not dip into the public purse whenever I like. We possess the *Code Napoléon* assuring everybody's rights and equality before the law; an independent judiciary; the opening of all posts; an army composed of the *élite* of the nation and no longer of mercenaries; there is liberty to write, think and believe within the limits of the law. Thus, when the peoples of Europe make revolutions to obtain the blessings we possess—and which they only obtained for a brief space under the Empire as the fruit of our victories—they naturally look to me because I represent these ideas, which are not yet the common property of Europe and which have been impeded by an impious sect which confounds '89 with '93. I repeat all this because my Ministers should always fully understand these fundamental ideas. I should like you to re-read my *Idées Napoléoniennes* which I wrote in 1837. My convictions have not changed. Your letter obliges me to recall our occasional differences. Nevertheless I sincerely desire to retain you since, despite certain divergences, you are still the best person to conduct our foreign relations. I recognize your great qualities and deep knowledge of affairs, but that things may go well you must fully understand and implement my thoughts.

Once again Walewski withdrew his offer of resignation. 'I cannot understand', wrote the Empress to Mme Walewski, 'why he thinks he has lost the confidence of the Emperor. Tell your husband that if I was with him at this moment I would prove him mistaken.' Eugénie was not told all the Emperor's secrets, and the disappearance of the Foreign Minister was expected in the Chancelleries—with regret in Vienna, with satisfaction in Berlin, and with eagerness by Prince Napoleon, the leading Italophil in France. He remained at his post till the end of the fateful year 1859, when he advised the Emperor to recall Thouvenel, whose ideas were closer to those of his master. This time the Emperor made no attempt to avert a change. 'Walewski's fall leaves no regrets,' commented Vieil-Castel. 'He quits the Ministry dishonoured by his wife, who has inscribed her name in capital letters on the list of the Emperor's sultanas.' Happily we are not bound to believe all the scandal which the malicious diarist purveys. Though he declined the offer of any Ministry except the Foreign Office and the War Office he never sulked. In visits to his successor and by correspondence with ecclesiastical dignitaries in Paris he continued to combat what he described as the triumph of revolution in Italy, to support the Pope, and to oppose the ambitions of Piedmont. His labours were in vain, for the Emperor had set in motion forces he could not control. His advice to help the insurgent Poles in 1863 and to break off relations with Russia was equally ignored.

On the home front Walewski, like Morny, favoured the thawing of autocracy by increasing the power of the Chambers. Unattracted by further departmental work he accepted the position of Minister of State and a seat in the Senate. A decree slightly enlarging the functions of the Legislature was a cheering sign. 'I hope England is pleased,' he wrote to Lady Sandwich. 'If not Parliamentary government, it is at any rate representative government, and it can no longer be said that the Emperor stifles political discussion.' The Cobden Treaty delighted him, for he remained an Anglophil to the end. As Minister of State he devoted special attention to culture, instituting a Commission de la Propriété Littéraire et Artistique, choosing the first members, and laying the foundation stone of the new Opera House.

The final phase of Walewski's career opened in 1865 when he succeeded Morny as President of the Chamber. 'If you think I might be of use,' he wrote to the Emperor, 'I believe it would please both the public and the Chamber.' Since the post could only be held by an elected Deputy he resigned his seat in the Senate and was returned without a contest. The experiment proved unsuccessful, for he lacked Morny's readiness of utterance and flair in managing a body growing more critical every year as the prestige of the ruler waned. He resigned in 1867 and begged the Emperor to restore him to the Senate. He had presented his friend Ollivier to the ruler as the only man capable of liberalizing the system, but died in 1868, too soon to welcome his call to the helm. In the words of Ollivier, the Emperor had lost the wisest though not the cleverest of his Ministers. Mérimée dismissed him as 'mediocrity or, rather, nullity personified. It is impossible to be more stupid.' He was not a statesman, complained the Emperor, who added that France possessed none. No one has claimed that he was a superman, but he had friends and admirers in Catholic and Austrophil circles, among them Richard Metternich who preferred him to any other servant of the Second Empire.

PART TWO

THE MINISTERS

9

PERSIGNY, *LOYAL SERVITEUR*

IF unselfish devotion to the man and the cause be the test of merit in the entourage of Napoleon III, Persigny claims the first place without a rival. He raised the banner at a time when the family had resigned itself to its fate after the death of the Duc de Reichstadt and showed no interest in the ambitions of the future ruler of France. Apostle, comrade, *loyal serviteur*, as he styled himself, he shared the trials and triumphs of his hero, equally convinced that a Second Empire was in the logic of events, as inescapable as sunrise after the gloom of night. Since the Bourgeois Monarchy failed to satisfy the political aspirations of France, and only a few doctrinaire Republicans credited the common man with capacity to rule, what alternative to a benevolent autocracy modelled on that of the mighty Emperor could there be? Of course dictators required a mandate, but France, he believed, was only awaiting the opportunity to welcome the bearer of a historic name. When the plebiscite for the Presidency confirmed his forecast he felt that the goal was in sight. Though there was nothing remarkable about him except the firmness of his political principles and his undeviating fidelity, he cannot be ignored. In the words of Hübner, the Austrian Ambassador: 'It is equally difficult to take him seriously and not to take him seriously.' It was a dedicated life.

Born in the same year as his master, Fialin, who later called himself Fialin de Persigny, was the son of a civil servant. Finding a military career too dull, he tried his hand at journalism. At this point the current of his life was changed by one of the accidents which constitute the romance of history. When some business took him to Augsburg he passed a carriage in which sat a dark young man. The coachman raised his hat, cried *Vive Napoléon!* explaining that he was the nephew of the Emperor. The idea of a restored Empire flashed across his mind and filled him with ecstasy as intense as that of a sudden religious conversion. Already a fervent admirer of Napoleon, he vowed, in his own words, to be the Loyola of the Second Empire. Nearly thirty years later he recalled in an address the exaltation of his early days. 'In dedicating myself to a great cause which has triumphed for the happiness and glory of France, I did not stop to consider whether I should find fortune or misery, but merely whether it was for the good of my country, resolved to bear poverty if it were to be my lot or to accept fortune modestly if it came my way.' They were no idle words, for his sincerity was never in doubt.

The first task was to fly a kite in the *Revue de l'Occident Français* of which only one number of eighty pages appeared in 1836. Taking as his watchword the proud boast of the Emperor, *J'ai dessouillé la Révolution, ennobli les peuples et raffermi les lois*, he pleaded for a Bonapartist restoration. 'Everyone in Europe expects a total renovation like the coming of the Messiah. I proclaim Napoleon's idea, martyred at St. Helena in the person of its glorious representative. The time has come to announce this precious legacy of the eighteenth century, the true law of the modern world.' He salutes the political genius of his idol as equal to his military prowess—the Concordat, the Code, the promotion of agriculture and industry, commerce and education. 'There is no other tradition for France and the West, a tradition more fruitful than all the Parliamentary Committees and constitutional treatises.' Mankind had never taken a step forward except through a man who embodies an idea.

The sole response from the family was an invitation from Joseph Bonaparte, now living in retirement at Denham. Except for a small gift of money nothing came of the meeting, but the young enthusiast never feared to stand alone.

> I shall continue my apostolate [he wrote to a friend]. I am not a member of the Bonapartist party but of the Napoleonic faith. My devotion is not purely dynastic; it is a religion, and I could not enlist under the banner of a party. I have never been tied to the princes whom I did not know: if I serve them it is due to my faith. Whatever their personal qualities, they embody a principle which will have its

inevitable consequences irrespective of their wishes. I will yield passive obedience to a leader on condition that he shares my faith and my goal. If I meet him I will place myself at his orders.

While Persigny was awaiting a leader, Prince Louis was waiting for followers. The young crusader was the first to salute him, and his earliest assignment was a tour through the land which was closed to his master, returning with such an encouraging report that the Pretender decided to test opinion himself. In the fiasco at Strasbourg in 1836 his henchman was at his side. Both were arrested, but Persigny escaped over the frontier. His flight, declared the prosecution, was particularly regrettable, for he was intelligent and resolute and knew most about the conspiracy. The Baden police were ordered to arrest him and hand him over to the French authorities. For some days he wandered about the Black Forest, whence he made his way to England and published a spirited defence of the enterprise, *Relation de l'entreprise du Prince Napoléon*. 'He knew that his family would have no fatherland till the voice of the people was heard. As heir to the greatest name of modern times he felt it his duty to restore to the people their rights.' Persigny was obsessed by the thought of what the Emperor had suffered. 'When the demigod was chained like Prometheus to his horrible rock,' he wrote from London, 'what right had I to complain? The memory of his long punishment never leaves me and gives me strength to bear anything. When I began to live in the faith of this great man I was prepared for anything. No torment will surprise me, nothing will cast me down.'

When the Prince returned from his brief exile in the United States the friends were longing for fresh adventures. At his wish Persigny published a little book anonymously in Paris entitled *Lettres de Londres, Visite au Prince Louis*, supposedly addressed to some French General. After painting the state of France in sombre colours, the author reminded his readers that the Emperor's nephew was available if his services were required, as Augustus was ready and able to complete Caesar's unfinished task. In the raid on Boulogne Persigny was again at his side. On the failure of the attack the little band of fifty scattered, the Pretender, Persigny, and three others putting to sea in a boat. Amid a hail of bullets from the shore they jumped into the water, were arrested and imprisoned in the citadel. A few days later, as the Prince stepped into the carriage which was to carry him to Paris for trial, his fellow-prisoner called out from a window of the fortress: 'Fear nothing. The shadow of the Emperor will protect you. You will triumph over your enemies.' When charged with being one of the leading spirits of the conspiracy, he stoutly replied: 'I had only to obey. I belong to the Prince and am his soldier.' Once again the rebels were lucky to escape with their lives. The Pretender was sentenced to life imprisonment in the fortress of Ham, the aide-de-camp to twenty years in the citadel of Doullens where he occupied himself by writing on the Pyramids. The friends were not to meet again till the fall of the Monarchy cleared the path to the Promised Land.

His old friend Falloux, though a zealous Legitimist, supplied him with books. When his eyesight was threatened he was transferred to a hospital at Versailles, where the Mayor procured permission for him to visit the Paris libraries once a week and to discuss his theories with Egyptologists. When Falloux attended these meetings he was impressed by Persigny's invariable serenity, as of one dedicated to a sacred cause. Such a man was no danger to the *régime*, thought Falloux, who, in 1847, obtained a promise of liberation through a son of Marshal Ney, aide-de-camp to one of the Orleans princes. All Persigny had to do was to write to one of the King's sons or, if he preferred, to the Minister of the Interior, basing his request on his state of health and the claims of his studies: he would not need to disavow the cause or his leader. After further discussions he was informed that a letter to Falloux would suffice. 'Impossible,' exclaimed Persigny when the kindly friend brought him the good news. 'I shall never ask a favour. That would imply a promise I cannot give. In a year we shall be in their place.' When they met again as deputies in the Chamber of the Second Republic a year later, Falloux revised his estimate of the man whom he had regarded as a harmless fanatic.

Released on the fall of the Monarchy, Persigny soon found himself one of the leading figures on the political stage, and he now assumed the title of Comte de Persigny, to which he had not the smallest claim. The prospect at the outset looked none too bright. Since almost everyone of importance, in and out of Parliament, was Legitimist, Orleanist or Republican, there seemed to be little room for a new party, and even after the triumphant plebiscite the President was a lonely figure. Though the country was behind him the Chamber was hostile and suspicious. The new Constitution exalted the Chamber at the expense of the President, who was forbidden a second consecutive term. Persigny urged him not to swear loyalty to 'this absurd constitution' till the Chamber agreed to consult the people. The plebiscite, he argued, had shown what the country wanted, and the Chamber was defying its will. The President, however, listened to Thiers, at that time a *persona grata* as the historian of the Empire, who tried to garrot him with Parliamentary strings in the hope that his popularity would wane and leave the path open for an Orleanist restoration with himself at the helm. Everyone who blocked the way to the Second Empire is denounced by Persigny in his Memoirs as a criminal. Ledru-Rollin is dismissed as a vain demagogue, a blind leader of the blind: Thiers as a moral monstrosity, all brain and scarcely any heart, without courage or character, crazed with vanity and convinced that he alone could govern France. Ambitious though he was, he had no nerve and was haunted by the spectre of mob rule, a new Terror and the scaffold. He even advised the removal of the Chamber to Châlons or Orleans.

Though the first elections in May 1849 returned a considerable group of extremists, commonly described as revolutionaries or socialists, Persigny, who now entered the Chamber, was not alarmed. France, he believed, wanted neither revolution nor socialism but a government under Louis Napoleon capable of preserving order. The inexperienced President allowed Thiers to choose most of the Ministers, and Persigny only succeeded in securing the appointment of his friend Falloux. Convinced that the plebiscite had furnished a mandate for a clean sweep, he vainly urged the Minister of the Interior to evict anti-Bonapartist functionaries throughout the country. The Republic, he cried, was a curse for France: what was needed was a combination of Legitimists, Orleanists and Republicans under the aegis of the President, the only rallying-point for the whole nation. The slogan anticipated by almost a century the demand of Goebbels to scrap all existing parties and rally round the Führer. Unlike the impetuous Persigny, the Prince knew how to wait while the

Chamber, the Ministers and the Republic steadily lost prestige. Persigny's advice to exclude the extreme Left from the Chamber was a further revelation of his Fascist ideology.

His first official task was a mission to Berlin in the summer of 1849 to arrange a Franco-Prussian *entente*, since at that moment both governments desired the weakening of Austria: Prussia because she wanted to strengthen her own position in the German Bund, France because she regarded Austria as the chief pillar of the Vienna settlement. The envoy was warmly welcomed by Frederick William IV, to whom he sang praises of his master, explaining that while the Legitimists represented merely the old aristocracy and the Orleanists merely the bourgeoisie, the masses were for the President. In Vienna he assured Schwarzenberg that his master wanted to reconcile the France of 1789 and of Napoleon with the old Europe. The envoy made such a favourable impression at Berlin that his appointment as French Ambassador was desired. He returned to the Prussian capital at the opening of 1850 with instructions not to meddle in internal affairs and not to commit his Government. His task was complicated by the fact that, while the President leaned to Prussia, the Foreign Office favoured Austria. Moreover, since Austro-Prussian friction had temporarily diminished, the friendship of France was no longer essential. Undeterred by a chilly atmosphere, Persigny continued to stress the identity of interests, Prussia aiding France to expel Austria from Italy, France accepting the aggrandisement of Prussia; but he angrily repudiated the charge that France demanded compensation in the Rhineland. Failing to secure definite results, and eager to be at his master's side in the approaching struggle in the Chamber, he returned to France at the end of 1850 carrying home an abiding impression of Prussian strength and a desire for further assignments in diplomacy.

The two most promising methods of preparing the way for the Empire were by the escape of the President from what Persigny called the suffocating air of the Élysée into the provinces and by winning over men of influence in the Chamber. Since the plebiscite the precedent of Caesar and the Roman Senate was in everybody's mind. Meeting the Austrian Ambassador at a party in February 1851, Persigny exclaimed in a loud voice, 'The Empire is coming, or rather it is here.' When the Chamber declined to remove the article in the constitution forbidding re-election of the President, he resolved that the constitution must go. Needless to say, he was in the secret of the *coup d'état* and was present at the final discussions when the guests had left the Élysée late in the evening of 1 December. He complained to Lord Malmesbury at Christmas of the hostility of 'certain English journals', by which he meant *The Times*.

> England finds it difficult to grasp the weaknesses of our Parliamentary system. Yours is the government of the upper classes who possess experience and are admirably mindful of public interests. In France the upper classes are absolutely unfitted for public affairs. Like our old *noblesse*, they are brilliant and frivolous, chivalrous and war-loving, but lacking the virtues needed in a free state, with the result that the parliamentary system involves disorder and anarchy. France is a great democracy which requires discipline, and Napoleon is the man to supply it. That is the secret of the immense acclaim. *The Times* asserts that the army forced the country to vote for him. How could an army of young soldiers, drawn annually from the bosom of the people, favour a military despotism? The truth is that it shares the national sentiment. The masses are intoxicated with delight and enthusiasm; no revolution was ever so easy and so popular. It may be asked if the army will plunge into adventures. The danger is not serious. There is not the slightest trace of bellicosity, least of all in the President. The officers only want peace and a tranquil life. So I trust that the good relations between our countries will be preserved.

Though designed for the key post of the Interior, Persigny felt that his notorious identification with the Bonapartist cause might make the seizure of power appear a party rather than a national enterprise. The post fell to Morny, and Persigny's assignment on the fateful morning was to take over the Palais Bourbon and close the session. During the opening phase of the dictatorship he was the most influential adviser, and the harsh decrees concerning the property of the House of Orleans were generally attributed to his pressure. He never understood that politics are the art of the possible, and shortly after the *coup* Mme le Hon reported to Flahault, father of her lover Morny, what sounded like the ravings of a maniac. The Rhine provinces, he declared, should be annexed so that the Powers might learn that they had a master before whom they must quail: that all the royal families and all the parties must disappear; that the President was the man to regenerate society and that the world must tremble before the Tuileries. All these prophecies, he added, would be fulfilled. Intoxicated by the fulfilment of his dreams he had lost touch with realities.

A month after the *coup d'état* of December 1851, Persigny reached the summit of his ambition, succeeding Morny at the Ministry of the Interior when the latter resigned in disapproval of the Orleans decrees. 'He is the President's evil genius,' commented Vieil-Castel in his usual malevolent way. 'He has great influence over him, though he is a mere vulgar intriguer, tortuous in his methods, a sort of insignificant cadet. He is the counsellor of violent measures and crooked means. The mere sight of him is enough to destroy any confidence in him. He is as much like a gentleman as chicory is like coffee.' A fairer verdict was pronounced by the Austrian Ambassador, who described him as *un bon garçon*. Though he was tactless and impatient, difficult to work with and had little control over his tongue, he possessed some sterling qualities, among them political courage, disinterested loyalty, decent morals and incorruptibility. His latest biographer classifies him as a type of the idealist adventurer.

Now for the Empire! When the Dictator set forth on his first official tour in that capacity, Persigny ordered the local Prefects to organize a rousing welcome. Joining him *en route* he found him so depressed by a chilly reception that he had drafted a speech disclaiming the intention to change his title. That the speech was undelivered, declares Persigny, was partly due to his protest. He rendered a further service when Fould, the Finance Minister, supported by a majority of his colleagues, fixed the Civil List at twelve million francs, six millions less than that of Louis Philippe and less than half of that of the last two Bourbon kings. Though the ruler seemed satisfied, Persigny pressed for a sum equal to that allowed to the Bourbons, and told Troplong, President of the Senate, that the Chief of State would be glad of twenty-five millions. Having secured the approval of the Senate, Troplong remarked to Persigny: 'If you had been a moment later the Senate would have voted twelve millions.' Many years later the Emperor complained of his difficulty in meeting expenses, and remarked to Persigny: 'And what if you had not changed the Civil List?' On the proclamation of the Empire he was nominated to the Senate. 'No one loves the Empire,' remarked the ruler in playful mood. 'I am a socialist, the Empress a legitimist, Prince Napoleon a republican. The only Bonapartist I know is Persigny, and he is mad.' Throughout the reign he was *plus royaliste que le roi*.

His first tenure of the Ministry of the Interior is memorable for his share in the transformation of the capital. A beginning had been made before the *coup* by continuing the Rue de Rivoli from the Louvre to the Hôtel de Ville, and when the President felt firm ground under his feet he instructed Persigny to make Paris the finest city in Europe. When the mayors of the chief cities were summoned for inspection there was no difficulty in selecting Haussmann, whose dynamic personality impressed everyone who met him. The timid Prefect of the Seine, who shrank from large capital outlay, was dismissed, and Haussmann proceeded to drive broad boulevards through the slums. After two years at the Interior, Persigny, who had shown little consideration for his colleagues, was requested by the Emperor to exchange his administrative duties for the position of Minister without portfolio. Resenting and declining the transfer, he resigned. 'I regret that for health reasons,' wrote the Emperor, 'you cannot remain a Minister without portfolio, and I hope your health will allow you to render further services.' His health, as everyone was aware, had nothing to do with it. He was consoled by his nomination as Grand Officer of the Legion of Honour and the expectation of an early return to the political stage.

Soon after he quitted office the Crimean War absorbed the Emperor and the country. The hot-blooded Persigny flared up when the Tsar declined to address the Dictator as *Mon Frère*: the insult, he argued, was not merely to the Emperor but to the nation. When the cautious Foreign Minister, Drouyn de Lhuys, advised that no action should be taken to oppose Russia's aims in the Holy Places on the ground that France would find herself alone, Persigny rejoined that if France looked on with folded arms Russia would regard her as a negligible quantity, and such a humiliating relationship would drift into war. If France were to dispatch a fleet to the Eastern Mediterranean to be ready for emergencies, England would assuredly follow suit. 'Persigny is right,' commented the Emperor; 'send the fleet.'

Since Drouyn de Lhuys seemed a half-hearted supporter of the war, he was replaced by Walewski, whose appointment created a vacancy in the London Embassy. A life-long Anglophil like his master, Persigny was the obvious choice when the Crimean War brought the old rivals closer together. In offering the post, the Emperor added that Queen Victoria desired his appointment, but even without such a cogent reason the selection of the Emperor's *homme de confiance* was itself a compliment. The new Ambassador quickly became *persona grata* in official circles and at Court. Though his tactless and frivolous wife, a granddaughter of Marshal Ney, was a social liability, his three years in England were a success. His troubles were in Paris, where his habit of reporting direct to the Emperor exasperated Walewski, his official chief. Finally the Emperor had to intervene and Persigny was recalled.

On his return to France he declined the Vice-Presidency of the Senate with the characteristic explanation that he had no wish for a sinecure and that in view of his services he must either be something or nothing. The intermezzo was brief, for a year later, on the outbreak of the war in Italy, Marshal Pélissier was recalled from London for a high command and Persigny returned to Albert Gate. He found the atmosphere at Westminster and Windsor less cordial after the Orsini plot, and the annexation of Savoy revived historic suspicions that France might be planning further adventures. Palmerston asked for his removal, and after a difficult year in London he was recalled to his former post as Minister of the Interior.

Persigny welcomed the slight relaxations of autocracy introduced in 1860, but there was no thought of permitting unfettered comment, as he explained in a circular to the Prefects reprinted in the *Moniteur*.

> A people must be united before it is free. Liberty of the press must follow, not precede, the consolidation of a new dynasty. So long as there are parties hostile to the established order they can only enjoy liberty in degenerate communities who, like the Greeks of the Lower Empire, prefer quarrelling and suicide to the safety of the state. Let abuses in society or government be exposed, the doings

of the Administration discussed, injustices revealed; let the movement of ideas stimulate social and political, commercial and industrial life. But I will stop at nothing to forbid attacks on the state from any quarter.

If the Emperor often moved too slowly, the impatient Minister tended to act in appointments and other matters too quickly. 'I think, my dear Persigny,' wrote the Dictator, 'that you can render me great services, but there must be fuller inquiries and greater moderation. Remember Seneca's words: "Nothing is great that is not calm.'"

Persigny's second term at the Ministry of the Interior was not a happy time. Detested by the Left as a henchman of the Emperor, he estranged the Right by his anticlericalism. 'He is more blinded than ever by the gabble of Prince Napoleon,' wrote Vieil-Castel in his journal on 1 April 1862. 'He has finished by persuading himself that the two worst enemies of the Empire are the Papacy and the conservatives. He is the worst Minister of the Interior we have had. He uses a paving-stone to kill a fly on the forehead of his master.' Such men find it easier to make enemies than to make or keep friends. Thick skinned as he was in the political arena, he was grievously wounded by the breakdown of his marriage. His wife, a social butterfly, had lost interest in her husband and her five children, incurred crippling debts, and, in the words of Vieil-Castel, had done enough to deserve ten separations. He was soon to lose also the most precious of his possessions, the confidence of his master.

The significance of the elections in 1863 as a political barometer was recognized by all parties. Since the phalanx of official candidates ensured a large majority, interest centred on the size of the Opposition. To make it as small as possible Persigny threw his abounding energies into the struggle, even gerrymandering marginal urban constituencies by including reliable rural voters. Mérimée compared him to a coachman flogging his horses and tugging at the reins. Angered by the growing audacity of the Opposition he overreached himself by an attack on Thiers, never an irreconcilable enemy of the Empire. The alarming increase of the hostile vote in the big cities pronounced the doom of the unpopular Minister who had overplayed his hand.

I believe your resignation to be necessary [wrote the Emperor], and I hope your devotion will understand my reasons. You would cause agitation and render verification of powers disastrous for the government. What was one to say of two unworthy deputies who owed their seats entirely to the most culpable official pressure? I recognize all the devotion you have shown me, and I am far from blaming you for not having succeeded everywhere; but your lofty and lucid mind is unsuited in a post where everything has to be prepared for in advance. How could one succeed when a candidature in Paris was arranged only ten days before the poll? I repeat that I bear you no grudge, for you have rendered me other services which I appreciate and of which I shall always retain a good memory.

The conclusion of the letter was even more wounding. 'I must add that the ill-considered conduct of Mme Persigny is very damaging. I advise you to take her for a journey; and I cannot help thinking that your exacting work has complicated your *ménage*, which causes me deep grief.' A few days later the *Moniteur* announced the name of the new Minister of the Interior 'in succession to M. de Persigny whose resignation is accepted.'

The fall of Persigny delighted not merely the Opposition but his critics on the Government side, and the Empress sent a message through Mérimée to Thiers expressing her satisfaction. 'M. Thiers will understand that it required courage on the part of the Emperor, with his good heart, to part with such a devoted friend.' Since he retained his seat in the Senate and the Privy Council, received the title of Duke, and joined the usual autumn house-party at Compiègne, he might well feel that his career was not over. 'It is always he who governs,' grumbled Thiers. A conversation was reported to him by a friendly Senator.

The Senator: His only passion is the Emperor and the Empire.
The Emperor: I know he loves me, but he is difficult.

Baroche complained that he bombarded the Emperor with his denunciations and intrigues. 'One is never finished with this gentleman, and one often wonders whether he is more dangerous in or out of office.' The ruler, however, was never an easy man to drive.

My relations with him were closer than those of anyone [wrote Persigny after the fall of the Empire]: but indecision, indolence and inability to control his *entourage* often paralysed him and led him to miss opportunities. I found it easy to convince his reason but very rarely could I mobilize his will. Since many people were jealous of my influence I begged him not to mention my name as his adviser; but he always told the Council 'that is Persigny's advice'. He thought I exaggerated the hostility of Ministers to myself.

By the time he lost his post dark clouds were gathering in the European sky. He had met and liked Bismarck during his mission to Berlin in 1850, when the young Prussian Junker was the militant leader of the Extreme Right. They met again twelve years later when he was Prussian Ambassador in Paris and Persigny Minister of the Interior. 'I know your influential part in the Emperor's success,' began the visitor, who proceeded to complain of the opposition in the Prussian Chamber, where the Liberals were striving to coerce the King and sabotage the army. 'Keep the support of the army,' replied Persigny; 'resist the deputies, and if necessary dissolve the Chamber.' 'That is also my view,' exclaimed the Ambassador, who shook hands warmly on taking his leave. A few days later he was called to the helm. Their third and last meeting took place in 1867 when the Chancellor accompanied his King to the Exhibition and accosted Persigny with the flattering remark: 'Have I not carried out your advice?'

Persigny sorrowfully contrasted Bismarck's hammer strokes with the growing inertia of his master. Like most other fallen Ministers he had the lowest opinion of his colleagues who remained in office. Now more than ever, he felt, his advice was needed, and he continued to give it without stint. 'In moments of crisis,' reported the Austrian Ambassador in May 1866, 'and when events threaten to shatter the world and the throne of his master, Persigny, the faithful and devoted companion of the Emperor in good and evil days, reappears on the scene.' The Emperor, he argued, should drop the policy of the sphinx and send him to Berlin and Vienna with plans of cessions and compensations which would avert a conflict. He was sure he would approve. Metternich was deceiving himself, for the ruler was now past vigorous initiatives and far-reaching decisions.

In a memorandum in 1867 Persigny described the failure to act in 1866 as a disgrace to the Empire. French policy, he complained, seemed to have lost its balance. France had abandoned the poor

Danes, who might easily have been saved by co-operating with England, and the Emperor had let down the army by allowing Fould to cut the estimates. On the eve of the Austro-Prussian conflict he awoke from a kind of torpor and summoned a Council to decide French policy. Drouyn de Lhuys, the Foreign Minister, and Rouher, the most influential of the Emperor's advisers, had nothing to propose. 'And you, Persigny,' the Emperor asked, 'why do you not speak?' France, was the reply, should desire victory for Prussia and then demand—and if necessary enforce—her withdrawal from the Left Bank of the Rhine and the creation of a new Rheinbund of German princelets under French patronage as in the days of Mazarin and Napoleon. Though the Emperor agreed, no action followed, a lamentable abdication attributed to the influence of the Empress who, in his opinion, objected not to the plan but to its author. She had never liked him, and in the autumn of 1866 she became an open enemy on learning of his advice to the Emperor to exclude her from meetings of the Council of Ministers. The penalty was his own exclusion from further discussions and the refusal of an interview.

> It is not the greatness of Prussia which so distresses me in the events of 1866 [he wrote in his Memoirs], but the terrible blow to the prestige of the Empire by the passivity of the Government. Till then, despite various checks and the Mexican fiasco, the whole nation had confidence in the firmness and skill of the Emperor. Now the Empire seemed shaken to its foundations and there was general stupefaction when we saw France inert and powerless, sanctioning the audacious ambition of Prussia without securing compensations. What obscured her judgment and paralysed her faculties? Partly the Emperor himself, partly his Ministers, some of whom were a curse. Thiers, though not a Minister, was the evil genius, ever ready to sacrifice the honour and interest of the country to vanity or vendettas, and condemning all intervention in German affairs. Rouher was equally to blame for throwing the Chamber into his arms. Fould was the worst of them all, clipping the ruler's wings by economizing on the army.

'How could you consent?' he wrote to his old master. 'Fould will disorganize the army for a miserable saving of twelve millions. It is incredible. The world will conclude that France cannot afford an army.'

Persigny was no less shattered by the deterioration on the home front. Unlike Thiers and Ollivier, who cast envious glances across the Channel, he continued to maintain that the Parliamentary *régime*, however attenuated, was condemned by experience and totally unsuitable to France. The common man deserved good government but was unfitted to provide it. The paramount duty of every government was to govern. The decline of grip was indicated by the toleration of press attacks on the Emperor. Ministers and bureaucrats had too much power, the Prefects—arms and eyes of the ruler—too little. When the fiery crusader presented these views in a lengthy memorandum, the Emperor doubted if enough competent men were available. 'Give them power,' was the reply, 'and you will get good men: in any case even the worst Prefect understands local needs better than any Minister.'

In the summer of 1869 Persigny implored the Emperor to assert himself.

> The Government inspires too little fear. Men are needed who, by their simple presence, would scare away evil passions, avert defections, gather round them good citizens, restore confidence, and stand up to the demagogues. Above all, courageous Ministers of the Interior and Justice are needed to collaborate with the Minister of War. The whole trouble in the state derives from the presence of two men [Rouher and Baroche] of whom the public is tired and almost ashamed. They are the real cause of the demoralization of the Empire, perfect representatives of the mean *bourgeois* system, the petty subterfuges and manœuvres, the lack of faith and conviction, morality and grandeur, recalling the reign of Louis Philippe, a system condemned by the recent elections. With these two men in office public contempt, the alienation of good citizens, the audacity of foes and public disaffection will increase. If you lack the courage to evict them your Government is doomed. That is the naked truth.

He was placing a copy of this indictment in safe keeping, he added, to safeguard at any rate the honour of his name, so that his son in case of need could prove that it was not his father's fault if the Empire foundered.

Persigny, a pioneer of Fascism, had no use for the Liberal Empire, for which he predicted a brief career. Visiting the

Austrian Ambassador a month after the appointment of Ollivier, he declared that it would be his task to save the situation by a new *coup d'état* by legal means. A conflict with the revolution, he added, was inevitable after the mistakes in recent years of Rouher and his friends. Instead of awaiting the battle it should be provoked. At the moment the Emperor was too irresolute to follow his advice, but he would be forced to recall him and adopt his secret plan. 'The eternal dreamer,' as Metternich called him, is best described in the words of his early friend Falloux as possessing both the virtues and failings of a fanatic.

When war was declared in 1870 Persigny offered his services and advice. It would be dangerous, he argued, to leave the capital exposed to evil passions and traitors without taking precautions; the first task was to suspend the liberty of the press and public meetings for the duration of the war. Unless the Ministry were changed the Emperor could not turn victory to good account. 'In these critical circumstances will you not make use of me? Am I, companion in hard times, condemned to remain an onlooker when the Emperor, his son and the dynasty are in danger? I appeal to your heart and ask you to employ me in Paris where my devotion may be of use to you, or else to let me fight in the ranks.' There was no reply. When the Empire collapsed on the news of Sedan he believed his life to be in danger and fled with his family to England.

Returning to France in July 1871 he died in the following year. His old master was informed of the stroke, and the dying man waited impatiently for some mark of affection. Some days after his death a letter arrived. 'My dear Persigny, I regret to learn you are ill and hope you will recover. Meanwhile I assure you that I forget our divisions and only recall the proofs of devotion you have given me over the long years. You know my sincere friendship.' The *Loyal Serviteur* had learned too late that the system of benevolent autocracy in which he so fervently believed may break down in a crisis owing to the folly or feebleness of the principal actor, who may be no wiser—or even less wise—than the meanest of his subjects.

10

THREE LAWYERS: ROUHER, BAROCHE, MAGNE

1. ROUHER

Most of the government business during the Second Empire was transacted by three competent and conscientious lawyers, Rouher, Baroche and Magne. Though there is no room in a dictatorship for a Prime Minister, Rouher held that position for several years in everything but name. Neither a member of the Old Guard, like Persigny, nor a relative, like Morny and Walewski, he served in complete loyalty, first in a departmental post, later as the official spokesman of the Government in the Legislature. There was nothing romantic or creative about him, but he proved a pillar of strength when the ruler was losing grip. With the exception of the *Loyal Serviteur* in the opening phase of the reign none of his servants stood so close to him and inspired such confidence. He was a model functionary, caring far more for good government, sound finance and social tranquillity than for any ideology. Belonging to the Right centre, he would have felt as much at home as a Minister under the July Monarchy or the Third Republic as in the Second Republic and the Second Empire. To speak of the Empire was to speak of Rouher, declared Jules Simon.

> He was the man of the militant Empire. He knew how to make himself agreeable and indispensable—agreeable as a good courtier, indispensable through his capacity to untie knots. A fellow-lawyer said that you could throw him out of the window but he would always fall on his feet. I did not regard him as a great orator or a statesman, but he was a skilful administrator and an incomparable debater.

Having won his spurs in the courts in Auvergne, Rouher, like most ambitious provincials, sought his fortunes in the capital. Till the fall of the Monarchy there was no need for political decisions, but the plebiscite for a President entailed a choice between Caviagnac, who had smashed the barricades, and Louis Napoleon, unknown to him except by name. Desiring to be on the winning side he voted for the General, and the overwhelming victory of the Pretender was a shock. His anxiety about his career was groundless, for he had earned a reputation for ability and honesty, and in the summer of 1849 he was appointed Minister of Justice. Having no direct ties with the President, he was not informed of the coming *coup d'état* till everything was ready. If, as Morny claimed, he had converted him, he was pushing at an open door. The Minister had been content with the Republic, but why should he sacrifice his post in its defence? Since the rivalry between the President and the Chamber was bad for business, he welcomed a firm hand at the helm. If compelled to choose between order and liberty he would always choose the former, on the principle that 'order is heaven's first law'. 'My political life dates from 1848, when I saw my country a prey to anarchy,' he explainted to his constituents. For the rest of his life he tended to identify Parliamentary government with bloodshed and barricades. Hating extremes, he distrusted hotheads, believing that politics, like business, should be approached with a cool brain. Equally opposed to clericalism and anti-clericalism, the most eminent servant of the Second Empire embodied the virtues and limitations of the bourgeoisie.

He had no wish to be identified with a conspiracy the success of which was in doubt, and on the afternoon of 1 December he discovered that documents bearing his signature were ready for dispatch to the provinces on the morrow. Justly resenting the use of his name he issued a protest: 'I know nothing of these and beg you to remove my name.' After the success of the *coup* it was safe to collaborate, and he served the Dictator as zealously as if he had been a Bonapartist all his life—muzzling the Press, dismissing untrustworthy magistrates, organizing addresses to welcome the *régime*, and helping to draft a Constitution.

A serious disagreement occurred within a month. Rouher was one of the four Ministers who resigned over the Orleans decrees, but he was indispensable. Three days later he was nominated to the Council of State with special care of legislation, justice, and foreign affairs. Three years later he returned to administration as Minister of Public Works, a post the importance of which was enhanced by the rapid development of industry and commerce, and his nomination to the Senate a year later set the seal on his fortunes. He shared the Emperor's enthusiasm for developing the national resources and, like his master, desired the state to assist individual enterprise. Chevalier received the same whole-hearted support in drafting the commercial treaty in 1860 as Cobden received from Gladstone, and the Cobden Treaty was followed by agreements with other countries. Living for his work, he needed no recreations, social or intellectual. 'I have not changed my profession,' he remarked in 1864; 'I remain an advocate, but I have only one client, France.'

He reached the top of the ladder when he was appointed Minister of State, free from departmental duties but charged with explaining and defending the policy of the Government. 'Rouher rules today,' complained Allain-Targé, a prominent member of the small Opposition; 'he has absolute power.' Maupas, another unfriendly witness, testifies that he dominated almost without limits. Ollivier coined for him the title Vice-Emperor. 'One hopes he will allow the Emperor some little share in governing,' wrote an ironical journalist; '*nous n'avons qu'un Rouhernement à défaut de Gouvernement*.' Only too glad to shift a mass of detail on to such broad shoulders, the ruler felt no twinge of jealousy when he heard the ablest of his Ministers described as Vice-Emperor, Grand Vizier or Mayor of the Palace. If he never felt entirely secure it was not from fear that his master might prove fickle but that his enemies might overbear his weakening will. Persigny would have been more than human had he not resented such a dominating influence, but his screaming indictment is more damaging to himself than to his rival.

> His great purpose in everything was to ruin what emanated from others, especially from myself. Sceptical, without conscience or convictions, he refused to accept a truth unless it could be turned to his own profit. His talent was incontestable. He governs the Emperor and runs the state. He attacks his foes from the rear with a smile on his face. What a misfortune for a country to fall into such hands.

From 1863, when the ranks of the Opposition were reinforced at the polls, vitality returned to the Chamber, and Government spokesmen had to cross swords with foes worthy of their steel. Morny's tact and ability as President of the Chamber helped to keep criticism within bounds, but Walewski, his successor, lacked flair and soon had to resign. Rouher's burden grew even heavier when he succeeded Fould as Minister of Finance in addition to his labours as Leader of the House.

From 1866 onwards the main battles were on foreign policy, in which Rouher had to find his feet; he was no traveller, had no intimate friends abroad, and took little interest in other lands. While plans for amending the settlement of 1815 chased each other across the ruler's mind, Rouher stood for the *status quo*, peace as the condition of prosperity, for the fostering of commerce by lowering tariffs, and modest expenditure on national defence. Like his master he entertained the friendliest feelings towards England but disliked her democratic system. The main problem after 1866 was that of Franco-German relations, for France's failure to extract compensation for her neutrality expressed her weakness to the world. Drouyn de Lhuys, who was identified with unrealizable demands, was succeeded in the Foreign Office by Thouvenel, with whom Rouher was in close agreement. Both were convinced that France needed peace, and the Great Exhibition was due in 1867. When Walewski longed to help the Polish patriots in the rebellion of 1863, Rouher had protested: 'War, whatever the cause, is not to the taste of the bourgeoisie, nor the country districts, nor the Chamber.' He had had no share in launching the Mexican adventure, but his views on Italy closely coincided with those of the Emperor—to combine maximum unification with Papal independence, and to withdraw French troops from Rome when the Pope possessed an army of his own. In Germany he regarded a confederation of the northern states as inevitable and desirable. The impulsive Empress naturally detested his preference for limited liability. The Emperor, she complained to the Austrian Ambassador, was worn out and at the mercy of the man he had made a Premier—'the cause of our decline, and he would dethrone us if he is not stopped'. Prince Napoleon was also amongst the critics. 'Rouher is a clever lawyer, not a statesman. He thinks only of meeting difficulties, so we live from day to day.' His best friend was the Emperor, who sent him the Grand Cross of the Legion of Honour in diamonds after a sharp attack in the Chamber. 'In the midst of your many labours and the unjust attacks on you a friendly gesture from myself may, I hope, make you forget the inevitable annoyances of your position and remind you of your successes and the services you render to the country every day.' Such a man, comments Ollivier, was most useful.

> One was always sure of support and he never made difficulties. The Emperor had no one else who could deal with every incident, avert embarrassments by expedients, steer his path between alternatives, defend every cause, even the most hopeless, wriggle out of urgent decisions by playing for time. As the Emperor's strength declined he insensibly allowed him greater importance every day in the conduct of affairs.

Rouher's most celebrated utterance was also the most unfortunate. The Second Empire was partially dependent on Catholic support, which could only be retained by the effective defence of the Temporal Power. 'We declare in the name of the French Government that Italy will not seize Rome. Never. France will never support this violence done to her honour and her Catholicity.' *Jamais* has stuck to his memory like 'the scrap of paper' to that of Bethmann-Hollweg and '*d'un coeur léger*' to that of Ollivier. Though he was merely voicing the well-known policy of the Emperor, the uncompromising adverb unloosed a storm. '*L'Empire Clérical a remplacé l'Empire Libéral*,' exclaimed a Deputy, and the declaration was regarded as a triumph for *l'Espagnole*. Prince Napoleon dispatched an article to Sainte-Beuve for *Le Siècle*, gloomily adding 'We are back to the sinister alliance of throne and altar.'

Rouher's fate was decided by the elections of 1869 when the large cities displayed general hostility. His first impressions were favourable, and a member of the Austrian Embassy found him with 'the smile of a victor' on his face. 'Just as I expected and told the Emperor, a majority of 200 for the Government which will be confronted by irresponsible demagogy. The Gambettas returned by Paris, that city of *frondeurs*, do not alarm us.' His master, interpreting more accurately the mood of the electors, bowed to the storm, and regretfully accepted the resignation of his ablest servant. 'I am weary and depressed by the attacks and insults with which I have been assailed for so long,' was the latter's comment, 'above all by the thought that these accusations reach the Palace of Saint-Cloud and are repeated by people very close to the Emperor. I have been in the firing line for six years and I must go.' Satisfaction in some quarters was matched in others by regret. Rochefort, commented Halévy, had been the pill which had caused the Emperor to dismiss his right-hand man. His old enemy Maupas records general relief at the fall of a man regarded as the chief obstacle to harmony now that the liberal tide had begun to flow. The victim accepted his fate with equanimity.

> I will not supply any pretext for mistrust [he wrote from his country home to Baroche]. I feel that the present Ministry is the only possible one. From the point of view of the dynasty I realize the evil dispositions of public opinion and the disorganization of the conservative party. Every day I find in the opposition press audacious attacks and crazy expectations; but the follies will help to rally our forces and, I hope, allow us to protect liberal institutions against the attacks of the revolution.

The Emperor, reported the Austrian Ambassador, had no illusions about the decline of his prestige, and seemed to despair of his ability to control the situation by concessions. Convinced that he alone could save the Empire, Rouher expected to be recalled to power when Ollivier succumbed to the combined attack of Left and Right. His first instinct was to return to the bar, but the death of Troplong, the veteran President of the Senate, created a vacancy which held him in public life. He regarded Ollivier as a mere stop-gap and the experiment of a Liberal Empire as doomed. Prince Napoleon, though no friend of Rouher, preferred him to the well-meaning idealist who now stood at the helm. 'I can only see Rouher, the only man of talent, as head of the Government. Unfortunately he is so unpopular that one cannot tell what would happen if he returned.' The Emperor continued to consult him on foreign affairs. The two men were equally anxious to preserve peace, but when the acid test came the ruler listened to less-experienced advisers.

Rouher was surprised at the initial disasters to French arms, though he believed that France could hold out longer than her foe. When in his official capacity as President of the Senate he visited the Emperor at the front, he was horrified by the confusion and conflicting counsels; Bazaine and MacMahon, he discovered, were equally incompetent. Fearing arrest on the fall of the Empire, he fled with his family to England, and his home in Auvergne was pillaged by German troops, who dispatched his papers to Berlin. Despite the *débâcle* he continued to believe in the necessity of the Empire on the ground that Bismarck could not deal with the Republic and that France, unlike Paris, remained loyal. Returning to the capital after the armistice he was elected for Corsica, and captained a little band of Bonapartist Deputies. His house formed the headquarters of the Bonapartist movement, where familiar figures such as Drouyn de Lhuys, Benedetti and Prince Murat refused to despair. Talk was heard of a 'return from Elba', this time a landing on the north coast. He paid several visits to Chislehurst and attended the funeral of his old master. 'I proclaim as my greatest honour', he told his constituents when he stood in 1875, 'my fidelity to the Imperial family whom you once welcomed with enthusiasm; the memory of the Emperor, that martyr of calumny, is dear to me.'

II. BAROCHE

Baroche was Rouher's political twin though the latter carried heavier guns. Both served the Second Republic; both welcomed the Second Empire; both were conservatives by temperament, caring infinitely more for honest government and social order than for political liberty; both disliked adventures abroad; both championed the Gallican tradition in dealing with ecclesiastical claims; both were dropped when the experiment of the Liberal Empire was launched. Both not only admired and liked the Emperor but sincerely believed that a quasi-dictatorial executive was the best and indeed the only instrument for saving the *Tiers Etat*, the backbone of the nation, from the mounting menace of the Fourth. Prince Napoleon's verdict, 'a lawyer without convictions who would plead any cause entrusted to him', did an able and conscientious public servant less than justice.

Born in 1802 of a good middle-class family, industrious and incorruptible, Baroche rapidly made his way at the Paris bar and entered the Chamber in 1847. When the Monarchy collapsed he accepted the Republic and explained his political faith as a candidate for the Constituent Assembly.

> I am republican by reason, sentiment, conviction—not as a provisional *pis aller* but as the only form of government which can henceforth ensure the greatness and prosperity of France. After our unhappy experiences of half a century I am convinced that Monarchy has had its day in France and has no longer any roots. In Lamartine's fine phrase, I desire a Republic which will win affection and respect and cause no one alarm except the enemies of the state and our institutions. It must be strong and energetic, wise and moderate, based on respect for the rights of all citizens and for the family and property.

When the supremacy of the bourgeoisie seemed to be threatened by the barricades, he was prepared to serve any *régime* likely to keep the mob at bay. 'We found ourselves pitched into a vast battlefield,' he wrote in a fragment of autobiography in 1855, 'one side furiously attacking, the other rallying to the defence.' The invasion of the Chamber on 15 May 1848 drove him still further to the right, and after the June riots he proposed mass deportation of the insurgents. Caviagnac was the hero of the hour, and in the plebiscite for the Presidency he voted for the republican General.

When his old comrade at the bar Odilon Barrot became President of the Council, Baroche accepted the post of Procureur-General, a position midway between that of a Minister and an official. His chief task was to appoint to the bench reliable supporters of the social order and to keep the press in step. Retaining his seat, he collaborated with the predominantly monarchist government and became Vice-President of the Chamber, edging away from the moderate republicans with whom he had associated. His anti-revolutionary zeal was rewarded by his appointment in 1850 to the Ministry of the Interior, the most important post after that of the First Minister, carrying with it the duty of speaking for the Government. To combat the republican Opposition was easy enough, for the conservative majority was overwhelming. Far more complicated was the problem of averting a clash between the President and the Chamber where both royalists and radicals dreaded a dictatorship. The dismissal of Barrot by the President in October 1849 and the nomination of Ministers of his choice had created alarm, and in April 1850 a deputy spoke openly of plans for a *coup*. The Government, retorted Baroche, was not responsible for the extravagances of Bonapartist journals. 'People who tell you that the Executive is planning a *coup* and a breach of the Constitution are committing an offence against the President and the Government and will be punished.' Had he belonged to the intimate circle of the President or possessed a little more imagination he would have known that the rumours of a *coup* were correct. An extensive tour in the south in the summer of 1850 revealed the extent of the President's popularity and his determination to increase it. 'I am very pleased with the political effect of my journey,' he reported to Baroche *en route*. The welcome was warmer in the villages than in the towns, where a few hostile demonstrations were organized. 'Prince,' replied Baroche, 'I can send you an excellent report of Paris. Your friends are delighted with the news of your journey, the socialists and other adversaries in consternation.'

What both men sincerely desired was the removal by constitutional means of the veto on the re-election of the President, but the prospect of such a vital change became more remote as his popularity waxed. Friend and foe agreed that the army, not the Chamber, would play a decisive role, and the dismissal of Changarnier from his command in Paris told its own tale. In defending the Government's action Baroche declared that such an exceptional step signified no menace to the Constitution, which the President would continue to respect. Danger, he added, came not from the Élysée but from the Royalist deputies who visited the Pretenders beyond the frontiers.

In one of the Ministerial shuffles of 1851 Baroche was moved to the Foreign Office, while continuing to represent the Government in debates on home affairs. Speaking in July on the revision of the Constitution, as to which Victor Hugo had asked 'Must we have Napoleon the Little because we have had Napoleon the Great? Augustulus after Augustus?', he contrasted the earlier conservatism of the poet with his present republicanism, an attack which was soon to be revenged in the burning verses of

Les Châtiments. Once again he repudiated the method of violence and declared that no one, least of all the President, approved *coups d'état*. Though the *coup* was a surprise, he welcomed it with a cheer. 'My colleagues and I in 1850-51,' he wrote later, 'by defending the authority of the Executive in some degree prepared the way for the glorious act of 2 December as devoted and loyal fellow-workers of the man destined to save France and civilization.' In the light of events his reiterated denials that the President entertained such a plan looked either insincere or naïve, and he was reproved by his old chief, Odilon Barrot, who had seen it coming. Since insincerity was foreign to his nature, the explanation can only lie in his astonishing failure to measure the vaulting ambition of the Man of Destiny whom henceforth he was proud to serve.

On 3 December 1851, the morrow of the *coup*, a decree instituted a Consultative Commission, a new name for the former Council of State, to conduct affairs pending the reorganization of the Legislature, to be presided over by the new Dictator, and in his absence, by Baroche. Unencumbered by the cares of a Department, the Vice-President shared with Rouher, Keeper of the Seals, and with Morny, Minister of the Interior, the main responsibility for launching the experiment of autocracy. Of the so-called Burgraves, the Monarchists who had escaped arrest, only Montalembert consented to join the Commission, some declining on grounds of principle, others doubtful whether the *régime* would last. Not till the heartening result of the plebiscite was announced did the Dictator feel firm ground under his feet. On the last day of the year, Baroche came to congratulate the new master of France.

> Has the will of a nation in any country ever been so solemnly displayed? Take possession, Prince, of the power which has been so gloriously conferred upon you. Restore the principle of authority, weakened for the last sixty years by continual turmoil. Combat without ceasing those anarchical passions which threaten the foundation of society. They are not merely detestable theories but are translated into facts and horrible outrages. May France at last be delivered from these men who are out for murder and pillage. Prince, on 2 December you have inscribed on your banner: 'France regenerated by the Revolution of 1789 and organized by the

Emperor'. May your wisdom and your patriotism realize this noble thought.

Baroche had too much self-respect for Byzantinism, and the words embodied his genuine convictions. The necessity of a strong executive as a bulwark against the social revolution was the core of his creed and the *Leitmotif* of his career from beginning to end.

The nominated Consultative Commission was speedily superseded by the nominated Council of State, in which Baroche helped to draft the new Constitution, the new franchise, and laws for the control of the press. In appointing him Vice-President of the Council the Dictator saluted 'the distinguished statesman who has stood at our side in very difficult times and has won fame by his talent and courage in defence of the great principles on which society rests'. The compliment was justified by the loyalty of a servant incapable of intrigue, and to preserve the *régime* he was prepared to defend measures which he disliked. The first test came with the Orleans decrees. Realizing that the Dictator had made up his mind, he helped to defeat the reference of the issue to the courts, and his subservience was particularly appreciated when four other Ministers resigned in protest. 'Baroche is a scoundrel,' snapped Vieil-Castel; but that was not the verdict of those who knew him best.

The Council of State, of which he was President, was superior to the Ministers, whose proposals for legislation required its approval before being presented to the Chamber. Having scrutinized a project in the Council he assisted the departmental Minister in the ensuing debates. The Austrian Ambassador described him in 1857 as the most distinguished member of the team, not indeed a statesman but an *homme d'affaires*. He disapproved the Crimean War and the Italian campaign, caring as little for national aspirations as for military glory. Like Rouher and Persigny, he regretted the slight extension of the privileges of the two Houses in 1860 as a needless weakening of the principle of autocracy, and took little interest even in the reconstruction of Paris. 'I pass no judgment on him as a statesman,' wrote Haussmann in his Memoirs. 'At the tribune he seemed to me a brilliant lawyer rather than a powerful orator. But in administration he was a bourgeois, imbued with the narrow conventional ideas of the middle-class Parisian and absolutely hostile to our great undertakings.'

When the elections of 1863 heartened the Opposition, the Emperor remodelled his Ministry. Persigny and Walewski were dropped, while Baroche became Minister of Justice and Culture and was promised a seat in the Senate. The Fould-Rouher-Baroche group was now in command. To his keen disappointment, however, he ceased to be the principal spokesman of the Government, and Rouher succeeded him as President of the Council of State. Though the greatest period of his life was over he continued to work loyally with Rouher, now the second man in France and at all times his most intimate friend. During the following years the Legislature was a battlefield for those who, like himself, wished to retain paternalism and those who, like Thiers and Ollivier, demanded the restoration of 'the essential liberties'. For Baroche and his conservative friends there was no incompatibility between autocracy and ordered liberty, since the nation had conferred on its ruler a mandate in more than one plebiscite. With such people as Baroche there was nothing to be done, complained Morny, who was ready for a limited advance; these old Liberals, he added, were more retrograde than an old Conservative like himself. Baroche, indeed, was only a Liberal in the sense that he favoured reforms in civil and criminal law. Persigny, an inveterate grumbler, attributed the unpopularity of the Government, of which he was no longer a member, mainly to the presence of Rouher and Baroche.

When his bosom friend Rouher resigned in 1869 Baroche followed suit. 'The presence of Rouher is indispensable to the Ministry,' he informed the Emperor. 'It is precisely because he is so useful that he is so violently attacked, though the rest of us are not spared. I am so convinced that the Ministry is impossible without him that if he withdraws I must beg the Emperor to accept my resignation as well.'

> Do not reproach me, dear friend [wrote Rouher], if I did not talk it over with you. I am so tired and depressed that no arguments would have had any effect. That you linked your fortunes to mine in Council illustrates our happy partnership. We have travelled a long ministerial road together, kept straight in the midst of

corruption, remained devoted to the Emperor amidst intrigues. We can return to private life without boredom, for we know how to occupy ourselves.

'I must tell you once more, my dear M. Baroche,' wrote the Emperor, 'how much I regret that you are leaving us after so many years of intimacy during which my confidence was commensurate with your services.'

> Sire [replied Baroche], I have been deeply touched by your affectionate note. It is with deep regret that I am compelled by the retirement of my friend to renounce this intimacy, as Your Majesty is good enough to call it, which I have been happy to possess for so many years. I entered your service on 22 December 1848. That was an honour, and the change in my situation will not alter my feelings. I belong absolutely to the Emperor and have served no government but his. What remains to me of life and strength is yours. Senator and member of the Privy Council, my devotion to the Emperor, the Empress and the Prince Imperial will remain the sole rule of my actions, happy if I can retain your confidence and occasionally enjoy our old intimacy. Your Majesty can count on me at any time, and all I ask is for the opportunity to prove my unalterable devotion.

These glowing words came from the heart, for Baroche never stooped to flattery and the Emperor had no wish for it.

The old Minister, nearing his seventieth year, retained his seat in the Senate, which under the Liberal Empire possessed greater privileges and responsibility. 'I hope this peaceful revolution will be good for France,' he wrote to his son. 'I am not worrying about my personal position. Is my political career over? If so I shall easily console myself with the thought that I have discharged my debt to the Emperor and to France by twenty years of service.' Though he had never desired a Liberal Empire, there seemed nothing left save to summon Ollivier.

> You may be surprised [he wrote to his son] to hear me speak of Ollivier as if I wanted him in power. I do desire it if he can find a majority. The situation is too serious for the friends of the Emperor to be side-tracked by questions of individual ambition. I have not much confidence in his character and capacity. Whatever his power of speech, I fear he is not up to the post he aspires to fill, but his programme is the Empire and Liberty, which is the same as ours.

Let him try. Any Ministry formed today without him would lead up to him and all opponents would turn towards him. I have advised the Emperor to take him, but do not imagine that I have become his friend. I have not seen him and do not want to see him. There are questions on which we could not agree. So do not believe reports in the press that I am to be Foreign Minister. I stand aloof. For ever? I do not know. The future is too dark to see ahead.

The experiment, he believed, would not last long, but for the moment no one was ready with a substitute. Even now at the eleventh hour the Emperor was more popular than the politicians, for a plebiscite on the recent constitutional changes gave him a five to one majority.

At all times a man of peace, Baroche disapproved the policy which resulted in war. 'Have I been convinced by the explanations of Gramont?' he wrote to his son on 17 July 1870.

> No, my friend, and we all grieve that the situation has been so badly handled, since it was not impossible to avoid a conflict without dishonour. Yesterday it was too late and France too compromised, so there is nothing for it but to put up a good fight. In Paris there is great enthusiasm, and crowds fill the streets day and night crying *Vive l'Empereur. A Berlin.* The Cabinet cannot complain of being badly served by its agents. It is the fault of Ollivier himself and M. de Gramont.

He blamed Thiers for denouncing the policy which issued in war, as strongly as he blamed Ollivier for the *gaffe* that he accepted responsibility for the conflict with a light heart. On the fall of the Empire he fled to Jersey, where he died a month later. 'What is there left for me to do in the world?' he wrote to a friend. 'Have I not had enough sorrows? Have I not been a witness of enough ruins? Am I fated to see still more? Has not a man lived too long if he survives everything he has helped to construct, the fatherland he has so loved and to which he has devoted his life, embracing in the same affection the country and the chief whom it chose?'

III. MAGNE

THE appearance of a large-scale biography of Pierre Magne in 1929 revived the memory of one of the pillars of the Second Empire. His career closely resembles that of his fellow lawyers Rouher and Baroche. He too had come to seek his fortunes in the capital and had held minor posts under Louis Philippe and the Republic; he too was industrious and incorruptible. Though no servant of Napoleon III reached the stature of Thiers and Guizot before him, nor rivalled the *panache* of Gambetta and Clemenceau after Sedan, the Emperor's team was well up to the standard of statesmen in nineteenth- and twentieth-century France. None of them possessed or strove to acquire sufficient influence to diminish his responsibility either for the triumphs or the catastrophes of the reign, and the ruler never excused himself at their expense. His relations with them were pleasant and sometimes affectionate, and when changes occurred they parted in peace. Magne was described by an unfriendly critic as merely a first-class clerk, but such functionaries were precisely what autocracy requires.

After years of experience in the Chamber and in subordinate ministerial posts Magne was prepared to serve any *régime* which could guarantee order and ensure the well-being of France. For him, as for Rouher and Baroche, ideologies had no charm. Though he was not in the plot to destroy the Second Republic he approved the *coup*, and his name was on a list of eighty men 'who justify the esteem and confidence of the country'. He was appointed to a Commission to assist the Dictator till a new Chamber was elected and was allotted the post of Minister of Public Works. Since 5 December, he reported cheerfully to a friend, Paris had enjoyed perfect tranquillity. 'Never have places of entertainment been more crowded, business brisker, the Bourse more buoyant, the whole population more confident about the social order. It is generally recognized that the act of December was a necessity; the Chamber itself would have acted if the President had not got his blow in first. Opponents begin to realize that he will have more votes than at his first election.' A few days later the plebiscite transformed the usurpation into a popular mandate.

Magne's enthusiasm for the new *régime* was cooled by its severity towards opponents, and the Orleans decrees caused him and other Ministers to resign. 'I parted from the President on the best of terms,' he reported to his wife. 'A public declaration was needed of my profound disagreement on a matter which I had energetically opposed in the Council; but I did not feel it necessary to refuse my services in an administrative position to a Government which is our only raft of safety. I left the Ministry from duty but with regret.' As President of the Section of Public Works, Agriculture and Commerce in the Council of State he was able to continue his work for the development of railways, a task as dear to the heart of the Dictator as to his own. Six months later he returned to office. 'I congratulate you and the public,' wrote his old patron, Guizot. 'You have won your spurs as an eminent administrator. I am delighted you are back again.' The Minister was in attendance during the President's triumphant tour in the South in the autumn of 1852 and heard the cry *Vive l'Empereur*! On the proclamation of the Empire he was rewarded by a seat in the Senate, and two years later he was promoted to the Ministry of Finance where his first task was to provide for the Crimean and Italian wars.

In 1860 Magne was transferred to the Privy Council in order that, freed from departmental duties, he should help to explain the Government's policy to both Chambers. 'In assigning this more important post,' wrote the Emperor, 'I wish to give you a new proof of my esteem and sincere satisfaction for all your services. As a mark of my appreciation I have decided to present you with a furnished house in Paris.' 'I cannot express my feelings on this striking mark of esteem and affection,' replied Magne. Ministers without portfolio, he explained to a friend, had the same status and salary as heads of departments and took part in the Council of Ministers. Since no single spokesman could cover the whole field of public business he was made responsible for finance, public works and Algeria, while Baroche and Billault dealt with other business at home and abroad. Magne was proud of the financial record of the Empire, which waged wars and developed the national resources without adding appreciably to the National Debt. When Fould, his successor at the Ministry of Finance, proposed a less cautious line he resigned. Every autumn he was a guest at Compiègne, where time was found for serious discussion amid the festivities.

Magne was often placed next to the Empress at meals and was exposed to a barrage of unpredictable queries.

Empress (2 December 1866): What do you say to my visit to Rome? Don't you approve?

Magne: I have never taken it seriously and never thought about it. If I may speak plainly, I think it very unwise from every point of view.

Empress: But surely, when a house is on fire it must be extinguished at once without worrying over difficulties. At all costs the Pope must be prevented from leaving Rome. None but myself can persuade him to remain and can secure certain concessions which in case of danger would justify the return of our troops.

Magne: His departure would be a sorry conclusion to our policy for the last fifteen years, so we must do our utmost to prevent it. I agree with your purpose but not with your method. Since we have no intention of armed intervention, your presence in Rome would imply the conditional return of our troops and would only be practicable if the Emperor were irrevocably resolved to implement his promise. If he decides to leave Rome, nothing will stop him and your intervention would be a fiasco. And if the return of French troops is not decided in advance, Catholics would be disappointed if he were to be exposed to a revolution. This visit seems to me to be both useless and dangerous.

The Empress took these arguments in good part, and when Walewski expressed agreement with them she remarked with a smile that she was not convinced. At the close of his visit she asked Magne if he had given further thought to the matter. When he replied that he had not changed his attitude she thanked him for his frankness. Frequent conversations with the Emperor throughout the reign were equally uninhibited. Unlike most dictators Napoleon III was a good listener, though he always decided his own course. The highest compliment to Magne was paid by Rouher in 1867 when the Emperor was considering ministerial changes. 'I should put him at the top of my list: a calm and lucid speaker, excellent judgment, a conservative liberal.' In the reshuffle he returned to the Ministry of Finance.

Magne, unlike Rouher, approved the loosening of the reins in 1869, and recommended Ollivier for the principal post. 'The foundation of the Liberal Empire fulfils the wishes of the country,' he wrote to the new Premier. 'I have worked for it with conviction and devotion, and I am resolved to serve it with all my heart.' He soon realized, however, that Ollivier was unequal to his task. Without political experience, vacillating and irresolute, he was primarily an orator, an artist greedy for applause and prone to take offence. The dislike was reciprocated, and despite the efforts of the Emperor it proved impossible to run in double harness. 'I cannot have him in my Ministry,' exclaimed Ollivier; 'I have no confidence in him.' Though he retained his position as Senator and member of the Privy Council, Magne had no share in determining the course which led to the fall of the Empire. Like Thiers, he realized the folly of the demand for a guarantee from the King of Prussia, for he was aware of the unpreparedness of the army.

On the eve of his departure for the front the Emperor summoned Magne to Saint-Cloud and spoke of his difficulties. The Ministry, he regretted, was not up to its task. He admired the eloquence of Ollivier, but he was not a statesman. He had no practical ideas, no centre of gravity. He, the Emperor, wished to assist the Empress Regent, as in 1859, by associating the Privy Council with the Ministers; but the latter—above all Ollivier—declined co-operation. Weary in mind and body, the ruler was no longer master in his own house. The two men never met again. Magne returned to his old post as Minister of Finance in the short-lived Palikao Ministry which succeeded Ollivier. His sympathy with his old master, now a prisoner at Wilhelmshöhe, was expressed in practical form.

> I beg you, Sir, to accept in evil days this mark of sympathy and attachment from an old servant whom in happier times you overwhelmed with kindness. I read in the papers that Your Majesty has made no financial arrangements for himself, and I believe it is true, as I know your disinterestedness. In 1860 you presented me with a house in Paris. Please, Sir, regard this property as yours and make use of it as you will.

'My dear M. Magne,' replied the fallen ruler,

> I am very touched by your offer, which proves your sincere devotion, but I cannot accept it. It is true I never thought while I was on the

throne of a nest egg in case of exile, but I have kept some property in Italy which, with the sale of jewels belonging to the Empress, will amply suffice for my modest establishment after my release. I thank you from the bottom of my heart for your generous offer.

When the end came in 1873 Magne paid tribute in words which do honour to both.

> I lived twenty years on terms of intimacy, saw him and talked with him almost every day, witnessed his joys and sorrows in good and evil fortune, stood at his side in matters great and small. His temper was always equable, his kindness invariable, so much so that people who approached him with distrust and hostility never left him without a sense of the real goodness of this exceptional man. He was always working and he read everything. The greatness and prosperity of his country and the amelioration of the lot of the working classes filled his thoughts. Manual labourers have never had and never will have a better friend. He had no love of discussion. His mind was synthetic and went straight to the conclusion, but he could listen to opinions he did not share. He was a remarkable writer and some of his utterances are little masterpieces. When he had to make a public speech he read the draft to the Council, where everyone expressed his opinion without reserve. It has been said that he lacked courage: I will only mention one incident. Who has forgotten his admirable behaviour during the riots? For several days crowds had gathered on the boulevards and become more and more menacing. While some way of dealing with them by force was under consideration, he appeared with the Empress in a phaeton which he drove himself unescorted through the angry throng. Of course it was very dangerous, for there had been several attempts on his life, and any fanatic could have killed him. Surprised by this evidence of trust, the crowd uncovered and saluted the courageous sovereign with shouts of *Vive l'Empereur!*

Alone of the old guard of the Second Empire Magne held high office under the Third Republic, serving as Minister of Finance for the fourth time in 1873 when France needed an expert of long experience and sound judgment to rebuild the national economy. He had never borne a party label and now, like most of his countrymen, he accepted the new *régime* without reserve. Such men are a precious asset to any *régime*.

II

OLLIVIER AND THE LIBERAL EMPIRE

ÉMILE OLLIVIER occupies a place apart in the drama of the Second Empire, for he had been a critic before he was called to the helm. Matched against Thiers, Gambetta and Clemenceau, he was a comparatively light-weight, but he was much more than a mere windbag. Fate dealt hardly with him by severing the thread of the Liberal experiment—largely his own creation—almost as soon as it was spun, and it is idle to speculate whether under happier circumstances it might have been a success.

His father, a zealous republican and a friend of Mazzini, had welcomed the fall of the Monarchy, had represented Marseilles during the Second Republic, was exiled at the *coup d'état*, and only returned after the general amnesty of 1859. The son, who was less of a radical, studied law in Paris, obtained an administrative post in the Department of the Bouches du Rhône, and rose to a Prefecture at the age of twenty-three. Sickened by local intrigues, he migrated to the capital in 1849 and slowly worked up a practice at the bar. Defeating an official candidate in a Paris constituency in 1857, he took the oath to the *régime* and joined a little group known as *Les Cinq*, of which he and Jules Favre, another eloquent young lawyer, were the principal spokesmen. 'It is unlikely,' he wrote, 'that the Emperor will issue his *Acte Additionnel* (a reference to his uncle's action during the Hundred Days), but it is not impossible. If he continues his autocracy I shall have no mercy on him. If he changes I must aid him.' With his silvery tongue he was soon a marked man. Montalembert described him in 1858 as to all appearances a real liberal.

He had never shared Victor Hugo's pathological hatred of the usurper, and his verdict, delivered after the Empire had passed into history, was one of acquittal. The principal actor, he declared, who had been denounced as a new Judas or Tiberius, a pickpocket and buccaneer, had implemented the wishes of an immense majority as subsequently expressed in a plebiscite. Realizing that a *coup d'état* was practicable only when already tacitly agreed by the general will, he hesitated. 'Yes, he hesitated. Not through lack of courage, for dangers never daunted him; the more menacing they were the calmer he became. Had he not heard the millions of voices crying out in every form and on all occasions: We are perishing; deliver us from our revolutionary enemies and our Parliamentary saviours? Yes, he had heard them. What then held him back? His oath.' A surgical operation was required by the desperate illness of the patient. The news of the arrest of leading generals and politicians was hailed with delight. The bloodshed on 4 December was an accident, the ensuing plebiscite an absolution and a mandate; the wholesale arrests and deportations were the work of his *entourage*. He promised George Sand a general amnesty but was overborne by Saint-Arnaud and others who warned him that the Reds were preparing civil war.

> While I deplore the necessity of a *coup* and the breaking of an oath, justice impels me to declare that 2 December was as salutary as Brumaire. Most of the protesters had advised or planned a similar action, and called it a crime merely because they had not committed it themselves. Posterity will pronounce no malediction on the Prince who, at the peril of his life and fame, saved France and Europe from a convulsion and the principles of 1789 from collapse. The Orleans decrees were not confiscation and were in accordance with precedent.

In listening to these glowing tributes we must bear in mind that praise of his old master was essential to the author's defence of his own record.

Though Ollivier accepted the *coup d'état*, he disapproved the deportations and regarded the proclamation of the Empire as a mistake. For the moment, no doubt, order was more desired than liberty, but he had always dreamed of combining a strong executive with representative institutions. The slight thawing of autocracy in 1860 evoked an eloquent appeal to the ruler which shocked his fellow republicans.

When one is the head of a nation of thirty millions and has been acclaimed by it; when one is the most powerful of sovereigns; when destiny has lavished its favours on you; when by a romantic experience one has exchanged prison and exile for a throne; when one has known every sorrow and every joy, there still remains one joy surpassing all the rest—freely and courageously to grant liberty to a great people, to ignore faint-hearted advisers, to put himself directly in the presence of the nation. He might find some people living in the past and others in the future, but the majority would ardently approve. For myself, a republican, I would admire and assist, all the more efficaciously because it would be wholly disinterested.

Seated in his presidential chair, Morny beamed on the eloquent young lawyer whose exhortation to the sovereign was at the same time an act of homage. Henceforth he was a national figure and the Liberal Empire was faintly visible on the horizon.

Ollivier's record in the Chamber, opposing or supporting the Government as he thought fit, was ratified by his Paris constituents in 1863 despite the challenge of an official candidate. The widespread repudiation of autocracy by the cities—the most arresting feature of the elections—strengthened his conviction that far-reaching constitutional changes were inevitable and that before very long the Government would invite his help. Returning to the Parliamentary arena after ten years, Thiers pleaded for what he called 'the necessary liberties', adding that, if they were granted, he would become a dutiful and grateful subject of the Emperor. Though this memorable utterance might have come from Ollivier, the two men drifted apart, Thiers remaining in the ranks of the Opposition while Ollivier steered steadily towards collaboration.

Everyone talked of his friendly relations with Morny, but few were aware how intimate they had become. All the advances came from the President of the Chamber.

'Well, I expect you are pleased,' he remarked after the concessions of 1860.
Ollivier: Yes, but you are either fortified or ruined.
Morny: How is that?
Ollivier: Fortified if it is only a beginning, ruined if that is the end.

At the end of 1861 Morny remarked to Ollivier, 'We are moving towards Parliamentary government and I am giving it a push.' After the close of the session in the following year, Ollivier accepted an invitation to Morny's official residence for their first heart-to-heart talk. He had always been both conservative and liberal, declared the host, who added that he looked forward to a constitutional *régime* and hinted at support of his visitor. Ollivier repeated that if the Empire granted real liberty he would support it, adding that he had no wish for office. Further conversations followed, but the proposal of a visit to the Tuileries was declined on the ground that his advice had not been asked. A few days later he declined an invitation to dinner at the Tuileries, and the project of a journal, directed by Morny and Ollivier and financed by the Government, was also firmly rejected.

At long last Ollivier made a slight response by accepting the charge of *rapporteur* on a plan to extend the right of association of employers and workers and public meetings. Civil liberties, of course, were no substitute for political reforms, but they were a welcome loosening of totalitarian strings. Though the selection of an avowed republican to examine a bill was resented by the Old Guard, Morny imposed his will on the ruler, who had been shaken by protests of his entourage. Unmoved by the shower of missiles from the Left as well as the Right, Ollivier enlarged the scope of the bill and defended it in the Chamber. 'I accept good things from any quarter. I never say "All or nothing." I say "A little day by day."' The bill in its final form went too far for the die-hards and not far enough for the republicans. The wrath of his old comrades was directed less against the details of the bill—a landmark in the annals of social legislation—than against the person of their old comrade, and after a stormy exchange in the Chamber Jules Favre declined to shake hands. A year later the death of Morny deprived him not only of a friend for whom he had come to entertain sincere affection but of the only member of the ruler's entourage who had long believed in liberalizing the Empire. Walewski, his successor as President of the Chamber, shared his liberal views but carried little weight at Court or anywhere else. For the next four years Rouher, described by Ollivier as the Vice-Emperor, possessed the full confidence of the Emperor and blocked the path to substantial constitutional reforms.

Ollivier accepted an invitation to dinner at the Tuileries in

May 1865, when the Empress was Regent during the Emperor's absence in Algeria. When the hostess praised his work on the Associations bill he replied that he would always be happy to aid within the limits of his principles. Though the exchange was friendly and unconstrained, he rightly concluded that she had no desire for constitutional changes. On joining a committee instituted by her to reform the prison system he obeyed a summons to the Tuileries. He found her alone, but a moment later the door opened and she exclaimed: 'The Emperor'. He shook hands warmly, remarking that Morny had often spoken of him with great appreciation. When the Empress invited him to repeat their conversation on his previous visit, he declared that his objections to the dynasty had diminished but the need for liberty had increased. 'What liberties are lacking?' asked the ruler. 'Free elections and a free press,' was the reply, 'and your Government is strong enough for bold measures.'

The interview had been staged by the ruler, not to learn Ollivier's opinions, which he knew already, but to form a personal impression. The verdict was favourable. 'He is not, as I have been told, out for himself. To see him is to realize that he is a man of character and convictions; Morny was right.' Ollivier noted in his journal that he was charmed, and the vision took shape of what they might accomplish together if the ruler would only grant liberty. When the Committee on prisons had finished its labours, the Empress graciously expressed the hope that it would not be the end. Meanwhile Ollivier continued his campaign in the Chamber for further concessions. The art of government, he argued, was to fulfil the legitimate aspirations of a people, and it must yield at the right time, neither too soon nor too late. 'For the Empire it is neither too soon nor too late: this is the moment.' The Emperor was loud in his praises exclaiming: 'He is a wonderful speaker', but while Rouher remained in control no progress was possible.

At the close of 1866, when the prestige of the Empire throughout Europe was at its lowest ebb, Ollivier was offered the Ministry of Education with the task of explaining the policy of the Government, but refused on the ground that responsibility without power was not worth having. Pressed by Walewski he drafted a memorandum on the changes he desired, above all greater freedom for the press, adding that he was incapable of defending causes in which he did not believe. The document was approved by Walewski, who renewed his appeal for collaboration in flattering words. 'Without you nothing is possible. You hold in your hands the destinies of the country. You will either save us or plunge us into the abyss.' Walewski showed the memorandum to the Emperor, who invited the author for a talk on 7 January 1867.

> *Ollivier:* The mainspring of your government has been confidence in your strength of will. Now people think you are ill and losing grip. If the *malaise* is not to become a serious peril, you must demonstrate your initiative, not by war but by bold liberal measures.
> *Emperor:* What sort?
> *Ollivier:* Above all the affirmation of peace. Appoint a Foreign Minister known everywhere as a man of peace. Then let your Ministers appear in the Chamber.
> *Emperor:* Are you not afraid that would mean reviving the Parliamentary *régime*?
> *Ollivier:* The Chamber would have no more power than today.
> *Emperor:* I agree that I must do something definite and liberal, but I am doubtful about the right moment. Should I not seem to be asking pardon for our reverses in Mexico and Germany? Would not concessions at this moment weaken me?
> *Ollivier:* I believe they would reassure public opinion.
> *Emperor:* Would it not be said that I had abdicated to my Ministers?
> *Ollivier:* That is what they are saying now. A new course would denote a new energy.
> *Emperor:* Would it not be best to postpone it till after the voting of the Address?
> *Ollivier:* That would look like submission to their demands. Announce your reforms in your Speech from the Throne, which would be all the more impressive because no one expects a liberal move.
> *Emperor:* My only wish is to do good. If I did not think I was of use to the country I would go at once. And you? I hear you are unwilling to take office.
> *Ollivier:* That is so; please do not press me. My support will be of most value as an independent.
> *Emperor:* So be it, but I only restore your liberty for the moment.
> *Ollivier:* Thank you, Sire. So long as you employ the immense talent of Rouher you need no one else.

Since collaboration with Rouher was impracticable the ruler would have to choose between them. Next day he wrote a grateful letter in his own hand. 'Our talk has left the best impression. It is a great satisfaction to converse with a man whose lofty and patriotic sentiments transcend small personal and party interests.' A second interview proved less rewarding, for it was easier to persuade the open-minded Dictator than his wife or his political chief of staff. In a talk with Ollivier the Empress urged postponement and consultation of the Council of Ministers, while Rouher was annoyed with Walewski for approaching their master behind his back. The Emperor announced his decision in the *Moniteur* of 19 January 1867, to 'extend public liberties without compromising the power entrusted to me by the nation'. The principal concessions were the substitution of the right of interpellation for the debate on the Address, and greater freedom of the press. This advance seemed too cautious for Ollivier and too adventurous for the Old Guard. After threatening to resign, Rouher stayed on at the urgent request of the Empress and received the Ministry of Finance.

Though Ollivier had to wait three more years before his demand for real authority was met, he was convinced that the Liberal Empire was bound to come and was impossible without him. Once again he appealed to the Emperor to assert himself.

> The reforms of 19 January have done more harm than good because they have been half-heartedly implemented. You must repair this error. You are surrounded by a Ministry and a Chamber equally unpopular and despised; get rid of them. Appoint a homogeneous and liberal Ministry, dissolve the Chamber and hold an election. If you think the plan too rash, try another. Don't abdicate in favour of Rouher. Create a constitutional government. I am sorry to write like this, but I am too attached to you to withhold this warning.

The Emperor thanked him for his advice, but explained that a captain does not change his crew when there are clouds on the horizon. 'I regret to discover that our country is less ripe for reforms than I thought. Look at the papers, and tell me if they do not disgust you with liberty of the press. Though not discouraged I am sad to witness the trend of events.'

The elections in May 1869 revealed the growing strength of

the republicans; votes for the Government were only four to three, in Paris only one in four. Rouher strove to prevent the election of his rival, not only in Paris, where he lost his seat, but in the Var. Here, however, the Emperor intervened, and Ollivier, standing as an Independent, was returned. Though there were only forty Opposition members in the new Chamber, eight more than in the old, their influence was immensely enhanced by the knowledge that the great cities were behind them. Interpreting the verdict as a notice to the Old Guard to quit, Ollivier secured the support of 116 Deputies, not including thirty Republicans, for a request for responsible government. The Emperor accepted the plan with the proviso that Ministers would continue to depend on himself alone. Some minor increases were granted in the powers of the Chamber, but of wider significance was the dropping of Rouher from the colourless caretaker government now installed.

In 1860, comments Ollivier, the Emperor could give or withhold liberty; in 1867 he had much less choice; in 1869 he had no option. It imposed itself on him both as a necessity and as his salvation. His only choice was between a grudging and a confident advance. Of the agents of the *coup d'état* Morny and Saint-Arnaud were dead, while two survivors, General Fleury and Maupas, welcomed the experiment. 'The authoritarian Empire,' declared the former Prefect of Police, 'has reached its last hour; the Liberal Empire will form the impregnable foundation of the dynasty. We are entering a new era, and we must be blind not to have faith in its future.' Hearing rumours that Persigny was out of favour and planned to lead the opposition to the new course, Ollivier appealed to his old friend for support on the ground that the irreconcilables would find less to attack under a more flexible *régime*. 'You are aware I did not advise the change,' replied the impenitent authoritarian; 'but I am too devoted to the country and the Emperor to place my own opinions above the public sentiment. I have never believed and never shall believe that a Bonapartist *régime* can support liberty in any form, but the men of December like myself must recognize that our role is finished. It is not for us to lead the new generation along the new path, for we should excite mistrust.'

Summoned to Compiègne Ollivier spoke from his heart:

Persevere in the new course but take a firmer line with the declared enemies of the Empire. The more liberty is allowed, the stronger the Government must be. To expose a hesitant Ministry to an unbridled press is not liberalism but abdication. Do you imagine that if I were in power I would tolerate Gambetta and his friends preaching revolt? Though the press must remain free I would punish sedition in every shape; but only a homogeneous Ministry of a constitutional character could undertake that task.
Emperor: I could not accept your friend Prince Napoleon. He is always criticizing, and he takes a malign pleasure when things go wrong.
Ollivier: Give him another chance, say as Minister of Marine in an Ollivier Cabinet.
Emperor: Will you give me your collaboration?
Ollivier: Yes, Sire, if you think it necessary, but not with your present Ministers.
Emperor: It would be painful to dismiss them at this moment; perhaps in a month.

By the end of 1869 all obstacles had been removed. The caretaker Government was dismissed, and on 28 December the *Moniteur* published a letter from the Emperor inviting Ollivier to propose members of a homogeneous Cabinet representing a majority in the Chamber to aid him in working the new constitutional system. At last Ollivier was ready for the call. 'Sire,' he wrote, 'it needs a violent effort on my part to plunge into the conflict, and I do so only because I have faith in Your Majesty. I count on your support against intrigues and on your benevolence towards my failings. We shall have painful times but we shall triumph. What glory you will deserve in history when you have instituted free government and barred the way to revolution. In this enterprise, worthy of a great heart, I offer you everything I possess of goodwill and brain.' Ollivier, reported the Austrian Ambassador on 25 November, was described by the Emperor as an honest man, very energetic and very able, incompetent only in foreign affairs. He coveted the Foreign Office, but his request was refused. The Emperor, reported Metternich, was very sincere in his constitutionalism; but his habits and traditions, above all his personal pre-eminence, forbade the complete self-effacement which the majority would desire and even demand.

The new team, installed on 2 January 1870, was under no illusions as to the extent of its authority. The hostility of the Empress to the liberal experiment was notorious, not merely because she had always believed in autocracy but because she resented the diminution of her influence. There were certain limits in foreign and domestic policy, explained the Emperor to Metternich, which he would never allow to be passed. 'If I bow to the necessities of the situation I am not throwing away my arms. Do not imagine I am abdicating; the future will prove it.' A similar declaration was made at his New Year reception. 'When a traveller after a long journey sheds part of his burden, it gives him fresh strength to continue his march.' 'Ollivier has talent,' he remarked to Metternich, 'He is young and may go far if properly guided. He has two precious qualities which make me forget his failings. He believes in me and is the eloquent interpreter of my ideas, especially when I let him think they are his own.' He was the first of his Ministers, he added, to understand him.

The new chief accepted the system under which the ruler presided at Cabinet meetings; though not fully democratic, dyarchy was as much as could be obtained under the Empire, and indeed he never wanted more. There was no Prime Minister; the Ministers of War and Marine were appointed by the Emperor and Ollivier himself was only Minister of Justice: *primus inter pares*. Though he claims that never was a Government more worthy of respect for merit and character, and Daru, the Foreign Minister, declared in the Senate: *Nous sommes d'honnetes gens*, their names made little impression. Ollivier was a general without an army, for the Old Guard which had run the Empire for nearly two decades liked him as little as the republicans. A few independents, among them Prince Napoleon and Montalembert, rejoiced, and Thiers exclaimed: 'Our opinions are represented on the Government benches: all good citizens should give their support.' Friend and foe wondered how it would work and whether it would endure. Would the Emperor who had once broken a solemn oath remain loyal to his new servants? Could the lifelong apostle of the Führer principle take any form of democracy in his stride? Jules Ferry, a future Premier, scourged it as 'the bastard of autocracy'. 'His task,' Lord Clarendon wrote to Lord Lyons, the British Ambassador, 'requires tact, experience, firmness, knowledge of men and a few other qualities in which he seems singularly deficient, and I cannot think his Ministry will last.' Probably nobody at home or abroad thought that it would except Ollivier, whose self-confidence throughout life knew no limits. The most optimistic spectator was Metternich, who describes him as very democratic, a man of high principle, devoted body and soul to the Emperor.

The new crew ran into a storm in the first week when Victor Noir, a Republican journalist, was killed in a brawl by Pierre Bonaparte, first cousin of the Emperor. Though he claimed that he had fired in self-defence when his home had been invaded and was acquitted after a trial, the incident unleashed a tornado of abuse against the Empire, in which Rochefort screamed the loudest and was sent to prison.

Ollivier defined his programme as a pacification of parties by liberty and a spirit of goodwill, and his declaration against the system of official candidatures delighted everyone except Rouher and other die-hards. Friendly relations continued with Grévy, a future President of the Republic, but Gambetta and Jules Favre, leaders of the left wing republicans, severed personal contacts. Ollivier's unsolicited and almost unanimous election to the Académie Française, hitherto regarded as a stronghold of the royalist Opposition, was an encouragement. His lofty mission, as he conceived it, was to rejuvenate the Empire and to improve the lot of the masses. 'Try to suggest something in the interest of the people,' the kindly Emperor used to say. Ollivier consulted Le Play, France's leading sociologist, but nothing of importance was achieved in the brief remaining period of peace.

The Liberal Empire needed a new constitution to supersede the pattern of 1852, and in April it was ready. The nominated Senate was transformed into an Upper Chamber sharing legislative power with the elected Chamber. The ruler retained the power to appoint and dismiss Ministers, who were also responsible to the Chamber. 'The Emperor', declared Article X, 'governs with the concurrence of the Ministers, the Senate, the Corps Législatif and Council of State.' He reserved the right to order a plebiscite, since changes in the constitution required nation-wide ratification. The separation of powers seemed to be partially realized, the ruler partly limited by the Chamber, the Chamber by the referendum. To complete the edifice Ollivier vainly advocated a Supreme Court on the American model.

At this point the Emperor announced a plebiscite for 8 May to approve or reject the new constitution.

> I believe that everything is illegal without your assent. I appeal to all of you who since 10 December 1848 placed me at your head, who for twenty-two years have sustained me by your votes and rewarded me with your affection; show me a new proof of confidence which will banish the menace of revolution, place order and liberty on a solid foundation and facilitate the eventual transmission of the crown to my son. Almost in unanimity eighteen years ago you conferred on me widest powers; be equally willing today to approve the transformation of the *régime*.

Ollivier followed with a rousing circular to the Prefects. 'The Emperor addresses a solemn appeal to the nation. In 1852 he demanded force to assure order; order assured, he now demands force to defend liberty. The vote is on the liberal transformation, not on the Empire itself. To vote *Oui* is to vote for liberty. In the name of tranquillity and liberty, in the name of the Emperor, we invite you all to unite your efforts with ours; this is a counsel of patriotism.' The voting was absolutely free, and a five to one majority, commented the jubilant Minister, registered the victory of liberty. With a programme of political appeasement and social amelioration, what honest citizen could advocate a monarchist, republican, or socialist revolution? Convinced that the nation was with him, Ollivier never worried over the abstention of two million voters. The Emperor, whose distress from stone in the bladder increased from month to month, was relieved that much of his burden had been assumed by a man whom he trusted and liked, and he constantly expressed his appreciation. 'I am grateful for your talent and devotion displayed every day. So long as you pursue this energetic and patriotic course my support will not fail.' More than ever before, he assured the Chamber, they could look ahead without apprehension. 'Wherever we turn,' echoed Ollivier, 'there are no troublesome questions; never has peace in Europe been better assured.'

His role during the crisis is defended in the fourteenth volume of his apologia. His main thesis is that, like his colleagues and their master he acted as the overwhelming majority of Frenchmen desired. The news of Prince Leopold's acceptance of the Spanish crown which reached Paris on 3 July was not merely a shock but a complete surprise: to the Empress it was 'the explosion of a bomb'. Such flouting by Madrid and Berlin of the customary courtesies of consultation had seemed unthinkable. 'This is very serious,' wrote the Foreign Minister the Duc de Gramont to Ollivier late the same evening. 'A Prussian prince at Madrid—we must prevent this intrigue.' Ollivier describes his anger and grief as he recalled his patient efforts to avert a conflict which many had believed to be inevitable. It was Bismarck's work, he said to himself; he was not the man to draw back and France must accept the challenge. And then? 'Without pronouncing the word I felt in my heart the sorrowful approach of war. If it must be, Bismarck and Prim, not France, would bear the entire responsibility.'

The attitude of the Government was explained to the Chamber on 6 July by the Foreign Minister in a brief statement which, after careful consideration of the wording, had received the unanimous approval of the Ministers in the presence of the Emperor.

> We do not believe that respect for the rights of a neighbouring people obliges us to allow a foreign power, by placing one of its princes on the throne of Charles V, to upset to our detriment the existing equilibrium in Europe and endanger the interests and honour of France. This eventuality, we quite hope, will not occur, for we count on the wisdom of the German and the friendship of the Spanish people. Were it otherwise, strong in your support and that of the nation, we should know how to fulfil our duty without hesitation or faltering.

Though the ugly word War was avoided, the final sentence was clearly an ultimatum and interpreted as such by the world. Re-reading it long afterwards, Ollivier prided himself on his share in the drafting of a declaration which replied with a dignified warning to an intolerable provocation. That evening the Austrian Ambassador found him in high spirits after it had been received with frantic applause.

> We have had enough humiliations from Prussia [he began]. French policy is no longer directed by people like Rouher and La Valette.

> It is I, a Minister of the people, springing from the people, feeling with the people, a Minister responsible to the nation, responsible for its dignity and the prestige of the Emperor, who have conducted this affair with a patriotic resolution you know me to possess. No more hesitations, no more vacillations. The Council was unanimous. We decided we must act. We carried the Chamber and we shall carry the nation. In a fortnight we shall have 400,000 men on the Saar. This time we shall fight as in 1793. We shall arm the people and they will race to the frontiers. I, of all people, have been forced to take up the Prussian challenge in this matter which concerns the dignity and honour of France, I who have shown my sympathy for German nationalism and have been regarded—perhaps am still regarded—as a Prussian.

Marshal Le Boeuf, Minister of War, declared that France could win the struggle by rapid action, and the Emperor had hopes of Austria and Italy. Prince Leopold's cancellation of his acceptance satisfied Ollivier; but at this moment, when the storm clouds seemed to be dispersing, the Emperor and Gramont, without informing the other Ministers, instructed the French Ambassador to secure an assurance from King William that he would veto a renewal of the candidature. Ollivier justly resented his exclusion from a crazy decision which might provoke war. His first instinct was to resign, and his reputation would stand higher had he done so.

> For the old decrepit Empire I had substituted a young Liberal Empire resting on seven and a half million votes. I felt deeply hurt by this renewal of autocracy. I was tired and needed to recover my breath. The idea of giving the signal for war upset me. The occasion to go was excellent and I was violently tempted to seize it. On further reflection this seemed an act of culpable egoism playing into Bismarck's hands. I had no doubt what would happen—the King would decline a guarantee. By remaining I hoped to persuade the Council and the Emperor to accept the refusal, though by not resigning I should be associating myself with an act I deplored.

The disagreement was speedily ended by Bismarck's provocative publication of an edited version of the Ems dispatch which converted Ollivier to a declaration of war on 15 July. Replying to a warning by Thiers in the Chamber he uttered the words which have earned him an unenviable immortality. 'Today my colleagues and I assume a grave responsibility. *Nous l'acceptons d'un coeur léger.*' 'A light heart when the blood of nations is about to flow?' exclaimed a Deputy. 'Yes,' replied the Minister, 'with a light heart. Do not think I mean with joy, I mean without remorse, with confidence, because war is forced on us, because we have done everything honourably possible to avert it, because our cause is just.' That such a virtuoso of language should utter words so liable to misunderstanding is attributed by his admiring biographer to the surge of emotion which swept over him amid the plaudits of the Chamber—a very poor excuse for a veteran of debate.

Once converted to belligerence, Ollivier indulged in the same wishful thinking as the ignorant Parisian crowds who shouted '*A Berlin*!' A fortnight later he invited Maxime du Camp for a talk. 'The Emperor', he began, 'did not want war, but he consented when he saw that I did.' He talked on and on, intoxicated by his own verbosity, visualizing a victorious France dictating to Europe, acclaimed by the people, a beacon to which the eyes of the world would turn.

> *Ollivier:* I believe in the collapse of Germany.
> *Du Camp:* What if it were the collapse of France?
> *Ollivier:* You don't love your country. If one loves it one believes it invincible. It is a crime to doubt it. If you loved it as I do you would be certain of its triumph. Prussia is doomed. We have only to stretch out our hand to take Berlin.

When reproached by his friend Prince Napoleon for gambling the fate of France on a candidature for the Spanish throne he exclaimed excitedly: 'If in presence of the national sentiment we had shirked the conflict, you would have been kicked out, you, your family and the whole dynasty.' He could not guess that within a month the catastrophe he foretold had occurred as the result of the declaration of war for which he was jointly responsible. On the evening of 9 August, when he and his colleagues were overthrown in the angry Chamber without the necessity of a vote, he complained bitterly of the ingratitude of France in evicting him, unmindful of his services and at a moment when he alone could save her. When Count Vitzthum, Austrian Minister in Brussels, expressed to the Emperor the surprise of his Government that he had not contented himself with the withdrawal of the candidature, he received the reply: 'We had gone too far to retreat. That is the fault of one of my Ministers.' Vitzthum expected to hear the name of the bellicose Gramont, but to his surprise the Emperor continued: 'That is M. Ollivier, an excellent man, but without understanding of great affairs.' That they had gone too far was the fault, not of the Minister, but of the ruler himself.

On the overthrow of the Ministry the broken-hearted man fled to Italy in fear of his life. The same themes recur again and again in the *Lettres d'Exil* covering the years 1870 to 1874. His feelings on receiving the news of Sedan, he assured his old master, were too deep for words. Neither of them had willed the war in order to take the Rhineland or prevent German unity; their hands had been forced by the Ems telegram. 'Courage, Sire, right is on our side. Providence has pronounced against us; let us bow in resignation and confidence. Perhaps, spoiled by years of prosperity, we need this affliction.' He found solace in the conviction that he had taken the only honourable course, the course which the country desired, since dishonour was worse than defeat. Moreover, he expected to return to public life when the storm abated. At the end of 1870 he vainly begged the prisoner at Wilhelmshöhe to sponsor his candidature for a seat in Corsica, but after fresh attempts in the seventies and eighties he accepted his fate. Anxiously searching his conscience in his solitary mountain retreat while the conflict raged beyond the Alps, he could discover no single error of judgment.

That his share in producing the catastrophe was far less than that of the Emperor, Gramont and Le Boeuf was true enough, for he had not been consulted about the fateful demand for a guarantee that a fresh offer for the Spanish throne would be declined. He had not seen Colonel Stoffel's grave reports from Berlin on the Prussian army, and had been assured by the Minister of War that France had never been so prepared. He was unaware of the slender foundations on which the Emperor based his expectations of aid from Austria and Italy, and he could not foretell that the French Command would prove so incompetent. He had wholeheartedly supported the declaration of war, but for that he saw no reason to apologize. 'I know I am the object of universal execration,' he wrote in June 1871. He professed himself unruffled by the storm, for some day France would be grateful to him for preserving her honour. Some day there might be a Bonapartist restoration. Some day France might recover and hit back. 'Our task is to understand the duties imposed on us by our misfortune,' he wrote to Prince Napoleon when the fighting was over; 'if we do, one day we shall enter Berlin. My only thought will be to prepare for that day. Henceforth one single passion, one single aim—*la revanche nationale*. It would be a holy war.' He would train his son in this idea and curse him if he rejected it. We might be listening to the strident tones of Juliette Adam or Paul Déroulède.

Ollivier's affection for his old master never waned. 'If he made mistakes,' he wrote to a friend, 'is this the time to reproach him? Is it not more generous to recall his fine and great qualities, his kindliness, his humanity, his love for the people and France, the magnanimity with which he renounced his autocracy, above all his misfortunes, the insults and infamies hurled at him? Poor, poor man! I forgive him everything and I could not restrain my tears when I read his latest proclamation which is simply admirable.' The Empire was the Emperor, he commented, when the news of his death arrived. 'While he lived I felt certain of a restoration. Now my eyes are covered by a thick veil.'

In 1876 Ollivier reiterated his familiar complaints to Maxime du Camp. Had he remained at the helm he would have prorogued the Chamber, arrested irreconcilable Deputies, muzzled the press, suspended the right of assembly, governed by decrees, and proclaimed a *levée en masse*. Then France would have won the war, annexed Rhenish Prussia and the Bavarian Palatinate, and secured her natural frontiers. This programme had been approved by the Council of Ministers under the presidency of the Empress on 8 August, and his fall had prevented its implementation. Placing his hand on his heart he concluded his fatuous monologue with the words ' *Moi, j'ai pardonné à la France*.' France, on the contrary, whispering, like Augustus to Varus, *redde meas legiones*, has never forgiven him. He and Bazaine were the scapegoats for *l'année terrible*.

Ollivier was denounced, not merely by royalists and republicans but also by Bonapartists who sought to shift the blame from the Emperor. The latter spoke kindly of him, but only in private.

'He is as innocent as myself and had equally little wish for the war. I like him. His intentions were good, and only events prevented their fulfilment. Every attack on him falls on me too.' The Empress, on the other hand, castigated him almost as fiercely as her *bête noire* Trochu. 'So long as I am alive nothing will be done for him. It is he who destroyed us.' Rochefort, as usual, was for sterner measures than mere ostracism. 'Ollivier must die and the jury will acquit the assassins.'

To Maxime du Camp he was the Attila of eloquence:

> His words were the curse and the doom of France. He was not a bad man. The poor fellow, unaware of his ignorance and his failings, confused words with deeds, honestly believing he had acted because he had talked. Like his hearers, he yielded to the charm, a singer in love with his voice. In listening to him one forgot the face of a defrocked priest, his squint, his dirty nails, his shabby appearance, his untidy hair. We only saw the orator's gestures which seemed to beat time to the marvellous eloquence, the grandeur of the images, his sonorous voice, the incomparable harmonies of his phraseology which stirred even the most apathetic. He possessed the strange faculty of speaking at any moment on any subject. Some power seemed to take control for which he was not responsible and to which he yielded as if he were obeying an irresistible impulse. That he was built up into a statesman is incomprehensible; that he was entrusted with the destinies of France was a crime.

Such extravagant vilifications usually breed a reaction. The passions of 1870 had begun to cool when Ollivier died in 1913 at the age of eighty-eight, and in recent years attempts have been made to challenge the harsh verdict of his contemporaries.[1]

---

[1] Pièrre Saint-Marc's biography (1950), which utilizes his journals and correspondence, presents him as a man of noble character and an unselfish patriot with a political record of which his descendants might be proud. In his striking study (1957) *The Political System of Napoleon III*, Theodore Zeldin argues that the Liberal Empire was a skilful and workable compromise between the autocracy of which France was weary and an omnipotent Chamber on the British model which the Emperor would never have accepted and which, in Ollivier's opinion, was unsuited to France. Steady progress towards liberty with the assent of the sovereign was infinitely preferable to changes extorted by violent means. Evolution, not revolution, was what the country needed and what he had tried to provide. That he failed was he fault of the Iron Chancellor.

12

DURUY AND THE SCHOOLS

THE most personally attractive of the Emperor's servants was one of the relatively few scholar-statesmen of France. It speaks well for the Dictator that he won not only the respect but the abiding affection of a man who disapproved the *coup d'état* and made no secret of his republican ideology. The greatest educational reformer in the history of his country, author of both large-scale histories of the classical world and of school books which sold by the million, he filled the post of Minister of Public Instruction for six creative years. The Emperor knew that he had no political ambitions and was perfectly satisfied with an academic career. His Memoirs and the affectionate biography by Lavisse reveals a personality of exceptional nobility. Born in 1811 into a family which for seven generations had worked in Colbert's Gobelins factory in Paris, Victor Duruy was trained as a weaver, but his brilliant record at school and college marked him out for a wider career. Among the pupils at the Collège Henri IV were the Duc d'Aumale and the Duc de Montpensier, who invited him to the Tuileries. Though he liked Louis Philippe, he found the Bourgeois Monarchy too spineless abroad and too static at home, and was neither surprised nor distressed by its collapse. Desiring the Second Republic to stay, he voted against Louis Napoleon in the plebiscites of 1848 and 1851.

Entering the Emperor's study one day Marshal Randon, Minister of War, noticed Duruy's *Histoire des Romains* on the table, and observed that he knew the author. 'It is a good book,' was the reply, 'and I should be charmed to have a chat with him. Ask him to come at one o'clock tomorrow.' A long talk ensued, ranging over the whole field of Roman institutions, which gave equal pleasure to both. 'I do not share all his ideas,' reported the Emperor to the Marshal, 'but he is an intelligent man.' The historian was particularly struck by the gentleness of the master of France. 'When he wished to please, his blue eyes were full of seduction, and at that moment his words were as soft as velvet.' They were not to meet again for nearly three years, but Duruy's services were requisitioned in 1860 when the problem of Italy and above all of the Papacy filled the ruler's thoughts. His memorandum on the Papal States summarized their history, argued that their possession was detrimental to the spiritual influence of the Pope, and advised that nothing should be left to him except the Vatican quarter under the guarantee and with the financial assistance of Catholic states. The memorandum, published anonymously, increased the confidence of the Emperor, whose views were much the same. Even now, two years were to elapse before his help was requested for a larger task, the biography of Caesar. Could he demonstrate the thesis that the greatness of a man of genius should be measured by the survival of his influence? Duruy's answer was provided in talks in which the Emperor read to his visitor the portion of his Preface embodying his thoughts on the role of Men of Destiny.

The more he saw of the Professor the more he admired him, and the plan of utilizing his abilities took shape. 'I am old and weary,' explained Mocquard, the faithful Political Secretary, 'the Emperor wants someone capable and discreet from the University world to assist me.' As Inspector-General of the University, replied Duruy, he could not join the Cabinet secretariat, but he would come for two hours a day without official title and without pay. His offer was accepted, but it was disappointing to discover that Mocquard only gave him routine letters to draft. On the third day the Emperor entered the room.

The Emperor: Well, M. Duruy, what are you doing?
Duruy: Routine complimentary letters, Sire.
The Emperor: Drop it and come along with me.

For the next few days the talk was entirely of Julius Caesar, above all of the conception of 'providential men'. 'What we call Providence,' declared the free-thinking historian, 'used to be called Destiny, a mysterious personage created to explain the inexplicable, which we have banished from our teaching; for the principle of education is to consider the merit of an act. Teachers must tell their pupils that we are not slaves but architects of our own fortunes.' 'Possibly,' rejoined the Emperor, who held to his thesis that when society was going to pieces legality might be infringed. 'One does such things at times,' was the rejoinder of the austere historian, 'but it is better not to recall them.'

Duruy expected to be offered the succession to Mocquard, but the ruler had something more suitable in view. When Duruy announced in 1863 his approaching tour for four or five months to the provincial *lycées*, the Emperor regretfully exclaimed 'That is a very long time.' News of his appointment as Minister of Public Instruction reached him *en route*. Hastening to Fontainebleau he inquired: 'How could Your Majesty think of making me a Minister?' '*Cela ira bien*,' was the reply, and so it did. His predecessor Fortoul had tried to subject Universities to the will of the ruler. Professors had to swear fidelity, while the Government nominated the Council of Instruction and the Academic Councils. Professors, hitherto irremoveable, became dismissable by the Emperor, Professors in the Lycées by the Minister, assistant masters by the Rector. A further step towards authoritarianism was the abolition of history and philosophy courses. Duruy's first task was to loosen the grip of the Government on a sphere of national life where academic autonomy was the breath of life.

The views of the new Minister were set forth in a Memorandum for the Emperor. Universal suffrage must be matched by universal elementary education; illiteracy must cease and teachers must be adequately paid; secondary education was no less important not, merely vocational but cultural.

> Since France is the moral centre of the world, let us provide for those who are destined to the liberal professions, to high positions in the state, to literature and science, philosophy and history, and thus to justify the aristocracy of intellect. The mass is climbing up; do not allow the bourgeoisie to stand still, for to stand still is to fall back. And let us not forget the girls.

It was the most generous educational programme ever presented by a French Minister, and with the Emperor's encouragement he proceeded to carry it out. No progress had been attempted in primary education since Guizot laid the foundations in 1833.

O

There were still millions of illiterates; in thousands of communes there were no schools for girls and many possessed no school at all. Children were often excluded by poverty owing to the paucity of free places, and many only attended for a brief period. Teachers, above all women teachers, received starvation salaries and no pensions. In secondary schools the position was no better. Vocational education was unknown, the teaching of history halted on the threshold of the modern world, and philosophy was barred by clerical influence as a danger to faith. Higher education was starved by meagre grants, inadequate buildings and lack of laboratories. In Duruy's term of office the whole face of education was transformed. Primary education became free and compulsory, the curriculum of secondary schools was widened, adequate salaries attracted better teachers, philosophy was restored to its place, school libraries were stocked, some provision was made for adult education, and an *École des hautes Études* was instituted for the *élite*.

An avowed *libre penseur*, like most of the leading Intellectuals of his generation, Duruy found his chief antagonists in the Church, which he regarded as instinctively and irrevocably hostile to modern civilization; and the longest chapter of his Memoirs is devoted to the running battle. Though the Emperor required the support or at any rate the acquiescence of the Church for the stability of his *régime*, he was no more a *croyant* than the Minister and shared his uncle's dislike of clerical interference in matters of state. When Duruy was attacked by some of the bishops, with Dupanloup at their head, the Emperor asked why he did not defend himself; but the Minister had no taste for controversy. There was nothing of the fanatic and propagandist about him, for he respected beliefs which he did not share. The most precious achievement of 1789, he declared, was tolerance. 'I had excellent relations with the bishops, who confined themselves to their spiritual duties,' he records in his Memoirs; 'but the Church, a state within a state, regards the Ministry of Public Instruction as its chief foe, particularly in regard to the primary schools. The Emperor was well aware of its ambitions and its feud with modern society, especially after the Syllabus of Errors issued in 1864.' There were, however, limits to the power of the Minister, who failed to avert the dismissal of Renan from his chair of

Hebrew at the *Collège de France* decreed by the Council of Ministers for the sake of public order threatened by demonstrations against the author of the *Vie de Jésus*.

The Empress and the Minister had little in common except devotion to France, but they liked and respected each other. The Empress, he declared, possessed a noble heart and lofty moral stature. For her share of the duties of the throne she had chosen charity. Every week she brought her gifts incognito to the poorest dwellings, and she visited cholera patients during an epidemic. Though she had been accused of exerting a sinister influence on policy in regard to Italy and war, he had never seen any ground for the charge. He always found her very gracious, despite their differences on the Temporal Power. The Emperor was an ideal chief. On entrusting the Ministry to him he merely exhorted him to 'keep alive the sacred flame for all that is noble and great', leaving him to settle details. Trusting him to the full and sharing his ideals, he usually took his side in the conflicts in the Council of Ministers, where he encountered as much opposition to his requests for funds as Haussmann in his campaign for a finer capital. The ruler also defended him against Dupanloup and his other enemies in the Church, and when the Vatican organ made his dismissal the price of Catholic votes in the next elections he encouraged him to defend himself. Except for disagreement on the vital issue of democratic institutions, the two men were very close to one another. On his master's credit side he listed two fine and far-reaching ideas—the liberation of nationalities and the welfare of manual labour. 'I do not think any sovereign has been more preoccupied with the good he could do. How often have I seen him enter the Council with projects to assist the weak and the poor. His hand was open—too open—for he could not refuse appeals. The Governor of the *Crédit Foncier* tells me he often had to advance a month's instalment of his Civil List.'

The most convinced liberal in the Council employed his influence to promote the extension of public liberties, less through intervention in debate than in letters to the ruler, who in the later years of his reign was ready for some cautious advance. 'Do not regard as enemies or *frondeurs* those who do not think precisely like ourselves or who are independent friends. Do not wish to be surrounded only by valets or enemies.' One day the

Emperor surprised the Council by remarking: 'If the press is free in Europe, how can it fail to be free in France?' Duruy congratulated him and urged him to persevere in this attitude against timid counsellors. 'Despite all your power,' he wrote, 'I defy you to suppress the *Débats*, which has already received two warnings and which a third would kill. We cannot walk backwards.' In another letter he wrote: 'Today in Council I heard the words *consummatum est* in reference to reforms. The people always has new needs which the government must satisfy.' The ailing Emperor, however, found concentration and application increasingly difficult.

> He hovered over the Empire rather than governed it. If he had had the passion or even the taste for government, as many precise ideas as generous sentiments, as much will as goodwill, he would not have written the *Vie de Caesar* at a moment when so many subjects demanded the closest attention. It was only from a lofty distance that he interested himself in education, and his encouragements were limited to confidential little notes.

Though he had not the slightest wish to overthrow the *régime*, Duruy never believed that it would be more than an intermezzo between the Second and a Third Republic. That it was losing prestige during his six years of office was obvious to friend and foe, and neither a small dose of liberalism nor any other expedient could save it. It was a paradox that this lifelong liberal should lose his post at the very moment when the experiment of the Liberal Empire was launched in the summer of 1869, since the new system was believed to require a new team, and the conservatives Rouher and Baroche were hustled off the stage at the same time as the progressive Minister of Education. 'I shall take new men for a new situation,' declared the Emperor. 'I accept any men and any ideas, retaining for myself merely the task of resisting the revolution.' His dismissal was conveyed in a friendly letter.

> My dear M. Duruy, It is one of the evil aspects of the situation that I must part from a Minister who possessed my confidence and who had rendered great service to public instruction. If politics have no bowels of compassion, the sovereign has, and he must express his regrets. I have appointed M. Bourbeau your successor. I hope to see you one of these days for you to tell me what I can do to show my sincere friendship.

The letter, in the Emperor's own hand, was scarcely legible, for he was now a sick man.

The ex-Minister retained some slight contact with affairs through his nomination to the Senate, but he ceased to count, and he watched the decline of French influence with grief and apprehension. He had approved intervention in Italy, but he regretted the failure to assist Denmark, deplored the Mexican entanglement, and desired the dispatch of an army of observation to Metz in the summer of 1866. After the revelation of Prussian power he urged preparations for the grim conflict which he, like most observers throughout Europe, fully expected.

> We are confronted with a young, ambitious state [he wrote to the Emperor] which wishes to become a great continental and a great maritime power, and will only feel confident of keeping what it has got after humiliating France as it has humiliated Austria. War is inevitable some time; not that I suggest the Prussians will attack Strasbourg or Metz, but their restless ambition will hurl them into some enterprise where they will come up against us.

He was particularly alarmed about the superiority of Prussia's artillery. When the storm broke he was horrified by the clumsy handling of the crisis. After the *débâcle* he returned to his historical writings and compiled his Memoirs, taking no part in the politics of the Third Republic. He remained the moderate and thoughtful liberal he had always been, hating extremes and disliking the rabid anti-clericalism of certain politicians no less than the clericalism which had striven to clip his wings.

13

HAUSSMANN AND THE BOULEVARDS

ON the crowded stage of the Second Empire Baron Haussmann was the nearest approach to a superman. In the words of Rouher everything in him was great, both his qualities and his faults. The dynamic Prefect of the Seine was in power longer than any Minister. While the names of most of the Emperor's agents are forgotten, that of the fashioner of Paris as we know it remains familiar to us all. Now that the French colonial empire is crumbling, the transformation of the capital into the finest city in Europe stands out as the principal legacy of Napoleon III. That the master-builder could have achieved little without the enthusiastic support of the Dictator is obvious. It is equally clear that no other functionary possessed the drive required to effect such revolutionary changes in face of vested interests and financial apprehensions. The substitution of broad boulevards for narrow streets had also a military significance, for the 1848 battle of the barricades could not be allowed to recur.

Born in Paris into a Protestant family from Alsace, Haussmann took a degree in law and opted for a career in administration. As a godchild of Prince Eugène Beauharnais and the son of an Orleanist journalist he had plenty of backing, and from a maternal grandfather he claimed the title of Baron, to which he had as little right as Morny to the title of Count. Beginning at the bottom of the ladder he learned his trade in the provinces, and on the fall of the Monarchy he felt entitled to ask for a Prefecture, preferably in the neighbourhood of Bordeaux where he had found a wife. On the election of Louis Napoleon to the Presidency he was summoned to Paris, where he would be informed whither he would be sent.

The President: The Var. Have you any objection?
Haussmann: No, but you could hardly send me further away from Bordeaux.
The President: The Var is a danger spot on the Italian frontier and needs a strong man.
Haussmann: I shall try to justify your confidence.

Such was the first meeting of the two men whose names were to be indissolubly linked in history. Their next was in 1850 when the President visited the Department of the Yonne to which Haussmann had been transferred.

In November 1851 at the age of forty-two, he was promoted to the Prefecture of the Gironde, which embraced Bordeaux. Hastening to Paris to thank the President, he arrived on 1 December in time to attend the historic reception at the Elysée on the eve of the *coup d'état*. 'I cannot tell you at this moment why I am sending you to Bordeaux,' remarked the host, 'but I want you to start tomorrow as early as possible. Fetch your instructions from the Minister of the Interior.' Finding Thorigny, the Minister of the Interior, at the reception, he asked for instructions on the spot. The Minister, unaware of the plot, looked blank and replied that he had none to give. When Haussmann reached the Ministry before daylight on the following morning he learned the reason of the President's mysterious command. The sight of troops in the streets and in the courtyard told its own tale. To his request to see the Minister he received the revealing reply: 'Which? M. Thorigny or Comte de Morny?' 'The Comte de Morny.' He was the first caller on the new Minister, who explained the need to win Bordeaux for the new Dictator.

On his arrival the new Prefect evicted his predecessor and burned the proclamations already printed announcing the state of siege. When the news of the fighting in Paris arrived some demonstrations occurred; many arrests were made but few were detained. His intimate knowledge of the city proved useful, and the smoothness of the transition was noted with satisfaction at the Elysée. After the plebiscite had confirmed the authority of the new master, Mixed Commissions were set up in each Department composed of the Prefect, the Advocate-General and the local commands. Of 1,500 charged at Bordeaux seventy-four were sentenced and twenty-seven transported to Cayenne or North

Africa. The next task was to secure the return of all official candidates to the Corps Législatif. To serve the Dictator required no sacrifice of principle from the functionary who had always regarded a benevolent and efficient autocracy as the ideal form of government. In May 1852 he was summoned to Paris for instructions on the coming visit of the President to the South, including Bordeaux, where a programme speech would be delivered. Persigny, Minister of the Interior, assured him of his confidence and affectionate esteem, and the President was more cordial than ever. Greeted in Bordeaux with organized cries of *Vive l'Empereur*! the Prince explained his intentions and ideals, and pronounced the celebrated formula: *L'Empire c'est la paix*.

The more the Emperor saw of Haussmann the more he was impressed. Here was the man to carry out his dream of making Paris the model city. Summoned to the Ministry of the Interior in June 1853 he was selected from a group of five Prefects. Inviting each of them separately to dinner, Persigny had no difficulty in making his choice. The portrait in his Memoirs many years later is the most elaborate and penetrating that we possess of the man he describes as one of the most extraordinary figures of the time. When asked to describe events in his Department at the time of the *coup* and the difficulties he had overcome, he recounted his campaign against the opposition in the Bordeaux municipality and his face shone with pride. While the words poured forth in a flood the Minister could not hide his satisfaction. Rough work lay ahead, requiring an experienced, resourceful and thick-skinned official, a born fighter who could hold his own against all comers and scorned red tape. Persigny rejoiced to think of letting loose this tall tigerish animal among the foxes and wolves who would oppose the generous aims of the Emperor. In his letter of acceptance the new Prefect wrote that he belonged to the Emperor without reserve.

For the following sixteen and a half years the Prefect of the Seine and the Dictator marched forward in unbroken harmony. While the latter rejoiced in the prowess of the most dynamic of his agents, Haussmann felt for his master a growing regard which shines through the Memoirs compiled long after the fall of the Empire. As an eye-witness of Orsini's bomb attack he admired the sang-froid of the intended victim, whose first words were

'Look after the wounded.' Too gentle and trustful, calm and benevolent by nature, he harboured no lingering resentments even for grave offences. 'I only once saw him angry. Some sudden contrariety occasionally brought a light into his gentle and even caressing eyes. There was rarely an exclamation, never an unsuitable outburst. He remembered every service. He pardoned his adversaries, once they were disarmed, too easily for prudence, for he did not always take sufficient account of their record and believed in the sincerity of political conversions.' In his closing days at Chislehurst the fallen ruler declared that Haussmann had always given him good advice and wise warnings. 'He was a great administrator; I did not realize his political worth soon enough.'

When the new Prefect took the oath at Saint-Cloud the Emperor declared that the first task was to introduce fresh blood into the Municipal Council. They should not hurry, rejoined Haussmann, who hoped to win them for his plans. The ruler produced a map on which his schemes were indicated in different colours according to a scale of priorities. Whole chapters of Haussmann's Memoirs are devoted to the first days of office. In addition to the Dictator he could count on Persigny, the Minister of the Interior, who received him with open arms. 'This excellent man from our first contacts had felt affection for me. He valued my work in the Gironde, above all the incomparable reception of the President in October 1852.' His predecessor, who had been relieved of his post owing to his dread of lavish expenditure, had many friends on the Municipal Council, including its President, Delangle, who in the course of an official welcome pointedly regretted the retirement of the former Prefect and declared his agreement with his cautious views, adding 'We will support you in all measures within the resources of the city.' With Piétri, Prefect of Police, the only functionary whose status limited his authority, a good deal of friction occurred. Though every Prefect was traditionally under the jurisdiction of the Ministry of the Interior, Haussmann, with Persigny's assent, dealt directly with the Emperor. That some of the Ministers disliked his privileged position as well as his policy and tried to obstruct it troubled him not at all. In his own words, he felt that not merely his master but all Europe was looking on as if he were a general planning a long campaign. 'I spoke to my employees like a commander to his troops.'

The most formidable opposition to his schemes came neither from the Municipal Council nor from the enemies of the *régime* but from Ministers and above all from Baroche. The transformation of Paris necessitated wholesale destruction, and the masterful Prefect, who had little use for legal niceties, issued a decree facilitating expropriation. In 1858 he demanded fresh powers which Baroche, as President of the Council of State, declared to be unnecessary. In a long memorandum to the Emperor the conservative lawyer pleaded for full inquiry and fair compensation in every case, and complained that many expropriations had been both needless and illegal. Counter-attacking in the Council of Ministers, Haussmann charged his accuser with hostility to the whole plan, which would be one of the glories of the reign. Baroche, he declares in his Memoirs, argued his pseudo-liberal thesis with passion, and the Emperor, who was present, took little interest in the details of administration and finance. When the Prefect's request for wider powers was refused, the kindly ruler sought to comfort him with the words 'How right you were, but it was too late.' The duel was renewed when he demanded the incorporation of suburban communes in the capital, and again the Emperor gave way, consoling him by admission to the Council of State.

How were these gigantic projects to be financed? The Municipal Council replied 'from the annual budget', a principle which limited the advance to a snail's pace. From fresh taxation? Here the veto of the Emperor barred the way. From the State? But the State contribution was necessarily small. Only large loans, euphemistically described by the Prefect as productive expenditure, could supply the need. Old projects already approved and in some cases begun, among them the continuation of the Rue de Rivoli, the completion of the Louvre, the improvement of the central market and the development of the Bois de Boulogne, had to be finished. The new banks, the Crédit Mobilier and the Crédit Foncier, had plenty of money to lend on moderate terms.

Haussmann confidently proclaimed that the increasing population and prosperity of the capital provided ample security for the enormous loans. 'Give Paris lungs,' he argued, 'and it will pay for itself.' The revenues of the Municipality were rapidly increasing, and he was delighted to discover that they had been underestimated by his timid predecessor. His aims were summarized in memoranda under four heads: (i) To uncover historic and public buildings, palaces, churches, etc. (ii) To improve public health by clearing away insanitary areas. (iii) To construct broad boulevards, healthier and better suited to the movement of troops in case of riots. (iv) To open up the approaches to the new railway termini. He quoted the injunction of *Le Roi Soleil* to Mansard, 'Build, build: we will supply the money and the foreigner will pay it off.' Though he knew little of the history of the city he arranged for the collection of illustrative documents at the Musée Carnavalet.

The most spectacular achievement was the construction of boulevards, based on a master plan of two great arteries north-south and east-west, with many connecting roads. He was assailed with loud cries of vandalism, extravagance, robbing the people of their homes, compensation claims degenerating into a ramp. That the whole scheme cost more than expected was inevitable, but it appeared to him and the Emperor a trifle in comparison with the enormous improvement in appearance, convenience and public health. Less outwardly impressive but no less vital to the welfare of the city was the supply of pure water from outside the Paris basin, the network of sewers, and the measures for the disposal of sewage. He was also the first to deal with cemeteries in relation to public health. The most popular of the changes was the beautification of public parks and open spaces, including the Champs Elysées and the Bois de Boulogne. Further improvements were effected in the *quais* and bridges, the building of the most sumptuous Opera House in Europe, churches and schools, asylums and homes for incurables, markets and abattoirs, town halls, theatres, barracks, hospitals, the restoration of Notre Dame and the Elysée. Though thousands of dwellings were demolished, many more were built. When Jules Ferry charged him with lacking all sense of legality, he replied that he was working for the welfare of the community and enjoyed the complete confidence of the Emperor.

Haussmann was never fully satisfied with his official status. He dreamed of the creation of a new Ministry of Paris, himself at the helm, with the title and rank of Minister, carrying with it the right to speak in the Conseil d'Etat and freedom from all control except that of the Emperor. Annoyed by opposition to two of his schemes in the Conseil d'Etat in 1860, he threatened to resign unless he was allowed to plead for them on equal terms. He enclosed a draft decree for the Emperor's approval: 'The Baron Haussmann, Senator, Prefect of the Seine, has the rank of Minister and the right to sit in our Council of State. He will assume the title of Minister of Paris.' That, replied the Emperor, was impossible; but his powers were increased and he was allowed to attend the Conseil d'Etat as an Extraordinary member. The Emperor's decision was due to the resistance of important Ministers, especially Rouher and Baroche, who treated the Prefect with marked coolness when he took part in the Conseil d'Etat. Vieil-Castel, who believed the worst of everybody, regarded him with contempt and resented the Emperor's favour. 'A cunning scoundrel like Haussmann, if enterprising and useful, will be well treated and spoiled. His hand will be pressed and he will be received with beaming smiles.' A partial consolation was found in his election to the Académie des Beaux Arts and the calling of a boulevard after his name.

His finest hour was the Great Exhibition of 1867. He had served on the Committee which began its work in 1863. All the celebrities visited the Hôtel de Ville where they were suitably entertained, and no Frenchman of his time received so many foreign decorations. His portrait at this proud moment was drawn by Mme Baroche, whose husband was no friend. 'He is very big. But like most of his buildings he excels by size rather than by grace or harmony, a Titan, not an Apollo. An Attila of expropriation, he destroyed Paris in order to make it greater than all France.' A commonplace talker with conventional ideas, she continued, he only became eloquent and interesting when dilating on his own achievements. In such a man neither taste nor modesty could be expected, yet he deserved a place in history and would have it. Rouher was often called the Vice-Emperor, declared Thiers; the real Vice-Emperor was the Prefect of the Seine. Rouher required the skill of a tight-rope walker to combine his jealousy of Haussmann's influence with his sincere respect for their common master. The ideal of a renovated capital, he argued, was excellent, and the busy ruler could not be held responsible for any mistakes in carrying it out. Though Haussmann was roughly handled in the Senate and the Chamber, no one questioned his personal incorruptibility. He multiplied irregularities and cared nothing for rules, declares Ollivier, but he was obsessed by the artist's passionate longing to witness the completion of his work. Jules Ferry, one of the most persistent critics of the Empire in the Chamber, spoke of *les comptes fantastiques* of Haussmann at a time when *tout Paris* was enjoying Offenbach's melodies in *les contes fantastiques* of Hoffmann. During the Great Exhibition master and servant looked back on the long struggle.

> *Haussmann:* If I had foreseen all the difficulties, jealousies, calumnies, intrigues, I would have refused the invitation.
> *Emperor:* I too have had my difficulties [taking his hand affectionately]. I understand you, for you are not the only person to suffer from injustice and ingratitude. They are aiming at me through the man who serves me with rare fidelity. I, too, am faithful, and will remain so to the end in the promise of my friendship.

The offer of a large sum to provide for the years of his retirement was declined on the ground that this was needless. 'You have given me something of inestimable value—your affection.'

As a firm believer in benevolent autocracy Haussmann frowned on the Liberal Empire, and the appointment of Ollivier in January 1870 closed his official career. He would not work with him, he declared, nor would he be associated in any way with the new *régime*. 'The Liberal Empire!' But was it not already liberal in the best and widest sense? Resting on universal suffrage, was it not the complete expression of the country? What former ruler was so constantly concerned with the wellbeing of the people? The Parliamentary Empire! I would have nothing to do with it, convinced that it would lead us to disaster. So I decided to leave the Hôtel de Ville without compensation and without alternative plans.' The Emperor, by this time in failing health and with a weakening will, told him that he must resign. 'Nothing of the sort,' was the reply. 'They must either dismiss me or keep me.' The bitterness remained for the rest of his life.

From his villa on the Riviera the fallen Prefect witnessed 'with stupefaction' the virtual abdication of his old master. 'A Napoleon with the almost nominal sovereignty of Louis Philippe: what a bad joke!' That he had changed his views he did not believe, but he had always been easily impressed, and Ollivier had a golden tongue. 'To restore the Parliamentary *régime* which he had overturned, to abandon the power he had exercised with distinction for seventeen years, was the limit.' Returning to Paris in May 1870 he was agreeably surprised to find the Emperor dissatisfied with his modest role as a constitutional ruler, and with a low opinion of his new Ministers and their chief. When they were alone after lunch at Saint-Cloud on 13 June the host amazed his visitor by his opening words.

> *Emperor:* I wish to change my Ministry. Yes, I never imagined such incapacity. We must form a *Grand Ministère* together at the close of the session.
>
> *Haussmann:* I will do my best to help, but I have no wish to return to public life. Some subordinate appointment would be the limit of my ambition. With my convictions I should be a misfit in any Cabinet. That is why in the past I declined the portfolios you offered me, and confined myself in the discussions of the Council to the affairs of Paris. If I were still of use it would only be on condition of having my hands free in any task assigned to me, of course under the authority of my master.
>
> *Emperor:* Do you imagine I should offer you a minor position?
>
> *Haussmann:* You would replace the Parliamentary Liberal Empire by the Authoritarian Liberal Empire?
>
> *Emperor* (decisively): Yes. My recent experience proves that with us power, to be respected, must be in a single hand and strong.

Haussmann proceeded to develop his programme in a series of interviews with his old master with a view to the restoration of autocracy, reserving for the decision of a plebiscite any serious conflict with the Legislature. Agreeing on the essential issues they differed about the timing of a new *coup d'état*. The Emperor intended to wait till the end of the session and the departure of the Deputies. Such delay, protested his visitor, would be dangerous, for no one knew what irremediable errors the inexperienced Ministers might commit in the meantime. The Emperor responded 'I will see to that.' When Ollivier read this extraordinary story in Haussmann's Memoirs many years later he exploded:

> If this is true; if, after giving me so many proofs of confidence and friendship; if, in the evening of the day on which he had thanked me

for my talent and devotion he had described me as a nitwit, he would have been the basest of men. If, on the morrow of the plebiscite, he had contemplated a *coup d'état* against the national verdict, he would have been the most imbecile of politicians. Such an outrage on his memory as this narrative has never been known.

Did Haussmann, never a friend of Ollivier, invent or misrepresent the utterances of the Emperor? We cannot tell.

On the outbreak of war he returned to Paris, went straight to the Tuileries, and offered his services. Finding the Empress and some officers in the council room he was invited to join them. After a General had urged the declaration of a state of siege, someone pointed out that there were no troops in the capital. Asked by the Empress to speak, Haussmann argued for such a declaration as essential for the safety of the dynasty and the capital, the necessary troops to be summoned from Algeria and elsewhere. At her request he was asked how to draft the proclamation, which he did without leaving the table. No other task was assigned to him before the Empire collapsed. A few months later the Tuileries and Saint-Cloud, the scene of many eager exchanges with his old master, and the Hôtel de Ville, where he planned his reforms and had ruled like a Dictator, went up in flames. The boulevards remained. *Si momentum requiris circumspice.*

PART THREE

FRIENDS AND FOES

14

THE ARMY

EVERY political adventurer needs the army in order to arrive and survive. Throughout his reign Louis Napoleon met with far less antagonism from the soldiers than from the politicians, the Church or the Intelligentsia. The legend of *Le Petit Caporal* lingered on, and the campaigns in the Crimea and Lombardy proved that Frenchmen had not forgotten how to fight. Though he had learned soldiering in Switzerland and had written on artillery, the new master was as much a civilian at heart as the Prince Consort or Louis Philippe. Such trifling opposition as he encountered was overcome before the *coup d'état*, and with Saint-Arnaud at the Ministry of War he knew that his cause was in safe hands. After the triumphant plebiscite Cavaignac and Changarnier withdrew into private life, and Lamoricière, the only other prominent antagonist, faded out after an intermezzo as Commander of the Papal forces. MacMahon and Montauban, Pélissier and Bazaine, had no political ambitions and were willing to serve under any *régime*. Instead of *Liberté, Egalité, Fraternité*, sneered Karl Marx, it was *Cavalry, Infantry, Artillery*. The Emperor could retort that he had been drafted by the people and was ready at any moment for another unfettered nation-wide vote.

1. FLEURY

Comte Fleury was the first officer to mount the band-wagon. Meeting the Prince in London after his return from the United States in 1837 he was captivated for life. 'His grave and firm features,' he writes in his Memoirs, 'his benevolent expression, his simple and distinguished manners, impressed me so much that in Africa my thoughts often reverted to him.' The burning Bonapartist faith of Persigny decided him to choose a military career with an eye on the future. 'Soon there will be an Empire, with its pomp and glory and influence in Europe. Join the army and you will return to us as a high-ranking officer. Some day you will command a regiment of the Guards.' The next decade was spent in Algeria where the dragging war provided a training for all the generals of the Second Empire, known in popular parlance as *Les Africains*.

During a period of leave after the fall of the Monarchy, Fleury attended a reception given by General Cavaignac, head of the Provisional Government; and among the guests was a General who in a few chance words rekindled his Bonapartist sympathies. 'The Orleans are finished, and the future belongs to Prince Louis Napoleon. He will be elected a Deputy and within two months you will see him President.' He arranged a meeting in the Prince's hotel, where Fleury was so warmly received as to attract the attention of the other guests. After asking a few questions, the host remarked: 'I must have further talk with you. Come and see me tomorrow morning.' The young officer was too excited to sleep. Next day the Prince explained that, since his life was in danger, he needed an aide-de-camp who would live in the hotel, watch over his safety, and accompany him when he walked to the Chamber or rode in the Bois de Boulogne. He proceeded to arm his visitor with the pistol and leaded cane which he had been carrying. Fleury was filled with affectionate respect which growing intimacy confirmed. Convinced that his new master would shortly become President, he drew up a list of household appointments to be ready for the call.

The result of the plebiscite was a surprise to almost everyone except the Prince, Persigny and Fleury, for Cavaignac was regarded as their saviour by the bourgeoisie. Fleury joined Persigny, Mocquard, the faithful secretary, and a few other close friends at the first dinner in the Elysée, and at the reception which followed the host received his guests with the dignified simplicity of a *grand seigneur*. After enumerating the appointments to the military and civil Household, Fleury adds with legitimate pride: 'The real aide-de-camp, master of the Court and organizer of everything was myself. The Prince's gratitude was my reward.'

The President called him 'my great organizer', and charged him with running the palace and stables. It fell to him to inform Changarnier of his dismissal, and when the President finally decided to seize power it was Fleury who recommended Saint-Arnaud, under whom he had served in Algeria, as Minister of War. The importance of his role was recognized by Morny, who exclaimed: 'The *coup d'état*! Neither Saint-Arnaud nor I made it, but you, for you gave us the means.'

Fleury was present at the historic reception on the evening of 1 December 1851, and next morning at six he was summoned to the Prince, whom he found in his dressing-gown, calmly drinking his coffee. Ordered to report whether the troops were at their appointed stations, he remarked that they would have to buy food if operations were prolonged. That had not occurred to the chief conspirator, who handed him 50,000 francs. Such, declares Fleury, is the answer to the calumny that the National Bank was robbed of millions to cover expenses and reward friends. Never, he adds, had the salvation of France been achieved at so small a price. Though he received a slight wound in the head, he was in the highest spirits and noticed a look of satisfaction on all faces. 'The most absolute ruler in history', not in the least intoxicated by power, asked him to adjust the civil and military household to the new situation, nominating him First Equerry and aide-de-camp.

Since a frontal attack on the *liaison* with 'Miss Howard' would have been fruitless, Fleury urged his master to marry into some royal house. The problem was happily solved by an even prettier face.

The Prince President: Je suis bien amoureux d'elle.
Fleury: Then you must marry her.

Once again it was his duty to arrange for a Household reviving the glamour of the Bourbon kings. As First Equerry he was responsible for the organization of the visit of the Emperor and Empress to England in 1855 and the return visit of the Queen and Prince Consort—a triumph for the *régime* hitherto frowned on by the older dynasties. The birth of the Prince Imperial was a doubly happy event for Fleury, since his grateful master promoted him to the rank of General. He remained chief adviser in regard to military appointments, was employed on confidential missions to foreign courts, and, like Persigny, experimented in diplomacy as Ambassador at St. Petersburg. His Memoirs, which close in 1867, breathe a genuine devotion and disprove the legend that no man is a hero to his valet.

II. CAVAIGNAC

Cavaignac was a stop-gap between the fall of the Monarchy and the emergence of Louis Napoleon. Acclaimed as the saviour of society from the nightmare of the barricades, he seemed poised for a long term of power; but he lacked political ambition and nherited strict republican principles from his regicide father. It was part of the Prince's luck that his only serious competitor never felt at home in the political arena.

Cavaignac learned his trade in Algeria, and on the fall of the Monarchy was appointed Governor-General. His tenure was brief, for Lamartine turned to him as the only person who could save the Republic. The first offer of the War Office was declined on the ground that he needed more troops in Paris. 'As a politician, if I were condemned to become one, I would never sacrifice my convictions as a soldier in the middle of his career. I am today ignorant of the army. If its state is unsatisfactory it must be reorganized. If disgruntled it must be reassured, and, if needed, more troops must be raised. If I am to become a Minister I must know the thoughts and will of the public which must express itself.' A month later, when a republican majority resulted from a general election, he was returned simultaneously in Paris and in a rural constituency. His hour struck when the Chamber was invaded by a mob on 15 May to the ominous cry *Vive la Sociale*! At the request of Lamartine he took command of some troops of the National Guard and expelled the intruders. The same firm hand was requisitioned when the National Workshops scheme broke down and the angry workers raised barricades in the narrow streets. When the idol of the bourgeoisie was pressed to continue at the helm, he surrendered his quasi-dictatorial powers and received the thanks of the Chamber. 'I am invited to make a *coup d'état*,' he explained, 'but I never will. I don't want to set an example to others who cherish ambitions. The only legitimate sovereign is the Assembly to which I owe account of my temporary power.' Appointed Chief of the Executive Council and authorized to choose his Ministers, he piloted the Government through the summer and autumn, leaning neither to the Right nor to the Left.

Proclaiming his pride in his father, who sat in the Convention of 1792, Cavaignac uttered a warning in ringing tones. 'We are the irreconcilable foes of those who say the Republic is evil or inadequate and strive for its overthrow. In this struggle we are prepared to throw in everything—our responsibility, our tranquillity, even our honour, if the Republic ever demanded such a sacrifice. Whoever objects to it is our deadly enemy.' He wrote to Changarnier, Military Commander in Paris, in similar terms. 'The nation is irrevocably committed to the republican cause. To desire anything else is to betray its interests and its will.' These resonant declarations cooled the ardour of the Monarchists and destroyed his chance of the Presidency. When Louis Napoleon was chosen by a decisive majority, he thanked the Chamber for its confidence and handed in his resignation amid general applause. After taking the oath to the Constitution the new President paid a well-earned tribute to his competitor 'for his loyalty and sense of duty which is the first quality of a Chief of State'. When, however, he held out his hand to the General there was no response. Many years later Marshal Canrobert expressed the opinion that this demonstration of enmity between the two leading actors on the political stage was a fatal error, since the only chance for the survival of the Republic lay in their collaboration.

Retaining his seat in the Chamber, Cavaignac resisted all attempts to make him lead the opposition when the President's loyalty to the Republic became suspect. Caring nothing for party, he spoke and voted as an Independent, opposing the credit for the expedition to Rome, the restriction of the franchise, and the attempted revision of the Constitution in the interest of the President. Despite his blameless record he was arrested at the *coup d'état* and imprisoned, first in the capital and later at Ham. Released a month later, he requested to be placed on the retired list, 'the only situation compatible with my honour and my devotion to liberty'. His remaining years were spent quietly in his country home.

III. CHANGARNIER

As the star of Cavaignac paled, that of Changarnier rose high in the heavens. He had won fame in Algeria and had followed Cavaignac as Governor-General. A few weeks later and without his knowledge, he was elected for the Department of the Seine. Reaching Paris on the morrow of the barricades, he offered his services to Cavaignac and was appointed Commander both of the National Guards of the Seine and of the regular troops in the capital. When the Prince entered the Chamber he was introduced to the General with the words: 'Here, General, is our new colleague who is eager to make your acquaintance.'

Changarnier voted for Louis Napoleon in the plebiscite. When asked how to avert the restoration of the Empire he naively replied: 'Rest assured that force will back the law and that he will not try to occupy my headquarters in the Tuileries.' His suspicions, however, were aroused when the President was about to sign the decree for his appointment, and he discovered that he would be wholly subordinate to the Minister of War. A threat of resignation procured the promise of a new text, and he rode at the President's side when he migrated from his hotel to the Elysée. It was now the turn of the fiery republican Ledru-Rollin to complain that Changarnier had too much power. That the Republic was in greater danger from the President than from any General was indicated when the former remarked at a meeting of the Council that a dictatorship was required for the public safety. When it was pointed out that the first result of such a change would be general bankruptcy, the President replaced his manifesto in his pocket unread.

The General's growing stature was recognized when Thiers inquired whether he would like to be President of the Council; if so the Prince would welcome him. The offer was declined, as he had similarly declined a Field Marshal's *baton*. 'If some day', he explained, 'my conscience disapproves something, it will be easier to refuse if I owe him nothing.' He underestimated both the resourcefulness and the popularity of the President when he remarked at table one day that at his first escapade he would conduct him to Vincennes. 'If the army has to choose between myself and this adventurer and plotter not a soldier would hesitate.' How could he be so sure? He was shocked at a dinner to officers at the Elysée in August 1850 by cries of *Vive l'Empereur! Vive le Désiré! Aux Tuileries!* In November his second-in-command was removed to a post in the provinces for vetoing cries of *Vive l'Empereur!* at military reviews. He retaliated by reminding the troops that acclamations were forbidden by the regulations. He described the President as a melancholy parrot and believed himself much better qualified for the post of Chief of State.

Breaking-point came in January 1851 when a Bonapartist organ published an announcement by the General that he alone was entitled to give orders to the troops in the capital. When questioned by Prince Napoleon he rejoined that he had never denied the rights of the Chamber, and was so long and loudly applauded that the Prince's reply was inaudible. Alarmed by his popularity, Persigny hurried to the Elysée, where he found the President and Morny, who agreed that the General must go. But how would he react? When some Ministers who opposed his dismissal resigned, Persigny informed them that the President would appoint an extra-Parliamentary Ministry, with himself at the Interior, in order to dismiss him in a constitutional way. Thereupon they withdrew their resignations and consented to his eviction. The President wrote of the outcome: 'I deeply regret to announce my decision to suppress your post. My weighty motives will in no way diminish the memory of your past services. Despite our separation I shall continue to count on your collaboration if the fatherland is in danger.'

The 'weighty motives' were explained by Baroche, Minister of the Interior. Owing to the exceptional and exorbitant importance of his command he had become, without his knowledge and perhaps in spite of himself, the hope of various parties who desired neither a royalist nor a Bonaparte restoration. Baroche might have delivered his message in a single sentence: the Government was afraid of him. The General vigorously defended himself in the Chamber.

> I had no wish to serve or to be an instrument of any party. Like all honest men I merely desired the execution of the laws, the preservation of order, and the security of the whole country, and I am proud to have contributed to provide these benefits. Despite envious

insinuations dictated by ingratitude I have joined no faction, no conspiracy. My sword is condemned to a temporary rest but it is not broken. If ever needed it will obey the inspiration of a patriotic heart and a resolute mind.

He was followed by Thiers who denounced the President for disuniting the moderates. The dismissal of the popular and respected soldier was generally interpreted as a prelude to a *coup d'état*, and Thiers exclaimed prophetically: *l'Émpire est fait*.

At the eleventh hour Persigny, with the approval of his master, made a final attempt to win the General. The triumph of the President, argued the *loyal serviteur*, was assured. If necessary he could dispense with the approval of the Chamber, but he would prefer to keep within the law. People would therefore be grateful if the General would go to the tribune and advise his friends to allow the President to be elected for a second consecutive term. The appeal was ignored, and with this refusal the last hope of averting a *coup d'état* disappeared.

Though Changarnier was warned at the end of November 1851, he refused to fly. After spending the evening of 1 December at the theatre, and assuring his friends that nothing would happen before the New Year, he returned home and was awakened early next morning by the invasion of his bedroom. Springing up he pointed his loaded pistol at the head of the Police Commissioner in command of the little force. 'General,' cried the latter, 'you do not recognize me. Why should you kill the father of a family?' 'If there were only four of you', was the reply, 'you would all be dead.' He was carted off to prison, where he found Cavaignac and other friends, thence to Ham. When released, he settled in Belgium, where he received messages of sympathy from the Comte de Chambord, Queen Amelia, the Duc d'Aumale and other royalists. Indignantly declining the oath of allegiance demanded from officers on active service, and convinced that the new *régime* would be short-lived, he strove for the union of the rival branches of the Royal Family. The rejection of his appeal to serve in the Crimean War was a bitter blow.

Changarnier returned to France when an unconditional amnesty was proclaimed in 1859, but he was never employed again. Early in 1870 the Emperor offered him a Marshal's *bâton*, adding, 'I desire to link your great name with my reign.' Fearing that acceptance might be interpreted as adhesion to the *régime*, he declined. Six months later it was the ruler's turn to reject a request for a command. Despite the rebuff, the old soldier travelled to Metz and sent in his name. The Emperor immediately appeared, shook hands, adding: 'All the commands are allotted, but we shall be happy, my dear General, to have your advice. I am touched by your devotion. Where do you come from?' When the visitor had told his story the Emperor exclaimed: 'From you that does not surprise me. But you must be hungry and tired.' He was invited to stay for lunch and next day accompanied the ailing ruler to the front. Everywhere he was acclaimed, and Plètri, the Emperor's secretary, exclaimed: 'You restore us all to life.' The vendetta of twenty years was over, but a few days later the Empire ceased to exist. It was Changarnier's fate to witness both its stormy birth and its tragic end.

IV. LAMORICIÈRE

Though less of a potential menace than Changarnier, Lamoricière's hostility was unconcealed. It could not last, he declared to Nassau Senior four months after the *coup*.

> *Lamoricière:* In France nothing lasts. I will not insult my countrymen by supposing that it will attain the average duration of a French usurpation. But I am alarmed about its successor. A constitutional monarchy, I fear, is too good for us, a despotism too bad.
>
> *Nassau Senior:* Thiers thinks that if he is overthrown by the upper classes there will be a restoration, if by the lower a republic.
>
> *Lamoricière:* The upper classes are too timid and disunited. The *noblesse* will do nothing and can do nothing; they have neither talents nor knowledge nor courage. Nor will the peasants, for our revolutions pass over them almost without their noticing.
>
> *Nassau Senior:* Will the army dethrone him?
>
> *Lamoricière:* No, it is too disunited.
>
> *Nassau Senior:* The *coup d'état* was a civil conspiracy, employing a fraction of the army as its instrument. Do you look to the bourgeoisie?
>
> *Lamoricière:* Not for action. They will talk and write against him, undermine his influence, expose his character, ridicule his person, and gradually make him hateful and despicable to the mass of the people. Then, like Charles X and Louis Philippe, he will be

overthrown in a day. The army will be neutral, neither attacking nor defending him, and will let the mob destroy him.
Nassau Senior: You mean the people of the towns?
Lamoricière: I mean the manual workers of Paris, Rouen, Lyons, Bordeaux and Marseilles.

The General underestimated the strength of the *régime*, which was soon to be reinforced by victories on the battlefield and the birth of an heir. A few years later he found a temporary outlet for his energies in the command of the little army of Pio Nono, which removed him from the unsympathetic atmosphere of the capital and the Court.

V. SAINT-ARNAUD

If Morny was the brain of the *coup d'état*, Saint-Arnaud was the strong right arm. Like a dozen other soldiers he had made his name in Algeria and felt no desire to terminate his military career. With the fall of the Monarchy, however, successful Generals found themselves in demand from one or other of the factions competing for power. Watching from afar the rivalry between the President and Changarnier, he was impressed by the skill and stature of the Prince, whom he had never seen. 'There is a man,' he exclaimed in November 1850, on reading a well-phrased Presidential message.

> You are making *coups d'état* in Paris [he wrote in January 1851]. You sack Changarnier, the most rancorous of scoundrels. He will seek his revenge. The President's entourage gives him bad advice, and his pose as the strong man has increased his difficulties. All this mess would be funny if it did not presage a very near future much less amusing.

Rumours that he was about to be recalled filled Saint-Arnaud with alarm. 'Never could I have a command more congenial, more important, more interesting than mine,' he confided to his brother. 'I would gladly pay to have two more years and two more stars.' He had prepared an expedition which was certain to succeed and would earn him a fine military reputation outside politics.

I am not worn out like several of my colleagues in Africa. That is how I feel, but fate will decide. I am a soldier and must fulfil my destiny. If I am summoned to Paris I will tell the Prince that I am first and foremost a soldier and have no wish to be a politician except on my own terms. So no Empire, no *coup d'état*, the constitution, obedience to the laws at home, wholehearted devotion to France abroad. That is my programme. If it is rejected I shall walk out with a pension.

In March 1851 Fleury wrote to say that the Prince held him in high esteem, and that he could retain his post till he was promoted General of Division. When a friend remarked that he was useful in Algeria the President replied: 'Yes, but he will be equally useful in France where the situation is tense. I must have him.' On receiving this news Saint-Arnaud resigned himself but continued to hold his head high. 'I will not be anyone's man, and I shall be guided by duty, heart and conscience.' His eagerly awaited nomination was announced in a gracious autograph letter from the President, dated 30 June 1851, the first he had received. 'Now my reputation is established,' was his comment, 'and they will have to reckon with me.' A month later he quitted Africa for ever.

They want to turn me into a politician [he wrote to his old friend the Duc d'Aumale], and the President wants me in Paris with a command. I obey because there is danger there, but with regret. I have grown up in Africa and I shall never love the Republic; but I will shed my blood to prevent France becoming a prey of the horrible *canaille* which seeks to devour her. Honest men must combine to save society.

The first interview with the President confirmed Fleury's report that the General was a man of energy who might be useful in the *coup d'état* provisionally fixed for 17 September. There was a conspiracy to imprison him, explained the ruler, and now that the Chamber was in recess it was the moment to act. On thinking over what he had learned, Saint-Arnaud wrote to inform the President that he could not count on him. If, however, as he advised, the *coup* was postponed till the Chamber was in session he would be ready to close its doors. The whole army would obey his orders, he assured Persigny, and would follow the lead of the capital. 'Tell the President I am quite ready to come to the

Elysée to convince him.' A friendly interview ensued and he was promised the Ministry of War. To his brother he confessed that he would rather die a thousand deaths than submit to the disgrace of being ruled by the *canaille*. General Lamoricière had said to a friend: 'When you see Saint-Arnaud at the Ministry of War, it means the *coup d'état*.' At the end of October the appointment was announced and the *coup* was fixed for 2 December. Among his qualifications was a capacity to lie without blushing. A few days before the *coup*, when all preparations had been made, he informed a Committee of the Chamber that he would die to defend the Constitution, baring his breast as he spoke.

'This is a solemn moment,' wrote the Minister of War to his mother in the early hours of 2 December. 'In two hours we shall take part in a revolution which, I hope, will save the country. This Chamber, crazy, blind and factious, will be dissolved, and an appeal to the people will decide the fate of a nation wearied by uncertainty and anxiety. We shall have a stable government and I am confident all will go well.' The dissolution of the Chamber and the arrest of military and political notables took place without resistance; but on the following day there were signs of trouble, and the Minister threatened drastic reprisals.

> Citizens of Paris: The enemies of order and society have started the conflict. They are out for pillage and destruction. Remain calm. Loitering in the streets impedes the movements of the brave soldiers, your protectors. Anyone found at a gathering to organize resistance will be regarded as an accomplice and court-martialled. Anyone caught constructing or defending a barricade will be shot.

The threat of death was inserted by Morny, Minister of the Interior, in the belief that it was the quickest method of ending resistance. After the bloodshed of 4 December the Minister of War congratulated his troops. 'Soldiers: You have saved the country from anarchy and pillage and saved the Republic. You have proved, as always, brave, devoted, indefatigable. France admires and thanks you. The President will never forget your devotion.'

Far from saving the Republic the army had destroyed it. A month later the Orleans decrees led Saint-Arnaud, an intimate friend of the Duc d'Aumale, to offer his resignation. 'My dear

General,' replied the President, 'I appreciate the delicacy of your feelings, but I cannot accept it. Firstly because I cannot deprive myself of your services, for I am tenderly attached to you. Secondly because the national interest, the overriding factor, is against it. *Restez donc pour la France et pour moi. Votre ami,* Louis Napoleon.' The General withdrew his resignation and accompanied the Dictator on his triumphant tours in the provinces, receiving a Marshal's *bâton* and a seat in the Senate on the proclamation of the Empire, simultaneously with Castellane and Magnan. His gratitude increased when the kindly ruler provided a dowry for his daughter. 'What a heart! He is more than an Emperor, he is a man. He is more than a man, he is a friend.' Further laurels were added by the cordon of Grand Officer of the Legion of Honour, and he received the highest distinction attainable by an officer on his selection as Supreme Commander of the French forces in the Crimean War. He had little time to wear his laurels, for cholera carried him off in September 1854. 'No one can share your grief more than myself,' wrote the Emperor to his widow. 'He has associated his name with the military glories of France when, with Lord Raglan, he won the battle of the Alma and opened the way to Sebastopol. I have lost a tried friend, and France has lost a soldier ever ready to serve in the hour of danger.' Having helped to make history he received a public funeral and found his resting place in the crypt of the Invalides.

VI. RANDON

If Marshal Randon had possessed a more flexible conscience his name would be as familiar as that of Saint-Arnaud, for he was cast for the leading role in the *coup d'état*. He had fought at Borodino and Leipzig, and throughout life regarded himself as the servant not of any party but of France. He had shown his mettle when as a young officer he witnessed the return from Elba and was one of the little group which marched away rather than violate their allegiance to Louis XVIII.

Learning his trade in Algeria, he earned a reputation for efficiency and reliability which caused the President in 1849 to appoint him to the command of the Third Division at Metz.

His refusal to lead the expedition to Rome on the ground that he was a Protestant was followed by the rejection of the Embassy in Vienna on the plea that he lacked diplomatic training. These manifestations of independence enhanced the regard of the President who, in the course of a provincial tour in 1850, visited Metz and made the Commander Grand Officer of the Legion of Honour. At the close of the year a fresh reason emerged for desiring the aid of a senior officer, in the eviction of Changarnier. Though the Ministry of War was a glittering prize, he refused to act against a fellow officer. When Changarnier was gone the President renewed his offer. 'I hope you will reconsider your decision, which I should greatly regret and which would impede the formation of the Cabinet. Today we are on the brink, and at such a moment a brave officer should not withhold his services.' Though 'on the brink' sounded rather mysterious, he could no longer refuse, convinced as he was that a strong government was more essential than respect for the Constitution.

Though the Prince prided himself on his knowledge of mankind, he had not taken the measure of his Minister of War, who records in his Memoirs the soundings by Morny and Persigny and finally by the Emperor himself. France, argued the latter, could not forever be plagued by agitation, and it was the duty of every citizen to rescue her from a situation endangering social order and damaging to her standing in the world. His rejection of the appeal is described in his Memoirs: 'Was there no other way of averting the danger? Why not await a favourable moment when the Chamber, opposing the opinion of the Conseils Généraux, unleashed a conflict in which the President would be defending the Government in the name of the law? With Paris and the Departments tranquil, how could a *coup d'état* be justified?' 'As the head of the army responsible for discipline,' he explained to the President, 'I should find it difficult to address the troops, and I could not support any act seducing them from their duty to support the law of the land.' If the decision to stage a *coup* was irrevocable he must resign. He received a friendly letter from the President. 'I need not tell you that I regret the separation from one who has given me so many proofs of his devotion, and rendered real services to his country by his skilful administration of the Ministry of War. You can rely on my high esteem and friendship. I shall expect you tomorrow at Saint-Cloud.' The *solatium* of the Governorship of Algeria was declined. Unaware of the date fixed for the *coup*, he only learned of it, like everyone else, on the morning of 2 December. A few days later the offer of the highest post in Algeria was renewed and accepted.

After six rewarding years in his new sphere, Randon was shocked by the appointment of Prince Napoleon to the newly created office of Minister of Algeria and the Colonies, and promptly tendered his resignation. 'My dear Marshal,' replied the Emperor, 'you have rendered signal services to Algeria, and I should be grieved if the new Ministry seemed to belittle them.' The experiment only lasted a year, after which the Emperor was begged to reinstate the popular Governor. 'No,' he replied, 'I have other plans for him.' His meaning soon became clear with the campaign in Italy and the expeditions to China, Syria and Mexico. The Minister of War worked in harmony with the Emperor through the testing years, but after the Sadowa fiasco in 1866 he was dismissed. 'My dear Marshal,' wrote the ruler, 'I have decided to replace you by Marshal Niel. I regret to terminate your services. My main reason is to spare you the trying debates in the Chamber. I have nothing but praise for your zeal and devotion during eight years. I hope our relations will not change, for I shall always be happy to give you new proofs of my friendship.' The desire to spare the septuagenarian Marshal a fatiguing task was a transparent pretext: the real reason was that France was smarting under the humiliation of 1866, which was widely attributed to the unpreparedness of the military machine. The injustice was deeply resented. When he asked the Government to defend him against his calumniators the Emperor merely expressed his sympathy and ordered the publication of his apologia in the *Moniteur*.

On the outbreak of war the Emperor invited his old servant to return to Algeria. 'You alone, my dear Marshal,' he declared in an interview in the Tuileries, 'can hold it while the troops are transferred to Europe. Old settlers and the Arabs alike know you and respect you and will not make trouble.' The offer was accepted with an expression of regret that he was too old to go to the front. Taking his hands, the harassed ruler exclaimed: 'I, too, my dear Marshal, am rather old for waging war and I am far from well.' His sorrowful expression and air of being weighed down by anxiety made a profound impression on the visitor. Delay in receiving the official notification of the appointment was interpreted as a sign of ministerial hostility and determined him to withdraw his acceptance. A pressing letter from the ruler failed to move him, for his health at the age of seventy-five was rapidly failing. He lived just long enough to witness the disasters of Sedan and Metz and the invasion of France.

VII. CANROBERT

Canrobert made his name in Algeria and took little interest in domestic politics. Returning to France on the fall of the Monarchy, he voted for Cavaignac in the plebiscite. On his defeat he asked to be presented to the victor, whom he found walking in the garden of the Elysée.

> Small in stature, his eyes were dull but very gentle. While fixing them on me they seemed to be looking far away. His long dark oiled hair fell over his ears and neck. His thick moustache covered the lower lip. His handshake resembled that of a paralytic. After some commonplace remarks in an Alsatian accent I withdrew. He struck me as very timid and embarrassed by the presence of a stranger. Beneath this apparent *gaucherie* he concealed a will of iron.

That his initial judgment was shared by Changarnier he discovered on being invited to the Tuileries, the headquarters of the Paris command. He heard an aide-de-camp declare that the General (Changarnier) would only have to lift his finger to send the President to Vincennes. His surprise became stupefaction when at table the host and his guests, among them several generals and colonels, oblivious of the presence of the waiters, boasted that he could be swallowed in a single mouthful. That such wild talk would reach the ears of the President had no terrors for his short-sighted critics, who felt sure of their superior strength.

Canrobert knew nothing of the coming *coup d'état*. At six in the morning Edgar Ney, son of the famous Marshal, knocked at his door and found him up.

Ney: You are not at the head of your troops?
Canrobert: Why should I be at such an early hour?
Ney: So you don't know what is happening? The *coup d'état*! You must take command of your troops.
Canrobert: Any order must come from the commander of the Paris troops. When he sends me his instructions I will obey.

At that moment a written order arrived to take command of his brigade and occupy the Madeleine. Writing in old age he explains that it was impossible to disobey, even for those who, like himself, would have preferred to stand aloof. The *coup*, he adds, was popular with the army and the people, for the Chamber had few friends. Not a shot was fired till the second day after the *coup*, when the General found himself in the thick of the fight and narrowly escaped death when a bullet fired from a window in a narrow street led inexperienced troops to panic. Riding from company to company he shouted his orders to cease fire. He was shocked by the arrest of Cavaignac and Lamoricière, who had given no offence. There were rumours of his arrest, and his letters were opened in the post. His apprehensions were groundless, for he was soon promoted to the rank of General of Division.

The more Canrobert saw of the Dictator the more he liked him:

> He was kindly and gentle to humble folk [he wrote after the Empire had disappeared], sympathized with misery, and tried by every possible means to lessen it. This sentiment coloured his whole life and is a key to many of his ideas. Never intoxicated by his elevation, he always remained easy of approach, and was never arrogant, bitter, vindictive, or ill-tempered. The only time I saw him angry was on one occasion during the Italian campaign. Affectionate by nature, he was not merely the most devoted of sons but the most tender of companions. 'How I regret,' he used to say, 'that my mother did not live to see me sovereign of France. God knows how she and I have suffered ever since my infancy. I always believed I should become Emperor of the French, improbable as it seemed.' He loved to do good. A journalist said of him that he hated the tyrant but loved the man. He forgave injuries and gratefully rewarded all services. Misfortunes, injustice, calumny, never upset him. He never put the blame for his own mistakes on other shoulders. In danger he was perfectly calm. He cared nothing for money and had no love of war. He sympathized with oppressed nationalities and wished them liberated without bloodshed. His ideal was William of Orange,

not Napoleon. I often disapproved his policy, but he was always so good to me, in such a touching and natural way, that I shall never forget it.

Canrobert's affection was reciprocated, his services in the Crimea being rewarded by a Marshal's *bâton* and a seat in the Senate. Henceforth he ranked among the pillars of the Empire and earned fresh laurels in the Italian war. Invited to take Morny's place in the Privy Council in 1865, he declined on the ground that he was a soldier and wanted nothing more. The reply annoyed the Emperor, who suspected some hidden motive and ceased to discuss his plans with him. The decline of the ruler's health now became sadly visible. 'He had no longer any will and could not stand up to pressing demands. More and more a fatalist, he let things slide. His kindliness also increased, and people got what they asked from him under the cloak of philanthropy. He was shattered by the uncompensated victory of Prussia in 1866 and by the sudden realization that the next victim might be France.' Though the ruler realized his neighbour's strength better than his Ministers, and found a zealous ally in Italy, the Parliamentary Opposition prevented adequate preparation for the worst. In 1869 he was in such agony that he cried aloud and it was thought that the end was near. On a visit to Saint-Cloud the Marshal found everyone in consternation. As he was leaving, two members of the staff wearing the Crimean medal accosted him with the words: 'We shall keep him, shan't we? He is so good to us. We all love him.' The General's last service was his command at Gravelotte, and his career ended with Bazaine's surrender of Metz.

VIII. CASTELLANE

Since Castellane, like Canrobert, cherished no political ambitions, his relations with the Emperor were uniformly friendly. He had reached the status of General of Brigade in his sixtieth year when the Monarchy collapsed and, like many other senior officers, was placed on the retired list. His Indian Summer was still to come. Smarting under his dismissal, he begged the newly-installed President to reinstate him. The Prince was sympathetic, but explained that nothing could be done at the moment since he was merely a figure-head. That was an understatement, for in the summer of 1849 he and several other elderly officers who applied were recalled. He visited the Elysée to express his gratitude, and the friendly reception ripened into affection. He seized the opportunity to urge the appointment of a competent Minister of War. 'He listened most attentively. His brief replies were sensible and those of an honest man. I was very pleased with him.' He promised to find work for his visitor, who was soon appointed to a provincial command.

Within a few months of the plebiscite which carried the Prince into the Elysée, Castellane began to hear talk of 'the Emperor', and in October 1849 he heard Persigny say that it was the only salvation. Changarnier believed he could avert it, but the President struck first.

> General Castellane [he remarked to an officer] will have been distressed by what I have to do to his friend General Changarnier; but he is too much of a soldier not to understand that the laws of hierarchy cannot be violated with impunity. He wanted me to be a mere figure-head, and I declined. I am loyal in my promises. Tell your General that his loyal collaboration touches me deeply and that I will gladly do my best for him to prove it.

Changarnier, declares Castellane, had hoped to succeed the Prince in the Presidency when his four-year term expired. The vacant post was offered to Castellane, who declined on the excuse that he was more useful in Lyons, the real reason being his instinct to play for safety. Though at the moment he was a *persona grata* at the Elysée, he explains, he would probably have aroused jealousy or suspicion and might have found himself in the wilderness within three months. Two interviews with the President failed to move him, but they parted good friends. He was one of the first to be nominated a Senator and to receive a Marshal's *bâton*. He accepted the *coup*, was chosen to sign the register at the Emperor's wedding, and was occasionally summoned to the Tuileries and Saint-Cloud to advise on military administration and appointments. The exceptional favour he enjoyed seemed to him at times something of a liability. 'It has the immense disadvantage of arousing envy,' he wrote in 1854, 'fortunately tempered by my absences.'

Too old for active service in the Crimea, Castellane strove to dissuade the Emperor from leaving Paris.

> *The Emperor:* I am thinking of visiting the Crimea because it is believed we can destroy the Russian army. With the 15,000 Piedmontese, the English and the Turks, there will be over 150,000 men. The Russian army once annihilated, I shall embark with the army, leaving the Turks in control.
> *Castellane:* There might be a reverse, and think what that would mean to the sovereign. I understand Your Majesty's wish, but I would prefer to see you commanding on the Rhine.
> *The Emperor:* So would I.
> *Castellane:* Your project is causing the greatest disquietude. The other day I asked a sub-Prefect about the reaction to the news. He replied that everyone said: What a misfortune!

Leaving the Emperor with the impression that the plan was postponed, if not abandoned, the Marshal was warmly thanked by the Foreign Minister for his opposition to 'that fatal plan', and by the Minister of the Interior, who declared that the Ministers were unanimous.

The Emperor never resented criticism and Castellane continued to speak with the frankness of a trusted friend. On a visit in 1861 he was greeted with the usual inquiry as to how things were going in Lyons.

> *Castellane:* Your Majesty wishes to know the truth. Well, there is disquiet. France takes little interest in Italy, and Your Majesty is too good-natured. You are continually giving money to people who feel no gratitude and would never be found at your side in time of need.

The old warrior saw the Emperor for the last time in the summer of 1862 during a visit to Auvergne and died in the autumn.

15

THE CHURCH

AMONG the maxims bequeathed by Napoleon and treasured by his nephew was the necessity of friendly relations with the Church. The Concordat, which restored the traditional religion, and the Organic Articles, which the Vatican never recognized, impressed him as a model of constructive statesmanship. Believing in nothing except their star, both rulers would have agreed with Voltaire: *Notre crédulité fait toute leur science*, and with Gibbon's description of the cults of the Roman Empire: 'to the believer all equally true, to the philosopher all equally false, to the magistrate all equally useful'. Political adventurers need as much support as they can get wherever it may be found.

At the Restoration the relations between Church and State became warmer. Though Louis XVIII was an eighteenth-century sceptic, he was surrounded by clericals with his brother Charles at their head, determined to revive as much as possible of the institutions and the spirit of the *ancien régime*. When the latter ascended the throne as Charles X in 1824 he threw caution to the winds. Burning with anger at its persecution during the Revolution, the Church grew increasingly ultramontane, with Joseph de Maistre as its spokesman and the Jesuits flocking back after an absence of fifty years. Yet sufficient elements of Gallicanism and undimmed memories of the ideas of 1789 survived to challenge the slogan of Throne and Altar. No one understood better than Louis Philippe, the most prosaic of rulers, that what little was left of the *mystique* of monarchy perished in the revolution of 1830. While Ozanam was founding the Society of St. Vincent de Paul, and Dom Guéranger was reviving the Benedictine Order at the Abbey of Solesmes, Saint-Simon and Proudhon, Comte and

Marx attracted large numbers to their secular ideologies, Michelet and Quinet thundered against the Jesuits as the enemies of liberty, and the Freemasons, unlike their English comrades, became increasingly anti-clerical. The rapid development of industry and the consequential drift to the towns accelerated the secularization of thought.

The status of the Church improved under the Second Republic with the Falloux Law and the recovery of Rome for the Pope by French arms. It improved still further under the Second Empire; indeed, except for the brief intermezzo of Charles X, it had never enjoyed such consideration since 1789. The hierarchy and the village *curé*, though mainly royalist in sympathies, stood firmly behind the Dictator, who was acclaimed as a new Constantine, a new Charlemagne, a new St. Louis. His desire to be crowned by the Pope was frustrated by the latter's demand for the abolition of the hated Organic Articles. The new master seized every opportunity of demonstrating his respect for the Church, supporting its charities and missions, restoring its edifices, and allocating part of the Orleans millions to pensions for aged and infirm priests. On a visit to Bayonne on the outbreak of the Crimean War he declared: 'It is the duty of the sovereign to approach the altar in order to ask heaven through the intercession of its consecrated ministers to bless his efforts, to enlighten his conscience, to give him strength to do good and combat evil. I thank you, Monseigneur, for the wishes you have addressed to heaven for me, and I beg you also to ask protection for our armies, to pray for those who fight as well as for those who suffer.' When the bishops piled incense on the altar of 'the Christian Prince', the chosen instrument of God, the Emperor told Persigny that their flattery disgusted him but was none the less useful. Neither clerical like the Empress nor anti-clerical like Prince Napoleon, he invariably paid outward respect to beliefs which he did not hold, and wished, like Frederick the Great, that 'everyone should find his own way to heaven'. The honeymoon was brief, for 'the new St. Louis' became Judas when his support of Italian nationalism threatened the territorial possessions of the Pope.

1. FALLOUX

Comte de Falloux, one of the noblest spirits of the age, was one of the few Legitimists who took an active part in political life. Entering the Chamber in 1846, he welcomed the eviction of Louis Philippe, whom his party had never forgiven for 'usurping' the throne. Regarding the Second Republic as a mere intermezzo, he resolved to make the best of it and was offered the Ministry of Education and Cults which he declined on the ground of health. That was a pretext, as he explained to his closest friend Montalembert.

> If I could hope to serve the cause of religion, I would not hesitate to sacrifice my feeling, but do the Bonaparte tradition, the education of Prince Louis and his Italian record justify such hopes? To collaborate with him is to enter on a slippery slope. If, as I believe, France has made the wrong choice, give her time to discover her mistake. Let us remain the servants of order, servants of society, without forfeiting our right to tell the country the truth. To lend weight to our words, let us preserve our best qualification, that of disinterestedness.

Pressure from Dupanloup was required to overcome his resistance. 'You are going to throw Italy into convulsions, abandon the Pope to his worst enemies, plunge France back into anarchy and compromise the Conservatives.' Falloux, now more than half converted, demanded guarantees from Thiers, the unofficial commander of the Royalist force.

> *Falloux:* I accept if you will vote for the liberty of teaching.
> *Thiers:* I promise. I share your convictions. We have been on the wrong track, my friends and I, in the field of religion. Now let me hasten to Prince Louis.

His acceptance was welcomed by Lacordaire, who saluted him as the first Catholic Minister since 1789, by which he meant the first Minister who put the interests of the Church before everything else. Very different was the verdict of the intransigent Veuillot. 'I have never counted on him. Though a fervent Christian, he was never one of ours, never what we call a Catholic *avant tout*, though perhaps he thinks he is. I urged him not to accept office, though I dared not tell him my reason, namely that he would leave our ideas outside the door. I was not mistaken. He is a man of compromise with much more ambition than is generally believed.' Veuillot was hard to please, and what he approved displeased most of his countrymen.

During his brief tenure of the Ministry of Education and Cults Falloux piloted through the Chamber the law which bears his name and registers the high-water mark of clerical influence in the schools. His task was facilitated by the haunting memories of the barricades in 1848 and the resultant craving for order. Victor Cousin, the fashionable philosopher of the time, though himself a freethinker, meeting a friend on the fall of the Monarchy, exclaimed: 'We must throw ourselves at the feet of the bishops; they alone can save us.' 'You go to mass,' commented Mérimée, 'but you are a hypocrite, for you no more believe in it than myself.' It was the beliefs of his domestics, rejoined the Professor, which made them serve him with honesty and devotion. Demagogy was the enemy, echoed Thiers to another *esprit fort*, and the clergy should help in the struggle. Every well-to-do bourgeois, scoffed a Catholic *croyant*, wanted everyone except himself to go to mass. Had not Voltaire, himself a wealthy bourgeois, desired his lawyer, his tailor, and his valet, to believe in God in order to lessen the danger that he might be robbed and his wife take a lover? Falloux, universally respected and conciliatory by temperament, displayed a Parliamentary skill recognized by friend and foe. 'If you have not seen him at the Conference table,' testified his ministerial colleague, Tocqueville, 'you do not know the power of his personality.' Ollivier in old age described him as the nearest approach to a statesman he had known. Success, however, would have been impossible without the aid of Thiers and the royalists. Primary schools were to be inspected by the village *curé*, while the state monopoly of secondary education was ended by permitting members of Religious Orders to establish private schools and to become teachers without a university degree. Four archbishops were placed on the governing body of the University of Paris, priests on the Academic Councils in the provinces, and religious instruction became compulsory for boarders in secondary schools. When chronic ill-health closed his political career, Falloux lived in the hope of a Bourbon restoration.

'France', he declared, 'is vigorous enough to recover but sick enough to need to be saved; so she should hurry up and unite the two royalist camps.'

When the expected blow fell on 2 December 1851, Falloux was arrested in the Chamber, where members of the Opposition had gathered as the news spread through the capital. His first visitor was an old friend from the other camp.

> *Persigny:* Will you ever forgive me for not warning you?
> *Falloux:* I should not forgive you if you had. Would it have changed my duty?
> *Persigny:* I have felt greatly upset about you.
> *Falloux:* You are returning my visit to you in the Luxembourg.
> *Persigny:* I tried to put you on the list to be released directly the little riots are repressed. Morny backed my appeal and the President consented, but the Prefect of Police argued that for the last month you had been among the most active in opposition.
> *Falloux:* That does me honour. Don't worry about my health. Let us remain friends. Try to give your Prince good advice, which he sorely needs.

The two men, each unswervingly loyal to his cause, respected each other and embraced as they parted.

When they met again three weeks later Persigny, now Minister of the Interior, sought an interview.

> *Persigny:* I can't bear the life I am leading. Even my strictest orders fail to exclude the swarm of petitioners. Just now there were seven or eight who had pestered me with letters. I came out with a pistol in each hand exclaiming: 'Be gone or I'll fire.' I have never asked anything of the President and I never will. Let others follow my example. I am ashamed to think I am on the stage and you are in the audience. But that is your choice, so tell us frankly what you think of us.
> *Falloux:* I don't attach much significance to the curtain-raiser; *I* await the main performance.
> *Persigny:* Yes, the Empire. I'll tell you the simple truth. What is holding it up? Himself alone. A fit of modesty made him dizzy after the *coup*. He takes his proclamation of a ten-years' Presidency seriously; not that he thinks of waiting all that time, but he feels it is too early to move. All his entourage tell him the contrary. Morny and I, who rarely agree, are at one about this, on the ground that the Empire is the natural consequence of the plebis-

cite. We have not convinced him, but we shall keep at it. But I need another six weeks at the Minister of the Interior.
Falloux: What could destroy your credit with the Prince?
Persigny: Our temperaments. I am headstrong and uncompromising. I go to him resolved to control myself, but in a few minutes I break out, and five times out of six I leave the Council at odds with everyone, to Morny's delight. I am the better politician, but he is cleverer at the game. The President will keep me to make the Empire and then pack me off. No matter so long as he remains faithful to Napoleonic traditions in home affairs. To avoid disaster he must avoid war and have heirs.

Falloux abstained in the plebiscite following the *coup d'état* which closed his political career. Abstentionism was the *mot d'ordre* of his master the Comte de Chambord, but his decision to withdraw was due to conscience alone. The monarchists had the opportunity of reorganizing their forces, but it had been ruined.

> I had also learned [he records in his Memoirs] that the republican blend of violence and incompetence could only lead France to bloody anarchy; there was not a serious or beneficent reform in their programme, and they find no use for true liberty. Thus I could not be surprised that the country permitted an audacious adventure which appeared to promise order. I decided neither to applaud nor to oppose. I was equally resolved not to harbour bitterness which would identify me with the demagogues.

Disapproving alike Republicans and Bonapartists, the austere Legitimist was almost the loneliest man in France.

When Falloux, as 'Directeur of the Academy', in accordance with precedent informed the Emperor in 1860 of the election of Lacordaire a quick exchange of reproaches took place.

Falloux: I come to announce and present for sanction the election of Père Lacordaire in succession to M. de Tocqueville.
Emperor: I sanction it with pleasure, but I find it rather strange and not calculated to afford me satisfaction.
Falloux: I see no cause for surprise. The Academy chooses men of talent and character, and the election has been ratified by all sound sections of opinion.
Emperor: I recognize his talent and say nothing against him. But I am sensitive to the attacks on me from every quarter, including your friends and the clergy.

Falloux: The Emperor himself raised these questions.

Emperor: I accept discussion, but I never expected such violent attacks.

Falloux: The Emperor confuses passion and conscience. The former almost always gives way; conscience never.

Emperor: You cannot deny that the parties are trying to exploit the present situation.

Falloux: They should not have been given the pretext.

Emperor: The clergy have had no cause to complain of me and are showing themselves ungrateful.

Falloux: The clergy have shown deference to the Empire, sometimes almost adulation.

Emperor: Allowance should be made for my difficulties. I am attacked for everything, as if I did just what I liked amidst such complications.

Falloux: Naturally everything is attributed to the Emperor.

Emperor: You are free, I am not. The Pope is unreasonable and has refused me the simplest things.

Falloux: He accepted all plans of reform. It is the French Ambassador who refused guarantees of neutrality and territorial integrity.

Emperor: I have always been attached to the cause of Italy and I cannot turn my guns against her. I could propose exchanges, for the Pope cannot retain his territories intact; such matters are arranged at a Congress.

Falloux: The only practicable solution is to retrace your steps on a road full of peril for yourself and France. Let us hope there will be no persecutions of the Church.

Emperor: Not during my reign. You know my sentiments for Pius IX. They are unchanged.

Falloux: No single will can guarantee it. The future of your son is at the mercy of the party of revolution.

Emperor: I realize the danger.

Falloux: This is a struggle not with parties but with consciences, which are invincible.

Emperor: I have been glad to see you and hear your views.

The Dictator shook hands with affection and sadness, and the main impression left on Falloux by the talk was one of melancholy. When asked about the interview he replied that they had to deal with Orsini as much as with the Emperor. The conversation was reported to the Pope, who agreed that the ruler's course was partly determined by fear of the dagger. Falloux's later years brought him little joy. The Empire fell as he had foretold and the intransigence of his revered master 'Henry V' barred his return to the throne of his ancestors. Though he had never loved the Empire it had provided far more of what he regarded as essential to the moral and spiritual welfare of France than the Third Republic with Gambetta's war-cry that clericalism was the enemy.

II. MONTALEMBERT

When Falloux left the political arena Montalembert succeeded him as the principal spokesman of the Church. His *émigré* father had fought against the Revolution under Condé and later in the English army, receiving a peerage after the Restoration. Born in England in 1810, his son Charles married an Englishwoman and found much to admire in the England of the Reform Bill. Unlike the older nobility he preferred the *juste milieu* of Louis Philippe to the intransigence of Charles X, though he deplored the chilly Gallicanism of the Tuileries.

The early life of Montalembert was dominated by Lamennais, the most dynamic figure in the French Church after the death of Joseph de Maistre. Starting as a Legitimist and Ultramontane, the temperamental Breton Abbé swung over from Right to Left, avowed himself a republican, and called for a new spirit in Church and State. People, he declared, were afraid of liberalism: Catholicize it and society would be reborn. The Church must accept contemporary society, for which tradition and authority had largely ceased to count. Of course the Church was unpopular, for it was identified with autocracy and the *ancien régime*, and in some cities priests could not walk the streets in their cassocks. The gulf between the priest and the citizen would not be bridged till the Church depended on the people, not on the throne.

The movement required an organ, and in 1830 *L'Avenir* was launched with 'God and Liberty' as its watchword. 'Unite them, and all the vital and permanent needs of human nature will be satisfied.' Two of the finest spirits of the younger generation, Lacordaire and Montalembert, responded to the call, and flung themselves into the fray. Ignoring the sound maxim *Le mieux est l'ennemi du bien*, they demanded the separation of Church and State, forfeiting the salary which in their view turned the priest into an official; henceforth they must be prepared for voluntary poverty. Lacordaire even went so far as to propose that they should leave the cathedrals and carry the altars into the barns. Down with the Concordat! Liberty of teaching! Liberty for the Religious Orders! Break the chains! Give the Church her chance! Aflame with enthusiasm, the two young apostles set forth for Rome to crave the blessing of the Pope. They were too sanguine, for Liberal Catholicism has never appealed to the Vatican, and in this case their programme was for something like a revolution. When two Encyclicals frowned on the movement, *L'Avenir* ceased to appear, the young zealots reluctantly obeyed, and Lamennais, who declined to surrender, passed out of their lives. For the rest of his days the old crusader, denounced as 'Robespierre in a surplice', turned his back on the Church and sought salvation in the people. Two years later his little book *Paroles d'un Croyant* found readers in many lands. Moving ever farther to the Left, he poured forth a stream of books and articles, spent a year in prison, welcomed the Second Republic, and sat on the Constituent Assembly till it was suppressed in 1851. Dying in 1854, he was buried without religious rites, for he had long broken not merely with the authorities of the Church but with its Creed.

Frustrated but undaunted, Lacordaire and Montalembert continued their campaign. Convinced that a religious revival must begin with the young, they looked to the Orders, whose zeal exceeded that of the secular clergy, and demanded permission for them to open schools of their own. It was uphill work, for the bishops had no stomach for a fight. When charged with unlicensed printing, Montalembert claimed to be tried by his peers and seized the opportunity to advertise his beliefs. He founded Committees throughout France, purchased the journal *l'Univers*, and asserted the rights of the Church with a vigour and persistence unknown since Joseph de Maistre. Unlike Lacordaire, he was a born fighter.

The fall of the Monarchy was followed by the abolition of the House of Peers, which Montalembert had used as his tribune. He accepted the Republic as an interim solution, was elected for a

Paris constituency, and helped Falloux to carry through his law. Though himself a liberal monarchist, he was strongly attracted to a new deputy named Prince Louis Napoleon. 'Who knows', he wrote to a friend, 'if this man, exposed to such humiliation, is not chosen by God to chastise the pride of our Scribes and Pharisees.' Believing that he was likely to do more for the Church than Cavaignac as President of the Republic, he visited him on the eve of the plebiscite.

> *Montalembert:* The Catholics have no candidate, and will vote only for someone who provides satisfactory guarantees. They merely ask what they asked of the Kings and will always demand liberty of instruction and association.
> *Louis Napoleon:* I would not, for three million votes, make engagements contrary to my convictions. I love liberty sincerely, but I am not well versed in this question of teaching. I will study it. As to religious associations I confess I have little love for convents. I realize their past services but I think them unsuited to our times. There are often abuses in Switzerland.
> *Montalembert:* I do not know to what you refer, and I do not believe there are any in France. If there were it is for the Church to correct them, as it has the right to do. The State should stand aloof unless there is some public scandal.

In recording the interview in his journal Montalembert added: 'I was much pleased by his manners and conversation, and still more by his truly liberal views. We shook hands, and I carried away a very favourable impression. I cannot imagine how his reputation for incapacity arose.' Any lingering doubts were removed by his election manifesto declaring that the protection of religion involved liberty of instruction. 'I am for Louis Napoleon,' he confided to a friend, 'as the sole means of rendering the Republic, if not acceptable, at any rate tolerable to honest folk. 'The hour has come,' he wrote. 'We have ploughed the soil and sown the seed; Falloux alone can reap the harvest. I am happy to have prepared the way.'

The Roman revolution of 1848 stirred Montalembert to the depths. 'The Pope, the Pope! I am thinking of him every moment.' Cavaignac's announcement that France would defend his person by the dispatch of a small force was described as inadequate; France, the traditional protector, must also defend his authority.

When Pio Nono fled to Gaeta in the Kingdom of Naples, Cavaignac called off the enterprise and Montalembert turned to Louis Napoleon, who accepted a formula promising support for 'all suitable measures to guarantee the liberty and authority of the Pope'. Backed by the Monarchists under Thiers and Molé, the champions of the Church secured the dispatch of a force under Oudinot sufficient to overthrow the Roman Republic of Garibaldi and Mazzini. After Victor Hugo had argued that the Pope must be compelled, if necessary by force, to grant liberal reforms, Montalembert delivered the greatest oration of his life. 'The Church is a mother. We are the sons of the Crusaders, and we will never yield to the sons of Voltaire.' Friend and foe alike realized that the nineteenth century would never haul down the flag. Thiers congratulated the most eloquent of men, and the Pope expressed his gratitude. On a visit to Rome after the passing of the Falloux Law he was acclaimed as 'this great soldier of Christ, more influential than any bishop'. 'Never has religion been more favoured in France' was the comment of the Vatican.

In the contest for power between the President and the Chamber Montalembert stood by the former. 'There are a thousand reasons for supporting him and none for abandoning him,' he explained to his friends.

> I see in him neither a principle nor a personality, and my feelings for him are a thousand leagues this side of the idolatry which Legitimists profess for their prince and their principle. I see in him a man who has rendered the greatest services to France, society and religion. I feel I am in his debt, and so, I believe, are the country and the whole world. I thank him for appointing the most trustworthy Catholic since Suger a Minister, for having restored the Temporal Power of the Pope, for having accorded to the Church liberty of teaching and association. I am revolted by the stupid ingratitude of those who, blinded by the few months of security they owe to him, renew against him this eternal barrage of criticism and antagonism which renders all power and all security in France impossible.

Falloux gently rebuked his friend's enthusiasm.

> *Falloux:* Don't you see that he wants to restore the Empire?
> *Montalembert:* No, he has neither the energy nor the power. In any case the best way of preventing it is to keep in with him and exert a moderating influence.

The President invited him to the Elysée and delighted him with his views. 'I found him always gentle and friendly, often sad and constrained, often a baffling reserve, above all in moments of crisis and danger. I wish he were more animated.' Montalembert brought him a Papal benediction from Rome. The President gallantly replied 'I am sure it will bring me happiness.'

In the autumn of 1851 there was thunder in the air, and Montalembert implored the President to have patience. 'Halt on the fatal incline where, without intending it, you will drag us down too. I beseech you not to destroy the unhappy party of order, not to disappoint the decent people who have trusted you. You have never had a more sincere and disinterested friend than myself. Perhaps you may condemn me to become your adversary, but my conscience forbids me to leave you without giving you a final proof of my attachment.' The President, after listening patiently, replied that he would never change his principles. 'I believe I am called to defend order and civilization, and I will make any sacrifice to fufill my mission conscientiously. I may err in the means, but my object will never change.'

The *coup d'état* and the arrest of some of his friends were a shock to Montalembert; but he soon recovered, and visited the President, whom he found as calm as ever, on the day after the massacre. 'My mission and my intention,' he explained, 'is to restore order. My attitude to religion and the Pope is unchanged: I desire their triumph.' He promised to preserve liberty of teaching. To the complaint that he had restored universal suffrage he replied: 'Don't worry. I accept it as the source of power, not as the organ of government.' Partially reassured, Montalembert on the eve of the plebiscite urged Catholics to support the new *régime*.

> December 2 put to flight all the revolutionaries, all the Socialists, all the bandits of France and of Europe. To vote against Louis Napoleon is to approve the socialist revolution; to substitute dictatorship of the reds for the dictatorship of a man who for three years has rendered incomparable services to the cause of order and of Catholicism, to abstain, is to shirk the duty of good citizens. To vote for him is not to approve all he has done. It is a choice between him and the total ruin of France. It is to arm the only possible Government today with the force needed to overcome the army of

> crime, to defend our Churches, our homes, and our women against the greed which respects nothing, the enemies of property-owners and even of the *curés*. If he were unknown I should certainly hesitate to confer on him such power and responsibility; but I recall such doings as the liberty of instruction, the restoration of the Pope by French arms, and the Church restored to the plenitude of its dignity with its councils and synods, the increase of its colleges and its charities. Who else can guarantee the continuance of these benefits? I am for authority against rebellion, for conservatism against destruction, for society against socialism, and, as always, for Catholicism against the Revolution.

Montalembert's satisfaction was shared by almost all the bishops and clergy as well as by the Vatican. Now at last, they believed, the danger from *les rouges* had passed away.

> I neither knew nor advised, nor applauded the *coup d'état*, neither the moment nor the method [he wrote to a friend]. They should have waited till the Chamber rejected the revision of the Constitution for the second time, and should have reached agreement with the Conservative minority to issue a joint appeal to the country. But now it is done I shall not refuse my support to a prince who desires order, risks his life against demagogy, and is more sympathetic to religious interests than any ruler of France for the last sixty years.

On the eve of the plebiscite he published a letter in *L'Univers* exhorting Catholics to cast an affirmative vote, firstly because he was the defender of order, secondly as a champion of the Catholic cause.

Montalembert was soon to regret his flaming manifesto, as Lacordaire, who had abstained from public comment, had expected. 'God can use militarism for good purposes', he wrote a few days after the *coup*, but, like everyone else, he wondered how the new master would use his power. In his visits to the Elysée Montalembert found him friendly but reserved. Though his advocacy must have influenced many voters, he received no thanks, for the President resented his importunity. When he naively observed that no one would accept the position of a nominated Senator, the host replied with a smile that plenty of good citizens could be found who were willing to receive 30,000 francs a year. By this time the autocrat had had enough of his advice, and the visits to the Elysée ceased. Disillusion hardened into hostility, and the offer of a Senatorship was declined. 'I decline this derisory offer,' he noted in his Journal, 'without concealing from the Minister my indignation at the President's conduct, using my name as a signboard, deceiving France and Europe which believed I was his adviser, whereas he consulted me about nothing.' Informed of his refusal, the Dictator, who never gave way to anger, wrote in a friendly tone: 'I regret to hear that your feelings towards me have changed. I cannot understand it for I entertain real friendship for you, and I should be grieved if anything were to come between us.' It was his last letter, for a few days later the Orléans decrees shattered what little was left of the friendship. 'How unworthy!' exclaimed Montalembert. 'Rewarding the clemency of Louis Philippe on two occasions by the spoliation of his children!' 'Starting confiscation again, unknown in France for fifty years, on the morrow of a revolution designed to save the rights of property he strikes this perfidious blow! Finally, to legitimize this act of brigandage he offers the Church the supreme insult of five million francs of stolen goods! I am thunderstruck.' On the same day he resigned his seat on the Consultative Commission, which had never met. His resignation was announced in the *Moniteur* without the explosive letter which provoked it, and the President remarked that he was delighted to be rid of him.

Montalembert entered the Chamber in the hope that, despite its fetters, he might exercise a certain influence by his eloquent voice if not by his vote. Thoroughly disillusioned, he described the ceremony of the oath of homage at the Tuileries as the saddest moment of his political career. That he had ceased to count was partly due to the divisions in the Catholic camp. Should the Empire be supported? Yes, of course, replied Louis Veuillot. No, declared Montalembert in a brochure *Les Intérêts Catholiques au XIXe Siècle* which demanded Parliamentary government as the only guarantee of liberty. He knew its faults, but what was the alternative? And which was best for the Church, autocracy or limited power? 'I admit it is easier to bow down before a master, imploring his support, speaking only to praise, but where will it end? *Respice finem*. Beginning as an accomplice and a dupe, it ends as a victim.' The Church had prospered under Louis Philippe, and the *Loi Falloux* had been passed under the Second Republic. Catholics should neither identify their cause with absolutism nor strive for its overthrow. The manifesto caused a final breach with Veuillot and a reconciliation with Lacordaire who had regretted his friend's short-sighted enthusiasm for an autocrat. Montalembert proceeded to fight both the Empire and Veuillot in *Le Correspondant*, which he purchased in 1856 and for which he received the collaboration of Falloux, Lacordaire and Dupanloup. Recognizing the sincerity of the two chief gladiators, the Pope declined to intervene. In the election of 1857 the Government mobilized all its resources and secured the defeat of its most formidable Catholic antagonist.

An article in 1858 issued a challenge which the Government could hardly ignore. 'When I feel the stifling fog closing round me with its servile and corrupting vapours, I hasten to breathe a purer air and take a bath of life in free England.' The Ministers, with the Emperor in the chair, decided to prosecute. 'I regret it,' remarked the ruler, 'but I could not prevent it, and I hope it will serve as a warning.' There was a veritable conspiracy of men of letters against the Government, he complained to Lord Clarendon. 'Avoiding frontal attacks and proceeding in the most insidious fashion, they introduce the most hostile and insulting allusions to myself. In striking a man so illustrious as Montalembert, I had to make an example which would instil a healthy fear into this party.'

The announcement of a trial brought expressions of sympathy from the Orleans princes and other friends, and the veteran Berryer, the brightest ornament of the Paris bar, pleaded his cause in court. Rebuked by the presiding judge for declaring that there was no liberty in France, the orator retorted that the truth of his statement was clearer than daylight, and that the expression of legitimate regrets should not be held a crime. After deliberating for an hour the Court imposed a sentence of 6 months' imprisonment and a fine of 35,000 francs. The verdict was welcomed by the defendant as a purification from his former error. While friends counselled him to avert imprisonment by flight, the *Moniteur* announced on 2 December that the Emperor, 'on the occasion of 2 December', had cancelled the sentence. It was a shrewd thrust, for Montalembert had accepted the Man of

December: but he had already appealed, and a second trial was held. Once again Berryer turned the defence into a demonstration; and once again a sentence of imprisonment was inflicted, reduced from six to three months; and once again the Emperor, realizing that the prosecution was a boomerang, cancelled the verdict.

A year later the Emperor's intervention on the side of Victor Emmanuel filled the champion of the Temporal Power with anger and grief and ended his political career; but he welcomed the growth of opposition in the Chamber and the Liberal Empire. 'It is a veritable abdication,' he exclaimed, 'the solemn and complete inauguration of the Parliamentary *régime*.' He liked and trusted Ollivier without sharing all his ideas. A dying man, his sufferings ended on the eve of the *débâcle*, and his old rival Veuillot admitted in the *Univers* that of all the laity of his time he had rendered the greatest and most devoted service to the Church.

III. VEUILLOT

Louis Veuillot, ill-educated son of a manual worker, was the Rochefort of the Church, equally ebullient and equally reckless in attack. Passing through Rome in 1838 in the course of a tour, the young journalist underwent as sudden a conversion as Saul on the road to Damascus, passing in a flash from indifference to burning faith. 'At the corner of a street', he joyfully reported, 'I met God. He signalled to me. I hesitated. Then He took me by the hand and I was saved.' Presented to Gregory XVI, he left the Eternal City a new man, aflame with the vision of a Christian France.

Returning to Paris he joined the staff of the obscure paper *L'Univers*, of which he soon became Editor and which he used as his bludgeon for the rest of his life. The paper, he proudly declared, held the place in the press which the Jesuits occupied in the Church. 'What are you going to do?' he was asked. 'Make a revolution,' was the reply. To turn back the hands of the clock wound up by the rationalists of the eighteenth century was beyond the power of any man or any group of men, but he dedicated himself to the campaign, caring nothing for money, office or fame, ready at any moment to sacrifice a friendship or to die for his faith. In 1844 he spent three weeks in the Conciergerie for attacking the University, and in the following year he joined Montalembert in founding the *Comité de la défense de la liberté religieuse*. The fiery crusader soon broke with his more moderate colleagues, and in 1849 Dupanloup described his organ as a running sore in the bosom of the Church. Scorning all compromise, he applauded the Inquisition, the St. Bartholomew massacre, the revocation of the Edict of Nantes, and other crimes of the Church which in his eyes could do no wrong. To Veuillot Christianity was a flaming sword, not the gospel of love.

Craving for absolutism in Church and State, he welcomed the *coup d'état* and rejoiced in the verdict of the plebiscite.

> France [he wrote] will reject Parliamentarism as she rejected Protestantism or she will perish in trying to spew it out of her mouth. The people have said: 'My orators bore me; clear them out and govern me. We must support the Government, for it stands for social order. We must support it today in order to earn the right to counsel it later. To the friends of order we say: The President is your general. If you do not share his triumph you will share his irretrievable defeat. Rally to him. Tomorrow will be too late for your safety or your honour. May God protect France!'

Warnings that he was playing with fire fell on deaf ears.

> *Falloux:* You have gone too far to draw back, but I beseech you to be less ardent. I know the President better than you. Never expect from him a sincerely Catholic policy. The expedition to Rome was a move against Austria, not in favour of the Church. When you have removed all obstacles in his path you will see where he will lead you. Think of your reputation and be neutral.
> *Veuillot:* Do you expect your opposition to succeed?
> *Falloux:* We are too divided. Probably neither we nor you can hold up the current. But we need not facilitate and applaud the object of our fears. Don't tie yourself to an unknown quantity. Don't commit yourself and the Catholics you represent. Save your dignity of tomorrow by preserving your independence today. Preach neutrality.

After this friendly admonition Falloux was shocked to find in the next issue of *L'Univers* a bitter attack on neutrality and fresh adulation of the Dictator. 'Flagrant treachery!' he exclaimed.

They never met again. The Catholics, wrote Veuillot in 1854, owed the Emperor not only support but gratitude.

> He has shown himself on all occasions liberal, enlightened, benevolent. This attitude has not been political stratagem, as some ungrateful people declare, but the natural consequence of his good intelligence and lofty qualities. In the situation into which France had been thrown by revolutions she was ripe for a master. It has pleased God to give her a King, a chief whose personal qualities justify the choice of Providence. What he has done for religion and social order no one else could have done nor perhaps desired to do. The Church enjoys a liberty unknown for centuries. Though stronger in its political constitution under the old Monarchy, it was less free. When the Church is free, every other legitimate liberty is safe or striking root under its shield. I recognize in him a mind truly great, truly liberal, and I venture to say truly royal. He is not afraid of the liberties of the Church, that is to say of good conduct, the sentiment of justice, of the legitimate aspirations of true liberty. We Catholics must accept the Government as a gift of Providence, deserve its continuance, and not be discouraged even when we think it sometimes makes mistakes.

Veuillot declined a decoration and a seat in the Chamber or the Council of State on the ground that he preferred to work in absolute independence. His allegiance was to Rome, not to France. It was said of him that he would have appealed from God to the Pope, and that his fidelity to the Church took the place of all the other Christian virtues. 'When the Church is attacked, I feel like a son who sees his mother being assaulted.' Every event at home and abroad was judged by the same confessional test. He welcomed the Crimean War in the hope that the schismatic Tsar would be excluded from the guardianship of the Holy Places, and was rewarded by a message from the Tuileries. 'Tell M. Veuillot that I am delighted by his approval which assures me the support of honest men.' His *éloge* on the death of Marshal Saint-Arnaud was reproduced in the *Moniteur*. 'He served his country and honoured God. His deeds will open to him the gates of history, his faith the gates of eternity.' For a second time a decoration was declined. 'I give myself,' he explained, 'so why should I seem to have sold myself.' An invitation to be presented to the Emperor was also declined. Their first and last meeting occurred after the Orsini plot, when he begged the ruler to issue a letter recommending the stricter observance of the Sabbath.

How wise Veuillot had been in repelling the advances of the Dictator was proved in 1859 when support of the House of Savoy seemed likely to threaten the Temporal Power. When the celebrated brochure *Le Pape et le Congrès*, inspired by the Emperor, proposed the amputation of the Papal States in return for a guarantee of the remainder, the Pope's denunciation was reproduced in *L'Univers*. The Emperor retaliated by suppressing the journal which had been his most stalwart supporter for many years, but the frowns of the Tuileries were compensated by the smiles of the Vatican. Undaunted, Veuillot pursued his campaign in a series of volumes, two of which, *Le Parfum de Rome* and *Les Odeurs de Paris* contrasted the city he adored with the modern Babylon he despised. When his paper was allowed to reappear in 1867, he continued to lay about him with his big stick. Like all fanatics he was a man of one idea, repelling as many readers as he won for the cause. In the words of Leroy-Beaulieu, historian of the Catholic Liberals, he introduced civil war into the Church. That in France clericalism bred the anti-clericalism of the Third Republic was due to this militant layman more than to any priest.

IV. DUPANLOUP

The Church could boast of two outstanding figures, but since Lacordaire turned his back on politics Dupanloup had to carry on the fight with little help from the hierarchy. At the fall of the Monarchy the Bishop of Orlèans enjoyed a high reputation as a writer and spiritual director. As chaplain to the Duchesse d'Angoulème, daughter of Louis XVI and Marie Antoinette, and religious instructor to the Comte de Chambord and the Orleans princes, he was closely allied to the dynasty; but he was ready to work with any *régime* which gave the Church a fair deal. A high compliment had been paid to his tact when he was called to the death-bed of Talleyrand when that hoary sinner needed a passport for his last journey. Less of a crusader than Montalembert and less of a pugilist than Veuillot, the brightest ornament of the

Church preferred the velvet glove to the iron hand. No French priest of his time had more friends or fewer enemies.

Intervening in politics only when he believed the vital interests of the Church to be involved, he accepted the Republic and pressed Falloux to take office when it was offered to him. Having voted for Cavaignac in the plebiscite for the Presidency and having had no dealings with Louis Napoleon, he was horrified by the *coup d'état* and the spectacle of 'a whole nation at the feet of a single man'. When Montalembert consulted him about the attitude to be adopted to the Dictator, the Bishop advised against any public pronouncement. The Orleans decrees were an even greater shock, and the proposed allocation of part of the proceeds of the sale of property to raise ecclesiastical salaries provoked the exclamation that he could not find words to express his contempt for the proposal. A long letter to the Dictator conveyed his views in respectful terms.

> I learn that you have most kindly thought of raising the salaries of ecclesiastics. God, who knows your intentions, will not fail to reward you. He also knows that the Bishops have not asked for it. Since, however, some prejudices against the clergy still prevail, charges would be brought against us from which we should suffer and religion too. No doubt if our incomes were larger we might give more alms and provide more hospitality; but there is a far higher consideration—the dignity of our character. If you wish to render effectual help to religion you might reconstruct ruined churches now open in poor districts.

When the President passed through Orleans shortly before the proclamation of the Empire, the Bishop and his Vicar-Generals gathered on the platform and the Bishop bowed respectfully without a word. 'Monseigneur,' said the Dictator, 'I hope one day to have the honour of being received by you in your cathedral at the head of your clergy.' For the second time the Bishop bowed in silence and the train moved on. After the brief ceremony he remarked: 'Do you know why I do not love despotism? Among other reasons because it degrades the soul and inspires the ruler with a contempt for men in proportion to their servility.'

That a man with such a large heart and such conciliatory temperament should clash with the fiery Veuillot was inevitable. In 1854 a controversy arose as to the suitability of the classics for school-children, some of the clergy complaining that Christian teaching was endangered. Dupanloup, who loved the classics, assured the teachers that they could be safely retained in expurgated texts and taught in a Christian spirit. Accused by the intransigents, with Veuillot at their head, of desiring a renaissance of paganism, he retaliated by forbidding his diocesan seminaries to read *L'Univers*.

Dupanloup had never loved the Emperor and nearly broke his heart over his Italian policy. Though sympathizing with the desire of Italians to remove the Austrian yoke, he was not prepared to assist Victor Emmanuel to despoil the Pope. Assurances as to his independence and personal safety failed to reassure him, for promises were as scraps of paper, as easy to break as to make. 'As a devoted son of the Holy Roman Empire,' he exclaimed, 'I protest against the revolutionary impiety which seeks to rob the Pope of his patrimony. They say they will only take the Romagna. Allow me to ask by what right they will take the Romagna? Why not the rest? The Emperor to give M. de Cavour an absolutely free hand! I cannot believe it.' One shock followed the other as the Pope was pressed back till Italy emerged as a nation-state. In 1861 state functionaries were ordered to sever relations with the audacious prelate.

> Anyone who has observed the facts and is actuated by a real devotion to the Emperor must consider the attitude of the Bishop of Orlèans as exhibiting a political hostility arising from the complicated nature of the questions in which he has thought it his duty to intervene. In entering the field of political controversy a bishop plays into the hands of the enemies of the Government to which he owes his See and all his prerogatives.

The circular proved a boomerang, for the ill-advised order for a social boycott was ignored.

Seven years later, when the Empire was in decline, the Emperor visited Orleans and the two men engaged in conversation for the first time. Tact was required on both sides. 'Your Majesty', declared the Bishop, 'will find that the people of Orleans have not changed, for they have maintained inviolate their patriotism and their religion. Your Majesty will feel here, perhaps more than in any other portion of your Empire, that France is and ever will be the most Christian nation on earth.' Turning to the Empress, who, as everyone present was aware, shared his views on the Temporal Power, he added: 'May Your Majesty see the young Prince, her love, her hope and her joy, grow daily in virtue and in that noble piety which, as Bossuet said to the son of Louis XIV, is the making of a man and a prince.' The speech healed the breach with the Tuileries and was published in the *Moniteur*.

For Dupanloup the most poignant grief of *l'année terrible* was not the defeat of France and the collapse of the Empire but the capture of the Eternal City, for to such an ardent soul the Papacy counted for infinitely more than his fatherland.

> A last and long-planned enterprise [he complained] has been perpetrated at Rome, thanks to the humiliation of France and our abandonment of the task. Rome is invaded. Italy has accomplished the dishonourable work, and the Pope is robbed of his rights. All treaties are set aside and the efforts of the Catholic world have been in vain. Where to find refuge?

His bitterest reflection was that the Emperor had some share of responsibility. Veuillot's legacy to France was a militant ultramontanism which fostered an equally aggressive anti-clericalism. When both Gallicanism and Liberal Catholicism were trampled underfoot by the Vatican Council, the two armies entered on a running fight which on more than one occasion came near to wrecking the Republic.

16

THE PARTIES

ROYALISTS and Republicans, though equally hostile to the Dictator, found it impossible to combine their forces. Active resistance was impossible, not merely because it was too perilous, but because after the horrors of 1848 France was in no mood for further turmoil. Few believed that the Second Empire would last longer than the First, perhaps not so long. What could not be altered by constitutional or unconstitutional methods must be endured, not in grovelling subservience but in watchful waiting. However widespread the discontent in the country, particularly in the large cities, there was little sign of it in a Chamber packed with official candidates.

'Looking at the situation broadly,' wrote the Duc de Noailles to the Duchesse de Dino after the *coup d'état*, 'the state of the Chamber, the division of parties, the impossibility of fusion, the menace of socialism and the secret societies, the imminence of danger in 1852, the event is welcome. That is what all thoughtful people feel and how I have felt from the first moment.' Writing from his country home in Auvergne the veteran Baron de Barante reported that the local folk were as indifferent as they had been in all the excitement of sixty years which did not affect their material interests.

> The bourgeoisie welcomes the severe repression of the reds who threatened them with massacre and pillage. So there is gratitude without enthusiasm for the President. His seizure of power is not resented, but no one expects it to last long. If there is a plebiscite there will be forced consent to a *fait accompli*. No government has ever been less able to allow the slightest liberty. Hitherto every new system has benefited some party; everything has now been done in

the interest of a person. So no liberty of the press, no deliberations, no control of the administration, no respect for the laws, perhaps disorder in the finances, posts filled by whim or favour. It is despotism in all its cruelty. The President has failed the Republic, which would never willingly have surrendered its authority. In this sense we have moved towards a better situation, and the Monarchy will perhaps have a chance of restoring the liberty it provided for thirty years and which we misused.

Guizot, another veteran royalist, who withdrew from active politics after the fall of the Monarchy and his own Ministry, described the *coup* as a ridiculous and shameful act, but after all that had happened since 1848 inevitable and deserved. France was now paying the penalty for the destruction of Constitutional Monarchy, the only satisfactory government for a civilized community.

I. THIERS

Thiers spoke for the group of elderly Constitutional Monarchists who remembered the First Empire and had no desire for a second. Napoleon, he declared, the apostle of the ideas of 1789, was made for France and France was made for him, but autocracy was no longer required. When Louis Philippe fled across the Channel, his former Minister hoped and expected that his grandson, the Comte de Paris, a lad of eight, would ascend the throne in due time; meanwhile the Republic was accepted as a stop-gap, for there was no alternative. 'I thought of the Presidency,' he confided to Falloux, 'but I must give it up. Perhaps we should allow Louis Napoleon to be elected, or even elect him ourselves, without wearing his livery. If I were to fail, it would be a serious set-back to the cause of order. If I succeeded, I should have to marry the Republic, and I am too virtuous to marry a girl of such evil reputation.'

Thiers' policy as the head of the largest party in the Chamber was to steer the ship of state between the Scylla of revolution and the Charybdis of dictatorship. Had he been an Englishman, he would have been a pillar of the Whigs. Claiming paternity for the formula *Le roi règne mais ne gouverne pas*, he promised support to any wise and honourable decisions and any Government which would assure order and security. When Cavaignac, an avowed Republican, declined all commitments to the Monarchists, the latter had no alternative but to support Louis Napoleon for the Presidency if he could satisfy them about his intentions. His draft manifesto proved too radical for Thiers, who proposed certain modifications. On their acceptance and after the decisive plebiscite Thiers exclaimed: 'He is not Caesar but Augustus.' He had urged the Legitimists to follow his example, arguing that the rule of '*un crétin qu'on mènera*' was the surest road to the return of the Monarchy. 'You are making a great mistake,' he exclaimed to Falloux who refused to swallow the bait. 'I am profoundly convinced,' replied the Legitimist leader, 'that you will be deceived. With Prince Louis the first day will be the best, and the day after will be detestable.' 'I will answer for everything,' rejoined Thiers, convinced that the President would prove wax in his hands.

After the plebiscite Thiers became for a time the chief adviser to the inexperienced President. For the inauguration ceremony he advised a frock-coat and the trimming of his moustache. Declining an invitation to take office, he chose a Ministry under Odilon Barrot with Drouyn de Lhuys at the Foreign Office and Changarnier in command of the Paris troops. 'Rely on the power which placed you in power,' was his advice. 'My sympathies are Orleanist, but if you establish order by good government I will support you.' The position of unofficial counsellor left him free to change his course if an agreement between the Bourbon and Orleans claimants should enable the Monarchy to be restored. Meanwhile the wings of the President should be clipped. He had never taken his orders from Louis Philippe, he assured his English friend Nassau Senior, and when the King tried to impose his will in 1840 he had resigned. The last word should rest with the Ministers enjoying the confidence of the Chamber. The division of power between the sovereign and his advisers spelled weakness and confusion, and France always needed a firm hand at the helm. Under the reactionary Charles X he had ranked as a man of the Left, under the Bourgeois King as a man of the Centre; now he emerged as a man of the Right. Since universal suffrage granted by the Republic went too far for his taste he helped to secure its limitation. Like most of his fellow royalists, he was haunted by the spectre of social revolution and rated order above political liberty, though he loved them both. 'Whom do we wish to exclude?' he exclaimed during a debate on the limitation of the franchise in May 1850. 'The class of vagabonds, the common people. The friends of true liberty, the true Republicans, are afraid of the vile multitude which has destroyed all republics—this wretched mob which has handed over the liberty of all Republicans to the tyrants, which exchanged Roman liberty for bread and circuses, which murdered the Emperor, who cowardly surrendered Rome to the barbarians, which surrendered the liberty of Florence to the Medici, which murdered the de Witts, applauded the murder of the Girondins, and would applaud yours and mine.' While the timid bourgeois statesman could never envisage the manual worker as a fully responsible citizen, the President, with a more modern mind, shrewdly detected in the Fourth Estate a potential ally.

When Thiers visited his old master Louis Philippe on his deathbed in 1850, the eldest surviving son, Prince de Joinville, assured him on behalf of the family: 'If ever you need us, we are ready.' They agreed that the time for action had not arrived. The three most controversial decisions of the Government—the limitation of the franchise, the expedition to Rome, and the *Loi Falloux*—received his support, and during his first year of office the President gave no cause of offence. When, however, he dismissed Odilon Barrot the honeymoon with the Monarchists ended. The first pitched battle was fought when the Chamber blocked a revision of the Constitution which would have allowed the President a second consecutive term and declined to increase his salary. 'Not an extra day nor another *sou*,' declared Theirs. It was a Pyrrhic victory, for there is nothing like a rebuff to stimulate the ambition of a would-be dictator.

When the Man of Destiny struck on 2 December 1851, Thiers was arrested and on his liberation he retired to Belgium, returning after the proclamation of the Empire. Though free from Victor Hugo's pathological hatred of the Dictator he regarded him with increasing apprehension and disdain. The Emperor, he declared to Nassau Senior at the end of 1852, would mean war, not only because he imitated his uncle but because he would not long submit to the settlement of 1815. Resenting the contemptuous hostility of the European monarchs, he was certain to seek compensation in military adventures which, if successful, would diminish regrets for loss of political liberty. 'I feel certain that, as soon as he finds us craving for a new excitement, he will stop our mouths with a war.' France, he added, was a bellicose country and would not try to hold him back. Though he disapproved both the Crimean and the Italian conflicts, Thiers took no part in politics during the first decade of the Empire, busying himself with the completion of his majestic *Histoire du Consolat et de l'Empire*. 'Tell him,' said the Emperor to Mérimée, 'that I regard his book as the greatest monument that has been erected to the glory of my uncle.' 'One of these days you will return to politics, which you like best,' remarked Nassau Senior. 'Not under this man,' rejoined Thiers; 'under another dynasty. We shall see.'

Thiers returned to the Chamber in 1863 when free speech had once more become possible. Till then Persigny, Rouher and Baroche had worked the system of autocracy which they believed essential to good government, and the militant Opposition had been confined to *Les Cinq*. Before the election the Duc de Broglie invited his old Monarchist associates to meet for consultation at his home. Standing for the Chamber, which he advocated, involved taking an oath to the Empire but with the intention of fighting it by all constitutional means. Though Thiers was not present he approved his attitude, stood for the Chamber, and was elected. With Legitimists, Orleanists and Republicans a little more adequately represented, Thiers, at the age of sixty-six, became the unofficial leader of the Opposition. Since it would have been futile to have urged the restoration of the Monarchy, he pleaded for 'the essential liberties'—civic and religious, liberty of the press, the unfettered choice of candidates, the right of Parliament to initiate legislation, and the right of the majority to determine policy. Everyone, including the Emperor, knew that he was no firebrand. 'I have always defended order and liberty,' he declared with truth. 'I am a son of 1789. I have advised my friends to take the oath. I shall never speak as a party man.'

His popularity waxed when the Minister of the Interior launched a clumsy attack in the *Moniteur*. His election, argued Persigny, would damage the policies of the Emperor, for he was a former servant of 'a *régime* which for eighteen years exhibited only impotence at home and weakness abroad'. When a deputation from the parties of the Left inquired if he would oppose the *régime* he replied, 'Yes, but within the limits of the Constitution.' 'I have seen M. Thiers,' reported Mérimée from Fontainebleau to Panizzi soon after his election:

> I found him very sensible and less annoyed than he had a right to be, for he owes his success to Persigny's attack. He talks very nicely about the Emperor and seemed resolved to leave the Opposition. I think he is aiming at an intermediate attitude. He would like some advance but thinks it would strengthen the Empire, and there is the snag. Yet it is good that he formally accepts the *régime* and wishes to improve and not to overthrow it. I feel sure we shall see him here one day.

That was not to be. He remained an Orleanist, but preferred the Empire in its later and more liberal phase to a radical Republic. 'I have no objection to an Opposition Deputy going to the Tuileries,' he remarked. 'I have been measured for my uniform, and I shall be delighted to wear it if the Emperor takes a step towards liberty.'

The Ollivier experiment in 1870 changed a former foe into a friend, if not a wholly disinterested friend. When the Austrian Ambassador asked for his views, the old statesman believed that he had been sent by the Emperor:

> I am very satisfied [he began] and no longer distrust the Emperor. My friends and I are very attached to the Orleans princes by duty and gratitude, but we are above all servants of the country, and we should not dream of making trouble by trying to bring them back. I am not lying when I say that if one of them were to set foot in France I should be the first to advise his arrest. If the Emperor continues along the path of ordered liberty we will support him with all our strength. As for myself and many members of the Left, we will rally to the new Government in perfect confidence.

Further concessions, such as the nomination of mayors by the municipal councils, were needed. Ollivier, he added, was too young and inexperienced to retain his place for long, a remark betraying his expectation of the succession in due course.

When the acceptance of the offer of the Spanish crown by the Hohenzollern prince appeared to confront France with a choice between humiliating acquiescence and war, Thiers offered his services. Far from expressing gratitude, the Emperor complained that he was a wretched *démolisseur* who had ruined everyone who had accepted his aid. Moreover, war was not certain and this was not the time to change the team. 'Tell him that the Emperor counts on the patriotism of the historian of the Consulate and Empire just as much as if he were in office.' After Ollivier announced in the Chamber the demand for guarantees, Thiers, amid a storm of interruption, courageously explained why he had not risen to his feet. 'Your decision may involve the death of thousands. You are breaking on a question of form. Some day you will regret your haste. Insult me as you will, I am ready for anything in order to spare the blood of my fellow-countrymen which you are prepared so imprudently to shed.' Prussia, he added, had gravely offended in supporting the candidature, but there was no case for war. The old patriot was a voice crying in the wilderness, and the country plunged to its doom like the Gadarene swine. His finest hour was still to come.

11. DUC D'AUMALE

In addition to onslaughts from the capital and the Chamber, a stream of criticism flowed from the exiled branches of the Royal Family. The childless Comte de Chambord was not taken very seriously, for that unbending champion of the *ancien régime* could count on Berryer alone to voice his claims. Far more formidable was the House of Orleans, represented by the sons of Louis Philippe, above all by the Duc d'Aumale, soldier, historian, and owner of Chantilly with its priceless treasures. The four volumes of his correspondence with his former tutor Cuvillier-Fleury reveal his unswerving loyalty to the Orleanist cause and his settled hostility to the Second Empire. Though he believed constitutional monarchy on the British model as practised by his father was the best form of government for France, he was ready to accept a republic if clearly desired by the nation; and even during a detested dictatorship he was resolved never to threaten the tranquillity of the state. No one was less of a *frondeur* than this stainless patriot. 'I do not complain,' he wrote when the revolution of 1848 drove his family into exile and ended his career as Governor-General of Algeria. 'I only suffer for my dear and venerable parents, for my friends, above all for France. My conscience is clear. Never despair of the fatherland. All good citizens should serve it more zealously than ever. My most ardent desire is to return as a simple citizen and do my duty.' In his study at Twickenham hung the sword which the great Condé had carried at Rocroy; underneath, in large letters, was the single word combining expectation with resignation, '*J'attendrai*'. He found partial consolation in recording the fortunes of the early Condés with the aid of the rich family archives. One of the worst features of the Second Empire was the exclusion from France of the writings of exiles, and the ban on the first two volumes, published in 1863, was only lifted in 1869. Exile seemed more difficult to bear when Louis Napoleon, who had twice attempted to overthrow the legal government of France, was allowed to return, to enter the Chamber, and to stand for the Presidency of the Republic.

The gradual revelation of the Prince's dictatorial ambitions filled him with apprehension. 'Louis Napoleon will have his hour,' he wrote in January 1851 when Changarnier, his only serious rival, was dismissed from his command. 'I don't envy his record in history, and what will the country be like when he goes? I know of no precedent in a Pretender in whom complete self-absorption makes up for a mediocre heart and mind.' Yet there was no case for despair. Changarnier might return, and an accord between Legitimists and Orleanists would constitute a powerful force to resist Bonapartism and repair the harm it was certain to do. The restoration of the Monarchy seemed to lie in the logic of events. Meanwhile frigid abstentionism was dictated not merely by self-respect but by the need to be ready for the call. 'On all sides I see boastfulness, depression, humiliation, ruin for the country.'

After the *coup d'état*, inaugurating what he described as the rule of the police, the confiscation of Orleans property confirmed his gloomiest anticipations. Still more audacious was the accusation that Orleanists were conspiring. His old tutor Cuvillier-Fleury argued that the best weapon against a government blinded by its omnipotence was patience, not conspiracy. 'I can't understand where they discovered a conspiracy,' replied the Duke. 'I know that the most insignificant letters are opened by the *cabinet noir*.'

For a high-ranking officer it was gall and wormwood to be refused a command in the Crimean war. The military victories, synchronizing with the birth of an heir, pointed to a longer duration of the dictatorship than he had anticipated. The Orsini bomb, reported his old tutor from Paris, had further strengthened his position, since nobody knew what would happen if he were to disappear. Yet the Duke's belief in a time limit remained unaltered, and his detestation waxed from year to year. 'Except for the embellishment of Paris,' he wrote, 'this government will leave nothing but ruins. Already it has destroyed much more than the Republic: like the harpies in the fable, it fouls whatever it touches.' When all Europe was talking in the spring of 1859 of the approaching conflict with Austria, he feared that the Emperor would launch the country on a very dangerous venture. 'Lovers of France and liberty, and real lovers of Italy too, should cry Peace! Peace! From a war commenced in this manner no good is to be expected for liberty, nor for France, nor for Italy.' A fresh blow was the omission of the princes from the amnesty which followed the victorious campaign. While doubting the sincerity of the constitutional concessions in 1860, he hoped they might be a first step.

The Duke's sole public attack on the *régime*, *Lettre sur l'histoire de France*, an Open Letter to Prince Napoleon, was provoked by a speech in the Senate on the record of the Bourbons. 'If a single member of the Senate or the Corps Legislatif', he wrote in April 1861, 'had felt able to refute the Bonapartist credo of Prince Napoleon, I should never have thought of taking up my pen. But since the opposition in both Chambers is exclusively Catholic or Republican and the press is muzzled, I felt it could not be left without a reply, all the more when it was placarded in the forty thousand communes.' Within a few days a flaming rejoinder adorned the windows of Paris bookshops signed Henri d'Orléans. Only a small number were offered for sale, for the censorship was certain to pounce; but hundreds were given away at the Bourse, and other copies were smuggled in from abroad, while foreign journals reproduced it whole or in part. The author was delighted with its reception. 'The results seem to have been good in Paris and that is the chief thing,' he wrote from Twickenham to his brother Prince de Joinville. 'Not bad here, especially in unofficial circles. I am compared to Junius, and that means a lot. The official world says: "It is true, but silence would have been better." In the event of a prosecution I should like to have Dufaure.' The respected advocate accepted the task. The case for the defendant was that the Orleans princes had lived in England for many years in retreat, calm, dignified and respected. Their attitude was enshrined in the familiar lines of La Fontaine:

> Cet animal est très méchant
> Quant on l'attaque il se défend.

The most effective ripost was the reminder of his father's leniency to the conspirator of Strasbourg and Boulogne and the kindly reception to Queen Hortense at the Tuileries. Despite attempts to close the frontier, the brochure was widely read all over Europe. That Prince Napoleon shirked a duel for which Aumale had appointed his seconds in advance increased his unpopularity.

Congratulations, however welcome, could do little to assuage the smart of exile. 'I have read Haussmann's speech,' he wrote. 'I have been in rather low spirits for some time, and this has not cheered me up. I see Paris, my real Paris, the Paris of the Parisians, vanishing piece by piece.' Despite his dislike of the author, he bought a copy of the *Histoire de Jules César*, the *édition de luxe*, for the collecting of rare books and sumptuous editions was a passion. The humiliation of France in the summer of 1866 increased his anxiety for the fortunes of France, and the opening of his letters illustrated the servitude and spiritual degradation of the country. Ollivier's experiment brought a faint ray of hope. 'The good folk engaged in this patriotic venture have my best wishes. I feel sure they took office—with banners flying—to implement the liberal policy they have always professed.' When the war came he offered his services, only to meet the same rebuff as in 1854 and 1859, this time from the statesmen of the Third Republic. 'There would be no merit in it,' he wrote on 2 August, 'for I no longer cling to life.' Returning to the land of his birth after the *débâcle* he presided at the historic trial of Bazaine. In reply to the Marshal's excuse for the surrender of Metz—that there was no government at that moment—he uttered the words with which his name will for ever be associated: '*Il y avait toujours la France*'. No Frenchman has loved his country more fervently or more unselfishly, and it is one of the sins of the Second Empire that it denied him and his brothers the opportunity of service.

III. BERRYER

The most uncompromising, though not the most formidable foes of the Empire were the Legitimists, the party of the old nobility and the heirs of the *ancien régime*. The death of Charles X in 1836 and of his son the childless Duc d'Angoulême in 1844, left his grandson, son of the murdered Duc de Berry, head of the elder line. Henri V, however, as his followers called him, laboured under two crippling disqualifications—his marriage was childless, and he stoutly declined to move with the times. While the Orleanist princes, like their father, realized that they were living in the nineteenth century, the heart and mind of the Bourbon prince were anchored in the past, and his refusal to recognize the tricolour flag destroyed his chances of mounting the throne. His dislike of the Orleanists was even greater than of the Bonapartists and the Republicans, and he never forgave them the 'usurpation' of 1830. Living in exile since his boyhood, he remained a shadowy figure unknown to his countrymen.

His standard-bearer was the most eloquent and the most eminent advocate in France, famous above all for his role in political trials. Born in 1790, Berryer followed Louis XVIII to Brussels during the Hundred Days and returned with him after Waterloo. Ardent Royalist though he was, he pleaded for a lenient sentence on Louis Napoleon just as he had defended Marshal Ney without sharing his views. 'If I could only act as well as Berryer speaks!' exclaimed Rachel, the queen of the European stage. Entering the Chamber in 1848 he strove in vain for the union of the two branches of the Royal Family on the basis of the accession of the childless Comte de Chambord to be followed by the Comte de Paris, grandson of Louis Philippe. He was among the notables carted off to Vincennes at the *coup d'état*, and the figures of the plebiscite surpassed his worst expectations. 'Can I witness without grief France proscribing by millions of voices the rights and institutions essential to the strength and dignity of Christian nations?' For the venerable advocate, as for Richard Hooker, law was 'the voice of God'.

Till his death in 1868 Berryer kept in touch with the Comte de Chambord by correspondence and visits to Frohsdorf, his home in Austria. 'What does Berryer think?' was the instinctive reaction of the lonely exile who knew nothing of the mind of France, and the friendship of the two fighters in a rearguard action never waned. In the opinion of Berryer, more could be achieved in the Courts than in the Chamber where freedom of speech was severely curtailed. His first chance came when the Orleans decrees outraged the feelings of circles without any political or personal attachment to the family. On his election to the Academy in 1854 he declined to make the customary visit to the head of the state, explaining that his arrest in 1851 rendered even such formal homage impossible. His most spectacular triumph was his defence of Montalembert, who was charged with attacking the Empire in an article on England's political system. Though the Count called himself a Liberal and his advocate approved dynastic autocracy, the latter vindicated the right of his client to complain that the liberties enjoyed beyond the Channel were denied to France. The Court was packed with celebrities, and the President of the Tribunal, fearing a demonstration when the sentence was pronounced, ordered the police into the room. By common consent Berryer's speech was no less damaging to the *régime* than the incriminated article.

Like other ardent Catholics, Berryer was shocked by the Emperor's intervention in Italy, denounced him as 'the great conspirator', and exclaimed 'God save France, for He alone can!' The implicit threat to the Temporal Power evoked a similar cry of distress from the Comte de Chambord, who declared himself ready to shed his blood for a cause which was that of France, the Church and God himself. When the powers of the Chamber were enlarged in 1863 the septuagenarian lawyer entered the arena, and for the first time found himself in disagreement with his master, who regarded any recognition of the Empire as apostasy. As the only Legitimist Deputy he was the loneliest figure in the Chamber, a leader without an army. After listening to his first speech, Thiers exclaimed that he felt fifteen years younger, but it was of no avail. He witnessed the decline of the *régime* without surprise, and died shortly before the *débâcle* in the conviction that the disappearance of the Bonapartists when the hour struck would automatically restore the Monarchy.

There was not a word of exaggeration in the tribute of the Comte de Chambord. 'France loses one of the noblest of her children, the cause of right its most eloquent champion, myself one of my most faithful friends. I shall never forget the force, the glory and the honour of his life, his unchanging devotion, the sincerity of his faith, the warmth of his heart, the elevation of his character, the power of his words, the ascendancy of his genius.' In his funeral oration Dupanloup saluted 'this great advocate, so helpful to the accused, so faithful to the defeated, the champion of the weak and the unfortunate. His place is secure among those rare orators in the Chamber and at the Bar whose memory will never die. How often have I heard him in Court and in the gravest of political debates lifting up his voice for God, for religion, for all that a Christian holds most dear. My beloved friend, the Church is not ungrateful.'

IV. JULES FAVRE

The Republican opposition, though far smaller numerically than the Royalists, fought with the gloves off and exerted wider influence. To enter the Chamber it was necessary to take the oath to the Constitution, a condition as unacceptable to certain Republicans such as Ledru-Rollin who spent the two decades of autocracy in London. In the later phase of the Empire, however, several of its most militant foes followed the example of the *Sermentistes* in the expectation that it might be more effectively assailed by sapping and mining from within. That their labours were not wholly in vain was proved by the constitutional concessions doled out at intervals.

'You can form no idea of our anger for the first four or five years,' wrote the veteran Republican Jules Simon in his Memoirs long after the Empire had passed away. 'We were caught in a trap, which was not flattering to our *amour-propre*; secondly, we had been beaten hollow; and finally we were treated with unprecedented severity. We were driven from our posts and the press was closed to us. We lived in perpetual fear of arrest or exile.' A week after the *coup* the resumption of his course provided the opportunity for a demonstration. 'Gentlemen, I am Professor of Ethics. The law has been publicly violated by the man who was charged with its defence. Tomorrow France is to declare if she approves or condemns it. If there were to be only a single vote in condemnation in the ballot box I declare it will be mine.' The challenge, pronounced in a ringing voice, brought the audience to its feet. The audacious Professor was instantly suspended, and on his refusal to take the oath deprived of his chair. France, he declared, had been the victim of a surprise and would wake up. The Orleanists, who had formed a working alliance with the President, had dropped him: the more they had backed him in the past the more they detested him now. Whom had he left? A handful of discredited and ridiculous Bonapartists. Leave them in their isolation and they will soon be gone. The *coup* was merely a third flare-up on the model of Strasbourg and Boulogne. This time it was much more serious, since the Pretender was now in office; yet his civil servants thought of nothing but turning against him when the hour came and then he would find himself alone. Jules Simon, like many other intellectuals, failed to realize how popular was the ruler in the provinces, among the timid bourgeoisie and with the Catholic hierarchy.

Jules Favre, Berryer's only serious rival in eloquence at the bar, and described by Proudhon as the Cicero of the Republic, had been a professed Republican since the revolution of 1830. Welcoming the fall of the Monarchy, he accepted the post of Under-Secretary to Ledru-Rollin, Minister of the Interior in the Provisional Government, and entered the Chamber as member for Lyons, his native town. When Louis Napoleon was returned in 1848 by several constituencies without announcing his candidature, Favre was appointed *Rapporteur* of a Committee to examine the validity of his election, and concluded that any citizen duly elected was entitled to take his seat. Though Lamartine and Ledru-Rollin disagreed with him, his argument was accepted by the Chamber. It was an irony of fate that the most persistent foe of the Dictator was the Republican who had opened the door. For the rest of his life he was censured for the action he had taken in 1848; but he had acted honourably as a champion of legality. When the Prince, while postponing his return to France, announced his readiness to fulfil any task the people might impose on him, Favre began to suspect that they were dealing with no ordinary candidate. Despite his apprehensions he preferred him to Cavaignac in the election to the Presidency. Long before the *coup* occurred, however, it was clear that the President was out for power, and when the blow fell Favre joined Victor Hugo in a vain attempt to rally the Chamber. Though the Prince was heard to remark that not a hair of his head should be touched, Favre was hidden by friends till the storm blew over. For the next six years he was busy at the bar. His greatest moment was the defence of Orsini, who gloried in his crime and was ready to pay the price. The trial turned into a flaming demonstration of the Empire which aroused attention in all the capitals.

A few months later Favre returned to political life. With the press in chains, meetings forbidden, and official candidates in every constituency, the Opposition could cut little ice, but *Les Cinq*, of whom he was the acknowledged chief, quickly made themselves felt. One of them, Darimon, recalls the icy reception they received from Royalists no less than Bonapartists, old acquaintances cutting each other in the lobbies and corridors, though none of the little group was an extremist. 'The Emperor has done horrible things,' he remarked to a friend, 'but I feel personal sympathy for him.' At home he pleaded for the liberty of the press and the unfettered choice of Deputies. Abroad he approved the collaboration with Victor Emmanuel but regretted the blocking of his road to Rome. For the Mexican adventure he had nothing but censure.

The Opposition were reinforced by the return to the Chamber of Thiers who echoed the demand for 'the essential liberties', but was simultaneously weakened by the defection of Ollivier. Despite his long record of opposition Favre was criticized for his moderation by impatient younger Republicans like Rochefort and Clemenceau; but he had no more use than they for the Liberal Empire, which he regarded as a veneer to cover the nakedness of autocracy. When the storm burst he joined Thiers in opposing the declaration of war, and on the news of Sedan he demanded the deposition of the Emperor. His brief experience as Foreign

Minister during *l'année terrible* was the most poignant chapter in his honourable career, and his only consolation was the knowledge that he had no responsibility for the trials of France.

His last sight of the Emperor had been when he paid the usual courtesy visit on his election to the Academy. In 1868 'The Emperor struck me as much stouter,' he reported, 'but in excellent health. His head is right down on his shoulders, his cheeks are pendulous, his whole appearance is unattractive. His hair is thinning, and falls on both sides of his head, and seemed to be dyed. During the audience, which only lasted two minutes, he seemed very embarrassed.' 'The last time I saw you', he remarked, 'was at the camp at Châlons. I congratulate the Academy on its choice of such an eloquent man. Your predecessor, M. Cousin, wrote a very fine book. He was very talented and patriotic. A pity he is dead. Death strikes everywhere.' All this was said with such embarrassment that he hesitated at every word. 'Yes Sire,' replied Favre, 'but men of stature leave traces which do not fade.' The Emperor bowed and the painful interview was at an end.

V. ROCHEFORT

Newspapers only began to play a part during the closing phase of the Empire, since every Dictator starts by muzzling the press. Journalists, among them Thiers and Armand Carrel, had helped to overthrow Charles X in 1830, and their influence increased when Émile de Girardin, the Napoleon of the press, inaugurated cheap papers and therefore large circulations with *La Presse* in 1836. Though an ardent supporter of Louis Napoleon against Cavaignac in 1848, he found his wings clipped by the *coup d'état*; his organ lost its interest and part of its clientele when its independence was gone. Dr. Véron, 'le grand Véron', the wealthy Editor of *Le Constitutionnel*, was scarcely affected by the censorship, not only because he was an avowed supporter of the *régime*, but because he was more interested in literature than in politics. When the political climate began to thaw and the Liberal Empire came in sight, the spearhead of the attack on the *régime* passed from the Chamber to the press.

Whatever the system, declared Rochefort's biographer, he was sure to oppose it, and whatever government he joined he was sure to resign. In assessing the significance of his vitriolic attacks on the Empire we must bear in mind that he was no less a thorn in the flesh to the Third Republic. Dipping his pen in gall, he fought for a Republic under the Empire and for the *Communards* against the Versailles Government, emerging from ten years' imprisonment to champion the frothy adventurer Boulanger and to scream at the innocent Dreyfus. With the passage of time the public became bored by the din of his tin whistle, and the longer he lived the more his influence declined. His sole virtues were his incorruptibility and his readiness to risk his life for the cause in which he believed at that particular moment.

Born in 1831, the son of a Legitimist father and a Republican mother, the Marquis Henri de Rochefort began life as a clerk in the Hôtel de Ville, a humdrum occupation relieved by the composition of vaudevilles and political journalism. His pathological hatred of Louis Napoleon originated with the *coup d'état*. December 2, he records in his Memoirs, was a day of stupefaction. Except for a few cries of *À bas le tyran*, Paris seemed too stunned to speak. Next day the tension mounted, shops were closed, and many people stayed at home. December 4 was the day of barricades, but only a few. One might have thought that the conspirator in the Elysée had set out to seek the combatants he required to justify his claim to have saved society. During his perambulations he stumbled over a corpse. The Emperor's marriage was received, according to Rochefort, with indignant stupefaction, and the Dictator's unfortunate compliment, 'She will have the virtues of Josephine' provoked his critic to recall the notorious frailties of Napoleon's wife.

By the time the Dictator took a downward plunge in 1866 and 1867 Rochefort had made such a reputation as journalist on the *Figaro* and other organs that his services were invited by the Orleanists. The offer was declined, not merely because he was a republican but because he planned a battering-ram of his own with the sole purpose of overthrowing the Empire. The soil, he explains in his Memoirs, had been prepared by the growing unpopularity of the *régime* far more effectively than by any opposition propaganda. To raise the capital presented no difficulty, and the title *La Lanterne* had already occurred to his mind. The addition of a hangman's cord to the picture on the cover carried a message which required no verbal explanation. The first issue of the weekly was on sale at forty centimes in the kiosks and received a welcome far exceeding his most sanguine dreams. Leaving his room for his midday meal on the morning of publication he found a woman outside the Bourse doing a brisk trade. Hastening to the printers he learned that the 15,000 copies they expected to suffice were already sold, and that 120,000 were required.

The first number opened with sentences revealing the tricks of a born demagogue:

> France, says the Imperial Almanach, contains 36 million subjects, not counting the subjects of discontent. I am profoundly Bonapartist, but I must choose my hero in the dynasty. I prefer Napoleon II who represents my ideal of a sovereign. No one will deny that he occupied the throne since his successor calls himself Napoleon III. What a reign, my friends! No taxes, no useless wars, no distant expeditions which expend 600 millions to earn 15 francs. No Ministers duplicating their functions at 100,000 francs each. Yes, Napoleon II, I love you, I admire you without reserve.

Paradoxes were part of his technique. 'We have received bad news; the Emperor is well.' When an anonymous correspondent informed him that Queen Hortense was not the author of the popular song *Partant pour la Syrie*, and that this revelation would be particularly wounding to her son, Rochefort announced, 'Every heart beat when the band struck up *Partant pour la Syrie* (music by Dalvimore).' 'You he insults,' exclaimed the Emperor to Persigny, 'with me he goes further by insulting my mother.' In his own words his audacity waxed with every issue, and the strokes of his tomahawk became more merciless as he strove to batter down the Empire. No other journal had met the popular demand for a fight with the gloves off. The second number broadly hinted that the ruler was a bastard. A veto on its sale in the kiosks was welcomed as a sign that his poisoned arrows had hit the mark and as the best and cheapest advertisement.

On the seizure of the eleventh number Rochefort fled to Brussels, where he was received with open arms by Victor Hugo who saluted him with the words: 'You are the brother of my sons.' He had read every issue of *La Lanterne* and rejoiced in its tornado of abuse. Copies of the paper were smuggled across the frontier in shoals, and the Belgian Government in turn requested Rochefort to leave the country. Feigning obedience he remained in Belgium, dating his articles from capitals he had never seen. A fierce encounter with the son of Baroche, Minister of Justice, whom he had furiously assailed, was described by Victor Hugo as a duel between the Empire and the Republic. His contributions to *Le Rappel*, a daily started by the sons of the poet, led to a boom in that paper.

The coming of the Liberal Empire enabled the notorious *frondeur* to stand for the Chamber in Paris in May 1869 as *candidat radical*. His election address, issued from Belgium, appeared in *Le Rappel*.

> My only qualification is an unbreakable determination to fight. Last year I founded *La Lanterne*, and I only left France to carry on my work. What I have written amid persecutions and hatred I shall repeat from the tribune without flinching or compromise, and with the authority of a mandate from the people of Paris. The time has come to unmask these irresponsible augurs who cannot look at one another without a smile, while we alas cannot look at one another without tears. France will only escape from her sickly slumbers by a salutary crisis. I am one of those determined to provoke it.

When Jules Favre announced his candidature for the same constituency Rochefort declined to withdraw. 'I am opposing him because his opinions are not mine. The concessions he hopes to extract from the Government some day do not suffice, and all the magic of his eloquence has failed to obtain them in eighteen years.' On his defeat he was elected by another Paris constituency, and in consequence was allowed to return from abroad. The first task was to found another paper, *La Marseillaise*, the sale of which in the kiosks was forbidden. A poor speaker, he was out of his element in the Chamber but demonstrated his hostility by absenting himself when the Emperor came to open the session and deputies took the oath.

On 10 January 1870 the death of Victor Noir, a member of the staff of *La Marseillaise*, at the hands of Pierre Bonaparte, first cousin of the Emperor, provoked Rochefort to blistering rage.

I was foolish enough to believe that a Bonaparte could be anything but an assassin. I thought an honest duel was possible in this family where murder and ambush are traditional. We weep for our dear friend Victor Noir murdered by the bandit Pierre Napoleon Bonaparte. For eighteen years France has been in the bloody hands of these cut-throats who, not content with shooting down republicans in the streets, lay traps for them and murder them indoors. People of France! have you not had enough?

In the Chamber he asked whether they were living under the Borgias or the Bonapartes. Paris seethed with excitement when the funeral of Victor Noir occasioned mass demonstrations at which the cries of *Vengeance*, *Mort à Bonaparte*, and *Vive la République* were heard. Rochefort received a six months' sentence, and only regained his liberty on the proclamation of the Republic. He had done more than any Frenchman except Gambetta to destroy the prestige of the Empire.

VI. GAMBETTA

While Thiers voiced the dislike of the Constitutional Monarchists for autocracy in any form, Gambetta spoke for the younger generation, which turned to republican principles as the glamour of the Second Empire began to fade. On the eve of the plebiscite in 1848 the precocious *méridional* wrote to his parents: *Vive Cavaignac! A bas Bonaparte!* On reaching Paris in 1857 the penniless law student consoled himself with wishful thinking. 'France is waking up,' he reported; 'the time is near. I know I am too impetuous, but there is so much suffering that one may be forgiven for an instant of enthusiasm.' Listening to Jules Favre's defence of Orsini he commented: 'When shall I deliver my own speech?' Two years later at the age of twenty-two he poured out his heart to his parents. 'I am burning to speak. Why should one hide it, dear good father? I am consumed by ambition, and that is no crime.' When briefs began to arrive he made contact with Jules Favre and Ollivier, declaimed the burning verses of *Les Châtiments* in the cafés, studied the orations of Mirabeau and Danton, and gloated over every rebuff to the *régime*. 'The political horizon darkens,' he declared in 1862; 'the sound of cracking can be heard. Public opinion is anxious. The industrial and financial crisis and the general malaise cloud the horizon. Surely we are in for a change.'

His chance came in 1862 with his first political case. Fifty-four men were arrested for a plot against the Empire which the Opposition believed to have been faked by the police. Counsel for the defence included most of the leaders of the bar, Gambetta being engaged for a mechanic named Buette, who escaped with a trifling sentence of three weeks. The performance of the young advocate, who had passed from the defence of the accused to an indictment of the *régime*, impressed Crémieux, a veteran republican lawyer, who appointed him his secretary. When the elections of 1863 swelled the little group of *Les Cinq* into a formidable opposition including Thiers and Berryer, Gambetta often attended debates, thirsting for the moment when he too would stand at the tribune. That the Empire could and would be overthrown he became increasingly convinced.

In 1865 Gambetta visited Comte de Paris at Twickenham to urge collaboration with the Republicans to destroy the Empire which they equally abhorred. In the year of Sadowa he reported that the Government was losing ground daily. 'Defections all round. Everyone expects an early collapse. 1869 will be a year of decision.' Stars in their courses seemed to be conspiring against the *régime*, for in 1868 the *Affaire Baudin* boiled up. A book on the *coup d'état* had revived the memory of the obscure Deputy, the earliest and best-known casualty in the street fighting. The Republican journals saw their chance, appealed for a national monument, and secured the support of 220 Deputies with Berryer at their head. When the Editor of *Le Rappel* was charged with exciting hatred and contempt of the Government, Gambetta sprang to his defence in the first resounding oratorical triumph of his career in which he was compared to Catiline.

> Grouped round a Pretender hitherto unknown to his countrymen, without talent, honour or rank, are types always ready for violence, men by whom institutions and laws have been sabred for centuries. They say they saved France. Where were all the leading figures—Legitimists, Orleanists, Republicans—who defended legality? In prison or *en route* to Cayenne. That, gentlemen, is how one saves France. For seventeen years you have been the absolute masters,

but you have never dared to celebrate the second of December. Well, we will celebrate it every year till the country regains control and exacts expiation in the name of liberty, equality and fraternity.

The young advocate had surpassed and surprised himself, and the ovation in court was taken up by the crowd outside. Thiers and Berryer, Jules Favre and Ollivier, were impressive speakers, but never in the annals of the Second Empire had such a lava-flow of rhetoric been witnessed in the Chamber and the courts. The Empire had received a shattering blow, for the ruler had been in the dock. When the young tribune resumed his seat, he had become a national figure. Thiers, whose flow of words never approached boiling point, distrusted his hot Italian blood; Italian rulers of France, Mazarin and Napoleon, had done her no good. Gambetta, though sincere enough, was carried away by his own eloquence, a blend of Rienzi and Mirabeau, and his anti-clericalism was deplorable. 'I become the enemy of your friends, Adam,' he remarked. 'Your Gambetta is a political and social danger.' Even before his success he was compromising the constitutional opposition, and how would it be with his enhanced authority? Adam and his wife Juliette were unshaken by such criticism, which they interpreted as the jealousy of a septuagenarian. Thiers, however, was not his only critic. Jules Simon, no friend of the Empire, denounced him as a fanatical atheist, and George Sand declared that Thiers was the only statesman in the ranks of the Opposition.

Striking while the iron was hot, Gambetta entered the Chamber, where he repeated the triumphs of the courts, for the process of disintegration had gone too far to be halted by the Ollivier experiment. In his maiden speech he fired a broadside against the Empire and boldly demanded the establishment of a Republic, though not by force. 'You are only a bridge between the Republic of 1848 and the Republic to come,' he cried, 'and this bridge we shall cross.' His words carried more weight than those of Rochefort, unpredictable as a volcano. Himself a *petit bourgeois*, there was nothing about Gambetta to alarm the well-to-do bourgeoisie, no flirtations with socialism, no menace of 1792. In a two-hours' speech on 5 April 1870, he defined the Liberal Empire as a contradiction in terms. If, as he believed, sovereignty resided in the nation, the Chamber must have the last word. 'If some power can override it, the sovereignty of the nation is infringed.' Universal suffrage, its most perfect expression, led logically to a Republic, though the change should be made by consent. 'The new Constitution did not establish government by the people, merely its semblance. Autocracy remained intact, with its most dangerous prerogatives—the right to make treaties, declare war, and alter institutions at the ruler's will.' When the storm broke he urged caution. 'You can only count on the sympathies of Europe and the assent of France if you can prove that you have been deeply insulted. Your Ambassador has neither sent you an indignant dispatch nor asked for his passports.' His attitude changed overnight when Bismarck edited and circulated the Ems report, and the young tribune became not only the voice, but the right arm of France.

VII. MME ADAM

That Gambetta learned to behave in polite society was mainly due to Mme Adam, *la Grande Française*, the presiding genius of the most influential political salon since Mme de Staël. Juliette Lambert, born in 1836, was reared in the ideology of her father, an unworldly Jacobin doctor to whom *Liberté, Egalité, Fraternité* was a gospel, not a formula. So profound was his sympathy with the underprivileged that he thought of marrying her to a manual labourer, a plan which made no appeal to the ambitious and fastidious girl. The alternative was little better, for at sixteen she was forced into a loveless union with a middle-aged lawyer. When they separated after the birth of her only child, Mme Lamessine settled in Paris at the age of nineteen, determined to make her career. Her first book, on Love and Marriage, attracted the attention of George Sand and opened the portals of the literary world. In 1864 she started a salon frequented by Jules Ferry, Henri Martin the historian, Gaston Paris the medievalist, Challemel-Lacour, publicist and diplomatist, and other celebrities. On the death of her husband in 1868 she married Edmond Adam, a wealthy banker twenty years older than herself, who enabled her to enlarge the range of her hospitality. A rigid *abstentioniste*, she frowned on the *sermentistes* who, like Grévy, took the oath to the Empire in order to undermine the fortress from within the walls. No exception to the rule was allowed for her husband who in 1869 announced his intention to stand for Parliament, for the word compromise found no place in her vocabulary. In vain did he cite the example of other stalwart republicans, and on the day that he was due to take the oath the stronger will prevailed. The candidate explained to the astonished electors that he had changed his mind, and the couple returned to Paris, Juliette prouder than ever, she wrote in her sparkling memoirs, to bear his name.

The outstanding event in the annals of the salon was the arrival of Gambetta in 1868. Every salon required not merely a loyal clientele, but a tame lion.

Juliette: We must introduce him to our circle.
Adam: He has the manners of a schoolboy, no standards of conversation or dress. His accent is impossible and he is overbearing in discussion.
Juliette: But is he out of the ordinary, is he of real significance?
Adam: Yes. But he is bohemian, vulgar, uncouth, a man of the crowd, a Danton.
Juliette: We'll invite him.

'Is he inevitable?' she asked one of her guests. 'No,' was the daunting reply, 'impossible.' Daudet, he added, described him as a noisy Gascon, a kind of commercial traveller in politics, provincial to his fingertips, ill-dressed and blind in one eye. For a moment she wavered, for a salon can be ruined by a single discordant element. Her husband thought the verdict too severe, and at last Gambetta was invited to meet a few intimates. One of them, the Marquis de Lasteyrie, grandson of Lafayette, arrived early and remarked to the hostess: 'I shall tell Thiers about this dinner, for I know he is greatly intrigued by *le jeune monstre*.' The guest arrived in an ill-fitting suit, a cross between an overcoat and a frock-coat, with a flannel shirt visible behind the waistcoat. Seeing everyone else in evening dress he excused himself. The only way to rehabilitate him, decided the hostess, was to take him into dinner herself. He understood and whispered in gratitude, 'Madame, I shall never forget this lesson.' Henceforth the place of honour was his without a rival in sight. At the dinner-table he argued that the Empire must be fought with every available weapon. 'Boycotting the Chamber is childish. To grapple with an enemy you must follow him up. When one visits the sewers one must wear scavenger's boots.'

When the young lawyer leapt into fame by his speech on the Baudin monument Adam was in court and Juliette's father, the old crusader of 1848, expressed a longing to kiss his shoes. Though Juliette believed that her *protégé* would deliver the *coup de grâce*, it required a stronger instrument than the human voice. With heart and head aflame she was incapable of grasping realities. That the Empire was sagging was clear to friend and foe, but that the army might be equally brittle was beyond her grasp. For her and her husband the Prussian spectre began to loom up in 1869 when their friend Nino Bixio, former comrade of Garibaldi, met them in Genoa after a visit to France and Germany by order of Victor Emmanuel.

> *Bixio:* He wished to learn the condition of the French and German armies, for he is convinced that Bismarck is meditating war against France. I share this conviction. Within a year you will be attacked, and since you are unprepared you will be smashed.
> *Adam:* Silence, Bixio, or I will chuck you into the sea. France beaten by the Prussians! Never!
> *Bixio:* My poor Adam, how blind is France!

On returning to Paris Adam repeated the conversation to Thiers, who confessed that it confirmed his own fears. A year later, when Adam and Juliette were the guests of George Sand at Nohat, the declaration of war burst upon them like a thunderbolt. *Vive la France*! exclaimed Maurice Sand. They all repeated the words with trembling lips, and the two women burst into tears. When the news of Sedan reached the capital Juliette made her first public speech to the crowd outside the Chamber of Deputies. 'The Republic is not decreed, it is made; it is your own child. *Vive la République*.' The bitterness of defeat was in some slight measure assuaged by the overthrow of the hated Empire and by her conviction that the curtain would rise on a new drama in which her political Messiah, the hero of the national defence, would play the principal rôle.

VIII. CLEMENCEAU

Though the most dynamic figure of the Third Republic only began to play a leading part during the Franco-German war, his voice had been heard during the Second Empire. Descended from a Vendée family of lawyers, Georges Clemenceau followed the traditional career till he abandoned it for active politics. The strongest influence in his life was that of his father, an unbending republican and *libre-penseur* who agreed with Gambetta's celebrated ejaculation, *Le cléricalisme, voilà l'ennemi*. The most dramatic incident of his youth was the arrest of Dr. Benjamin Clemenceau by a panic-stricken government on a vague charge of disaffection. A month in prison in Nantes was followed by a sentence of deportation. When the handcuffed victim was placed in the prison van, his son, a student at the *Lycée* at Nantes, burst out: 'I will avenge you!' The savage sentence was remitted, for by the time the prisoner reached Marseilles, the chorus of protest from citizens of Nantes persuaded the authorities that it would be unwise to exalt an obscure provincial doctor into a political martyr. Father and son were grateful heirs of the men of 1789 who had drafted the Declaration of the Rights of Man. Both were Positivists, convinced by Comte's interpretation of the history of the human mind as an evolution in three stages—the theological, the metaphysical, and the scientific. Both believed, if not in perfectibility, at any rate in the possibility of progress with the aid of science, reason and liberty.

Settling in Paris at the age of nineteen to pursue his medical studies, Clemenceau brought introductions from his father to left-wing celebrities, among them Blanqui the veteran Communist, Arago the scientist, and Michelet the democratic historian. More interested in the theatre and politics than in his studies, he contributed to obscure journals which circulated in the *Quartier Latin*. Sentenced to imprisonment for marching in a political procession, he spent ten weeks in jail, emerging as a fiercer foe of the Empire than before. A humdrum professional career could never content such a soul of fire, and after taking his degree he visited Mill at Blackheath, meeting also Herbert Spencer and Frederic Harrison. In the same year, 1865, he crossed the Atlantic to study the working of democracy as Tocqueville had done a generation earlier. It was not the Promised Land, he discovered, and in articles for the *Temps* he denounced the corruption of Tammany Hall and lynchings in Georgia. Yet he preferred a land of freedom to his country under a Dictator, and informed his father of his intention to settle there. When the astonished parent stopped his allowance he became a teacher of French in a girls' school in Connecticut and was attracted to one of the pupils. The guardian of the orphan girl, a Protestant pastor, insisted on a religious ceremony, but the young rationalist declined. The demand was withdrawn and the ceremony took place in the City Hall of New York in the summer of 1869. The couple had nothing in common, and after the birth of three children they parted. Seven years of loveless marriage had done nothing to sweeten the temper of a man who was not fashioned for domestic bliss.

Returning to France after four years in the New World, Clemenceau found republicanism becoming fashionable, the Empire tottering to its fall, and the names of Rochefort and Gambetta on all lips. He had left his country because the *régime* allowed no scope to an ardent republican, and he reappeared when the Liberal Empire permitted the Opposition to raise its head. His detestation of the *régime* was almost as fierce as that of Victor Hugo. He had always been a Jacobin who frowned not only on dictators but on the aristocracy. 'All those Emperors and Kings, Archdukes and Princes,' he wrote to a friend when the Great Exhibition of 1867 brought the world of privilege to Paris, 'are grand, superb, generous, sublime, their princesses anything you wish. But I hate them with a merciless hatred, as people hated in 1793 when that poor fool Louis XVI used to be called the execrable tyrant.' The Tiger, *le tombeur des Ministères*, the *enfant terrible* of the Third Republic, waited in the wings for a call, and when the Empire collapsed he plunged into the fight. Though he had taken no active part in the attack on the *régime*, he deserves mention among its implacable foes.

IX. THE SOCIALISTS

On the extreme left stood a group of thinkers far less interested in forms of government than in social change. While the politicians from Thiers to Gambetta and Clemenceau spoke for the bourgeoisie, the socialists, whose significance in French history dates from the Babeuf conspiracy in 1796, claimed to represent the downtrodden proletariat. Saint-Simon, though a member of the *Noblesse*, exercised wider influence after his death in 1828 through his disciples Bazard and Enfantin than during his life, and the term socialism became current about 1830. Though usually described as the father of French socialism, he never advocated the rule of the common man. Society, he argued, should be guided by industrialists and scientists, who were best fitted to develop the resources of the country and to raise the standard of living for the common man. Though the *École Saint Simonienne* quickly disintegrated owing to the rivalry of its leaders and certain doctrinal extravagances, particularly the attack on marriage, the attempt to shift the angle of vision from politics to economics coloured the outlook of many members of a younger generation, among them Louis Napoleon, before Karl Marx proclaimed a similar message with greater power. More of a doctrinaire than Saint-Simon, condemning alike competition and coercion as the root causes of suffering, Fourier, himself a bourgeois, advocated co-operative communities called *Phalanstères*, rich and poor living and working together in brotherly love; but he ignored the frailties of human nature and the first *Phalanstère* collapsed in 1832. A third dreamer, Cabet, expounded a similar ideal in his widely read utopia *Voyage en Icarie*. Fleeing to England to evade arrest, he became a disciple of Robert Owen, and founded a community which quickly came to grief.

The most arresting figure in the socialist camp lives in popular memory for his battle-cry: *La Propriété c'est le vol*. Burning with zeal to give the common man his chance, Proudhon thundered against those who owned property without working and the concentration of the means of production in relatively few hands. In his eyes the gladiators in the political arena were engaged in a sham fight. Political democracy was certainly desirable, but economic democracy—equal opportunity and equal pay—was the only rewarding goal. When Louis Napoleon entered the Chamber in 1848 he sought acquaintance with influential Deputies, among them Proudhon. 'He seems well-intentioned,' reported the latter, 'more obsessed by his uncle's glory than by his own ambitions. He is mediocre, and I doubt if he will go far. He spoke little, listened in a friendly manner, and seemed to agree with me in almost everything. He had not been taken in by the calumnies against Socialists.' The phase of amicable co-existence ended when the revelation of the Prince's ambitions unloosed a flood of invective which earned the socialist prophet a sentence of three years. Emerging on the fateful 2 December 1851, he renewed his attack, denouncing the latest 'act of brigandage' as the sequel to the escapades at Strasbourg and Boulogne. The arch-criminal, he added, was not the sole offender, for the plebiscite was the apostasy of France, though it was in the logic of events, he wrote to Michelet. 'The country needed this shock, for only thus could it learn.' *Le buffon de son oncle* was flagellated as a bastard, without virtue or shame, worse than Tiberius, Nero or Elagabalus, a disgrace to his name. 'You cowardly Frenchmen, kill him.' When the usurper migrated to the Tuileries Proudhon screamed *Canaille en haut, canaille en bas.*

Proudhon had a good heart, but his rage, not only against the Dictator but aganist traditional institutions and religious beliefs, brought him more foes than friends. After launching another broadside in 1858 he fled to Brussels to escape arrest and returned a year later under the general amnesty, resuming his propaganda for an equalitarian society till his death in 1865. In proposing equal pay for all who rendered service to the community, regardless of ability or technical skill, he assumed that the gulf between the classes would eventually be bridged by education. A firm believer in human perfectibility, he looked forward to the ultimate disappearance of coercion in every form. Governance of man by man, he argued, was oppression, a strange aphorism in the mouth of a socialist not far removed from philosophic anarchism.

Louis Blanc lives in history less as historian and politician than as the spiritual father of the *Ateliers Nationaux* of 1848 which by their failure smoothed the way for the Dictator. The plan had long been simmering in his mind, and in his *Organisation du Travail*, published in 1839, he denounced competition as the enemy of social well-being and proclaimed the right to work. 'To each according to his needs, from each according to his capacity', was the better way. The material needs of the community should be supplied by co-operative workshops. He formed the Provisional Government in 1848, and at his suggestion the principle of the Right to Work was proclaimed. When the scheme got completely out of hand and Cavaignac was called in to storm the barricades, he fled to Brussels, declined the general amnesty of 1859, and only returned when the Empire had disappeared. The respected spiritual descendant of Rousseau and the eulogist of Robespierre was at no time a serious menace to the Dictator.

The Socialist standard-bearers were as deeply divided as the Monarchists and the bourgeois Republicans. While Proudhon and Louis Blanc were what Napoleon contemptuously described as *idéologues*, Blanqui was a man of action, and the Blanquists were professed revolutionaries. A born rebel, he advocated Communism by violence, spent half his life in prison, and became the chief bogy-man of his time. He was condemned to death for his share in an armed rising in 1839, the sentence being commuted to life imprisonment. Released in 1848, he inspired the invasion of the Chamber and was sentenced to ten years. Back in jail in 1861, he escaped abroad, returning under an amnesty in 1869. He took part in the mass demonstration at the funeral of Victor Noir, played a part in the Commune, and was transported by the Versailles Government. Like Rochefort, he was always in opposition. His views and methods were so extreme, and therefore so distasteful to the bourgeoisie, that he was a nuisance rather than a serious threat to the successive *régimes*. Indeed his mere existence was an asset to the Dictator in his role as Saviour of Society who enabled honest citizens to sleep quiet in their beds.

17

THE WORLD OF LETTERS

I. VICTOR HUGO

THE brightest luminary in the literary world, like most other writers of his time, grew to manhood without pronounced political convictions. While his father General Hugo owed his promotion and allegiance to *le petit caporal*, his royalist mother detested the Empire, and her lover was executed for complicity in the Malet conspiracy. The young poet was quite content with the July Monarchy, accepted a peerage, made friends with the Duke of Orleans, and dreamed of high office when he ascended the throne. He witnessed the birth of the Second Republic without enthusiasm and the return of Louis Napoleon from his long exile without alarm. When the two men entered the Chamber at the same time at the by-elections in June 1848, the Prince called on him, as on other prominent Deputies, in the hope of gaining his support. 'I have come,' he explained, 'to clarify our relations. Do you take me for a mere adventurer? People say I want to be a second Napoleon. He and Washington can serve as models to ambition, the former a man of genius, the latter a man of virtue. As between the guilty hero and the good citizen I am for the good citizen. That is my ambition. I stand for liberty.' Hugo believed in his sincerity, describing him as inclined to melancholy, something of a somnambulist, distinguished, serious, gentle, courteous, and good company.

With the aid of his two sons Hugo founded a paper *L'Événement* to support the Prince in the belief that he would be loyal to the Republic, and on the eve of the plebiscite for the Presidency he issued a single sheet repeating the words *Louis Napoleon* one hundred times. So zealous was his paper that he was generally believed to be aiming at office. His ambition soared higher still, for he aspired to the position of an *Éminence Grise*. He was a guest at the first official dinner of the new President at the Elysée. 'This is a very improvised affair, just a few friends,' remarked the host; 'I thank you for coming.' Asked for his advice he replied: 'Reassure the bourgeoisie, look after the people, revive our glorious traditions. France is a nation of conquerors. When she is not winning victories with her sword she must win them with her brains. Realize that and all will be well. Ignore it and you will be lost.'

On his re-election in May 1849, Hugo found himself a lonely figure in a predominantly conservative Chamber, trusted neither by the Monarchist majority nor the Republican minority. 'I am not a politician,' he declared, 'merely a free man.' By the autumn he had ceased to be considered a supporter of the President, though he still dined at the Elysée. His paper went into opposition, explaining that the Prince's advisers stifled all his noble impulses. In the following year the *Loi Falloux* further estranged the man who shared Gambetta's sentiment: *Le cléricalisme, voila l'ennemi*. At this point he formally joined the Republican group in the Chamber with the words: 'Republicans, open your ranks and let me in. I am one of you.' His hostility increased with the revelation of the President's ambitions, which he attempted to block by opposing a revision of the constitution. When a prosecution was launched at *L'Événement* he declared open war. 'Because we have had a Napoleon the Great,' he exclaimed in the Chamber, 'must we have a Napoleon the Little?' Visiting his sons in the Conciergerie, he expected to join them at any moment.

The *coup d'état* filled him with almost pathological fury, and his first instinct was to resist; but the country was in no fighting mood. He escaped arrest by slipping away to Brussels, where he prepared a preliminary indictment of the oath-breaker, deferring a comprehensive record till more details became available. Regarding himself as the conscience of France at a time when her voice was silenced, he denounced *Napoléon le Petit* with all the ferocity of a Hebrew prophet. He had believed in the usurper and helped him to climb, and he had been tricked. He began by quoting the solemn oath to the Constitution and the words of the President of the Chamber: 'We take God and man as witnesses to this oath.' The vote of the nation and the oath he had taken, added the new President, would govern his conduct. 'I shall regard as enemies of the country all who try to change by illegal means what France has decided.' One article of the constitution declared that the Deputies could not be arrested except for a criminal offence, another that for the President to dissolve the Chamber or impede the execution of its mandate would constitute high treason. In that event authority would pass to the Chamber, and it would be the duty of the Deputies, regardless of the number and strength of the enemy, to cover with their bodies the sovereignty of the people, to employ all weapons for the overthrow of the usurper, to accept proscription with all its miseries, to confront the traitor with his oath, to forget their private griefs, their families, their ruined fortunes, their shattered affections, their bleeding hearts, to forget themselves, to have only a single wound, the wound of France, to cry Justice, to be implacable, to seize the abominated crowned perjurer, if not with the arm of the law, at least with the pincers of truth, to scorch in the flames of history every letter of his oath and to brand them on his face. The conscience of mankind should awake.

> On 2 December an odious, repulsive, infamous, unprecedented crime was committed, recognized as such even by its beneficiaries, a crime embracing all crimes—treachery, perjury, murder, spoliation, swindling, nocturnal massacres, secret *fusillades*, ten thousand citizens deported, forty thousand proscribed, sixty thousand families ruined. The author of this crime is a malefactor of the most cynical and degraded kind. His servants are the comrades of a pirate, not functionaries but accomplices. When France awakes she will start back with a terrible shudder.

The author proceeds to describe the culprit:

> A man of middle height, cold, pale, slow of speech as if half asleep, with a slight German accent, vulgar, childish, theatrical, vain. He has an *idée fixe*. He knows what he wants and gets there, ignoring justice, law, reason, honour, humanity. He is not a half-wit but simply a man of another age. Philip II of Spain would recognize him, Henry VIII smile at him, Caesar Borgia embrace him, Ali Pasha of Janina shake his hand. He has something of the Middle Ages and the Byzantine Empire. What he has done would seem quite

natural to Mahomet II and Alexander VI. To our time his actions appear hideous. His greatest talent is silence. He remains dumb and motionless till the hour strikes and he leaps on his prey. When he breaks silence he lies as other people breathe. If he announces an honest intention, be on your guard; if he affirms, do not trust him; if he swears an oath, tremble. Machiavelli has left descendants and Louis Bonaparte is one of them. You say it will last. No, no, no! If it did there would be no God in heaven and no more France. Every citizen worthy of the name has only one duty—to load his rifle and wait.

What of the triumphant plebiscite?

The Prince rubs his hands, concludes that it is all over, that he is absolved. Yet the moral question remains. There are two things which may be news to you called Good and Evil. You must be told that to lie is not good, to betray is evil, to murder is worse. It may be useful but it is forbidden. M. Bonaparte, you may be the master, you may have armies, guns and fortresses, but the human conscience stands up and proclaims: This you shall not do.

After two hundred pages of this vitriolic abuse the author finds some comfort in the title of his book. *Napoléon le Petit* would never rank with the master bandits of history.

Though he has committed enormous crimes he will remain shoddy, the nocturnal garrotter of liberty who has glutted his soldiers, not with glory like the first Napoleon, but with wine, the pigmy tyrant of a great people. As Dictator he is a buffoon, as Emperor he will be grotesque, at once hideous and ridiculous. Once stripped of success, the pedestal removed, the sword detached, a poor little skeleton; can one imagine anything more paltry and pitiful? Tiberius, Nero, Timur and other murderers were tigers. M. Bonaparte is only a hyena, part brigand, part knave—Napoleon the Little, no more, no less. Think of it. At the head of the greatest people on earth, in the middle of the greatest century in history, this personage has made France his prey. *Grand Dieu!* You are a monkey, not a lion, a parrot, not an eagle, a comedian.

'I feel Bonaparte is beginning to smell a bit,' wrote Hugo when the Empire was proclaimed. 'The Montijo marriage will finish him.' When his Belgian publisher complained of his intemperate language he replied that in such a case pinpricks were useless. 'Perhaps I may offend the bourgeoisie. What matter, if I can arouse the people? Jeremiah, Isaiah, Tacitus, Dante, were they not violent? It will be time for moderation when we have won.' Permission to return to France if he promised to cease his attacks was scornfully rejected. France's greatest poet had grave faults, but he never lowered his flag. 'I forgive them and I pity them,' he remarked of former comrades who purchased return to their fatherland by laying down their arms. For the writer who could earn large sums by his pen unrelenting defiance was much easier than for men who found it difficult at all times to make a living. Though the Empire lasted far longer than he anticipated, he never doubted that he would witness its downfall. The success of *La Lanterne* encouraged him and his sons to launch *Le Rappel*, with Rochefort among the contributors, which started with a sale of 50,000. Prosecution increased its popularity, and the *régime* staggered under a rain of blows from many quarters. The Liberal Empire might prove a palliative, but few expected it to arrest the decline.

After launching the first of his broadsides in *Napoléon le Petit*, Hugo proceeded to compile a voluminous record of the *coup d'état*, which had to await publication till the Empire had disappeared, since his Belgian publisher feared retaliation from the Tuileries. *Histoire d'un Crime*, he declared in a preface added in 1877, had been commenced twelve days after the *coup*, completed in the following May, and very little revised. Once again the author writes in a rage, the strokes of his battle-axe falling on everyone who failed to oppose the usurper, including fellow-travellers such as Mérimée and Montalembert. The Dictator is presented as the perfect Machiavellian, calculating, passionless, completely amoral. That he broke his oath is true enough and bad enough, but there was no premeditated massacre. That every participating General received a million francs and every participating soldier two gold crowns—all stolen from the Banque de France—was a pure invention. It was equally untrue that the soldiers were as savage as their chiefs, made no prisoners, filled their pockets with loot, and spent the night drinking and smoking cigars. Though the larger record contained some new information, the exaggerations and inventions weakened its impact.

Of Hugo's three boardsides the most enduring is *Les Châtiments*, published in Brussels shortly after the proclamation of the

Empire. Conscience could not be crushed, declared the Preface, for it was the thought of God. The hundred poems are divided into sections, each bearing a slogan of the Dictator: Society is saved, Order is restored, the Family restored, Religion glorified, Authority consecrated, Stability assured. Comparing the Man of December to a night burglar and Paris to a cemetery, he opens the attack with *Nox*, the longest of the items. Haunted by the memory of the corpses he had seen lying in the streets, he flagellates the murderer who had the effrontery to stage a pompous ceremony in Notre-Dame.

> Cet infâme apportait à Dieu son attentat.
> Comme un loup qui se lèche après qu'il vient de mordre
> Caressant sa moustache, il dit—J'ai sauvé l'ordre.
> Anges, recevez moi dans votre légion.
> J'ai sauvé la famille et la religion.

The outbreak of war opened the frontier to the old gladiator and rendered possible the publication of *Les Châtiments* in France. A poem entitled *Au moment de rentrer en France*, composed in Brussels on 31 August, was added to the new edition.

> Je vois en même temps le meilleur et le pire.
>   Noir tableau.
> Car la France mérite Austerlitz, et l'Empire
>   Waterloo.

The ink was scarcely dry on these lines when the news from Sedan brought France the liberation for which the poet had longed and fought for nearly twenty years. But at what a price! More than ever he felt it his right and his duty to denounce the man who had not only broken his oath and shed French blood but had brought the invader to the capital.

II. MÉRIMÉE

If Victor Hugo was the most celebrated and the most formidable foe of the Emperor in the literary world, Mérimée was his most distinguished friend. The author of *Colomba* and *Carmen* was drawn into the Imperial circle neither by strong ideological sympathy nor by political ambition but owing to a long-standing friendship with the mother of the Empress. When travelling in Spain in 1830 he met the Comte and Comtesse de Teba and caught his first glimpse of Eugénie at the age of four. 'Chance took me to Spain,' he wrote long afterwards, 'where I found some very kind people. There I saw a little girl to whom I used to tell stories.' His work as Inspector of Historical Monuments, in which he delighted, involved official visits to many lands. During one of these journeys in 1836 he wrote to Stendhal: 'On my return I will introduce you to an excellent friend whom you will like for her intelligence and personality. She is an admirable friend, but there has never been a *liaison*. She is a perfect type of the Andalusian women. She is the Comtesse de Montijo, formerly Comtesse de Teba, of whom I often told you.' The friendship developed when the Comtesse brought her two daughters to Paris for their education, and when the fall of the Monarchy threatened him with the loss of his post she offered him hospitality in Spain. His duty kept him in Paris, he replied, but the future was dark. After the bloodshed of the barricades he was haunted by the spectre of mob rule and concluded that France needed a Man.

The leader for whom he was looking soon appeared, but his election to the Presidency introduced a fresh element of discord. 'You cannot conceive the violence of parties,' he reported to Countess Montijo in January 1851 when Changarnier was dismissed.

> Happily the fury is so far confined to the upper class. The people care as little about the President as about the Chamber, perhaps even less. The crisis is prolonged, the *rouges* may cut in between the Deputies and the President as they did between Louis Philippe and the Third Party. Changarnier, the terror of the *rouges*, has been replaced by a tough man—all right against a revolt but lacking *sang-froid* and commonsense. I fear that in dismissing him the President has cut off his right hand with his left. We are incorrigible. The French nobility has committed so many follies that the bourgeoisie has kicked them out. And now the bourgeoisie seem even more extravagant. At present you can't talk politics in Paris. You have only known three or four parties. Now there are twenty, and not one of them knows what he wants except the *rouges* who may triumph some day.

Filled with such dark apprehensions Mérimée welcomed the *coup d'état*. 'This looks like the final battle,' he wrote on the eve of the historic 2 December, 'but who will win? If the President loses, I think the heroic Deputies will have to make way for Ledru-Rollin. I return home after meeting nothing but madmen. The face of Paris recalls 25 February 1848, but now it is the soldiers who terrify the citizens.'

The Emperor's marriage opened a new and exciting chapter in Mérimée's career. Having no political ambitions, he begged the Empress to exact an oath never to ask a favour. Taking him at his word she received his oath in the most solemn manner, while inviting him to bring to her notice cases of hardship. He declined the post of Director of the National Archives but gratefully accepted a seat in the Senate with its welcome salary of 30,000 francs. 'My first thoughts must go to you,' he wrote to Countess Montijo, 'I feel a little stunned. Fould tells me that the Empress warmly embraced her husband when he gave her the news.' For the Empress he felt real affection, for the Emperor liking and respect. He was particularly struck by his courage. 'Does the fear of assassination greatly disturb him?' inquired Nassau Senior in 1857 after the attempts on his life. 'Not at all,' replied Mérimée. 'He is brave but also a fatalist.' When the Archbishop of Paris was killed, Mérimée discovered in Nice a light coat of mail capable of resisting a dagger, and sent a description to the Empress. On his return to Paris she told him that she might have persuaded him to wear it for one day, but no more. 'If we were to take precautions,' she added, 'we should think of nothing else.' Her courage was equal to his and indeed greater, since she fully expected to end like Marie Antoinette. This conversation occurred shortly before the ordeal of Orsini's bombs, which neither of the sovereigns allowed to alter the usual routine in the slightest degree. That the Empire had come to stay Mérimée never believed. He thought the ruler was far more liberal than his entourage, for he realized that France would not for ever tolerate the Constitution of 1852. When Nassau Senior remarked in 1850 that he was good in private life and bad in public affairs, Mérimée replied that it was too soon to decide that he was a bad politician. Europe was very sick, but he was not the cause.

Mérimée cared little for the glamour of the Court. 'We have plenty to do here,' he reported to Panizzi from Compiègne in 1865. 'Your servant is director of the theatre, author and actor.

In his moments of leisure he has to undertake researches into Roman history. He is free to do what he likes between one in the morning and eight. We eat too much. I am half dead. The life we lead is a terrible strain on nerve and brain. We emerge from overheated rooms, drive in open carriages in icy weather, and return to a tropical temperature. I wonder how the ladies stand it.' Despite such discomforts he never missed the November house parties, where he was regarded as something of an institution. Writers and artists, invited for the first time, asked the oracle what clothes they should wear.

When the Emperor embarked on a biography of Julius Caesar he asked Mérimée, who was equally interested in the subject, to send him a memorandum and invited him to name a sum for his services, 'Sire,' was the response, 'I have all the books at home. I can manage with two quires of paper, a dozen quill pens and a bottle of ink. Let me make it a present.' It was never written, for verbal exchanges proved more satisfactory. He had no illusions as to the academic significance of the book which he had helped to produce.

> I think you are too severe on the *Life of Caesar* [he wrote to Panizzi in 1869]. Would you like the author, instead of saying things simply and sincerely, to have followed the German historians who in their desire to abandon the beaten track chose the most absurd side-tracks? But I wish he had taken my advice to confine himself to reflections instead of telling the story without anything that is new. The reflections of a man in a position beyond the range of writers would have provided something original and very interesting. The great fault in my opinion is that one might say that he is standing before a mirror to portray his hero.

Everyone realized that it was primarily a political tract.

A more rewarding task for Mérimée was to encourage artists, preserve historic buildings, and promote archaeological research. He was less happily occupied as a member of the first Commission for the publication of the correspondence of Napoleon. 'The fifteenth volume is printed but not yet published,' he reported to Panizzi in 1864. 'I think you know I am no longer a member. It was disagreeable enough under the Marshal [La Valette], and it will doubtless be a good deal worse under a prince [Prince Napoleon]. Moreover this second commission will probably be extremely suspect and I have no wish to share the responsibility.' He had been sounded about continuing his services but declined. It was a wise decision, for the omissions from the official enterprise were to fill four supplementary volumes when the Empire was gone.

Mérimée lived just long enough to witness the downfall of the *régime*. 'Our bellicose nation is badly rattled by the thought of war,' he reported to Panizzi when the crisis began. 'You saw the panic on the Bourse after the declaration of M. de Gramont. I don't see how there can be war unless for some unknown reason Bismarck wills it.' When the storm burst he added that at the moment the war was very popular, with plenty of volunteers and troops leaving for the front in confident mood. He was less sanguine. 'I fear our Generals are not geniuses, and defeat would mean a Republic.' On 1 August, after the first disasters, he found the Regent firm as a rock, though she realized the horror of the situation. 'The Emperor may seek death, for he could only return to Paris as a victor and victory is impossible. Nothing is ready, disorder everywhere.' 'If we had Generals and Ministers', he lamented, 'nothing would be lost, for there is plenty of enthusiasm and patriots. But in a state of anarchy the elements are useless. We are on the road to a Republic, and what a Republic!' I know nothing more admirable than the Empress at this moment. She has no illusions, yet she displays a heroic serenity which must cost her a great effort. Every day we hear of some new folly on the part of the late Ministry—here no food, there no munitions, complete illusion about the number of troops.' Each letter was now more despairing than the last. '*Finis Galliae*,' he wrote on 21 August. 'We have brave soldiers but no General. Here in Paris there is only disorder and folly. I think the Emperor is seeking death. I am expecting the proclamation of the Republic in a week and the Prussians in a fortnight. I envy those who have fallen on the banks of the Rhine.' When the news of Sedan rang down the curtain he moaned, 'A French army capitulates, the Emperor a prisoner. Everything collapses at the same moment.' A month later he too was gone.

III. SAINTE-BEUVE

Sainte-Beuve, like Mérimée, welcomed the *coup d'état* and tepidly supported the Empire by tongue and pen. As a child he had seen Napoleon reviewing the troops in Boulogne, but he never displayed interest in the Bonapartist cause till the battle of the barricades filled him with dread of mob rule. He had too little faith in human nature to care for democracy. Louis Napoleon, he believed, was the only man to tame 'the ferocious beast', to throw a plank across the abyss, and to inaugurate the Welfare State. In 1852 he accepted the Cross of the Legion of Honour which he had twice refused under Louis Philippe. He appealed to the Constitutional Monarchists, the men of 1830, not to sulk in their tents but to serve their country, and he transferred his *Lundis* to the official *Moniteur*. The new master, he declared, held in his hands the power of Louis XIV and in his heart the principles of the Revolution.

His adhesion earned no gratitude in the Dictator, who never pretended to care about *belles lettres*. Among the papers discovered in the Tuileries after the *débâcle* was a Memorandum by Sainte-Beuve dated 1856 which pleaded for some official encouragement to literature, succour for writers in distress, and access to the Emperor independently of the Minister of Education. French literature, he added, had become a democracy, and the great majority of authors were workers living by their pen. He was not speaking of the Professors and Academicians but of the rank and file who had always been neglected, which was bad for them and bad for society. If the Emperor were to take an interest in them as he did in manual workers, and offer prizes, he would earn their gratitude. The appeal evoked no response. The celebrated critic had never felt much enthusiasm for the Emperor, and he felt increasingly disillusioned as the reign advanced. His friend Princess Mathilde procured him an invitation to Compiègne, but he found the atmosphere too frivolous for his taste and the experiment was not repeated. On the other hand he aspired to a seat in the Senate, not in order to play a part in politics, for he was as unpolitical as Mérimée, but because the salary would relieve him of financial anxieties. The first attempt of the Princess in 1864 failed, but she succeeded in the following year. His lingering respect for the Emperor disappeared when he rather pleasantly observed: 'I read you with pleasure in the *Moniteur*,' three years after he had transferred his *Lundis* to another paper.

Rarely intervening in debate in the Senate, for he was a poor speaker, his most notable utterance was a denunciation of the ecclesiastical attempts to exclude from public libraries writers who were the glories of France. 'Your list, Gentlemen, is incomplete,' he sarcastically exclaimed. 'The name of Molière is missing, *Tartuffe* is missing.' There should be no *Index* in France, no classification of books as good and bad. The Emperor, he added, honoured Renan with his esteem and George Sand with his friendship. A more unexpected declaration of independence occurred when he transferred his *Lundis* from the *Moniteur* to the *Temps*. When the editor of the official journal demanded the omission of a sentence the impenitent author published the whole article in the *Temps*. His challenge to authority led to his exclusion from the salon of Princess Mathilde, who regarded his connection with an oppositional journal as a crime beyond forgiveness. 'The Empire is very sick', he wrote, 'and as I am inside the door I should be the first to suffer if it goes.' *Felix opportunitate mortis*; the ailing old man missed the *débâcle* by a few months.

IV. GEORGE SAND

George Sand had no respect for tradition or authority in any sphere. As a republican and socialist, a friend of Mazzini and Louis Blanc, she could scarcely be expected to smile on a dictator, but her heart was too good to hate Louis Napoleon or anyone else. Contact was established when the prisoner at Ham sent her a copy of *The Extinction of Pauperism*, and she replied in a letter which was at once an expression of sympathy and a confession of faith. She had studied the plan with deep interest, though she was not clever enough to judge of its feasibility. Who was to carry it out? 'You should be grateful to us for resisting the attraction of your character, your intelligence and your rank, and for daring to tell you that we shall never acknowledge any sovereignty except that of the people, which seems to us incompatible with that of an individual.' The time for Personal Government was over.

You deserve to have been born in an age when your exceptional qualities might have secured our happiness and your glory. People say that you merely desire to be a French citizen, a sufficiently lofty role if properly understood. The heir to a great name concerns himself with the fortunes of the proletariat. That is your greatness, that should be the link between you and the republican millions of France. If it depended on myself, who have read your writings, I should trust your promises and open the prison doors.

The captive gratefully replied that a visit from her, for he was occasionally allowed visitors, would be a red-letter day.

The fall of the Monarchy filled the ardent democrat with delight. 'The Republic is the best of families,' she wrote estatically, 'the people the best of friends. The Republic for ever! What a dream, what enthusiasm, what admirable and orderly behaviour of Paris! I have just been there and witnessed the nobility, sublimity and generosity of the people in the heart of France. We are all excited and intoxicated at having gone to sleep in the mire and woken up in heaven. Now it is safe and we would all die to preserve it.' The warm-hearted woman had pitched her expectations far too high, for the new *régime* proved no more progressive than the Bourgeois Monarchy, and the streets of the capital were soon running with blood. Having lost her faith in the Second Republic she took the *coup d'état* calmly, reserving her wrath for the harsh police measures which accompanied and disgraced it. 'Let us hope the authorities will tire of their own rigour, which has been quite unnecessary,' she wrote. 'The eight millions who voted for the new master of France should teach them to rely on the people.' 'You have been told,' she wrote to Mazzini, 'that they voted under the dominion of fear. That is untrue. I have found in him good instincts and aims resembling our own.'

Convinced that the Dictator was better than his agents, she appealed to him in a series of letters which do honour to her courage and humanity, 'Prince, the friends of my youth and my old age are in prison or exile. Your heavy hand fell on all who call themselves Socialist Republicans.' Far from opposing the new *régime*, she regarded it as the last chance of salvation amid the corruption of morals and confusion of ideas. 'I cannot be its apostle, but I should regard it as a crime to reproach heaven, the nation, or the man whom God calls and the people accept.' Repression, however, had gone too far, and mass imprisonment and deportation of harmless folk must stop. 'Amnesty, amnesty soon, my Prince!' A letter of portentous length closed with a request for an interview, which was promptly accorded, in which her belief in his goodness of heart was confirmed. 'I obtained from you words of kindness which I shall never forget,' she wrote. 'You were good enough to tell me: "Ask me for whatever pardon you may wish."' When the individuals she brought to his notice were liberated she described herself as the only Socialist who remained his friend. Persigny, Minister of the Interior, to whom he referred her, with equal readiness promised pardon for any friend she might name. In her campaign to secure the release of all untried detainees she begged her friend Prince Napoleon to use his influence with the Government.

Once again she was to be disillusioned. Promises, she discovered, were not enough, for they remained in most cases a dead letter, thanks to the agents less pliant and kindly than the Dictator himself. 'Half of France has turned informer against the other half; the blind hatred and atrocious zeal of a furious police have been satiated,' she wrote to a friend. 'Paris is in chaos and the provinces a tomb.' A second interview with the President to save a friend from deportation opened her eyes to the vices of autocracy. 'He is neither debauched, nor a robber, nor bloodthirsty, but he is no longer in control if he ever was. Circumstances and party ambitions cast him into the whirlpool, and he flattered himself that he could control it; but he is already half submerged, and I doubt if he is now fully conscious of his actions.' She occasionally appealed to the Empress on behalf of friends in financial distress, and not in vain; but her friendship with Prince Napoleon was of little avail in her works of mercy, since he counted for less and less. Opening prison doors, arranging help for the stricken families of political victims, in one case rescuing four young soldiers from the firing squad, she was called the saint of Berry and *Notre Dame de Secours*. It was her finest hour. Though the ruler and the novelist never met again, for after the political amnesty of 1859 there was no occasion for further correspondence, she remained a welcome guest in the salon of Princess Mathilde and counted Prince Napoleon among her intimate friends.

When the *Vie de César* was published in 1864 she criticized its cult in an obscure newspaper.

> I have not had time to consider whether it would please the illustrious author or not [she wrote to Prince Napoleon]. While paying homage to the real talent of its composition, I cannot accept its thesis. To compare the work of Caesar with that of Napoleon I, blameable perhaps in certain ways but truly glorious, seemed to me real blasphemy. I should have said so had I not feared to trespass on the domain of politics at the request of the publisher. How old is that doctrine of the authority of a single ruler and how hollow nowadays! It is the fault of Caesar, the fatal path which always leads to disaster.

She had only a few years to wait till her generalization received a new and terrible proof.

George Sand lived to witness the collapse of the *régime* which she had tolerated but never fully approved. The declaration of war seemed to her a blunder and a crime. 'Paris must be mad,' she declared, 'the honour of France is in no way involved. To me this war appears a blunder, the singing of the Marseillaise an infamy. Men are ferocious and conceited brutes. What a lesson for nations which like dictators!' When bad news from the front poured in, she knew that the curtain was about to fall. 'The Empire is lost; it has lived its allotted span. The same men who confidently voted for it in the plebiscite would today vote unanimously for its overthrow. Alas! there is no longer the enthusiasm of the wars of the Republic. There is scepticism, disaffection, a determination to punish in the next vote.' If the ruler did not promptly abdicate, she declared, he should be deposed. Sedan cut the knot and she greeted the Third Republic with a cheer. 'What a glorious event, what a happy day amidst all our disasters! At last Paris has risen like one man. That is what she should have done a fortnight ago. Hurrah for Paris!'

V. FLAUBERT

No French writer of his time displayed less interest in the political scene than Flaubert, who lived for his literary work and felt equal disdain for the successive systems by which France was governed. In his voluminous correspondence there are singularly few references to public affairs. Politics, he felt, was a vulgar game, unsuitable for intellectuals and appealing to the worst elements in human nature. 'You ask what I think of all these happenings,' he wrote contemptuously on the collapse of the Monarchy. 'Well, it's all very funny. It is a joy to see some of the crestfallen faces and to witness the deflated ambitions. I don't know if the new pattern of government and society will be favourable to the arts; it cannot be more bourgeois, more mediocre, more stupid. Life is a dull show. I don't know if the Republic will help, and I greatly doubt it.' A year later he wrote to a friend in Corsica in his usual pessimistic vein. 'I don't know if the Corsicans are as stupid as the French, but here it is deplorable: republicans, reactionaries, reds, blues, tricolors, compete in ineptitude; it is enough to make decent folk sick!'

Though Flaubert liked the *coup d'état* no better than his fellow craftsmen, he blamed the people more than their new master. 'I was in Paris at the time,' he reported to a friend, 'I was nearly slaughtered several times, sabred, shot or blown to pieces by cannon, for there was something to suit all tastes. But I had a good view. Providence, knowing my love of the picturesque, always posts me to the first night when it is worth while. This time I wasn't sold. It was first rate.' The arch individualist resented even the mild yoke of the Academy.

> A worm-eaten and stupid institution. I detest all limitation, and I think an Academy is the most unsuitable thing in the world for the human mind, which has neither rule nor law nor uniform. Our dear country detests liberty. The ideal state, according to the socialists, is a kind of huge monster sucking into itself all individual action, all personality, all thought, directing everything, doing everything, a sacerdotal tyranny in these narrow hearts. Everything must be regulated, everything rebuilt on different foundations; there are no follies or vices which are not to be found in these dreams. Nowadays

man is more of a fanatic than ever, obsessed with himself. That is his only tune; he bleats for the infinite, as Montaigne used to say, and can find nothing bigger than this miserable life from which he is always striving to escape. Since 1830 France has been living in a crazy realism. The infallibility of universal suffrage is becoming a dogma to replace the infallibility of the Pope. The powerful army, the right of numbers, respect for the mob, has succeeded the authority of names, divine right, the supremacy of mind. The human conscience, worn out with fatigue, seems ready for slumber in sensual apathy. Republic or Monarchy, it will be a long time before we emerge from this situation. What is this quality but the negation of all liberty, superiority, nature itself? That is why I love art: there, at any rate, is liberty, in the realm of the imagination. There one is at once king and people, active and passive, viaticum and priest. No limitations!

The gloomy bourgeois novelist described himself as a bourgeoisphobe. When George Sand called him a mysterious being, he replied that he was devastatingly commonplace and was sometimes sick of the bourgeois inside him. 'Hate of the bourgeois is the beginning of wisdom.' Such a man, packed full of phobias, could never be really happy.

The approach to the Empire seemed to Flaubert a natural development in a country which lacked real love of liberty.

I read of the President's tours. Splendid! We must only have one idea and no longer respect for anything. If all morality is useless for future communities which, being organized like an automaton, will not need it, he is preparing the way. I am speaking seriously, for I believe that is his mission. 1789 destroyed Monarchy and the nobility, 1848 the bourgeoisie, 1851 the people. Nothing is left but an imbecile *canaille*, and we are all reduced to the same level of mediocrity.

He regarded women as bundles of emotion, and confessed that he preferred the dead to the living. Writing in the summer of 1853 he congratulated Victor Hugo on missing the ordeal in France where one could not move a step without being defiled. 'The atmosphere is heavy with poisonous vapours. Air! Air! So I open the window and turn my gaze in your direction. Mediocrity loves regulations. I hate all restrictions, corporations, caste, hierarchy, the herd. These things fill my soul with execration.'

The prosecution for immorality of the author of *Madame Bovary*, published serially in the *Revue de Paris* in 1859, challenged his conviction that liberty was the life-blood of literature.

> I have now learned [he wrote] that it is very unpleasant to be involved in a political affair, and that social hypocrisy is a serious matter. This time it has been so stupid that it is ashamed of itself and has beaten a retreat. The book is moral, eminently moral. I shall continue to write with conscience and independence for the sole pleasure of writing. I am not in the least upset. It is too silly. Every man of letters in Paris defends me; they all line up behind me, feeling that my cause is theirs. The police miscalculated. They thought they would go for the first novel which came along. Now, partly owing to the prosecution, mine passes for a masterpiece. I have plenty of what used to be called the great ladies on my side. The Empress has spoken for me and the Emperor says: 'Let him alone.' There is not a line in French literature of the last three centuries which is not equally dangerous to religion and morals. It is all so stupid that I end by being amused.

By an illogical compromise the court censured the novel and acquitted the author. Well might he describe the episode as one of the most inept follies of the reign, and he begged a friend to tell the Emperor so, for the prosecution proved a magnificent advertisement. A few months later the prosecution of Baudelaire led to the omission of some offending verses in *Les Fleurs du Mal* and to the increased sale of the expurgated edition. The misanthrope emerged from the ordeal with an even lower estimate of his fellows. 'I neither love life nor fear death,' he confided to a friend.

> I have no sympathy with any political party or, to be more accurate, I execrate them all because they seem to me equally narrow, false and puerile, living for the moment, without broad views and never rising above the conception of utility. I hate all despotism. I am a rabid liberal. What I have seen, felt, read, has left me with an inextinguishable love of truth. Goethe exclaimed on his death-bed 'Light! Light!' Yes, light, even if it consumes us!

Most of his closest friends, such as Sainte-Beuve, Gautier and the Goncourt brothers, were *habitués* of Princess Mathilde's salon before he joined them in the middle sixties. Though professing distaste for life in Paris, he enjoyed the friendship of the lively hostess, who became one of his chief correspondents. Since there was no obligation to support the Empire, he accepted the red ribbon of the Legion of Honour procured for him by the Princess, and was present at a ball at the Tuileries when the visiting sovereigns flocked to the Great Exhibition in 1867. Never either a declared supporter or a declared foe of the Empire, he thought that Rochefort's noisy squibs in *La Lanterne* went too far; and when Sainte-Beuve aroused the wrath of the Princess by writing for the *Temps*, an opposition journal, he took her side.

> His worst offence [he wrote to her] is to have displeased you. When you begged him not to write in that paper he should have desisted. Such are my political views. Yet I quite understand his anger at the rejection of his article elsewhere, and only a man of letters knows how these things hurt. So I excuse his rancour, but I should not excuse a break with a Government which has done so much for him. You call it treachery, but if he only writes on literature the harm is small. What I cannot forgive is that he has caused you grief, you who have been not merely so kind to him but so devoted.

When Flaubert was blasted out of his ivory tower in 1870 his first reaction was one of anger and disgust.

> I am shattered by the folly of my compatriots [he wrote to George Sand on hearing of the declaration of war]. The irremediable barbarism of mankind fills me with black sorrow. This enthusiasm, with no idea behind it, makes me wish for death. The good Frenchman wants to fight because he feels provoked by Prussia, because savagery is the natural condition of man, because there is a *mystique* in war which transports the masses. Have we reverted to racial wars? I fear so. The horrible butchery lacks even a pretext. It is the instinct to fight for fighting's sake. Hobbes was right: *homo homini lupus*. If only I was living among the Bedouins!

His chilly blood began to warm up as bad news streamed in. He bought a revolver in Rouen and began training the local militia; but he can hardly have been an inspiring chief, and he soon resigned on the ground that his men were too undisciplined. 'I defend this poor Republic,' he wrote to George Sand after Sedan, 'but I don't believe in it. It is even more foolish than the Empire and has no use for the Muses. The Latin races are finished. Now it is the turn of the Saxons who will later be swallowed by the Slavs. France needs a leader. A man! a man! We are entering an age of darkness. I hate democracy.' Though France is proud of Flaubert, he was never proud of France.

VI. THE GONCOURT BROTHERS

The de Goncourt brothers, a single mind and heart located in two bodies, took as little interest in politics as most writers of the time, and their voluminous journals rarely allude to current affairs. What little they knew and heard about politicians filled them with disgust. 'Lying phrases, sonorous words, humbug,' they wrote in 1863:

> Revolutions, alternation of the ins and outs, atrocious corruptions—that is about all. No trace of political morality. I look about for some disinterested opinion and find none. People are prepared to run risks in the hopes of some appointment and to pledge support to a party with prospects. A Senator professes the opinions of his place, and a young friend of mine is attached to the Orleans family because he has half a promise of a job if they return. There are scarcely two or three unpaid madmen or enthusiasts in a party, if you can find them, and it will be strange if you don't discover they are imbeciles. This causes disillusion, scepticism, acceptance of power in any shape, the political apathy which I find among my literary friends, in Flaubert's house as in ours. No need to die for any cause; live under any government however much you dislike it; believe in nothing but art and literature. Everything is a lie and a trap.

It might be Flaubert speaking.

The brothers had cause to remember the *coup d'état*, for their first book was due for publication on 2 December 1857. On hearing the news they hurried to the printer and found that he had burned the posters announcing *En 18—*, fearing the title might suggest a reference to 18 Brumaire. Though the Empire never interfered with them as it interfered with their friends Flaubert and Renan, they resented the utter indifference of the Court to them and their writings even when they had made their name. No summons to the Interior or Compiègne reached them, and they never angled for an invitation. Neither recognized adherents nor declared enemies of the *régime*, they were described by Gautier as Mathildistes, for they were among the chief ornaments of her salon, never forfeiting her favour and never losing their affection. 'We, more than anyone, had reason to complain of this *régime* of police and prosecutions,' they wrote in 1869. 'We shared the hatreds of writers for this government, the enemy of letters. In this bear-garden of a decaying Empire, where we possess no friend except the Princess, people try to discredit our talent with the calumny "*Courtiers*".'

When the news of Sedan reached Paris, Edward de Goncourt, broken-hearted at the death of his brother Jules, pronounced a verdict on his countrymen as severe as that of Flaubert himself.

> Empire, Republic, it is always the same thing. It is tempting to say it is the Emperor's fault. It is generous of me to write like this, I who as the result of four verses was the victim of a press prosecution. Yes, it is tempting. But if the Generals have been incapable and the officers not up to their task, that's not his fault; and if the French people had not been very sick his mediocrity would not have prevented victory. Sovereigns merely represent the moral stature of the majority of their subjects. Among my literary friends I know only one absolutely pure—Flaubert.

Two other novelists and poets regarded the Empire with more friendly eyes, though their contacts were of the slightest. Alfred de Vigny, former officer of the King's Guard, shocked his friends Victor Hugo and Lamartine by expressing approval of the dictatorship, but the Empire derived little profit from his adhesion. Invited by a Minister to compose a poem on the birth of the Prince Imperial, he politely declined. Though he accepted an invitation to Compiègne he had no taste for Courts and spent the closing years in his country home. Even more tenuous were the ties of Théophile Gautier who, confessing that he had no political opinions, accepted the Empire, wrote for the *Moniteur*, and was numbered among the *habitués* of the salon of Princess Mathilde.

VII. THE WORLD OF LEARNING

The world of learning gave the Dictator as little anxiety and as little moral support as the world of letters. In the preface to his *Catechism of Positivism* Comte welcomed the disappearance of the Parliamentary system but disliked the proclamation of the Empire and the muzzling of the press. Victor Cousin, the oracle of the University, detested the Empire but made no public protest.

> Our master possesses the three qualities most essential to success [he remarked bitterly to Nassau Senior in 1853]: he is bold, calculating and deceitful. His only chance of keeping us in subjection is to intoxicate and brutalize us by successful war. Yet with all his faults he is a gentleman in the English sense of the word. He has had the education and he has the manners and feelings of the aristocracy, but the Bonaparte dynasty goes out with Louis Bonaparte.

That was the only comfort.

The historians were as contemptuous as the philosophers. The veteran Guizot, apostle of the *juste milieu*, was one of the milder critics. Neither the upper classes nor the parties had rallied to the Government, he reported to his friend Lord Aberdeen.

> They take no overt action against it, but they talk, for we retain freedom of conversation. The present régime will not destroy it, for stronger governments have failed to do so. As a constitutional monarchist I will never serve any other régime, but I will raise no obstacle to the Government now at grips with anarchy. When dictatorship is struggling against anarchy we cannot hesitate in our choice. Having lost free government we must support the necessary government.

France, he wrote in 1849, knew she was in an inn where she would not remain but where she desired to rest awhile. The *coup d'état* was a disgrace to the country, but the humiliation was deserved. The overthrow of Constitutional Monarchy led to demagogy which in turn was bound to generate dictatorship. A year later he described the proclamation of the Empire as a shameful comedy. It had nothing to fear from the army or the mob, so it would doubtless last for some time; but sooner or later dictory sources. He had arranged them in his solitary meditations, remote from things and people, for he was dreamy and chimerical. When compelled to act, he was shrewd enough yet always inclined to strange ideas. He trusted in his star, as convinced of his right as Charles X. He had a sort of abstract worship of the people but very little taste for liberty and a contempt for assemblies. Willing to obey a nation, he was too proud to take orders from Parliament. There was something of the adventurer about him.

In the summer of 1850, when the President's ambitions had become the chief topic in political circles, Tocqueville believed that he lacked the nerve to seize the glittering prize. 'He is daring in his plans,' he remarked to Nassau Senior, 'but when the moment of execution comes he hesitates. His last chance was in January 1849 when he enjoyed the prestige of his six million votes and before his intellectual mediocrity had been detected.' When the sphinx-like conspirator struck in the following year Tocqueville's indignation knew no bounds. Brumaire had been supported by the educated classes who now repudiated the *coup d'état*. This man, he exclaimed to Nassau Senior, could not claim a decent supporter, and for a parallel one had to go back to ancient Rome. He had begun to conspire from the day of the plebiscite. How long would it last? asked his English friend. 'Till it is unpopular with the mass of the people,' was the reply.

> At present the disapprobation is confined to the educated classes. We cannot bear to be deprived of the power of speaking or writing. We cannot bear that the fate of France should depend on the selfishness or vanity or fears or caprice of one man, a foreigner by race and education, and of a set of military ruffians and infamous civilians fit only to have formed the Privy Council of Catiline. We shall get rid of him in a few years, perhaps in a few months, but there is no saying how much mischief he may do meanwhile to his neighbours. What I fear is that when he feels the ground crumbling under him he will try the resource of war.

Tocqueville passed away before his gloomy prophecy was fulfilled. Lanfrey's biography of the mighty Emperor, published in 1867, was the most damaging attack hitherto launched by a serious historian on the Napoleonic legend which had aided his hapless rise to power.

Though the Emperor disliked all attempts at clerical dictation, he had to avoid a major clash with the Church. The appointment of Renan, the only qualified candidate for the Chair of Semitic Languages at the Collège de France in 1859, was followed by an ecclesiastical broadside. While awaiting confirmation the distinguished savant received the Legion of Honour and was dispatched on an archaeological mission to Phoenicia. On his return the appointment was announced, and the new Professor delivered his inaugural address on the place of the Semitic peoples in the history of civilization; but the cup was dashed from his lips by a single phrase which described Jesus as *un homme incomparable*. Four days later the Minister of Public Instruction, though himself a *libre penseur*, suspended the course on the ground that he had professed doctrines injurious to the Christian faith and calculated to provoke regrettable agitation. As a *solatium* he was appointed Assistant Director of the Department of Manuscripts. The decree announcing the appointment added that he had received a salary during the two years since his initial nomination without discharging the duties of his Chair. Regarding this unfortunate phrase as a censure, he declined the new appointment, and the Emperor regretfully abandoned the attempt to secure his services. In 1869 he stood without success for the Chamber; if he had been returned he would have supported Ollivier. Though more of a Liberal than Sainte-Beuve and Taine, he felt too little confidence in the ultimate sanity of common man to qualify as a Democrat.

Renan's lifelong friend Taine, coming of age in 1849 on the eve of the elections to the Chamber, explained his reasons for abstention.

> I have only two settled political opinions. The first is that the right of property is absolute, anterior to the State, like individual liberty; the second is that all rights are reducible to one—that of consenting overtly or tacitly to the government. Forms are indifferent, since their legitimacy derives solely from acceptance by the nation. What suits France I do not know, so I cannot vote either for the Republic or the Monarchy. Besides I know too little of the character and opinions of the candidates. The two parties disgust me.

Asking and expecting little of any *régime* since he expected little of human nature, he was in no way outraged by a *coup d'état* so emphatically ratified by a plebiscite.

x*

The troops [he wrote] are for M. Bonaparte. The dissolved Chamber was unpopular. Everything is quiet. He will assume monarchical power under republican forms. The countryside is for him, and the democrats have been out of favour for two years. No one will make trouble. So our course is set for several years. For sixty years France has been in perpetual oscillation—from monarchy to republic, from liberty to authority, and so it will long continue. We are too much and too little democrats to tolerate either alternative, yet liberal ideas are gradually making headway and after seven or eight revolutions they will prevail. Sick from the Monarchy of the last century, we are now in a century of convalescence with relapses, and we shall not recover our health till the twentieth. We must get used to it and be patient; our children will be happier than ourselves.

Taine's acceptance of the *régime* did not involve degrading subservience.

You know [he wrote to his sister] that M. Bonaparte has broken his oath, destroyed public liberty, and killed defenders of the law. The Rector, a priest, has sent us the following circular: 'The undersigned teachers at Nevers declare their adhesion to the measures taken by the President of the Republic on 2 December and offer him their gratitude and respectful devotion.' My colleagues, even the most liberal, had the impudence to sign. I refused. I had no desire to inaugurate my career as Professor by an act of cowardice and a lie. Charged as I am to teach respect for the law, fidelity to one's oath, the cult of right, I should have seemed to approve perjury, usurpation and assassination. I know you would have done the same. It is less perilous than I expected. The Rector who, though weak, is kindly and honourable, sent in the list without mentioning my refusal. I believe he really felt that I alone have done my duty.

He told Prévost-Paradol that he thought the Dictatorship would last. 'He cleverly bases himself on universal suffrage, which asks for well-being not for liberty! He has the clergy, the army and his uncle's name. So no more political life for us perhaps for ten years, and we must devote ourselves to silence and *belles-lettres*.'

That he was *persona grata* in the salon of Princess Mathilde was no indication of adherence to the *régime*, which resented his independence. After a brief spell as examiner at the Military Academy at St. Cyr, he was informed by the Minister of War, Marshal Randou, that an officer with technical knowledge would replace him. The Emperor mildly remonstrated. 'My dear Marshal, some little measures create needless hostility, for instance the dismissal of M. Taine. He is a distinguished man with many friends among scholars and men of letters. I wish him to retain his post which he fills with distinction.' Far from contesting his merits, explained the Marshal, who resented the rebuff, he was too good for the job. The real reason, as everyone knew, was that complaints had come from parents who had been told that he was one of the unbelievers against whom Dupanloup and other ecclesiastics waged unremitting war. On the other hand he was permitted to continue his lectures on the history of art at the École des Beaux Arts.

The outbreak of war found Taine in Dresden, where he was collecting material for a book on Germany similar to his *Notes sur l'Angleterre*. Hastening home he found everything in confusion. The Government, he wrote on the morrow of Sedan, appeared the aggressor and deserved to fall, but the real aggressor was the country, which had rendered the war inevitable. Prussia was playing the detestable part of Napoleon and might have a similar fate when Europe, as in 1815, recognized the common enemy. No one more heartily detested the dragooning of the human spirit by irresponsible autocrats. 'We were in the hands of a gambler who played his last card, lost, and ruined us all.' The Man of December had ended as the Man of Sedan. His gravest offence was to unleash a conflict which led to the siege of Paris and the bestial atrocities of the Commune. Gazing into the abyss of human depravity, he recoiled in horror and disgust, wrathfully comparing *homo sapiens* to a chained gorilla. His remaining years were dedicated to a documented exposure of the *ancien régime*, the Revolution and the First Empire, in which he found as little to please him as in the Second Empire and the Third Republic. Trying every performer on the stage of history by his own lofty standards, he wrung his hands over the crimes and follies of mankind. 'Taine,' declared Paul Bourget, '*était votre conscience vivante*', a voice crying in the wilderness but without a message of hope.

BIBLIOGRAPHICAL NOTES

Chapter 1

La Gorce, *Histoire de la Deuxième République*, 2 vols., and *Histoire du Second Empire*, 7 vols., are classics. His views are summarized in his later book, *Napoléon III et sa politique*. The fullest account of the early years is by Thirria, *Napoléon III avant l'Empire*, 2 vols. Ollivier's apologia, *L'Empire Libéral*, 16 vols., is a primary source for the closing phase. Seignobos' two vols. in Lavisse, *Histoire de la France Contemporaine*, cover every aspect of the national life in the third quarter of the century. Simpson's admirable large-scale biography unfortunately ends with the second volume and the Crimean War. The best brief biographies are by Sencourt and Thompson. Guedalla, *The Second Empire*, is a colourful sketch. Robert Williams, *Gaslight and Shadow: the World of Napoleon III*, presents ten prominent figures. Zeldin, *The Political System of Louis Napoleon*, traces the evolution from autocracy to the Liberal Empire. *Histoire Socialiste*, edited by Jaurès, Vol. V (by Emile Thomas) describes the plight and progress of the Fourth Estate. Clapham, *The Economic Development of France and Germany, 1815–1914*, is a mine of useful information. Brogan, *The French Nation*, sets the Second Empire in the context of French history since Napoleon. The Emperor's early political writings are collected in *Œuvres de Napoléon III*, Vol. 1. Stéphane Pol, *La Jeunesse de Napoléon III*, contains the reports of his tutor Philippe le Bos. His letters to Mme Cornu, a friend from childhood, appeared in 1937, 2 vols. Earl of Kerry, *The Secret of the Coup d' Etat*, contains the correspondence of Flahaut with his illegitimate son Morny. The impressions of British Ambassadors are found in Lord Normanby, *A Year of Revolution*, 2 vols.; Sir Victor Wellesley and Robert Sencourt, *The British Embassy in Paris*, and *Conversations with Napoleon III*; and Lord Newton, *Life of Lord Lyons*, Vol. 1. Austrian views are recorded in Hübner, *Une Ambassade à Paris*, 2 vols.; Oncken, *Die Rheinpolitik Napoleons III*, 3 vols. (mainly the correspondence of Richard Metternich); and Salomon, *L'Ambassade de Richard de Metternich à Paris*. Oncken's lengthy introduction appeared in English dress in New York in 1928 entitled *Napoleon III and the Rhine*. Packe, *The Bombs of Orsini*, studies the Emperor's relations with the Risorgimento. Lynn N. Case, *French Opinion on War and Diplomacy during the Second Empire*, is full of new material. *Bismarck and the Hohenzollern Candidature for the Spanish Throne*, with Introduction by George Bonin, presents a complete translation of the German Foreign Office *dossier* captured by the Allies in 1945 which contains fresh proof that Bismarck, despite his denials, was pulling the strings in Madrid. Spuller, *Figures Disparues*, 3 vols., provides many obituaries.

Chapter 2

The best biography of the Empress is by Robert Sencourt. Her *Lettres Familières*, preserved in the Alva archives, appeared in 1935, 2 vols. Paléologue's *Conversations with the Empress Eugénie* are no adequate substitute for the memoirs she declined to write. Filon's biographies of the Empress and the Prince Imperial are affectionate and intimate tributes by the latter's tutor. Comtesse Stéphanie de Tascher de la Pagerie, *Mon Séjour aux Tuileries*, 3 vols., Mme Carette, *Souvenirs intimes de la Cour des Tuileries*, 3 vols., and Marquise de Taisey-Chatenoy, *A la Cour de Napoleon III*, are useful. Princess Pauline Metternich's Memoirs are vivid but scrappy. Magda Martini, *Marie Laetitia Bonaparte Wyse*, *Une Reine du Second Empire*, portrays the granddaughter of Lucien Bonaparte who broke with the Court after the *coup d'état*. Fleury et Sonolet, *La Société du Second Empire*, 4 vols. (illustrated); Bac, *Intimités du Second Empire*, 3 vols.; Bac, *La Cour des Tuileries;* Boulenger, *Les Tuileries sous le Second Empire*, and Bellessort, *La Société française sous Napoléon III*, are useful. The celebrated Journals of Count Horace de Vieil-Castel, 6 vols. (abridged English edition, 2 vols.) report the gossip and scandal of the capital.

Chapter 3

Mme André Maurois, *Miss Howard* (English translation) and Decamp, *Comtesse de Castiglione*, provide the first full account of the two best known of the amorous ruler's mistresses. There is a vivid sketch of the latter in eclipse in Bac, *Intimités du Second Empire*, Vol. 1.

Chapter 4

Count Egon Corti, *Maximilian and Charlotte of Mexico* (English translation, 2 vols.) utilizes the rich store of the Archduke's papers at Miramar.

Chapter 5

The best biographies of Morny are by Boulenger, Amédée-Thierry, and Christophe. Brousse, *La Comtesse le Hon*, describes the social and political role of the best-known of his mistresses. Alphonse Daudet paints a vivid but unflattering picture of his former employer as the Duc de Mora in *Le Nabob*. A more attractive portrait is presented by Ludovic Halévy, who knew him more intimately, in his *Carnets*, Vol. 1.

CHAPTER 6

The political convictions and career of Plon-Plon are mirrored in *Correspondance du Prince Napoléon et l'Empereur Napoléon III*. Flammarion, *Prince Napoléon*, is merely a sketch. Maxime du Camp, *Souvenirs d'un demi-siècle*, is a friend's tribute. A large-scale biography based on the Prince's papers is needed.

CHAPTER 7

The unfinished Memoirs of Princess Mathilde appeared in the *Revue des Deux Mondes* in 1928-9. There are good biographies by Ferdinand Bac and Marguerite Castillon du Perron. See also Bac, *Intimités du Second Empire*, Vol. III.

CHAPTER 8

The first brief biography of Walewski by Comte d'Ornano utilized family papers. The best and most recent is by Poirson.

CHAPTER 9

Since Persigny's Memoirs only describe certain phases of his career, Farals, *Persigny, Ministre de Napoléon III* (1957), is very welcome. Goya, *Un Roman de l'Amitié*, contains his correspondence with Falloux, a friendly political opponent.

CHAPTER 10

There are adequate biographies of the three lawyers, Rouher by Sohnerb, Baroche by Maurain (to be supplemented by Mme Baroche, *Second Empire, Notes et Souvenirs*), and *Le Ministre Pierre Magne*, 2 vols., by Durieux.

CHAPTER 11

Ollivier records and defends his career in *L'Empire Libéral*, 16 vols., supplemented by *Lettres de l'Exil, 1870-4*. A full and sympathetic biography by Pierre Saint-Marc appeared in 1956. Zeldin, *The Political System of Napoleon III*, salutes him as a courageous statesman.

CHATPER 12

Duruy, *Notes et Souvenirs*, 2 vols., is supplemented by Lavisse, *Victor Duruy*, an affectionate tribute by his distinguished pupil and secretary. His conflict with the Church is fully described by Maurain, *La Politique Ecclésiastique du Second Empire*.

CHATPER 13

Haussmann's *Memoirs*, 3 vols., must be checked by Chapman, *Baron Haussmann*, and Pinkney, *Napoleon III and the Rebuilding of Paris*.

CHAPTER 14

For the army chiefs see Fleury, *Souvenirs*, 2 vols.; Bapst, *Canrobert*, 6 vols.; *Journal du Maréchal de Castellane*, 6 vols.; Randon, *Mémoires*, 2 vols., and Rastoul, *Le Maréchal Randon*; Ibos, *Cavaignac*; Comte d'Antioche, *Changarnier:* Quatrelles l'Epine, *Saint-Arnaud*, 2 vols.

CHAPTER 15

For the Church see Maurain's massive monograph, *La Politique Ecclésiastique du Second Empire*; Gazier, *Histoire de la Religion en France*; Debidour, *Histoire des Rapports de l'Eglise et l'Etat en France, 1789–1870*; Bourgeois et Clermont, *Rome et Napoléon III*; Duroselle, *Les Débuts du Catholicisme social en France, 1822–70*; Leroy-Beaulieu, *Les Catholiques Libéraux de 1830 à nos jours*; Weill, *Histoire du Catholicisme Libéral en France*; Boutard, *Lamennais*, 3 vols.; Falloux, *Mémoires d'un Royaliste*, 2 vols.; Lecanuet, *Montalembert*, 3 vols.; Abbé Lagrange, *Vie de Dupanloup*, 2 vols.; Faguet, *Dupanloup*; Eugène Veuillot, *Louis Veuillot*, 3 vols.; E. Gauthier, *Le Génie satirique*; François Veuillot, *Louis Veuillot* and *Correspondance de Louis Veuillot*, 10 vols.; Hales, *Pio Nono*; Woodward, *Three Studies in European Conservatism*.

CHAPTER 16

The best introduction to the study of royalist opinion is in Nassau Senior, *Conversations with Tocqueville, Thiers, Guizot*, 4 vols.; le Duc d'Aumale, *Correspondance avec Cuvillier-Fleury*, 4 vols.; E. Daudet, *Le Duc d'Aumale*; Baron de Barante, *Souvenirs*, vols. 7–8; Geyl, *Napoleon: For and Against*, discusses the Napoleonic legend. No adequate biography of Thiers exists, but brief studies by Rémusat and Allison are useful. Lacombe, *Berryer sous la Seconde République et le Second Empire*, does justice to the leading Legitimist. Ollivier, *L'Empire Libéral*, Reclus, *Jules Favre*, and Darimon, *Histoire de douze ans*, defend the activities of *Les Cinq*. Rochefort tells his story in *Les Aventures de ma Vie*, vols. 1 and 2. Ducray's biography of Rochefort is a mere sketch. The best study of Gambetta is by Deschanel. Mme Adam's republican salon comes to life in her *Souvenirs*, vol. 1, and in Winifred Stephens, *Juliette Adam*, based on personal knowledge. Léon Daudet, *Clemenceau*, paints an intimate portrait of his father's friend. The best brief record of the Tiger is by Hampden Jackson. Weill, *Le Parti Républicain, 1814-70*, and *L'Ecole Saint-Simonienne*; Tchernoff, *Le Partie Républicain sous le Second Empire*; and Plamenatz, *The Revolutionary Movement in France, 1815-71*, describe the leaders of the Left. The best study of Proudhon is by Dolléans.

Chapter 17

The most comprehensive survey of the literary world is in Petti de Julleville, *Histoire de la Littérature Française*, Vol. VII. Bac, *Intimités du Second Empire*, 3 vols., is useful. André Maurois' biographies of George Sand, Victor Hugo and Dumas, and J. Richardson, *Théophile Gautier*, are full of new material. Mérimée, George Sand, Flaubert, Sainte-Beuve and Taine reveal themselves in their voluminous correspondence. Harold Nicolson, *Sainte-Beuve*, rightly admires his writings more than his character. The latest edition of the Journal of the de Goncourt brothers during the Second Empire fills vols. 1-4. Mme Octave Feuillet's *Souvenirs* illustrate the affection of herself and her husband for the sovereigns. For Quinet see his Correspondence with Michelet, and Mme Quinet, *Quinet après l'Exil*. Tocqueville lives in Nassau Senior, *Conversations and Correspondence with Alexis de Tocqueville*, 2 vols. For Taine see *Taine, Sa Vie et sa Correspondance*, vols. 1-3. Faguet, *Politiques et Moralistes du Dix-Neuvième Siècle*, 3 vols., is a classic.

INDEX

About, Edmond, 94, 124
Adam, Edmond, 273, 274-5
Adam, Juliette, 273; her early life, 274; and Gambetta, 275-6
Affaire Baudin, L', 272-3, 276
Alba, Duchess of, 19, 35, 37; her death, 45; the Emperor's letters to, 37, 38, 40-1, 44, 45
America and the Mexican enterprise, 75, 76, 80, 81
Army, the, and Napoleon III, 210; and the *coup d'état*, 1851, 212, 221
Augier, Émile, 94, 124
Austria, Napoleon III at war with, 22-23; expelled from the German Confederation, 26, 47; and the Mexican enterprise, 76, 77, 80; Walewski and, 133; Franco-Prussian attitude to, 143
Avenir, L', launching of, 237-8

Bacciochi, Count, 57, 59, 67
Balzac, Honoré de (1799-1850), 87
Barante, Baron de, on the acceptance of the *coup d'état*, 1851, 252-3
Baroche, Pierre-Jules (1802-70), 149, 152; and the Second Empire, 154, 160, 256; accepts the Republic, 1848, 161; his public appointments, 161, 162; and the *coup d'état*, 1851, 162-3; Vice-President of the Consultative Commission, 163; congratulates Napoleon III, 163-4; and the Council of State, 164; his foreign interests, 164; succeeded by Rouher, 165; his resignation, 165-6; and the Liberal Empire, 166; his death, 167; opposes Haussmann, 202, 204; and Changarnier's dismissal, 216-17
Baroche, Mme, 46; on Haussmann, 204
Barrot, Odilon, 163; President to the Council, 15, 59, 161; his dismissal, 162, 255; Thiers and, 254
Bazaine, Marshal (1811-88), in Mexico, 25, 77, 78; at Metz, 31, 32, 160, 227; his trial, 261

Beauharnais, Hortense de (1783-1837), 3, 7, 100, 120; and Comte de Flahault, 16, 85-6; and her son, de Morny, 86
Bellanger, Marguerite, Napoleon III's *liaison* with, 45, 68-9
Benedetti, Vincent, Count, 29-30, 160
Béranger, Pierre-Jean (1780-1857), 6, 10
Berryer, Pierre Antoine (1790-1868), 95, 272; defends Montalembert, 244, 245, 263; and the Comte de Chambord, 258, 262-4; his early life, 262; as the Legitimist Deputy, 263-4
Billault, Auguste, 109, 169
Bismarck, Prince Otto von (1815-98), 2, 26, 51; and war with France, 26, 29-30, 51, 276, 311; and the Ems telegram, 30, 186; the Prince Napoleon and, 113; Persigny's meetings with, 150
Blanc, Louis, 70; and the National Workshops, 280-1
Blanqui, Louis-Auguste, 281
Bonaparte, Jerome, King of Westphalia (1784-1860), 31, 99, 100, 101, 102; his character, 119, 121; settles in Florence, 120; under Napoleon III's régime, 123
Bonaparte, Joseph (1768-1844), 4, 120, 139
Bonaparte, Louis, King of Holland (1778-1846), 3, 5, 16, 85, 120
Bonaparte, Lucien (1775-1840), 5, 100
Bonaparte, Maria Letizia (Mme Mère) (1750-1836), 100, 120
Bonaparte, Pierre, 183, 270-1
Boulogne, Napoleon III's raid on, 8, 36, 100; Persigny and, 140
Bourbons, the, attacked by Prince Napoleon, 107-9, 260-1; de Chambord and, 262
Bourget, Paul, 128, 309
Broglie, Duc de, 256
Burgoyne, Sir John, 53

315

INDEX

Cabet, Étienne, 279
Canrobert, Marshal François, 16, 214; on Napoleon III, 225, 226–7; and the *coup d'état*, 1851, 225–6; his later career, 227
Carbonari rising, 4, 100
Carpeaux, Jean Baptiste, 124
Castellane, Marshal Esprit de, and Napoleon III, 227–9
Castiglione, Countess: sent to seduce Napoleon III, 22, 45, 61 ff.; her early life, 61; her beauty, 64–5; end of the *liaison*, 65–7; and Dr. Hugenschmidt, 67–8; her last years, 68
Cavaignac, Louis Eugène (1802–57), 15, 88, 161; defeated for the presidency by Napoleon III, 14, 155, 210, 211, and the *coup d'état*, 1851, 89, 90, 213, 214; Minister of War, 213; and the Republican cause, 214, 254; his enmity towards Napoleon III, 214; and Changarnier, 215; and Pius IX, 239–40
Cavour, Camillo, Count di (1810–61), 133; plans to evict Austria from Italy, 22, 23; and Countess Castiglione, 22, 45, 61–2, 66; and the Papal States, 24; and Prince Napoleon, 105, 108
Chambord, Comte de, 6, 20, 123, 235, 237, 248, 258; his dislike of the Orleanists, 262; and Berryer, 263–4
Charles X (1757–1836), 5, 230, 231, 237, 267
Charlotte, Empress, 25–6, 76; on the situation in Mexico, 79; returns to Europe, 80–1; interviews Napoleon III and the Empress, 81–2; her insanity and death, 82, 83–4
Changarnier, General Nicolas, 210, 225; and the *coup d'état*, 1851, 87, 89; his dismissal, 162, 212, 216–17, 219, 223, 228, 259, 288; Military Commander in Paris, 214, 215, 216, 254; votes for Napoleon III, 215; and the German crisis, 1870, 217–18
Church, the: and education, 194, 195, 233; at the Restoration, 230–3; Napoleon III and, 231, 241, 307; Falloux and, 232–3; Lamennais' new movement in, 237–8; Montalembert and, 238, 240, 243–5; urged to support Napoleon III, 241–2, 247;

Veuillot and, 245, 247–8; Dupanloup and, 248–51
Cinq, Les, 20, 95, 256; Ollivier and, 173, Gambetta and, 272
Clarendon, Lord, 69; on Ollivier's liberal Cabinet, 182–3
Clemenceau, Dr. Benjamin, 277, 278
Clemenceau, Georges, 26, 168, 173; his early life, 277; in America, 277–8; and the Third Republic, 278
Clotilde, Princess, marries Prince Napoleon, 22, 105–6
Cobden Commercial Treaty, 21, 135, 156
Coburg, Duke Ernst of, 26, 78
Comte, Auguste, 230, 303
Conneau, Dr. Henri, 2, 11, 43, 55, 70
Constitutionnel, Le, 2, 267
Cornu, Hortense, and Napoleon III, 2, 11, 42, 69–72
Corti, Count Egon, 73
Coup d'état, 1851, 16–17, 89–91, 155, 162–3, 255, 265, 267. Part played in by: Saint-Arnaud, 16, 17, 89–91, 219–21; de Morny, 16, 17, 89–91, 212; Princess Mathilde, 71; the army, 89–91, 217, 222, 223–4, 225–6; Prince Napoleon, 103; Walewski, 132; Persigny, 144, 217; Baroche, 163; Ollivier, 174; Montalembert, 241; Veuillot, 246; Dupanloup, 249; the Royalists, 252–3; the literary world, 286, 288, 292, 294, 304, 307–8
Cousin, Victor, 22; and the Church, 233; on Napoleon III, 303
Cowley, Lady, 31
Cowley, Lord, 132; on Napoleon III, 17, 23–4, 45–6; and the Empress, 36, 39, 46, 69; on de Morny, 97–8; and Prince Napoleon, 105, 108

d'Argenteau, Countess Mercy, 45–6
d'Aumale, Duc, 50, 191, 221; in exile, 259–61; his detestation of the Second Empire, 259–60; and the attack on the Bourbons, 260–1; returns to France after 1870, 261–2; *Lettre sur L'histoire de France*, 108, 260–1
d'Auvergne, Prince Henri de la Tour, 66
Daudet, Alphonse, and de Morny, 94, 97; on Gambetta, 275; *Le Nabob*, 94, 312

INDEX

de Souza, Mme, 86
de Vigny, Alfred, 302
Decaux, Alain: *La Castiglione, le Coeur de l'Europe*, 61
Demidoff, Count Anatole, marries Princess Mathilde, 121–2; returns to Russia, 123; his death, 127
Dino, Duchesse de, 64; on Napoleon III, 6–7
Drouyn de Lhuys, Edouard, 26, 132, 151, 157, 160; and Prince Napoleon, 103; and the Crimean War, 146–7; Thiers and, 254
Du Camp, Maxime, on the Empress, 42–3; and de Morny, 86; on Princess Clotilde, 105–6; Prince Napoleon and, 115, 117; and Ollivier, 187, 189, 190
Dumas *fils*, Alexandre, 124, 127
Dumas *père*, Alexandre, 124
Dupanloup, Felix Antoine Philibert, Bishop of Orleans (1802–78), 244; attacks Duruy, 194, 195; and Falloux, 232, 249; condemns *L'Univers*, 246, 249–50; his reputation, 248; and the *coup d'état*, 1851, 249; and Napoleon III, 249, 250–1; and the Italian campaign, 250; his tribute to Berryer, 264
Duruy, Victor (1811–94), 72, 313; his early life and opinions, 191; his relations with Napoleon III, 191–3, 195–6; on the Papal States, 192; and the biography of Caesar, 192–3, 196; as Minister of Public Instruction, 193; his educational programme, 193–4; and the Church, 194; the Empress and, 195; and the Liberal Empire, 195–6; his dismissal, 196–7; and the 1870 crisis, 197

Education, Duruy's reforms for, 193–5; the Church and, 194, 195, 232–3
Empire, the Liberal, 5, 190 n.; Ollivier and, 29, 32, 175 ff.; Prince Napoleon and, 113–14, 116; welcomed by Maupas, 180; Napoleon III and, 182, 184; its Ministers, 182; its new Constitution, 183–4; overthrown, 188; Duruy and, 196; condemned by Haussmann, 204–6
Empire, the Second, 17; proclamation of, 18; Bismarck and, 27; its decline, 28, 177; end of, 31–2; as an experiment, 32–3; Paléologue and, 46; de Morny and, 95, 97; Prince Napoleon and, 99, 104; Persigny and, 138, 139, 142, 145; Rouher as its Prime Minister, 154; Baroche and, 160; Magne and, 168, 169; Ollivier exonerates, 173–4; the Church under, 231; its acceptance by Royalists and Republicans, 252; Thiers' attitude to, 256–7; d'Aumale's hatred of, 259–61; hated by the Legitimists, 262; Rochefort's attacks on, 268–9; attacked by Gambetta, 272–4
Ems telegram, 30, 51, 186
Eugène, Prince (Prince Imperial), 26, 32, 35, 42, 67; birth of, 19, 38–9, 71; and the German war, 51–3; at Chislehurst, 54–5; his death, 55; Prince Napoleon and his birth, 104
Eugénie, Empress (Maria Eugénia de Guzman) (1826–1920), 17, 22, 29, 185, 251; her marriage to Napoleon III, 19, 36; her character, 19–20, 34; relations with her husband, 25, 32, 37, 38, 54; and war with Germany, 30–1, 51–3; escapes to England, 32, 53–4; her love of politics, 34, 35, 50–51; her appearance, 35; contemporary opinions on, 36, 38, 39, 42–3, 47–8, 48–9; gives birth to a son, 38–9; as a hostess, 39–40; and spiritualism, 40–41; her enemies, 42–4; and Orsini, 44–5, 289; appointed Regent, 45, 52; and her husband's *liaisons*, 45, 60, 61, 63, 67, 68–9; and the Italian campaign, 46–7, 170; and the Mexican enterprise, 47, 73–84; Persigny and, 48–50; 149, 151; her retirement at Chislehurst, 54–5; last years, 55–6; and Hortense Cornu, 71–2; and Prince Napoleon, 104, 108–9, 110; Princess Mathilde and, 124; and the Walewskis, 134; dislikes Rouher, 157; and Ollivier's liberalism, 176–7, 179, 190; her charitable works, 195; and Haussmann, 207; Merimée and, 288, 289, 291
Evans, Dr. Thomas Wiltberger, 32, 53, 67
Exhibition (1855), 104; (1867), 27, 51, 111, 157, 300; Haussmann and, 204, 205

INDEX

Falloux, Comte de, 244; and Persigny, 141, 142; Minister of Education, 232–3; and the *coup d'état*, 1851, 234–235; abstains at the plebiscite, 235; and Napoleon III, 235–6; later years, 237; reproves Montalembert, 240; and Veuillot, 246
Falloux Law, 231, 233, 239, 240, 255
Favre, Jules, 13, 99, 113, 270; and *Les Cinq*, 20, 173, 266; in opposition to Ollivier, 176, 183; and Napoleon III, 265–6, 267; and the 1870 crisis, 266–267; defends Orsini, 266, 271
Ferry, Jules, 182, 203, 205
Feuillet, Octave, 21, 94, 124
Feuillet, Mme Octave, 29, 314
Filon, tutor to the Prince Imperial, 54, 55, 311
Flahault, Comte de, 16, 21, 85–6, 87; on his son, 91
Flaubert, Gustave (1821–80), 21, 124; his disinterest in politics, 297, 299; on the *coup d'état*, 1851, 297; dislikes the Academy, 297–8; prosecuted for *Madame Bovary*, 299; and Princess Mathilde, 299–300; and the 1870 crisis, 300–1
Fleury, General, 59, 180; becomes a Bonapartist, 210–11; as aide-de-camp to Napoleon III, 211–12; and the *coup d'état*, 1851, 212; his later career, 212–13; and Saint-Arnaud, 220
Fould, Achille, 145, 151, 157, 169
Fourier, Charles, his *Phalanstères*, 279
Francis Joseph, Emperor, 23, 25, 31, 73, 106, 133; and his brother Maximilian, 76
Frederick, Crown Prince, of Prussia, 27, 51
Frederick William IV, King of Prussia, 131, 143

Gambetta, Léon Michel (1838–82), 26, 32, 168, 173, 183; as a young Republican, 271–2; and the Second Empire, 272–4, 275; and the 1870 crisis, 274; Juliette Adam and, 274–6
Garibaldi, Giuseppe, 24, 45; and Pius IX, 114–15
Gavarni, Chevalier Sulpice, 124
Gautier, Théophile (1811–72), 72, 87; and Princess Mathilde, 124–5, 299

Germany and Austria, 26, 47; moves towards war with France, 26–27, 29–31, 185; the Empress and, 51
Girardin, Émile de, 124; inaugurates cheap newspapers, 267
Goncourt, Edmond and Jules de, 124, 125, 127, 299; their disgust with politics, 301, 302; and the *coup d'état*, 1851, 301; Princess Mathilde and, 302
Gounod, Charles, 124
Gramont, Duc de, 167; and the 1870 crisis, 185, 186, 188
Granville, George Leveson-Gower, Earl, 30, 53, 132
Great Britain, and the Mexican enterprise, 75, 76, 77; Napoleon III and, 131
Greville, Charles Cavendish Fulke, on Walewski, 132
Guizot, François (1787–1874), 5, 88, 130, 131, 168, 169, 193; on the *coup d'état*, 1851, 253, 303–4

Halévy, Ludovic, 159; and de Morny, 88, 94, 97, 312
Ham, fortress of, Napoleon III's imprisonment at, 2, 10, 11–12, 57, 69, 70, 100–1
Haryett, Elizabeth. *See* Howard, Miss
Haussmann, Eugène-Georges, Baron (1801–91), and the reconstruction of Paris, 21, 146, 195, 198 ff.; his judgment on Baroche, 164–5; his early life, 198; and Napoleon III, 198–9, 200–1, 202, 204, 205, 206; and the *coup d'état*, 1851, 199–200; sent to Bordeaux, 199–200; made Prefect of the Seine, 200–1; his relations with the Municipal Council, 201–2; opposed by Baroche, 202, 204; financing of his schemes, 202–3; and the Conseil d'Etat, 203–4; and the Great Exhibition, 204, 205; condemns the Liberal Empire, 205–6; and the restoration of autocracy, 206; in the 1870 crisis, 207; d'Aumale and, 261
Hidalgo y Costilla, Miguel, 73, 75
Home, Daniel Dunglas, the Empress and, 40–1
Houssaye, Arsène, 94, 124

INDEX 319

Howard, Miss (i.e., Elizabeth Haryett), in Paris with Napoleon III, 14, 59; becomes Comtesse de Beauregard, 19, 45, 60; her early life, 57–8; her *liaison* with Napoleon III, 58–60, 212; marries Clarence Trelawny, 60–1
Hübner, Joseph Alexander, Count, 22, 27, 38, 78, 159, 181, 184; on Napoleon III, 17, 20, 33; and the Empress, 39–40, 45, 46–7, 50, 51, 53; on Prince Napoleon, 106; and Persigny, 138, 145, 150; on Baroche, 164
Hugenschmidt, Dr., 67–8
Hugo, Victor (1802–85), 2, 10, 15, 124; and the *coup d'état*, 1851, 16, 90, 266, 283–4, 286; attacks Baroche, 162–3; his hatred of Napoleon III, 173, 283 ff.; and Pius IX, 240; and Rochefort, 269–70; and Louis Napoleon's return from exile, 282; founds *L'Événement*, 282–3; becomes a Republican, 283; escapes to Belgium, 283 ff.; launches *Le Rappel*, 286; his return to France, 287; Flaubert and, 298; *Les Châtiments*, 163, 286–7; *Histoire d'un Crime*, 16, 286; *Napoléon le Petit*, 284–6

Ingres, Jean-Auguste-Dominique, 124
Isabella, Queen, of Spain, 19, 76, 103
Italy, Napoleon III and, 21–4, 114–15, 133; the Empress and, 45, 46; the Countess Castiglione and, 66; Prince Napoleon and, 106–8; Rouher's policy towards, 157

Jecker, Jean Baptiste, and the Mexican enterprise, 75, 96
Jesuits, their return after the Restoration, 230
Josephine, Empress (1763–1814), 2, 3
Juarez, Benito, 25, 75, 77, 79, 83

La Gorce, 2, 32–3, 310
La Guéronnière, *L'Empereur Napoléon III et l'Italie*, 23; *Le Pape et le Congrès*, 24
Labiche, Eugène, 102, 124
Lacordaire, Jean Baptiste Henri, 242, 248; welcomes Falloux, 232; Napoleon III and his election to the Academy, 235–6; joins Lamennais' movement, 237–8; and Montalembert, 244
Lamartine, Alphonse-Marie (1790–1869), 5, 13, 14, 213, 265
Lamennais, Félicité-Robert de, 102; and the French Church, 237–8; his last years, 238
Lamoricière, General, and the *coup d'état*, 1851, 89, 90–1, 210, 218–19; and Saint-Arnaud, 220–1
Lanterne, La, 269–70, 286, 300
Lavisse, Ernest, 26, 191, 310, 313
le Bas, Philippe, tutor to Napoleon III, 3–4, 310
Le Boeuf, Marshal Edmond, 186, 188
Le Hon, Countess, 144; and de Morny, 87–8, 93–4
Ledru-Rollin, Alexandre, 142, 264, 265; and Changarnier, 215
Legitimists, the, 262, 263
Leopold I, King of Belgium (1790–1865), 76, 77, 79
Leopold, Prince, of Hohenzollern-Sigmaringen, offered the Spanish throne, 29–30, 185, 186
Littré, Émile, 124
Louis Philippe (1773–1850), 5, 18, 19, 101, 191, 237; abdicates, 12, 22, 88; Princess Mathilde and, 122; and monarchy, 230; Falloux and, 232; Thiers and, 253, 255
Lyons, Richard Bickerton, Lord, 28–9, 30

MacMahon, Marshal Marie, 31, 160, 210
Magnan, Marshal Bernard, 89, 90
Magne, Pierre, 154; and the Second Empire, 154, 168, 169; and the *coup d'état*, 1851, 168; opposes the Orleans decrees, 169; his public appointments, 169; and the Empress's Italian policy, 170; and Ollivier's Liberal Empire, 170–1; his tribute to Napoleon III, 172; under the Third Republic, 172
Maistre, Joseph, Count de, 230, 237
Malmesbury, Lord, 144; on Napoleon III, 4, 12, 32
Marseillaise, La, 270
Mathilde, Princess (1820–1904), 25, 41, 292; hostess at the Elysée, 19, 29, 36,

102, 123; and Napoleon III, 31, 61, 120, 122–4, 127; her dislike of the Empress, 20, 42, 43, 51, 124, 127; and Miss Howard, 59; and Countess Castiglione, 62, 65; and Prince Napoleon, 100, 104; her family background, 119–20; her marriage to Demidoff, 121–2; in Italy, 122; her *liaisons*, 122, 124, 127–8; becomes the first lady, 123; her salon, 124–5, 299, 302; described by Sainte-Beuve, 125–126; disliked by Vieil-Castel, 127; after Sedan, 127–8; her death, 128

Maupas, Charlemagne de, Prefect of Police, 16, 89, 90; and Rouher, 156, 159; welcomes the Liberal Empire, 180

Maximilian, Archduke, Emperor of Mexico (1832–67), and the Mexican enterprise, 25, 47, 73–83; on his meeting with Napoleon III, 74–5; his experiences in Mexico, 79–83; his death, 83

Mazzini, Giuseppe, 21, 101, 173

Meilhac, Henri, 97

Meissonier, Jean, 124

Mérimée, Prosper, 21, 23, 233; and Princess Mathilde, 20, 124; and Comtesse de Montijo, 35; and the Empress, 37–8, 47, 288, 289, 291; on Prince Napoleon, 109, 110; on Walewski, 135; on Persigny, 148; and Thiers and the Second Empire, 257; his friendship with Napoleon III, 287, 288, and the *coup d'état*, 1851, 288–9; and Napoleon III's *Life of Caesar*, 290; and Napoleon Bonaparte's correspondence, 290–1; at the 1870 crisis, 291

Metternich-Winneburg, Prince (1773–1859), 18; and Napoleon III, 7, 29, 30, 153, 181, 182; and the Empress, 34; and the Mexican enterprise, 76, 77, 83, 84; on Ollivier, 185

Metternich, Princess Pauline, 20, 34, 64, 126

Mexico, the French enterprise in, 25–6, 73–84; de Morny and, 96. *See also* Maximilian

Michelet, Jules, 304

Miramon, Miguel, sometime President of Mexico, 25, 75, 83, 96

Mocquard, Jean François, Political Secretary to Napoleon III, 59, 60, 90, 211; and Duruy, 192

Moltke, Helmuth, Count von, 27, 31

Montalembert, Charles de (1810–70), 163, 173, 182; his birth and early life, 237; influenced by Lamennais, 237–8; and Napoleon III, 239, 240, 241–3; and the *coup d'état*, 241, 242; his disillusionment, 243; condemns the Second Empire, 243; prosecuted by Napoleon III, 244–5, 263; welcomes the Liberal Empire, 245

Montholon, General Charles, Marquis de, 10, 11, 70

Montijo, Comte de, 19, 35, 41

Montijo, Comtesse de, 19, 25; Mérimée and, 288, 289; the Empress's letters to, 51–3, 53–4

Morny, Charles-Auguste-Louis-Joseph, Duc de (1811–65), 20, 21, 22, 62, 75, 124, 135, 157; his birth, 16, 86; and the *coup d'état*, 1851, 17, 87, 89–91, 155, 212, 221; resigns, 18, 91–2, 145; his death, 25, 97–8; his personality, 85; his early life, 86–7; and Countess Le Hon, 87–8, 93; and his half-brother, 88–90, 92, 97; later appointments, 91, 92–3, 95, 163; his marriage, 93–4; his social accomplishments, 94; and *Les Cinq*, 95; and the Liberal Empire, 95–6, 165; and the Mexican enterprise, 96; Halévy on, 97; and Ollivier, 175–6; *Monsieur Choufleury restera chez lui*, 94, 97

Murat, Lucien, Prince, 101, 102, 160

Napoleon Bonaparte, 2–3, 5; idealized by his nephew, 3, 6, 7–11; Prince Napoleon and, 99, 110, 111; Princess Mathilde and, 125, 126, 128; and relations with the Church, 230

Napoleon II (Duc de Reichstadt), 4, 138

Napoleon III (Charles-Louis-Napoleon Bonaparte) (1808–73), contemporary judgments on, 2, 4, 6–7, 12, 17, 21, 24–5, 26, 27–8, 28–9, 32, 57, 74, 172, 201, 225, 226–7, 305–6; his idealization of his uncle, 3, 6, 7–11; his early life, 3–4; his ideals of government, 5, 6, 7–11, 28, 102, 133–4; banished to America, 7; in London, 7, 12; imprisoned at Ham fortress, 11–12, 57, 69–70; his actions after the 1848 Revolution, 12–14; as Prince-President of the Republic, 14–15, 88–90, 142; aspires to the Imperial title, 15–16; and the 1851 *coup d'état*, 16–17, 89–91, 212, 223, 241; as Dictator, 1852, 17–18; becomes Emperor, 18; his marriage, 19–20; increases the prestige of France, 20–1; and the reconstruction of Paris, 21, 146, 198, 200, 202, 205; and the map of Europe, 21; and Italy, 21–4; at war with Austria, 22–3; the Mexican enterprise, 25–6, 47, 74–84; outwitted by Germany, 26; his declining health, 29, 227; and the German war, 1870, 30–1, 186, 188; last years at Chislehurst, 32–3, 54; his wife on, 37; attempts on his life, 38, 44, 65, 200–1, 289; his *liaisons*, 45–6, 57–69; and Persigny's attack on the Empress, 49–50; reconciled to his wife, 54; his illegitimate children, 57, 59, 60, 61, 67; and the Duc de Morny, 85 ff., 97; and Prince Napoleon, 100–102, 105, 109–12, 115, 117; defends the Liberal Ministry, 114; and Count Walewski, 131, 132; desires the friendship of England, 131; his Civil List, 145–6; and Persigny, 148, 149, 153; and Rouher, 156, 157; and Baroche, 162, 166; relations with his Ministers, 168; and Magne, 169, 171; and Ollivier's liberalism, 177–81, 183, 189–90; his position under the Liberal Constitution, 183–4; and Duruy, 191–3, 195; the Army and, 210; relations with his Generals, 210–212, 217–18, 219–22, 223–5, 227–9; and the Church, 231, 241; and Lacordaire's election to the Academy, 235–236; and Montalembert, 242–3, 244–5; welcomed by Veuillot, 246; and Thiers, 258; and Rochefort, 259. Writings of: *Aux Manes de L'Empereur*, 10; *L'Idée Napoléonienne*, 8–10; *Les Idées Napoléoniennes*, 7–8; *Rêveries Politiques*, 6; *La Vie de Caesar*, 28, 70, 71, 196, 290

Napoleon, Prince (Napoléon-Joseph-Charles-Paul) ('Plonplon'), 11, 13, 25, 43, 187; his dislike of the Empress, 20; marries Princess Clotilde, 22, 105–106; and the Prince Imperial, 55; and de Morny, 97; his early life, 100; relations with Napoleon III, 100 ff., 110 ff., 115; ambassador to Madrid, 102; and the Second Empire, 104; at the Crimean War, 104–5; ministerial posts, 105, 224; and Italian affairs, 106–7, 111, 115, 134; his contempt for the Bourbons, 107–109, 260–1; advocates intervention in Poland, 109–10; complains of his inactivity, 110–12; and the Austro-Prussian conflict, 112–13; visits Germany, 113; approves the Liberal Empire, 113–14, 182; urges ministerial reforms, 116; his last years, 117; praised by George Sand, 117–18; and Rouher, 157–8, 159; on Baroche, 160; and Changarnier, 216; his anti-clericalism, 231

National Workshops, 14, 88, 280–1

Nicholas I, Tsar, 19, 93, 131, 146; and Princess Mathilde, 122, 123

Niel, Marshal Adolphe, 113, 224

Nieuwerkerke, Count Alfred de: Countess Castiglione and, 64; Princess Mathilde and, 122–3, 124, 127

Nigra, Count Constantine, 46, 124

Noailles, Paul, Duc de, on the *coup d'état*, 1851, 252

Noir, Victor, 183, 270–1

Normanby, Lord, 12, 59, 60, 132, 310

Oldoini, Marquis, 61, 62

Ollivier, Émile (1825–1913), 99, 165, 233, 245; and *Les Cinq*, 20; and the Liberal Empire, 29, 32, 116, 173, 176 ff.; on the Empress, 47–8, 50; and the 1870 war, 51; Morny and, 95, 175–6, 177; and Walewski, 135, 176, 177; and Rouher, 156, 158, 170; his defeat, 159; supported by Baroche, 166–7; his early life, 173; and the *coup d'état*, 1851, 174; appeals to Napoleon III for liberalism, 174–175; and the Associations bill, 176–7; interviews with Napoleon III, 177, 178, 181; his Liberal Ministry, 181–4; his behaviour during the 1870 crisis, 184–8, 189, 258; escapes to Italy, 188;

his responsibility for the catastrophe, 188–90; on Napoleon III, 189; du Camp on his eloquence, 190; biographies of, 190 n.; and Haussmann, 205–7; Thiers and, 257; *Lettres d'un Exile*, 188
Organic Articles, 230, 231
Orleans family: Napoleon III's decrees against, 18, 91–2, 123, 155, 164, 169, 174, 221, 231, 243, 249, 259, 263; the Duc d'Aumale and, 258; the Legitimists and, 262; and the Second Empire, 265
Orsini, Felice, attempts to assassinate Napoleon III, 22, 43, 44, 200–1, 260; defended by Favre, 266

Paléologue, Maurice, the Empress and, 31, 35, 46, 47, 51, 55, 311
Palmerston, Henry John Temple, 3rd Viscount, 20, 21, 147; and the Empress Eugénie, 38; and the Mexican enterprise, 76, 78; and the *coup d'état*, 1851, 132
Papal States, 23, 24, 47; Prince Napoleon and, 106–7; Duruy's memorandum on, 192; Napoleon III and, 248; Dupanloup's protests concerning, 250
Paris, Comte de (Louis Philippe d'Orléans), 6, 20, 262; Thiers and, 253; visited by Gambetta, 272
Paris, its reconstruction by Haussmann, 21, 146, 198 ff.; in 1870, 32
Persigny, Jean, Duc de (1808–72), 6, 22, 29, 108, 154, 211; and the Empress, 20, 48; his devotion to Napoleon III, 25, 59, 138, 140, 149, 234–5; on the character of Napoleon III, 27–8, 149–50; and the Countess Castiglione, 67; and the *coup d'état*, 1851, 89, 90, 144–5; advocates a Bonapartist restoration, 139–41, 142; present at Strasbourg and Boulogne, 140–1; his imprisonment, 141; after the fall of the Monarchy, 141–2; in Berlin, 143; becomes Minister of the Interior, 145–6, 147–9; and the Second Empire, 145, 256; ambassador in London, 147; dismissed by Napoleon III, 148–9, 165; his meetings with Bismarck, 150; and the

Austro-Prussian crisis, 151; deplores the attitude of the government, 152–153; and the 1870 war, 153; his death, 153; attacks Rouher, 156; and Ollivier's liberalism, 180, 182; and Haussmann, 200, 201; encourages Fleury, 211; attempts to win over Changarnier, 217; and the Church, 231; interview with Falloux, 234–5; and Thiers, 256–7
Persigny, Mme de, 147, 148, 149
Poland, Prince Napoleon and intervention in, 109; Walewski and, 129–30, 157
Pius IX (Pio Nono), Pope: Napoleon III and, 22, 24, 114–15, 231; the Empress and, 45, 46; and Queen Charlotte, 82–3; and Prince Napoleon, 107; frowns on Lamennais movement, 238; Montalembert and, 239–40; Dupanloup and, 250
Plonplon. *See* Napoleon, Prince
Poniatowski, Prince Joseph, 129
Poniatowski, Prince Joseph Michael, and the Countess Castiglione, 64, 65, 66, 67
Poniatowski, Princess Louise, 88
Popelin, ——, Princess Mathilde and, 127, 128
Press, the, under the Second Empire, 267; Rochefort and, 268–9
Prim, Juan, Marquis de los Castillejos, 29, 185
Proudhon, Pierre-Joseph, 15, 102, 230, 231; and socialism, 279–80, 281; and Napoleon III, 280
Prussia, French relations with, 1849–50, 143

Quinet, Edgar, condemns Napoleon III, 304

Rachel (Élizabeth Rachel Félix), 130–1, 262
Randon, Marshal Jacques Louis, Minister of War, 191, 223, 224; and the *coup d'état*, 1851, 222, 223–4; his early career, 222–3; appointed Governor of Algeria, 224; replaced by Niel, 224; and the 1870 crisis, 224–5; and Taine, 308–9
Ranke, Leopold von, 18

INDEX 323

Rappel, Le, 270, 272, 286
Reding, Baroness, 119–20
Renan, Ernest, 72, 99, 124; dismissed for *Vie de Jésus*, 194–5, 307
Republic, Second, 1848–52; establishment of, 12–15 102; end of, 17; the Church under, 231; Falloux and, 232
Republic, Third, 277
Republicans, the, 264–6; and the *coup d'état*, 1851, 252; their opposition to the Second Empire, 264; Gambetta and, 217 ff.
Rochefort, Marquis Henri de, 26, 94, 159, 183, 190; his hatred of Napoleon III, 268; publishes *La Lanterne*, 269–270, 286; in exile in Belgium, 270; elected to the Chamber, 270–1; attacks Pierre Bonaparte, 270–1; his imprisonment, 271
Rothschild, Baron Alphonse de, 22
Rouher, Eugène (1814–84), 29, 91, 114; and the Empress, 47–8; and Mme le Hon, 93, 94; condemned by Persigny, 151, 152, 153, 156; Prime Minister of the Second Empire, 154–155, 176, 177, 256; and the *coup d'état*, 1851, 155; his public appointments, 156–7, 159, 163, 165; his foreign policy, 157; his resignation in 1869, 158–9, 165; last years, 159–60; and Magne, 170; opposes Ollivier's liberalism, 179, 180, 183; and Haussmann, 198, 204–5
Royalists, the, and the *coup d'état*, 1851, 252–3; Thiers and, 253, 254, 256, 257; and Rochfort, 268
Russell, Lord John, 2, 108; and Walewski, 132

Sadowa, 26, 27, 224
Saint-Arnaud, Jacques Leroy de, 16, 17, 104; and the *coup d'état*, 1851, 87, 89, 90, 174, 219, 220–1; Minister of War, 210, 212, 220–2; in Algeria, 219–20; and Napoleon III, 219–22; eulogized by Veuillot, 247
Saint-Marc, Pierre, on Ollivier, 190 n.
Saint-Simon, Claude-Henry de Rouvroy, Comte de, 231; and socialism, 279
Saint-Beuve, Charles-Augustin, 19–20, 21, 314; and Princess Mathilde, 124,
125–6, 292–3, 299, 300; and the *coup d'état*, 1851, 292; appeals for encouragement for literature, 292; his *Causeries du Lundi*, 293
Sand, George, 72, 102, 124, 273; and Prince Napoleon, 117–18, 295, 296; and the Adams, 274, 276; and Napoleon III's *Extinction of Pauperism*, 293–4; welcomes the Second Republic, 294; and the *coup d'état*, 1851, 294; appeals for the release of the political prisoners, 294–5; criticizes the *Life of Caesar*, 296; welcomes the Third Republic, 296
Sardou, Victorien, Princess Mathilde and *Mme Sans-Gêne*, 128
Sedan, 31, 53, 117, 127, 188
Sencourt, Robert, 32, 310, 311
Senior, Nassau William, on Countess Castiglione, 65; and Lamoricière, 218–19; and Thiers, 256; and Napoleon III, 289
Simon, Jules, on Rouher, 154; on the Republicans and the Second Empire, 264–5; denounces Gambetta, 273
Socialists, the, 279–81; Saint-Simon and, 279; Proudhon and, 279–80
Solferino, 3, 23, 45
Spain, and the Mexican enterprise, 75, 76; Prince Napoleon and, 103
Stendhal (Henri Beyle), 35
Stoffel, Colonel, 113, 188
Strasbourg *putsch*, 7, 35, 120; Persigny and, 140
Syllabus of Errors, 24, 194

Taine, Hippolyte, 2; Princess Mathilde and, 124, 128, 308; and the *coup d'état*, 1851, 307–8; on the 1870 crisis, 309
Talleyrand (Charles Maurice Talleyrand de Périgord), 16, 85, 129, 248
Tascher de la Pagerie, Countess, on Napoleon III, 25; on Countess Castiglione, 63, 66, 68
Thiers, Adolphe (1797–1877), 6, 12, 15, 16, 26, 95, 96, 122, 173, 240, 263, 267, 272; President of the Third Republic, 32, 127; and the Mexican fiasco, 83; on Prince Napoleon, 101; condemns the 1867 Ministry, 114; and Walewski, 130, 131; Persigny and, 142, 148,

151; Baroche and, 167; and liberalism, 175, 182; on Haussmann, 204; and Chargarnier, 215, 217; Falloux and, 232, 254; and the clergy, 233; and the Second Republic, 253–4; on the limitation of the franchise, 255; and the *coup d'état*, 1851, 255; his attitude to Napoleon III, 255–6, 257; returns to politics, 256, 266; and the Second Empire, 256–7; and the 1870 crisis, 257–8, 266; distrusts Gambetta, 273

Thouvenel, Edouard, 134; becomes Foreign Minister, 75, 157

Tocqueville, Alexis-Henri, Comte de (1805–59), 2, 5, 233; his portrait of Napoleon III, 305–6; and the *coup d'état*, 1851, 306; *Democracy in America*, 305

Trochu, General Louis, 32

Troplong, Raymond, 145, 159

Troubetzkoi, Sophie, de Morny's marriage to, 93–4

Ultramontanism, 237

Univers, L', Veuillot and, 245–8, 250

Universities, the, under Fortoul, 193; their freedom under Duruy, 193; the Falloux Law and, 233

Vernet, Jean, 124

Véron, Louis, 2, 267

Veuillot, Louis-François, 24, 243, 245; and Falloux, 232–3; Montalembert's breach with, 244; his conversion, 245; and *L'Univers*, 245–6, 248; and the *coup d'état*, 1851, 246; Falloux admonishes, 246; urges Catholic support of Napoleon III, 247; his allegiance to Rome, 247–8, 251

Victor Emmanuel II, 22, 23, 31; desires a united Italy, 24, 107, 250; and Countess Castiglione, 45, 61–2, 68; disliked by the Empress, 46; his dissolute life, 46, 61; and French troops in Rome, 115; Austria and, 133

Victoria, Queen, 32, 33; and the Empress Eugénie, 36, 38, 55, 132; and the Walewskis, 132

Vieil-Castel, Count Horace de, 94, 311; on Napoleon III, 21, 24–5; on the Empress, 43; and the Castigliones, 63–4, 65, 67; and Prince Napoleon, 103, 105, 109; on Jerome Bonaparte, 121; on Princess Mathilde, 126–7; on Walewski, 131, 134; on Persigny, 145, 148; on Baroche, 164; on Haussmann, 204

Viollet-le-Duc, Eugène, 124

Vitzthum, Count Karl, 187, 188

Walewski, Count Alexander, 22, 41, 46, 71, 147, 157, 170; his jealousy of Napoleon III, 69; his early history, 129; in England, 129–30; serves in the French army, 130; Thiers and, 130, 131; his *liaison* with Rachel, 130–131; his second marriage, 131; ambassadorial appointments, 131–2; and the *coup d'état*, 1851, 132; becomes Foreign Minister, 132–4; his disagreements with Napoleon III, 133–5, 165; final phase of his career, 135; and liberalism, 176, 177–8

Walewski, Countess, Napoleon III and, 46, 69, 131, 134; her marriage, 131

Wellington, Duke of, 132

William I of Prussia, 27, 29, 51, 186

Württemberg, Catherine of, 100, 119

Zeldin, Theodore, on the Liberal Empire, 190 n., 310